ONE THOUSAND COPIES
OF THIS LIMITED FIRST EDITION OF

THE

COLLECTED WORKS

OF

KEN WILBER

HAVE BEEN ESPECIALLY
PREPARED FOR FRIENDS OF THE
AUTHOR AND THE PUBLISHER

ONE THOUSAND COPIES
OF THIS LIMITED FIRST EDITION OF

THE
COLLECTED WORKS
OF
KEN WILBER

HAVE BEEN ESPECIALLY
PREPARED FOR FRIENDS OF THE
AUTHOR AND THE PUBLISHER

The Collected Works of Ken Wilber

THE COLLECTED WORKS OF

KEN WILBER

VOLUME THREE

A SOCIABLE GOD

EYE TO EYE

SHAMBHALA
Boston & London
1999

SHAMBHALA PUBLICATIONS, INC.
Horticultural Hall
300 Massachusetts Avenue
Boston, Massachusetts 02115
www.shambhala.com

9 8 7 6 5 4 3 2 1

FIRST EDITION
Printed in the United States of America
♾This edition is printed on acid-free paper that meets
the American National Standards Institute z39.48 Standard.
Distributed in the United States by Random House, Inc.,
and in Canada by Random House of Canada Ltd

Library of Congress Cataloging-in-Publication Data
Wilber, Ken.
[Works. 1998]
The collected works of Ken Wilber. — 1st ed.
p. cm.
Includes bibliographical references and indexes.
Contents: v. 1. The spectrum of consciousness; No boundary. — v. 2. The Atman
Project; Up from Eden—v. 3. A sociable god; Eye to eye.
ISBN 1–57062–501–8 (v. 1: cloth: alk. paper).—ISBN 1–57062–575–1
(v. 1: Special edition).—ISBN 1–57062–502–6 (v. 2: cloth: alk. paper).—
ISBN 1–57062–576–X (v. 2: Special edition).—ISBN 1–57062–503–4
(v. 3: cloth: alk. paper).—ISBN 1–57062–577–8
(v. 3: Special edition).
1. Consciousness. 2. Subconsciousness. 3. Self-perception.
4. Psychology—Philosophy. 5. East and West. I. Title.
BF311.W576 1999   97–45928
191—DC21   CIP

CONTENTS

THE COLLECTED WORKS OF
KEN WILBER

INTRODUCTION
TO VOLUME THREE

I HAVE, FOR CONVENIENCE, divided my overall work into four general phases. Phase-1 was Romantic (a "recaptured-goodness" model), which posited a spectrum of consciousness ranging from subconscious to self-conscious to superconscious (or id to ego to God), with the higher stages viewed as a return to, and recapture of, original but lost potentials. Phase-2 was more specifically evolutionary or developmental (a "growth-to-goodness" model), with the spectrum of consciousness unfolding in developmental stages or levels. Phase-3 added developmental lines to those developmental levels—that is, numerous different developmental lines (such as cognitive, conative, affective, moral, psychological, spiritual, etc.) proceeding in a relatively independent manner through the basic levels of the overall spectrum of consciousness. Phase-4 added the idea of the four quadrants—the subjective (intentional), objective (behavioral), intersubjective (cultural), and interobjective (social) dimensions—of each of those levels and lines, with the result being, or at least attempting to be, a comprehensive or integral philosophy.

The works of these phases form a fairly coherent whole. It is not so much that one period was rejected and replaced by its successor, but that the works of each period remain, in my opinion, largely valid, and the succeeding works simply add new material, not erase old. Each phase was relatively true but partial, and had much of its partialness corrected by subsequent additions (or so I trust). Even the works of phase-1, if their occasional Romanticisms are removed, contribute useful foundation stones for this particular edifice.

The material in this volume is from a full-fledged phase-2. One of the main tasks of phase-2 was to explore the implications of a developmental and evolutionary view of psychology, religion, philosophy, and the human condition in general; and likewise attempt to expose certain fallacies that result from a failure to take a sufficiently developmental view into account. As such, the works in this volume are still, in my opinion, some of the most important I have done.

None of them has received quite the attention, or caused quite the controversy, as "The Pre/Trans Fallacy," so perhaps I should begin my commentary there. I discovered the pre/trans fallacy by looking at my own mistakes. By looking, that is, at why the Romantic viewpoint seems at first to make so much sense—and why almost everybody seems to start their study of spirituality with a Romantic view—and yet it cannot handle the actual data and evidence of phylogenetic and ontogenetic development. The general Romantic view is fairly straightforward: infants, and dawn humans, start out immersed in an unconscious union with the world at large (and the pure Self)—peacefully embedded in a type of primal paradise (either a literal earthly Eden, a foraging ecological wisdom, or an infant fusion "with the mother and the world in bliss"). Through subsequent development, this primal paradise is necessarily lost as the rational-ego emerges from this primal Ground, breaks and fragments this "nondissociated" state, and creates thereby a world of sin, suffering, ecological catastrophe, patriarchal brutality, and general malevolence. But the self (and humanity) can drop its overly analytic, divisive, and fragmented stance by returning to, and recapturing, the wholeness of the original embeddedness (but now in a mature and conscious form, or on a higher level). The original wholeness, now combined with analytic capacities, will result in a renewed heaven-on-earth, ecologically sound and balanced, and usher in a liberated nondissociated consciousness, which is spiritual in the deepest and truest sense.

As I explained in the introduction to volume 2, I started writing both *The Atman Project* and *Up from Eden* in order to prove that Romantic conception. If nothing else, it cannot be said that I do not understand that view, or that I have never had any sympathy for it. I was, in phase-1, its most ardent fan. But the more I tried to make the Romantic orientation explain the actual evidence, the more dismally it failed. During a long period of intellectual anguish, I slowly abandoned a strictly Romantic stance (while keeping some of its more durable truths), and moved to adopt the only view that seemed to me to be able to impartially handle the great preponderance of evidence—and that was a developmental or evolutionary model.

In tracing out my early, fervent embrace of Romanticism, I was able to reconstruct what I believe are the intellectual errors that led to that embrace—and they are all summarized by "the pre/trans fallacy" (PTF). The PTF simply says: in any recognized developmental sequence, where development proceeds from pre-*x* to *x* to trans-*x*, the pre states and the trans states, because they are both non-*x* states, tend to be confused and equated, simply because they appear, at first glance, to be so similar. Prerational and transrational are both nonrational; preconventional and postconventional are both nonconventional; prepersonal and transpersonal are both nonpersonal, and so on. And once we confuse pre and trans, then one of two unfortunate things tends to happen: we either reduce transrational, spiritual, superconscious states to prerational, infantile, oceanic fusion (as did Freud); or we elevate infantile, childish, prerational states to transcendental, transrational, transpersonal glory (as the Romantics often did). We reduce trans to pre, or we elevate pre to trans. Reductionism is well understood; elevationism was the great province of the Romantics.

The Romantics, and me in phase-1. The overwhelming preponderance of evidence points to the fact that infants (and early hominids) did not exist in a transrational heaven, but in a prerational slumber. The awakening of the rational, self-conscious ego out of this prerational, prereflexive slumber did indeed involve a painful awakening to the horrors of the manifest world, but that awakening was not a fall from a previous superconscious state, but the growth up and out of a subconscious immersion. The subconscious immersion is *already* fallen—it *already* exists in the manifest world of hunger, pain, finitude, and mortality—it just hasn't the awareness to fully register those painful facts. Likewise, the rational ego, far from being the height of ontological alienation, is actually halfway through the growth to superconscious awakening. (The ego isn't actually in the lowest hell, it just feels like it, much as frostbite doesn't really hurt until the affected part starts to warm up.)

But the Romantics, *correctly* realizing that Spirit is beyond mere rationality, and *correctly* realizing that the rational ego stands outside of, and even resists, nondual Spiritual consciousness, then made the classic elevationist PTF: they assumed the prehistorical slumber in paradise was the primal whole out of which humanity fell, and back to which humanity must return, in order to usher in a transrational heaven. And that deeply *regressive* view of human potentials would set the stage for all of the well-known downsides, even horrors, of Romanticism: an obsession with self and self-feelings (regressing from worldcentric to sociocentric to egocentric), hedonistic amorality (regressing from postconventional compassion to conventional care to preconventional impulse)—all of which claimed to be "beyond reason," whereas most of it was simply beneath it.

All of that became obvious to me as I reconstructed my own mistakes. And all of that I worked out in the concept of the pre/trans fallacy. The idea itself was initially presented in *The Atman Project*, which was the first major statement of phase-2; and it was worked out in detail in the essay "The Pre/Trans Fallacy," which was included in the book *Eye to Eye* (which is included in this volume).

In the almost twenty years since its publication, two types of criticism have constantly been leveled at the pre/trans fallacy. The reductionists aggressively attack it for allowing the existence of *any* transrational, transpersonal states (they are still ever so busy reducing all trans states to sneaky insurrections of infantile, prerational silliness). And elevationists indignantly attack it, often vitriolically, for claiming that infants and children (and dawn humans) are only prerational, without access to any sort of spiritual or transpersonal states. Both of these attacks are exactly what one would expect to happen if the PTF were true; still, both sides have presented my view as much more rigid than it ever was.

First, with the reductionists, I do not think that all, or even most, of those states that claim to be transpersonal or spiritual are actually that. Speaking as an authority on the topic, I can say that the human capacity for self-delusion is too enormous to take all such claims at face value. A highly critical, occasionally skeptical, and sometimes even polemical attitude must be our constant companion on the road to any sort of truth. The commodity most lacking in spiritual circles seems to be, indeed, a healthy skepticism, possibly because it is confused with lack of faith, a stance which, if understandable, is deeply misguided. Nonetheless, against the reductionists, I—and a colossal amount of cross-cultural evidence—refuse to dismiss all transpersonal, transrational, mystical states, as if they were only irritating irruptions from an infantile, primordial slime.

With the elevationists, I can agree, to a point, that various types of spiritual or transpersonal states are available to infants (and dawn humans), nor have I ever denied that. I will first address infants, and then the earlier stages of human evolution.

In particular, I see two major types of spiritual access in infants. One, what I have called "trailing clouds of glory," which refers to all the deeper psychic (or soul) awareness that the individual brings to this life and which is therefore present in some sense from conception forward (however you wish to construe that—as reincarnation, or simply as deeper potentials present from the start). Hazrat Inayat Khan probably put it best: "The crying of an infant is very often the expression of its longing for the angelic heavens [through which it has just passed on its way to earthly birth—what the Tibetans call the rebirth bardo]; the smiles of an infant are a narrative of its memories of heaven and of the spheres above." Notice that these potentials are not something that are part of the infantile stage itself—they are lingering impressions from other, *higher* spheres. (And therefore, what is *recaptured* in enlightenment is *not* the infantile structure itself, but the actual higher spheres! The Romantic notion that the infantile self *is itself* a primordial paradise remains therefore deeply mistaken.)

Two, the infant also has access to what I refer to as the three major states of consciousness: gross (waking), subtle (dreaming and deeper psychic), and causal (deep sleep, pure Witness, primordial Self). The early self (prenatal, perinatal, neonatal, infancy, and early childhood) has various types of access to all of those spiritual states (because it wakes, dreams, and sleeps). But so does the adult. In other words, the infantile state, in this regard, does not have access to something spiritual that is then *lost* or denied to the adult. (The strictly Romantic view is, again, significantly off the mark.)

So does the infantile self have access to any sort of "spiritual awareness" that is actually *lost* in subsequent development but can be *regained* in higher states of spiritual awakening? In a limited sense, yes: the trailing clouds of glory (whether in their prenatal, perinatal, neonatal, or later forms). But, to repeat, those "trailing clouds" are primarily a lingering contact or impression of higher, transpersonal, transrational levels; they are *not* potentials that are structurally part of the infantile self, so that, in recontacting these higher levels in subsequent development, it is not a *regression* to infancy that is occurring, but a *progression* to, and rediscovery of, the higher levels themselves. The fetal and infantile self does not live in perfect nirvana,* beyond all suffering and pain and

---

* Elevationists often use, as a counterexample to disprove this statement, the exis-

decay; it lives immersed in samsara, with all its hunger, pain, passing pleasure, screams, and occasional smiles—but it carries with it, buried in its bosom, the higher levels of its own potential evolution (and the higher states of subtle and causal consciousness), which it can *permanently* contact and bring into full consciousness *only* when its own development moves from prerational to rational to transrational.

Of course, any of the lower, *prerational* potentials (e.g., various proto-emotions, prana, emotional-sexual impulses) can *themselves* be repressed during early childhood development, and if that occurs, then, as I have strongly maintained all along, successful therapy generally involves regression in service of the ego (in order to recontact and reintegrate these lost or repressed facets). Moreover, if this repression is severe, it can slow or even completely cripple higher development into transpersonal and superconscious states. In that case, there needs to occur a spiraling return to early structures: a regression in service of ego (to repair the early, prerational trauma), and then a progression in transcendence of ego (having repaired the prerational damage, the self can more easily move from rational to transrational adaptation). So once again, even in this spiral of return-and-transcend, what is being contacted is not itself a higher state, but a lower state badly damaged and in need of repair. The Romantic view is again considerably off the mark.

Finally, the pre/trans fallacy says that *in any recognized developmental sequence*, pre and trans are often confused. It does not say that childhood is nothing but pre. As I just explained, there are types of transient access to spiritual states even in the infantile self. Rather, the pre/trans fallacy is meant to call attention to the massive types of confusion that occur even in fully recognized developmental sequences. For example, researchers from Piaget to Kohlberg to Gilligan agree that moral judgment moves from preconventional to conventional to postconventional modes. The pre/trans fallacy simply says that, given this recognized sequence, preconventional and postconventional are often confused, simply because both are nonconventional. And we have to look no further than the general New Age movement to find abundant evidence of preconventional impulse being confused with postconven-

---

tence of tulkus or reincarnated buddhas: fully enlightened beings who remain conscious through all the stages of bardo, infancy, and childhood. Well, of course, a fully enlightened being is an exception to the rule, but that is a trivial example, because fully enlightened beings are an exception to every rule.

tional liberation; prerational self-absorption being confused with post-rational freedom; preverbal hedonism confused with transverbal wisdom. Alas, it is almost always the Romantic orientation, with its sincere but confused elevationism, that drives the entire display, with self-obsession elevated to Self-realization, divine egoism exalted as divine liberation, and rampant narcissism paraded as transcendental freedom. But the important nugget of truth contained in the Romantic intuition is that, indeed, we have fallen from a union with Spirit (a union found, not in the dregs of an infantile past, but in the depths of the timeless present), and we can indeed *regain* that spiritual union—but *only* if we grow in a transcendence of ego, and not simply recapture an infantile self. (For an extensive discussion of childhood spirituality, see *Integral Psychology* in *Collected Works,* Volume Four.)

What, then, of the earlier stages of human development? And not just the dawn state of perhaps a million years ago, but also the early stages of tribal foraging and village horticulture? Are we arrogantly to pronounce them "inferior"? And are we really to claim they had no access to transrational, transpersonal spirituality? Romantic theorists bristle at the thought that anyone would so callously pronounce whole epochs to be "inferior" or "lacking in genuine spirituality." And rightly so. But then, I have never even remotely claimed such.

To begin with, however, let us note that the Romantics who get so indignant about those two claims ("inferiority" and "lacking true spirituality") make exactly those claims themselves—not about foraging tribes, but about you and me. The general anthropological Romantic claim is that original tribal consciousness (during the period Gebser calls "magical") was "nondissociated," a type of harmony and wholeness of self, culture, and nature. The Romantic theorists agree that this magical structure was prereflexive and prerational (in the sense of preformal-operational thinking as a central organizing principle of society; the society was instead organized around prereflexive nondissociated consciousness). But, they claim, far from being a "lower" development, this prereflexive consciousness was balanced, holistic, ecologically sound, and deeply spiritual. But, they continue, with the eventual rise of egoic-rationality (through several stages), this nondissociated state was brutally repressed, fragmented, and destroyed, and in its place was a nightmare called modernity, which is marked, first and foremost, by *dissociated consciousness,* which carries alienation, fragmentation, and shallow (if any) spirituality. In other words, in its place are you and I: we moderns are all, with a few exceptions, judged to be living in dissociated consciousness, an inferior, fragmented state, lacking a genuine spirituality. This Romantic view thus condemns literally *hundreds of millions* of modern people as having inferior consciousness and lacking a deep spirituality. So the first thing we should note is that charges of "inferiority" and "lacking spirituality" drop from the lips of these Romantics with an alarming ease and frequency. It is a very harsh system of ranking and value judgments that these Romantics have embraced, and it would do well for us to soften such brutal blows.

My view of the early tribal magical structure is, I believe, more nuanced. But let me first emphasize that I am talking about the original, prehistorical, tribal, foraging mode of perhaps 200,000 to 20,000 years ago (a similar case can be made with the horticultural mode of 10,000 to 3,000 years ago). Indigenous peoples living today are people *living today*; they have continued to undergo their own development for hundreds of thousands of years, and their exact relationship to prehistoric tribes is far from clear; moreover, they are usually inextricably intermixed with other cultures and modes. No, I am referring to the structure of the original, prehistorical, magical-foraging mode, to the extent we can reconstruct it.

To begin with, any society is a collection of individuals who themselves are at very different levels of development. At the same time, as I pointed out in *Up from Eden,* any given culture has something like a "center of gravity," or an *average mode* of consciousness, around which conventional, everyday realities are organized. The Romantics agree that the average mode of early tribes was "magical" (in the nonpejorative sense of prereflexive and nondissociated) and the average mode of modernity is egoic-rational (which is usually meant pejoratively but doesn't affect our main point about the average mode). I further suggested that in addition to the average mode, there is the *most advanced* mode, the mode displayed by those souls who were the most developed in any particular domain. During the magical foraging times, this definitely appears to have included the shamans, who, I forcefully argued, were the first great explorers of the genuinely transpersonal, spiritual domains. At the very least, these souls directly experienced the deeper psychic dimension of the human potential, evidenced in an extraordinarily sophisticated nature mysticism, journeys to upper- and underworld domains, actual psychic capacities, and—again at the very least—a unitive consciousness with the entire realm of nature. In *Up from Eden* I spent an entire chapter extolling these remarkable, authentic, and deeply spiritual feats.

At the same time, scholars of the shamanic state have pointed out that, although there might have been exceptions, the typical shamanic voyage did not include, for example, extended periods of absorption in the purely formless realm (causal cessation). In other words, by criteria that are acceptable even to shamanic advocates, the shamanic voyage did not include the causal domain. And therefore, at the very least, shamanic spirituality was not a path that traversed the entire transpersonal realm.

If, on the other hand, one performs (as *Up from Eden* did) a historical analysis on the succession or emergence of spiritual states accessed by the typical forms of the most advanced consciousness in each general epoch (magic to mythic to mental), one generally finds a succession of transpersonal states that move from shamanic (psychic) to saintly (subtle) to sagely (causal), with each of the succeeding states having access to their predecessors, but not vice versa—a true mark of a holarchy of development.

The advanced mode of the magical-foraging era was thus most definitely alive to profound realms of authentic spiritual development, even if we cannot believably claim that shamanism itself exhausted the entire terrain. To return, then, to the average mode: What of the actual nature of the prereflexive, nondissociated consciousness, or the "magical structure" of the *average mode* of foraging consciousness? Was it a truly integrated, holistic, harmonious whole?

The magical structure, no doubt, was an extraordinary mode of consciousness; if nothing else, it inhabited the first men and women who evolved beyond the great apes and hominids, and although some people will insist on seeing this as an insult to apes, it was a colossal evolutionary advance by almost any scale of judgment. Still, the question is whether it actually *integrated* self, culture, and nature, or whether it had not yet fully differentiated them in the first place. By calling this magical structure "nondissociated," the Romantics completely beg the question, avoid the issue. The great, glorious, catch-all prefix "non" always stands as a warning of a pre/trans fallacy begging to be made. For the real question is, not whether this structure was "nondifferentiated," but was this structure predifferentiated or was it truly transdifferentiated? "Nondissociated" can easily apply to both (which is exactly how it hides its PTF).

Approaching the question in this more precise fashion, the answer is more obvious. The magical structure was largely predifferentiated. On this, scholars from across a wide spectrum of approaches are in general agreement. Jean Houston, following Gerald Heard, calls this the preindividual and proto-individual period (that is, archaic to magic). Duane Elgin refers to them as constricted consciousness and awakening (proto) consciousness. Jürgen Habermas and his colleagues, who conducted extensive research reviews, calls them preconventional and predifferentiated. Robert Bellah, tracing religious evolution, calls them primitive and archaic (predifferentiated action systems). Erich Neumann called them pleromatic, uroboric, and preindividuated. This does not mean stupid, confused, or imbecilic; it means that various subjective, objective, and intersubjective domains were not approached in fully differentiated terms. Some see this as a good thing, others as a problem; but there is general agreement on the actual nature of the structure itself.

The broad conclusion: with the magical structure, the self, culture, and nature still lay interfused with each other. They were not integrated, for they had not yet separated, differentiated, and crystallized out from each other. This predifferentiation is what gives the magical structure its, well, magical charm, and makes it a misunderstood magnet for those who actually desire a transdifferentiated integration for the modern world. But the actual situation of the foraging mode was, apart from its many wonders, something less than an integrated paradise. Because the I, the we, and the it were as yet poorly differentiated, advances in each domain were hindered. Average life span was less than three decades; political systems were focused on body-bound kinship lineages; slavery was sporadic but by no means nonexistent; warfare had already begun; and sexual exploitation was definitely not unheard of. It is, *in its complete contours*, a consciousness that no Romantic I know would actually want to inhabit.

The fact that magic could be taken up and into mythic, and that mythic could be taken up and into the mental, is a development that—ideally—would carry the extraordinary accomplishments of each mode forward, building on their strengths, curtailing their partialness, and building together a more embracing, inclusive, encompassing future. Ideally, of course, is never the case, and cultural evolution has as often been the history of brutalities, repressions, oppressions, and worse, as human evolution sometimes progressed, sometimes brutalized its way toward tomorrow. *Up from Eden* is a chronicle of the undeniable advances, and the even more undeniable brutalities.

But the general point of phylogenetic evolution, as of ontogenetic, is that *whenever the wisdom of a previous stage is forgotten, a pathology results*. In *A Brief History of Everything* I outlined the major "lessons" that each age of humanity managed to learn, and the point here is that the great foraging lesson was: *Spirit is interwoven with earthbody*, which is our blood, our bones, our foundation, our support. We of the modern West have forgotten that lesson, and we are therefore in the grips of a global pathology that very well might kill us all.

That the Romantics want us to remember that incredibly important lesson is very much to their credit, and in that specific regard, I am a staunch Romantic. But when they go quite beyond that and dubiously inject characteristics into the magical structure—when they claim trans-differentiated integration for what most scholars would see as prediffer-entiated structures; when they claim that the shamanic voyage was a complete path across the transpersonal; when they claim that the mental structure itself is intrinsically pathological; and when they condemn mil-lions upon millions of people to living in an inferior state compared with magical indissociation—then perhaps we might not wish to follow them.*

In addition to "The Pre/Trans Fallacy," *Eye to Eye* contained nine major essays exploring the implications of a full-spectrum model of human growth and development. The overall spectrum of conscious-ness, as outlined in *The Atman Project*, contained almost two dozen basic levels (which are simply an elaboration of the Great Nest of Being, matter to body to mind to soul to spirit). I usually condense these into nine or ten major levels, and sometimes use even fewer, such as the traditional five I just gave (which are essentially the same five the Ved-anta uses), and sometimes only three: body, mind, and spirit (or gross,

---

* What about the final claim of certain sophisticated Romantics?—namely, that even if the magical structure is a less developed structure of consciousness (predifferenti-ated and not transdifferentiated), nonetheless a truly integral structure would result if the naturic wholeness of the magical structure were combined with the rational structure of modernity. I agree that would be a welcome integration, but it would simply be an integration of prerational and rational; it would not be profoundly transrational. Rather, that integration (of all previous structures) is exactly what the integral-aperspectival (centauric) structure is supposed to accomplish (according to Gebser, myself, and others). Moreover, the magical structure itself is not the only structure other than rationality that is supposed to be included in the integration: there are the entire realms of mythic-horticultural and mythic-rational-agrarian, all of which Romantic-tribalists generally despise. Finally, even if we toss in the most advanced mode (shamanism), this is, as we saw, a partial and limited approach to the overall transpersonal. From any angle, the foraging structure simply cannot per-form the Herculean feats the Romantics demand of it, but rather remains a very important but very limited mode.

subtle, and causal). The essay "Eye to Eye," which opens the book named after it, uses the simple three (the eye of flesh, the eye of mind, and the eye of contemplation) and suggests how even that simple scheme can shed considerable light on many recalcitrant philosophical and psychological dilemmas. "The Problem of Proof" carries this discussion forward and presents what amounts to a full-spectrum empiricism: sensory experience, mental experience, and spiritual experience, all of which are equally experiential, and thus all of which can be carefully validated using evidence that is open to confirmation or rejection by a community of the adequate.

"A Mandalic Map of Consciousness" presents a summary of the overall spectrum of consciousness, and "Development, Meditation, and the Unconscious" outlines five major types of "the" unconscious, and points out why these distinctions are crucial for understanding everything from the nature of development to the form and content of meditation. In my opinion, this outline of five different types of unconscious processes is an important contribution. One of the main conclusions is that meditation is not primarily a way to dig back into, or uncover, prerational impulses, but rather a way to carry development or evolution forward into transrational and superconscious states.

The next two essays ("Physics, Mysticism, and the New Holographic Paradigm" and "Reflections on the New Age Paradigm") are both attempts to point out what I believe are certain fallacies contained in those popular approaches, fallacies that, once again, I understood well by making most of them myself. I think it is of paramount importance, in trying to understand other theorists, to start by getting into a state of *strong sympathetic resonance* with what they are trying to say. I always try to assume the other's position until I feel I could argue it successfully in debate. Then, and only then, do I step back and intensely scrutinize it. If it fails in any major way, according to whatever wisdom I can muster, then I try to criticize it from a position of past sympathy. Even in the occasional polemical pieces I have written, I have rarely written polemically against any view that I did not myself once embrace; and, like a reformed smoker, I am occasionally insufferable for my condemnations. Many critics therefore assumed that I simply had a blind prejudice against these ideas and lacked the slightest compassion for their existence, whereas these critiques actually came out of an urgent desire to share mistakes that I myself had made. These two essays are prime examples of such. I stand by every conclusion in both of them, and only hope they can help to stem a certain regressive and elevationist tide that continues to dominate, as it always has, spiritual studies.

"Legitimacy, Authenticity, and Authority in the New Religions" came out of a series of seminars on the new religions, dealing with ways that we might be able to discriminate between dangerous cults (such as Jonestown and Synanon) and more beneficial movements (such as Zen or Kabbalah). This piece was written at the same time I did *A Sociable God* (which is contained in this volume) and suggests why and how a developmental view can help adjudicate authentic versus inauthentic religious involvement. "Structure, Stage, and Self" marked the first formal statement of phase-3 theorizing, so I will address that in a moment. And "The Ultimate State of Consciousness" returned, yet again, to the monotheme of all my writing: Always Already Truth. It is not uncommon for me, once I have devoted much of a book to the importance of development, to end on the theme of that which can *never* be reached by development or evolution at all, and that is the primordial Ground of Being, a Ground that, being the Condition of all conditions and the Nature of all natures, is always ever-present, and therefore could no more be reached or attained than we could attain our feet.

A Sociable God is an interesting book, I believe, for several reasons. To begin with, I wrote all of it in one fevered weekend. On a Friday afternoon I promised someone that I would have something soon, and on Monday morning put the manuscript in the mail. The entire book has a very terse, abstract, spartan, enormously condensed and crystalline style, for perhaps obvious reasons. It came out of a very intense intellectual space, and it conveyed ideas that I still believe are deeply important. It outlines the general spectrum of consciousness, focusing primarily on worldviews (archaic, magic, mythic, mental, psychic, subtle, causal, nondual). It then gives nine different ways that the word "religion" is commonly used, and points out that, at the very least, we need to distinguish between horizontal *legitimacy* (or how well a given religion provides meaning, integration, and value on a particular level) and vertical *authenticity* (or how well a given religion promotes transformation to higher levels altogether). Most religious scholars, in confusing these two scales, have seen the loss or disruption of a lower-level engagement that happened to be highly legitimate, and mistaken that for a loss of spiritual sensibilities altogether, when in fact it was often part of a larger movement to a more authentic stance. The classic example is the loss of the hegemony of a mythic-membership religion with the rise of modernity, which was not actually the loss of a transrational spirituality and its replacement by the devil of rationality, but was mostly the growth beyond prerational modes to rational modes *on the way to* the transrational. In this larger evolutionary view, the rational denial of God contained more Spirit than the mythic affirmation of God, for the simple reason that it contained more developmental depth. It was more authentic, even if it was occasionally less legitimate—it was a sick version of a higher level, compared to the previous healthy version of a lower level, so as we attempt to redress the ills of modernity, let us not forget the higher potential contained therein.

The criterion for depth—and the *scale of adjudication* used in *A Sociable God* (as in all of my works)—is *holistic embrace*: how much of the Kosmos can a given structure internally contain? Put objectively, how many types of holons does a particular self-organizing system contain in its own makeup? Put subjectively, how much love (Agape) is built into a structure? A quark is enfolded in an atom; an atom is enfolded in a molecule; a molecule into a cell; a cell into an organism. In each case, the holon gains more *depth*, because it lovingly embraces more of the Kosmos in its own makeup. Likewise with human holons: when my identity and sympathy expand from me to my family; from my family to friends, communities, even nations; from nations to all of humanity; and from humanity to all sentient beings without exception: what have I done?, except take more and more souls into my own, and increased thereby my own depth, by moving increasingly out of me and into the Kosmos at large, until what I call my "self" and what I call the "Kosmos" are one and the same undeniable Fact, and the Love that moves the sun and other stars now moves me just as well; and we are all embraced in a gentle compassion that knows no others nor outsiders, that refuses fragmentation and cannot remember sorrow's many names.

That scale—from egocentric to ethnocentric to worldcentric to Kosmic—is a scale of holistic embrace, and that scale is the one used in *A Sociable God* to adjudicate the authenticity of various cultural and religious engagements. Each higher embrace does not mean that individuality is increasingly obliterated, but that it is increasingly enlarged. A person who extends sympathy and caring from his own ego to his family, and from his family to his community, has not impoverished his self, but enriched it. Just so, to expand one's identity and sympathy from tribe to multitribe nation, and from nation to all humanity, and from humanity to all sentient beings, is simply to find a deeper Self in the midst of wider embraces. Kosmic consciousness is not the obliteration of individuality but its consummate fulfillment, at which point we can speak of Self or no-self, it matters not which: your Self is the Self of the entire Kosmos, timeless and therefore eternal, spaceless and therefore infinite, moved only by a radiant Love that defies date or duration.

That holarchy, or nest of increasingly holistic judgments, has been central to every work I have ever done, starting with *Spectrum*; and of course it was as well the backbone of *A Sociable God*, which was written right at the beginning of the eighties—right at the beginning, that is, of the aggressive colonization of all cultural studies by the extreme postmodernists. It would be a long time—almost two decades, really—before anybody could breathe the word "hierarchy" and not be lynched in "liberal" academia; before anybody could murmur the phrase "is better than" and not be brought before the postmodern tribunal and publicly branded a traitor to the cause. For the core of extreme postmodernism was the notion that all values are culturally relative; all realities are socially constructed; all truth is a subjective preference in the face of an essentially truthless world. Unfortunately, all of those statements are said to be true *for all people and for all cultures*, without exception. In other words, the extreme postmodernists were guilty of exactly the horrible sins they accused everybody else of: they pronounced a long list of *universal truths*, but with the further embarrassment that their universal truths were all self-contradictory. They claimed it was universally true that there are no universal truths, that it is a cultural invariant that there are no cultural invariants, that it is objectively true that there is no objective truth whatsoever. They claimed, in fact, that their position was superior in a world where nothing was supposed to be superior at all. Critics would eventually spot this duplicity and give it a technical moniker—"the performative contradiction"—but others would simply call it by its simpler name, hypocrisy.

And now, two decades later, as cultural studies itself awakens to a colossal hangover—an entire generation of scholarship often lost in performative contradictions—in narcissism and nihilism as a postmodern tag team from hell—we are in a position to pick up exactly where holistic hierarchies and value judgments left off: with ways of determining how to make sane, compassionate, and caring judgments based on degrees of depth, on degrees of love, on degrees of inclusion and holistic embrace. Pick up, that is, where numerous treatises, including *A Sociable God*, left off.

A Sociable God and *Up from Eden* are the books of phase-2 that particularly explored cultural worldviews. I would later (in phase-4) come to call this the Lower Left quadrant (the spectrum of collective or cultural consciousness, morals, worldviews, etc.). *The Atman Project* had already attempted to outline the Upper Left quadrant (the individual spectrum of consciousness). What both *Up from Eden* and *A Sociable God* further accomplished, I believe, was to *tie these two quadrants together*, and to believably show that individual and cultural *are inextricably bound by patterns of relational exchange*. That is, the human being is a compound individual, compounded of matter, body, mind, soul, and spirit (to use the simple five levels). Each level of the compound individual is actually *a system of mutual exchanges* with elements *at the same level of development* in the exterior world: matter with matter (physical food consumption), body with body (sexual procreation), mind with mind (symbolic communication), and so on. At every level, in other words, the subjective world is embedded in vast networks of intersubjective or cultural relationships, and vice versa, not as an afterthought or a voluntary choice, but as an inescapable pregiven fact. As I would later put it, agency is always agency-in-communion.

It is common to look at social evolution in terms of the various modes of techno-economic production, moving from foraging to horticultural to agrarian to industrial to informational (what I would call the Lower Right quadrant, or social systems). By supplementing that analysis with a focus on *worldviews* (which move correlatively from archaic to magic to mythic to mental to global),* *A Sociable God* was able to make a series of predictions that have held up quite well. One was that the breakdown of the civil religion (as discussed by Robert Bellah) would leave American culture open to several trends, including a retrenchment and even resurgence of fundamentalist religion, as well as a regression to narcissistic New Age agendas and intense self-absorption. It's not hard to find corroborative evidence for both of those in today's culture. But another, riskier prediction involved the fact that beyond the rational-egoic level is the first stage of transrationality, namely the psychic level, which supports a panenhenic, shamanic, nature mysticism. The

---

* It was *Sex, Ecology, Spirituality* that first specifically laid out the correlations of the Lower-Left quadrant (archaic, magic, mythic, rational, vision-logic) and the Lower-Right quadrant (foraging, horticultural, agrarian, industrial, informational) and further correlated those quadrants with the others. *A Sociable God* did not specifically discuss the Lower-Right quadrant, and *Up from Eden* tended to treat Lower Left and Lower Right as one dimension. It would be in phase-4 that these various distinctions and correlations were made. But *A Sociable God* and *Up from Eden* laid a foundation by correlating Upper Left and Lower Left in terms of a specific analysis of levels of structural organization and relational exchange.

prediction was that the most widespread, popular themes of a newly emerging spiritual orientation would therefore involve shamanic, panenhenic, nature mysticism and Gaia worship, focused on ecological consciousness and gross realm unity. More than I imagined, this has become the case. On the one had, this is altogether salutary, coming just in time, one hopes, to help stem a certain ecological catastrophe wrought, not by modernity per se, but by typical human greed, a greed which—most definitely present from the time of archaic foraging, but which at that time had not the means to express itself globally—finally found a way, by hijacking the fruits of modernity, to make itself suicidal on a global scale.

Alas, with this resurgence of nature mysticism has also come the standard, correlative distrust of all higher mystical states, including deity mysticism and formless mysticism. These are, as always, misinterpreted by panenhenic enthusiasts to be "other-worldly" and therefore supposedly anti-earth, anti-Gaia, and anti-ecological, whereas they actually transcend and include all of those concerns. But the nature mystics have come armed with angry words for souls who seek yet deeper and higher occasions, and I believe it will be decades before this particular fury runs its course.*

A Sociable God was also pioneering, in my opinion, in that it introduced a psychological model of *structures, states,* and *realms.* A person at almost any stage or structure of development (such as magic, mythic, rational) can have a temporary peak experience of any of the transpersonal realms (psychic, subtle, causal), and this gives us a grid of nine or more types of spiritual experiences. I outlined these different types of altered states or spiritual experiences (e.g., a magic, mythic, or rational peak experience of a psychic, subtle, or causal realm) and pointed out why these distinctions are crucial in understanding religion and religious experience. This "three-dimensional" model was, at the time, a novel integration of research on psychological structures (e.g., Piaget, Kohlberg, Gebser) and states of consciousness (e.g., Tart), and it has remained a central aspect of all subsequent phases of my work (phases 2, 3, and 4). A crucial conclusion was that higher development involves not just altered states but permanent traits—that is, the necessity of converting temporary peak experiences into permanent transpersonal structures. (See *Integral Psychology* for in-depth discussion of this model.)

---

* For an elucidation of the new Person-Centered Civil Religion, with its panenhenic outlook, see *One Taste*, September 23 entry.

Toward the end of this period I began not so much to question the evolutionary model as to appreciate both its strengths and its weaknesses. In particular, studies in developmental psychology were already starting to suggest that development does not proceed in a linear, monolithic fashion through a series of discrete ladder-like stages. Rather, overall development seems to consist of numerous different developmental lines or streams (such as cognitive, moral, affective, psychological, and spiritual) that progress in a relatively independent fashion through the levels or waves of the basic spectrum of consciousness (matter to body to mind to soul to spirit). If we simplify the spectrum of consciousness as going from preconventional to conventional to postconventional to post-postconventional waves, and if we use affects or feelings as an example of a particular stream, then we have preconventional affects (e.g., narcissistic rage, impulse gratification), conventional affects (belongingness, care, concern), postconventional affects (universal love, global altruism), and post-postconventional affects (transpersonal compassion, love-bliss, ananda). Likewise with cognition, morals, needs, self-identity, psychological development, and spiritual development (considered as a separate line), among many others.

Each of these developmental lines or streams traverses the same basic levels or waves, but each does so in a relatively independent fashion, so that, for example, a person can be at a very high level of cognitive development, a medium level of interpersonal development, and a low level of moral development, all at the same time. This shows how truly uneven and nonlinear overall development can be. A massive amount of research continued to demonstrate that the individual developmental lines themselves unfold in a sequential manner—the important truth discovered by developmental studies. But since there are at least two dozen different developmental lines, overall growth itself shows no such sequential development, but is instead a radically uneven and individual affair. Moreover, at any given time a particular individual might show much growth in one stream (say, psychological), while showing little or no growth in others (say, spiritual). None of this could be explained by a phase-2 model, but all of it made perfect sense according to phase-3.

Although I abandoned the strictly linear or "ladder-like" view of development by 1981, I am criticized to this day for presenting a rigidly linear view of development, where, it is alleged, psychological development must be fully complete before spiritual development can even begin. I never held that rigid a view even in phase-1, and I certainly abandoned anything remotely like that almost two decades ago. So I never know quite how to respond to these charges, other than to point out that they are untrue. But then, I have had a hand in this, as I sometimes continue to talk simply of "levels of development" as an introductory simplification (as I did in *A Brief History of Everything*); but still, one would hope that scholars in particular would view my work as a whole and correctly report my actual view.

In any event, I first presented that phase-3 model in "Ontogenetic Development: Two Fundamental Patterns" (*Journal of Transpersonal Psychology*, 1981), which appeared in *Eye to Eye* as "Structure, Stage, and Self" (included herein). The "two patterns" in the original title referred to the difference between the enduring basic structures (the major levels or waves in the spectrum of consciousness) and the transitional lines or streams that make their way through the basic levels. This understanding was implicit even in *The Atman Project*, where on several occasions I stated that "Although I have placed side by side such items as cognitive development, moral development, and ego development, I do not at all mean to equate them. . . . Loevinger, for one, thinks ego development is independent of psychosexual development. Kohlberg has shown that intellectual [cognitive] development is necessary but not sufficient for moral development. And so it goes, with all sorts of various developmental lines running parallel, independent, and/or correlative with all sorts of other developmental lines." That was written in 1978, during phase-2; but by 1981, with phase-3, I made all of those distinctions very explicit, and began to carefully present these different lines as the relatively independent streams that they are, while also continuing to emphasize the universal nature of the general waves in the overall spectrum of consciousness itself.

This move to phase-3 invalidated very few of the actual propositions of phase-2; it simply set them in a larger context. The pre/trans fallacy, for example, still applied to any developmental sequence, but it was now understood that there are many such sequences, so that a person could be preconventional in one line, conventional in another, and postconventional in yet another. The PTF was still valid, but one had to be sure one had a single developmental line each time one applied it. This changed none of the conclusions of phase-2, but opened them up to even richer elaborations.

From the beginning of phase-1 to the end of phase-2—from twenty-three years old to about thirty-one years old—I was living in various small apartments in Lincoln, Nebraska; was happily married to Amy Wagner; had left graduate school in biochemistry and was working as a dishwasher at the Red Rooster Restaurant; was meditating daily (with frequent retreats); and reading/writing at a terrifying rate. The last two years of that period saw a great burst of activity—*The Atman Project*, *Up from Eden*, and *A Sociable God* were all completed, plus many of the seminal essays in *Eye to Eye*. By the end of that period, Amy and I had amicably split after ten almost-always happy years (we simply grew in different directions), and I was on my way to Boston to try to salvage an integrative journal that Jack Crittenden and I had cofounded. Phase-2 was over, phase-3 was about to begin.

But I would always look back on the Lincoln years as my true education in all those things that mattered most.

A SOCIABLE GOD

*Toward a New Understanding
of Religion*

Foreword

O UR RELIGIONS, our Gods, and our selves may not be quite what we thought. That of course is nothing new. Indeed history can be read as an expression of their progressive evolution, as Ken Wilber has elegantly done in *Up from Eden*. For religion has been the driving force behind a vast range of behavior, calling forth the highest expressions of human nature and providing excuses for the lowest. Whole cultures have lived, killed, and died for their beliefs. Small wonder then that religion has been one of the central interests of psychology, sociology, and anthropology.

Throughout most of Western history religion was preeminent in defining our reality, and woe to the individual who suggested other views or even other methods of discovering truth (e.g., Galileo). Yet recent history, as if in recompense, has not been kind to religion; it has steadily lost ground to science and rationalism as the major purveyors of reality. Indeed, from the rational perspective, religion is frequently seen as a relic of prescientific thinking, an unfortunate carryover from less sophisticated times. God, if not dead, is at least moribund, surviving only through the unrequited longings of the psychologically immature.

Yet in recent years God has been staging a dramatic comeback, not only in traditional guise but in a full range of diverse forms, Eastern and Western, exoteric and esoteric, fundamentalist and gnostic. Christianity has seen both a fundamentalist revival and the reappearance of contemplative-mystical approaches. In addition, there has been an unprecedented influx of nonWestern religions and disciplines—yoga, Zen, TM, and all. Some of these differ so fundamentally from our traditional beliefs and practices as to call into question some of our most basic assumptions about the very nature of religion itself. Buddhism, for example, posits no supreme being or God and centers around a rigorous program of mental training explicitly aimed at controlled psychological processes and states of consciousness. On the morbid side, there is also no end of religious pathology; cults, Jonestown, and Moonies have become household terms.

Small wonder then that the study of religion, in any of its forms, has assumed new importance for both psychology and sociology. Sociologists have been particularly active in studying "the new religions" and in attempting to connect their emergence with larger social patterns and possible pathologies. They have therefore tended to link religious motivation to inadequacies at the social level, and immaturities at the psychological. And of course they are often correct since there is no shortage of evidence that religious immaturity and pathology reflect their psychological counterparts.

And yet the nagging question remains, Could we be missing something? Is this really all there is to religion? After all, the great saints and sages, Buddha, Christ, Lao Tzu, Shankara, Aurobindo, and others have been said to represent some of the highest levels of human development and to have had the greatest impact on human history. So at least said Toynbee, Tolstoy, Bergson, James, Schopenhauer, Nietzsche, and Maslow, among others. Thus we may ask, Are our guiding sociological assumptions, theories, and methodologies adequate to identify not just immaturity and pathology but also the heights of human experience and development that certain of the great religions claim are both possible and achievable through training?

It is the goal of this book to ensure that these heights are indeed identifiable, and it takes its psychological framework from recent developments in what has come to be known as transpersonal psychology.

The last two decades of psychological research have seen a dramatic surge of interest in areas such as the nature of consciousness and consciousness-modifying technologies, self-regulation of psychophysiological processes, and nonWestern psychologies. The general trend has been toward the recognition that there exist states of consciousness, levels of psychological maturity, and degrees of voluntary control beyond those formerly thought to define the human potential. Humanistic psychology first emerged in an effort to focus attention on these areas; transpersonal psychology followed when even the humanistic model proved inadequate to encompass the full range of phenomena being studied. The term "transpersonal" was chosen to encompass those experiences and states in which the sense of awareness and identity apparently went beyond *(trans)* traditional personality and ego.

In the West they were commonly called peak experiences and were initially assumed to occur only rarely and involuntarily. However, certain Eastern psychologies and religious disciplines were subsequently found to contain not only detailed descriptions of such states but also instructions and technologies for attaining them at will. Suddenly, and with no small surprise to Western psychologists, it began to become apparent that the esoteric core of certain of the great religions, Eastern and Western, which had formerly seemed nonsensical or even pathological, could be understood as technologies for the voluntary control of psychological processes and consciousness. To take but one specific example, meditation could now be seen as an attentional training strategy rather than as a regressive and autistic escape from the world, and this new interpretation now has significant support from empirical research.

Thus it was not that the great religions were necessarily pathological but rather that, prior to an understanding of the nature of such phenomena as state dependency, our own Western psychological framework had not been readily able to encompass such phenomena.

Of course this is not to say that all things Eastern or religious are of this ilk. There are clearly distortions, dogma, pathology, misunderstanding, and misuse around all religions. Indeed, the pragmatic core of rigorous mental training is often buried under exoteric trappings and dogma, or else reserved as an esoteric core for the few deemed able to meet its exacting demands. But where this core of mental training is found, it tends to display marked similarities among apparently quite diverse systems and to point to common psychological principles, worldviews, and transcendental states: the so-called "transcendent unity of religions," "perennial philosophy," and "perennial psychology."

The addition of a transpersonal dimension to traditional psychological models has thus allowed the meaningful reinterpretation of a major sphere of human activity. However, sociological theory has tended to lack a corresponding dimension and has thus sometimes been susceptible to an overly reductionistic approach in its studies of religion. This book therefore aims at adding a transpersonal dimension to sociological theory.

No one is more qualified to do this than Ken Wilber, who is recognized as the preeminent theoretician of transpersonal psychology. In his numerous books and papers he has provided an unparalleled integration of the world's major psychological and religious systems. In *The Spec-*

trum of Consciousness he suggested that the apparent conflict between different psychological and religious systems could be resolved by seeing them as addressing different and partly complementary structures of consciousness and levels of the unconscious. In *The Atman Project* he suggested a model for developmental psychology that extended through not only childhood and adolescence but also the various levels of enlightenment. In *Up from Eden* he applied this model to human evolution at large.

Now in *A Sociable God* he takes this same model and uses it as a developmental framework against which the various levels of social interaction can be assessed. This therefore provides a corrective addition to current methods of sociological analysis such as phenomenological-hermeneutics that have lacked critical criteria for hierarchical evaluation. It also provides a means for avoiding the trap of taking one level of social interaction and making it paradigmatic for all. For example, Marx interpreted all behavior in terms of economics, and Freud in terms of sexuality. Art, philosophy, religion, and all "higher" activities thus became expressions of economic oppression or sexual repression.

To this developmental framework Wilber also adds an analysis of the various epistemological modes, the ways in which we obtain knowledge. The fact that sensory, intellectual, and contemplative modes yield different realms or categories of knowledge that are not wholly equivalent or reducible one to another is often forgotten. Conceptual symbolic knowledge cannot wholly be reduced to the objective sensory dimension, nor the contemplative to the conceptual, without resulting in what is called category error. Thus the method for establishing the validity of each realm's knowledge is specific: analytic-empirical for objective data, hermeneutics for symbolic communication, and direct gnostic apprehension for the contemplative.

After delineating these general schemata, Wilber then applies them to specific, especially religious, issues confronting sociology today. First he performs the much-needed task of differentiating among the many and varied ways in which the term "religion" has been used, suggesting that much current confusion stems from imprecise or even mixed usage.

Next he turns to the evolution of religion and interprets its current status and directions against his developmental framework. Our current progression away from mythic belief toward increasing rationalization has been widely interpreted as evidence of an anti- or post-religious evolution. But Wilber reframes this whole movement by noting that this type of progression is an appropriate phase-specific shift as the prerational yields to the rational *on its way to the transrational*. From this evolutionary perspective our current phase is seen as antireligious only if religion is equated, as it often is, with the prerational rather than with any of several levels on the prerational–rational–transrational developmental hierarchy. This remarkable perspective also allows a method of determining what Wilber calls the authenticity of a religion: the degree to which it fosters development to the transrational levels. This he differentiates from "legitimacy," which he defines as the degree to which a religion fills the psychological and social needs of a population at its current developmental level. And all this leads directly to one of the more seminal parts of the book.

The current religious ferments and the new religions can be examined precisely in light of their responses to the current developmental phase of increasing rationality. Wilber suggests that three major types of sociological responses are now occurring: first, attempting to cling to the now outmoded mythic levels (e.g., "moral majority"); second, embracing the ongoing rational-secularization process (such as the liberal intelligentsia tend to do); and third, in a minority of cases, attempting actual transrational transformation, not by denying rationality but by embracing it *and* going beyond it via intensive yogic-gnostic practice. It is this latter group that Wilber suggests may provide effective catalysts for a broader-scale evolutionary advance, if indeed such is to occur. The importance of such widespread maturation to full development of the rational level, and then beyond, is difficult to overestimate. Our willingness and ability to correct the vast amounts of worldwide suffering from preventable causes such as malnutrition, poverty, overpopulation, sociogenic pathology, and oppression, as well as to avoid massive, if not total, self-destruction, may depend on it. The importance of Ken Wilber's contribution of a testable, critical, comprehensive, sociological model capable of guiding assessments of these evolutionary shifts is likewise not to be underestimated.

This could have been a very lengthy book. The number of novel ideas and suggested syntheses it contains within its few pages is remarkable. The author has chosen to give us an heuristic framework rather than a detailed text. Nonetheless, this outline may well be sufficient to keep both sociologists and psychologists busy researching and filling it out for many years to come, for it has suggested a way to move the psychology and sociology of religion to a new watershed.

Roger Walsh, m.d., ph.d.

Prologue

THIS BOOK IS an introductory overview of the psychology and sociology of religion, with particular emphasis on how modern sociological theory might benefit from a dialogue with the perennial philosophy—that is, from transcendental or "transpersonal" perspectives (hence the subtitle). In the terms of current sociology, it is an introduction to a "nonreductionistic" sociology of religion (or worldviews in general), and it is based on various tenets taken from modern functionalism (e.g., Parsons), hermeneutics (e.g., Gadamer), and developmental-structuralism (e.g., Habermas), all of which are carefully set in a context of transcendental or transpersonal possibilities (e.g., William James). The book is not "merely metaphysical" or "hopelessly idealistic," however, for it contains concrete methodologies and strategies for hypothesis formation and testing.

Of course, a transcendental or transpersonal sociology is, in part, a new type of approach; nonetheless, its topic is of direct and immediate relevance to any number of current social, psychological, and religious theories and topics, including the new religious movements in America, cults, the influx of Eastern mystical traditions, the breakdown of "civil religion," the psychology of religious experience, meditation, the process of sociological "legitimation" of worldviews, humanistic and transpersonal psychology, moral development, and so on—all of which, more or less, are woven together in the following pages by virtue of the scope of the topic itself. Scholars as well as educated laypersons concerned with any of those topics might thus find the book of interest.

I have, then, tried to provide the briefest possible statement of, and introduction to, a general transcendental sociology. *Brief,* for several reasons. For one, this is, in part, and as far as I know, the first attempt to broach the transcendental aspects of the subject, and first attempts deserve brevity. For another, I wished this book to be a concise statement of the *possibilities* of this field and not a rambling dissertation on its necessary content. The book itself, although scholarly, is meant to be accessible to the educated layperson interested in psychology, sociology, and religion, and brevity makes it that much more accessible. For scholars in these fields, my presentation of "just the skeleton" will allow them to add the meat and flesh of their own ideas, perspectives, and insights, without any further interference from me, thus arriving at a variety of fleshed-out products by virtue of their own additions (coproductions, as it were). I believe this skeleton is sound enough, and new enough, that no more need be presented in this initial outing; to do so would simply run the risk of overdetermining a new and fragile topic. Finally, by keeping the account sparse, I felt that the volume might more easily be used as an auxiliary text or for outside reading in any number of college or graduate courses on closely related topics.

But because this *is* a short introductory presentation, I have occasionally had to state my suggestions in a rather dogmatic and conclusive fashion. I would therefore like to emphasize that the following suggestions are, in fact, offered as hypotheses, and hypotheses that can potentially be tested—and potentially rejected—by a set of experimental methodologies. These methodologies are outlined in the last chapter. I might also say that this is one of those slightly awkward topics whose individual parts can better be understood once the overall topic is itself grasped, and thus this is one of those books that benefit from a second reading. At the least, the reader might, at the end, briefly reflect on the points that went before and see if they do not make a type of comprehensive sense perhaps not obvious at the first reading.

The word "transpersonal" might be new to some readers. For the moment, suffice it to say that it involves, in part, a sustained and experimental *inquiry* into spiritual, or transcendental (transpersonal), or "perennial philosophical" concerns. And it does so *not* in order to uncritically validate all so-called "religious experiences" but to attempt to develop legitimate and reproducible means for differentiating between authentic spiritual experience, if such indeed exists, and merely psychotic, hallucinatory, grandiose-exhibitionistic, paranoid, delusional, or other abnormal or pathological states. It is a *critical* discipline.

But because this book is, in part, one of the first attempts to bring a transpersonal or critical-transcendental dimension to sociology, it is faced with both a blessing and a curse. Blessing, in that one may, with only a modicum of intelligence, make pioneering observations, by simple definition. Curse, in that there are no precedents against which to judge the real value of those observations. This is quite different from even the recently introduced field of transpersonal psychology, for transpersonal psychology—under different names—actually goes all the way back to Plato, Augustine, and Plotinus, in the West, and Buddhaghosa, Patanjali, and Asanga in the East, and it can claim such contributors as Kant, Hegel, Bradley, Eckhart, C. G. Jung, William James, Jaspers, et al. This is because psychology itself, as a distinct discipline, goes back at least to Aristotle's *De Anima,* and transpersonal psychology, by whatever name, is simply the approach to psychology from the perspectives of the *philosophia perennis,* an approach that is thus as old as the perennial philosophy itself. Under the title "transpersonal psychology" it is, in a sense, a new and modern discipline, but it has a very old and very honorable history.

Sociology, on the other hand, is counted as perhaps the youngest of all the human sciences. Certain Renaissance and Enlightenment scholars—Hobbes, Locke, Rousseau, Machiavelli, Montesquieu, Vico—were sociologists of a sort. But it was not really until the nineteenth century, when the concept of *society* was finally distinguished from that of the *state,* that sociology emerged as a distinct discipline. The term "sociology" itself was not coined until 1838, by Auguste Comte, and its two great "founders," Émile Durkheim and Max Weber, wrote their first pioneering works in 1893 and 1920, respectively. A mere several decades ago.

Here is the catch: sociology, yet an infant, arose in an intellectual climate largely dominated by the then-fashionable scientific materialism, and many of its early proponents were overly influenced by mechanistic science (e.g., Comte) or material interactions (e.g., Marx), with the result that their sociologies are expressly reductionistic. Even that sensitive scholar Durkheim has recently been labeled, by Robert Bellah, as one of the two "great reductionists" in human sciences (the other being Freud). Being such a young science, sociology has only recently moved to correct these reductionistic trends, by, among other things, using models based on living and not mechanical systems (e.g., Parsonian functionalism) and introducing phenomenology and interpretive disciplines, or the study of the *meaning* of mental acts *as* mental acts and not merely as reducible to empirical-objective behaviorisms (Schutz, Berger, etc.).

All of that is good news, and all of that will be touched upon in the following pages. Beyond that, however, sociology has still not been opened to those concerns embodied in the perennial philosophy. On the one hand, this is because sociology is indeed an infant; it had not the advantage of being exposed to a Plato, a Spinoza, a Hegel, a Leibniz—all perennial philosophers of a sort. On the other hand, it is only recently that a modern, *experimental,* and systematic inquiry into the essential tenets of the *philosophia perennis* has been undertaken (largely by transpersonal psychologists), and so, prior to this, just exactly how to infuse sociology with genuinely transcendental or transpersonal concerns might not have been all that apparent anyway. In any event, I believe the time is now ripe for such an infusion.

The point is that the modern psychology of religion ought to have something to offer the modern sociology of religion, and this book is a short introduction to both.

1

The Background Problem
vis-à-vis Religion

THE AIM OF THIS BOOK is to suggest some contributions that transpersonal psychology might be able to make to the science of sociology, and especially the sociology of religion, by, first, sketching out the basics of transpersonal psychology and, second, transposing these basics into the categories and dimensions of modern sociological theory. That done, specific topics and problems—such as the new religions, cognitive validity of religious knowledge, some definitions of religion itself, hermeneutics and structuralism in religious universals, methodology of religious inquiry, and so forth—will be broached. It should be emphasized, however, that because of the large amount of theoretical ground that has to be covered quickly, this presentation will necessarily take place on a very tentative, generalized, and informal level.

The initial problem, for both the psychology and sociology of religion, is to provide theories and methodologies for determining or understanding the purpose, and perhaps secondarily the validity, of religious involvement. I would like very briefly to review the major sociological (and orthodox psychological) responses to this problem, in order to highlight the areas to which transpersonal psychology might eventually contribute.

Primitivization Theory

One of the first and apparently reflex approaches is "primitivization," which views religion in general as the product of lower or primitive stages of human development or evolution. In sociology, for example, Comte's famous "law of three" sees historical evolution as moving from myth-religion to metaphysics to rational science, in which case religion is simply viewed as a primitive consolation for a primitive mentality. Transposed by modern developmental psychologists, this phylogenetic development seems to find many parallels in today's ontogenetic development: the infant goes from prototaxic magical thinking to parataxic mythical thinking to syntaxic rationality.[87] Religion, it again seems, is prompted by fixations or regressions to infantile magic or childish myth, the latter being particularly marked by Oedipal object-relations and thus susceptible to paternal or especially patriarchal introjections and subsequent projections as a heavenly Father,[29] now loving, now vengeful, now jealous, now forgiving—everything you ever wanted to know about Jehovah. From primitivization sociology to rational-emotive theory to psychoanalysis to orthodox cognitive psychology, this "religious = childish" formalization has been pandemic, with Freud himself *(The Future of an Illusion)* leading the way.[31] Piaget also has extensively traced out the magical, mythical, "religious-type" thinking of early childhood and documented how such thinking tends to drop out as more formal and rational modes of thought emerge and develop.[70]

That particular developmental sequence—magic to myth to rationality—is not to be denied, as we will soon see in detail; problematic is its capacity to explain all, or even most, of the essential contours of religion. To give only the mildest objection now: even if all religious involvements were indicative of infantile-childish cognitions, that would at best explain their source but not their function or purpose—their *meaning* for those subscribing to them and their function in society at large.

Functionalism

It is not uncommon, then, that if a sensitive scholar first embraces primitivization as explanatory, he or she eventually moves on to some sort of functionalist approach (e.g., Parsons, Merton, Luhmann), if not to completely replace primitivization, then at least to supplement it.[62, 69] In functionalism or general systems theory, groups or societies are viewed as organic systems, with each of their "parts" (religion, education, customs, etc.) serving some type of potentially useful or necessary function. Religious symbolism is thus analyzed in terms of the salutary functions it serves in such specific areas as pattern maintenance, tension reduction, goal attainment, and so forth of the overall social organism. From this view, religious symbolism, if indeed it functions adequately (i.e., if it helps the system to reproduce itself), is to that extent *appropriate*.

In general functionalism, the functions and meanings of group or social activities are often divided into two dimensions, manifest and latent. The manifest function has a recognized value—it is more or less conscious, explicit, and expressed. The latent function, on the other hand, is neither recognized nor consciously intended—it is more or less implicit and unexpressed. Merton,[62] who introduced this distinction in sociology (cf. Freud's similar distinction in dreams), used the Hopi rain dance as an example. The manifest function of the ritual is to bring rain. However, such rituals also "fulfill the latent function of reinforcing the group identity by providing a periodic occasion on which the scattered members of a group assemble to engage in a common activity." The manifest meaning is apparent to the members of the group; the latent meaning, however, can usually be discovered only by specific functional analysis, that is, by the attempt to determine what the empirical and *objective* function of a particular relationship actually is and does, despite what the subscribers say or think it does (the manifest and subjective explanation).

When it comes to religion, then, various rites, symbols, and beliefs can be seen as serving legitimate functions. For even if, on a manifest level, the religious symbols are not objectively "true" (e.g., even if the rain dance does not actually bring rain), nonetheless on a latent level the rites and symbols serve a very necessary, useful, and to that extent "true" function: they help preserve and protect the overall integrity and cohesion of the group (they help the system to reproduce itself). Thus religious symbols, whether or not "objectively true," can nonetheless serve a legitimate purpose in the self-regulating social system. In short, religion serves some sort of function, perhaps hidden, and therefore has some sort of meaning, perhaps latent, in a given group or culture.

This, of course, is very similar to aspects of pragmatic psychology, such as that proposed by William James. Religious symbols can be appropriate units in the functioning of the psyche, regardless of the "objective truth value" of their supposed referents. For James, the very *belief* in spiritual realities could serve a salutary purpose that itself validated—indeed constituted—the truth-claim of the belief.[51]

There is clearly merit to this approach, and we will want to retain aspects of it in our overall formulation (even as we will find a place for a type of limited primitivization). But the functionalist approach in and by itself is expressly reductionistic. Religion is not actually a communion with some sort of true divinity, spirit, or godhead; it is really not much more than a safety-valve function. Its referent is not actual divinity; its *referent* is merely other symbols in a circle of social transactions. In other words, religion is not really religious; it is not about very God, but about various god-symbols, themselves composed of merely human social reciprocities.

If used exclusively, this approach heavy-handedly negates or at least re-interprets the actual validity claims of the subscribers themselves, and thus bypasses or reduces the central part, the subjective part, the phenomena it is asked to explain. Not surprisingly, it is forced to place the "real meaning" of religiousness exclusively in a latent dimension where it can hide from the objections of the subscribers. This is not to deny that there *are* latent dimensions and functions in a belief system, for there are; it is to object to the pandemic reduction of the manifest-subjective intentionality to a latent-empirical function.

Thus, for functionalism, Lao Tzu, Buddha, Krishna, and Christ were not really intuiting a transcendent ground of being, which is what *they* said they were doing (their manifest intent). The functionalist can find no objective evidence, no empirical referent, for this "transcendental ground," and therefore what these sages were *really* doing was serving some sort of merely latent function unknown to them. The transcendental ground, *as* transcendental ground, never enters the picture, contrary to everything the sages themselves actually had to say on the subject.

But there are orthodox objections to exclusive functionalist systems theory as well. Preeminent among them is the apparent fact that human goal states and values cannot be determined via empirical-analytic or merely objective methods.[32] For, unlike the merely biological systems that form the basis of the functionalist model, human interactions also possess conscious meanings, values, goals, and purposes, and these relations are not so much objective as they are intersubjective. Consequently, they are disclosed not so much by objective measurement and analysis as by intersubjective communication and interpretation, and these intersubjective interpretations slide through the system without leaving completely empirical-objective footprints.[38] For example, one cannot easily devise an empirical-scientific test that will disclose the meaning of *Hamlet*. *Hamlet* is a mental and symbolic production whose meanings and values disclose themselves only in a community of inter-subjective interpreters. Functionalism, in its attempt to be empirical and objective, often misses the essence of these intersubjective meanings and values. On the other hand, if one attempts to overcome this shortcoming by simply stipulating the goal values and states that will then guide analysis of the system, that amounts to a normative and interpretive as opposed to empirical approach, which functionalism claims to be. Trying to account for these normative-interpretive dimensions by feeding them back into the empirical functions of the system (e.g., Luhmann) is again to reduce the former to the latter.

PHENOMENOLOGICAL-HERMENEUTICS

As theorist-researchers begin to question this reductionism (in its psychological or sociological forms), it is not uncommon for them to move from exclusively functionalist analyses to something resembling phenomenological-hermeneutics: from at least one completely valid perspective, *the religious symbol is exactly what it says it is.* It is not merely a manifest function hiding the real latent function, or just a safety valve, or only a tension-reduction or social-cohesion mechanism—it is fundamentally what it says it is. If Buddha or Krishna was lucid and legitimate in his communicative meaning, and he said he was contacting a fundamental ground of being, then that is our only starting point. And if I want to *understand* that point, if I want to understand anyone else's symbols and meanings, then the best approach is some sort of *empathetic interpretation* (just as if I wished to understand *Hamlet* or any other symbolic communication). I must *reproduce* in *my* awareness via *interpretation* the *inner* world or meaning of Krishna or Hamlet or Job or whomever, there only to grasp its essential message.[32,49,46,68]

The science of such interpretation is generally called "hermeneutics," from the Greek *hermeneutikos,* to translate or interpret, and from Hermes, god of science, commerce, and eloquence. Hermeneutics has its modern roots in general phenomenology, or the attempt to discover the nature and meaning of mental acts *as* mental acts, and not merely as reduced to various objective, sensory, and empirical displays. For a merely sensory-empirical object—say a rock—does not necessarily point to or refer to anything other than itself. But a *mental* event—a concept or symbol—by its very nature points to or *refers to* other entities and events, including *other* symbols, which themselves can refer to yet other symbols, and so on in an *intersubjective* circle of symbolic meanings and values. In short, a mental act *as* mental act is what Husserl called *intentional*: it has *meaning* or *value* because it refers to or embraces other occasions, including other meanings and symbols and values. Phenomenology is an attempt to directly study this realm of intersubjective *intelligibilia,* not merely the realm of objective *sensibilia,* and hermeneutics is simply the branch of phenomenology that is especially concerned with interpreting the meanings of these intersubjective or intentional symbols.

Accordingly, if I want to understand the meaning of a particular religious system, I must not do so in a merely empirical, objective, reductionistic fashion. I must first empathetically understand the system by reproducing or entering its intersubjective and interpretive circle (the "hermeneutic circle"). Schools differ as to whether interpretation should be empathetic or actually participant (where feasible), but some form of *inside understanding* and *interpretive engagement* is deemed absolutely fundamental. The *meaning* of a religious expression is not solely or even especially to be found in, for example, its latent tension management, but rather in its manifest intentionality and its intersubjective acknowledgment. And the way you—as an "outside investigator"—determine that intersubjective meaning is to enter (not necessarily physically) the hermeneutic circle itself, the circle constituted by the intersubjective exchange of linguistic symbols, an exchange that is always set in a particular *historical* context. Hence the common title: historical-hermeneutics. If I want to understand the religious meaning of the word "sin," for example, I must take into account the *historical* context of the symbol itself, because what is "sin" to one epoch is not necessarily "sin" to another (whatever happened to gluttony and sloth, once "deadly sins"?). Merely defining "sin" objectively misses its historical referents and thus leads to bad interpretations, bad hermeneutics, ethnocentric bias, and so forth.[33,34]

This general phenomenological-hermeneutical approach has had an immense influence on both the psychology of religion—James's *Varieties* is a type of forerunner—and the sociology of religion—Ricoeur, for example, or Robert Bellah's "symbolic realism," which is a type of hermeneutic Durkheim, if I am allowed to say that. Likewise, I have watched many psychologist colleagues move from an initial fascination with systems theory and psychocybernetics (the scurrying of information bits through personless neurons) to a more comprehensive system that also includes an attempt to grasp the *meaning* of that information in terms of a self that shapes and is shaped by history. The self as history, hopelessly interlocked with other selves as history, constitutes not merely information but a *story,* a *text,* with beginnings and middles and endings and ups and downs and outcomes, and the way you grasp the meaning of a text is via good interpretation: hermeneutics.

There is obviously much to be said for phenomenological-hermeneutics, and we will be drawing significantly on many of its tenets as we proceed. But taken in and by itself, hermeneutics seems finally to suffer a series of unhappy limitations. Foremost among these is its radicalization of situational truth and its consequent lack of a universal or even quasi-universal critical dimension, a way to judge the actual validity, not just interpretive mesh, of a religious truth claim. Krishna may have been transcending, but was the Hopi really producing rain? How are we to differentiate the authentic from the less than authentic engagements? Hermeneutics of course denies that such a critical or universal dimension exists, thereby relativizing all cultural truths with the quite illogical exception of its own claim that such is always (i.e., universally) the case.

For hermeneutics, all religious expressions—indeed, all symbolic productions—are to be understood from the inside; *verstehenden* sociology at its extreme. If you are *in* the hermeneutic circle, consensual interpretive agreement is validation; if you are outside the circle, you are not allowed a judgment. In neither case can the circle itself be shown to be wrong, or partially wrong, or even just *partial.* Such theoretical absolutizing of cultural relativity often translates itself, in the field, into exasperation,[3] an exasperation apparently due in some cases, not to incorrect methodological application, but to a more native preunderstanding that not *all* religious expressions are "true" and that some form of critical appraisal is mandatory.

Hermeneuticists and symbolic realists, of course, reply that this exasperation must be due to methodological or interpretive malfunction, because there is no *external standard* against which religious expressions could possibly be critically appraised, without, it is said, committing reductionism. Thus, any attempt to say other than what the particular hermeneutic circle itself says is, in a priori fashion, charged with reductionism, and thus hermeneutics, in and by itself, under the guise that it is being "nonreductionistic," tends all too rapidly to slide into the limp notion that "*all* religions are true," a stance that precludes any sort of sustained critical appraisal. Hermeneutics has no teeth.

DEVELOPMENTAL STRUCTURALISM

Not only does exclusive hermeneutics deny those truths of functionalist systems theory that *are* partially true—for example, the possibility that there are latent functions performed by a text outside the knowledge of the text—it also overlooks the advances made in modern structural-developmental sciences, especially in the lines of Baldwin,[8] Piaget,[70] Werner,[95] Kohlberg,[54] and Loevinger.[57] For the seminal discovery of these disciplines is that psychological structures develop in a *hierarchic* fashion. Barring arrest, regression, or fixation, each stage of development includes, comprehends, or subsumes the basic elements of its predecessors but adds significant structures and functions not found in its predecessors—each stage "transcends and includes" its predecessors in a *nested hierarchy,* a development that is envelopment.[100] The senior level includes the junior but *not vice versa,* and it is that "not vice versa" that constitutes and establishes a very real hierarchy. Each senior stage displays a greater degree of structuralization, differentiation-integration, organization, functional capacity, and so on through a dozen variables found to define, via a developmental-logic, the meaning of the word *higher.* Thus, developmental psychologists speak unabashedly about *higher stages* of cognition (Piaget), ego development (Loevinger), interpersonal relations (Selman), moralization (Kohlberg), and even *quality,* as the psychoanalyst Rapaport explains: "*Structures are hierarchically ordered.* This assumption is significant because it is the foundation for the psychoanalytic propositions concerning differentiation . . . , and because it implies that the *quality of a process depends upon the level of the structural hierarchy on which it takes place*"[76] (my italics).

Accepting for the moment that psychology is always also social psychology, this overall hierarchization is extremely significant, because it apparently gives us—perhaps for the first time—a paradigm to *adjudicate the comparative degree of validity* of various psychosocial productions (including religious expressions). A similar approach has already been suggested by Habermas,[41] who wants to use, among other schemes, Kohlberg's stage-structures of moralization to adjudicate the developmental level of interactive competence evidenced in various individuals and, indeed, societies and historical epochs at large.

Before looking more carefully at this nested hierarchy paradigm, let us note that Habermas explicitly recognizes it as a corrective to historical-hermeneutic inquiry. Habermas utilizes some of the essentials of hermeneutics, such as its emphasis on narrative history and communicative competence, but he stresses that against hermeneutics, as a *narrative foil,* must be placed the hierarchic realizations of a developmental-logic. The fact of *levels* of narrative development *imposes* on any given narrative a competency status that is not and cannot be determined solely by empathetic interpretation of the narrative itself. There is, in other words, some sort of *external corrective* to the heremeneutic circle, and that external corrective is a scheme of developmental levels of narrative competence.

Finally, we note that, by virtue of nested hierarchy, each higher structure of consciousness is potentially capable of *legitimately criticizing* the partiality, but not the phase-specific appropriateness, of its lower predecessors, precisely as, for example, a person of formal operational thinking can criticize the lopsided egocentrism of preoperational thinking, or a stage-5 moral stance will criticize the lack of perspectivism of stage-2 stance. In other words, structural-developmentalism seems to give us that universal or quasi-universal critical dimension or external corrective apparently lacking in merely hermeneutic, phenomenological, or symbolic realist approaches.

OUR OVERALL APPROACH

With all of the above as background, we can now state that the crux of this book is the suggestion that there exists a nested hierarchy not only of psychosocial development but also of authentic religious development, and that, in fact, these two run precisely into each other as two ends of a single spectrum, and that, finally, the hierarchical nature of this spectrum will give us a critical-normative sociology of religion, one that is capable of *structurally analyzing* various religious expressions, assigning them a spot in the hierarchy, consequently adjudicating their degree of authenticity, and accordingly pronouncing that, in terms of an *overall critical sociological theory,* this or that religious engagement is *higher* than this or that other religious engagement, *precisely* as we now say, for example, a stage-6 moral response is higher than a stage-4 response. In addition to this developmental-structuralism, we will also find necessary, appropriate, but circumscribed roles for functional systems analyses, hermeneutical inquiries, and even a type of primitivization theory, attempting, as it were, to salvage the moments of truth of each of the approaches we have so briefly discussed.

Before we begin such a construction, we need some background information, particularly from the field of transpersonal developmental psychology.

2

The Nested Hierarchy of Structural Organization

THE ORTHODOX BASE

HERE IS A VERY SIMPLIFIED, streamlined, and composite version of the nested hierarchy of structural organization as discovered by orthodox developmental psychology (I have included a few of their Eastern psychological correlates for future reference).

1. *Physical:* the simple physical substratum of the organism (the first and lowest Buddhist *skandha;* the first and lowest yogic chakra; *annamayakosha* in Vedanta).
2. *Sensoriperceptual:* the areas of sensation (the second skandha) and perception (the third skandha) treated as one general realm; simple sensorimotor cognition (Piaget).
3. *Emotional-sexual:* the sheath of bioenergy, libido, élan vital, or prana (the fourth skandha in Buddhism, the *pranamayakosha* in Vedanta; second chakra).*
4. *Magical:* the beginning of the mental realms; this includes simple images, symbols, and the first rudimentary concepts, or the first and lowest mental productions, which are "magical" in the sense

---

* For simplicity's sake, I will usually refer to these lowest three levels as "the" *archaic* level.

42

that they display condensation, displacement, confusion of image and object, "omnipotence of thought," animism, and so forth. There is also a lack of perspectivism, or an inability to clearly take the role of other. This is Freud's primary process, Arieti's paleologic, Piaget's preoperational thinking (the third chakra). It is correlated with Kohlberg's preconventional morality, Loevinger's impulsive and self-protective stages, Maslow's safety needs, and so forth.

5. *Mythic:* more advanced than magic, with a beginning of concrete operational thinking (Piaget) and a beginning of perspectivism (or communal role-taking), but still incapable of the simplest hypothetico-deductive reasoning, consequently "mythic" in its operation (cf. Gebser); the overall "lower mind" (the fourth chakra, the beginning of *manomayakosha* in Vedanta and *manovijnana* in Mahayana). It is correlated with Loevinger's conformist and conscientious-conformist stages, Maslow's belongingness needs, Kohlberg's conventional morality, and so forth. Because of its overall *conformity* status, we often refer to this general level as "mythic-membership."

6. *Rational:* Piaget's formal operational thinking (the fifth chakra, the culmination of manomayakosha and manovijnana). It is the first structure that can not only think about the world but think about thinking; hence, it is the first structure that is clearly self-reflexive and introspective, and it displays an advanced capacity for perspectivism. It is also the first structure capable of hypothetico-deductive or propositional reasoning ("if a, then b"), which allows it to apprehend higher or purely noetic *relationships*. It is correlated with Loevinger's conscientious and individualistic stages, Kohlberg's post-conventional morality, Maslow's self-esteem needs, and so forth.

Figure 1 (page 44) indicates these general stage-structures and their hierarchical nature. I have placed a gap between each structure to indicate that they are largely emergent or discontinuous in development; that is, they cannot be fully reduced to or explained solely in terms of their predecessor(s)—what has come to be called emergent evolution[71] or milestone development[57] (which does not preclude the continuous and linearly unbroken development *within* each level, or what is known as "polar development"). Each line in figure 1 is evolution; each gap, revolution.

THE TRANSPERSONAL LEVELS

The problem of this section is, Where in figure 1 does religious expression belong?

Let us begin by noting that there is an increasing reacceptance, among developmental-structuralists, of the notion of phylogenetic/ontogenetic parallels: Primitive-paleolithic magic is similar in deep structure (*not* surface structure) to infantile–early childhood preoperational thinking; classic religio-mythic expressions are similar in deep structure to late childhood preoperational and beginning concrete operational thinking; and modern rational-science is top of the hierarchy with adolescent-to-adult formal operational and hypothetico-deductive reasoning.[5,66,95,105] As Arieti[5] explains,

> What is of fundamental importance is that the [two] processes to a large extent follow similar developmental plans. This does not mean literally that in the psyche . . . ontogeny recapitulates phylogeny, but that there are certain similarities in the . . . fields of development and that we are able to individualize schemes of highest forms of generality [deep structures, for example, as in figure 1] which involve all levels of the psyche in its [different] types of development.

If we accept for the moment that there is some sort of truth to that idea—for I think there most definitely is—then we are faced with certain

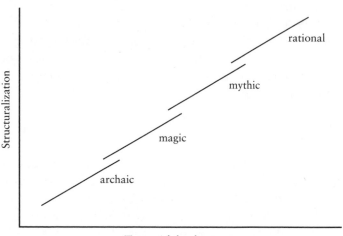

FIGURE 1

grave problems vis-à-vis legitimizing religious consciousness. For what we have, when figure 1 is seen to be not only an ontogenetic but also a phylogenetic/ideogenetic chart, is actually a very sophisticated theory of religious primitivization, an update and slight expansion of Comte's law of three. For, if we treat religion as a structure among other structures, and not something potentially shared by them all (we will investigate that later), then *increasing historical development* clearly shows an eventually *decreasing religiosity.* Paleolithic humans had magic religion: totem ritual that expressed the fusion of human and animal ancestor, voodoo-like rituals, animistic beliefs, and so on. Neolithic and Bronze Age humans had classical mythic religion: gods and goddesses controlling their fate, with petitionary rituals and prayers offered by humans to their heavenly fathers and mothers. And then, finally, comes the revolution of rationality (starting with Greece c. sixth century B.C., reaching its stride with eighteenth-century Enlightenment thought but only today beginning to claim a clearly dominant structural role).[105] This increasing rationalization brought the eventual retreat of religion (in any conventional sense) as a widespread, legitimate worldview, its place being taken increasingly by hypothetico-deductive reasoning, empirical-analytic inquiry, and technical interests, as sociologists from Weber onward have noted.

By this scheme there is no highly developed religious structure of consciousness, for the highest structure is rational-scientific. It appears that we have no choice but to capitulate to the primitivizationists, psychoanalysts, and such—religion is *basically* a primitive fixation/regression to infantile magic or childhood myth (rationalized, if necessary). Such a *developmental argument,* I believe, can even disarm Bellah's refutation of psychoanalytic reductionism, because here the analyst is not interpreting religious symbolism in terms of something foreign to the person himself, but rather is demonstrating that the religious symbol has its own internal structure that *places itself* in the history of hierarchic structuralization of the person's psyche. Analysis merely helps the individual to remember and reconstruct this history so as to more clearly see how it is presently opaque in its influence. To say this is reductionistic is to say that helping a person move from stage-3 morality to stage 4, 5, or 6 is reductionistic.

There are only two ways out of this impasse. The first is to claim that phylogenetic/ideogenetic evolution is in fact devolution—that there actually existed in the past a historical Garden of Eden on earth, perhaps in the Bronze Age of mythic religion, and that we have gone steadily downhill since. Since evolution is really devolution, the *earlier* stages are really *higher*. To empirical scientists this might seem a somewhat silly notion, but I remind the reader that such sober and respected religious scholars as Joseph Campbell[23] and Huston Smith[86] have more than flirted with this idea. I have also found that among sympathetic scholars of religion it is something of a point of honor to believe this. Nonetheless, for various reasons it is a concept I find thoroughly unconvincing, as only someone could who entitled a book on the subject *Up from Eden.*

The second way out of this impasse is to open the possibility that there are stages of structuralization higher than formal operational thinking. Ontogenetically, this would mean that an individual today can develop beyond exclusively rational forms of mentation to some sort of higher stage or stages of consciousness as yet unspecified. Phylogenetically, it means that evolution is still continuing and that human culture at large faces further and higher levels of (r)evolutionary structuralization.

But that idea reminds us immediately of Hegel,[45] who saw history as eventually transcending mental self-consciousness in the absolute knowledge of spirit as spirit. There are Aurobindo,[7] who maintained that evolution is driving toward supermind realization; Teilhard de Chardin,[91] who saw it culminating in omega point, or Christ consciousness at large; and the great Russian philosopher Berdyaev,[15] who concluded that evolution moves from subconsciousness to self-consciousness to superconsciousness (his words). Despite the excesses of some of these presentations, the point is that the general concept of evolution continuing beyond its present stage into some legitimately transrational structures is not a totally outrageous notion. Look at the course of evolution to date: from amoebas to humans! Now what if that ratio, amoeba-to-human, were applied to future evolution? That is, amoebas are to humans as humans are to—what? Is it ridiculous to suggest that the "what" might indeed be omega, *geist,* supermind, spirit? That subconscious is to self-conscious as self-conscious is to superconscious? That prepersonal gives way to personal, which gives way to transpersonal? That Brahman is not only the *ground* of evolution but the *goal* as well?

What is specifically needed, however, beyond these generalizations, is some sort of more precise specification of what the higher structure-stages of consciousness might be. For various reasons, I first looked to the psychological systems of Hinduism and Buddhism for possible answers; I later found these answers echoed in Sufism, Kabbalah, neo-

Confucianism, mystical Christianity, and other esoteric traditions. What struck me about these traditional psychologies is that, although they often lacked the detailed sophistication of modern Western psychologies, they were perfectly aware of the general features of the level-structures so intensively investigated in the West (i.e., physical, sensorimotor, emotional-sexual, lower mental, and logic-rational). Nonetheless, they universally claimed that these levels by no means exhausted the spectrum of consciousness—there were, beyond the physical, emotional, and mental levels, higher levels of structural organization and integration.

For instance, Vedanta Hinduism claims there are six major structure-levels of consciousness.[26] The first and lowest is called annamayakosha, literally the level made of physical food, or the physical body. The second is pranamayakosha, the level of emotional-sexuality (prana is an almost exact equivalent of libido). The third is manomayakosha, the level of mind. This level also includes, besides rationality, the "dream aspects" of mentation; dreams, says Shankara, are basically wish-fulfillments, composed of the person's "fantasy and desires." The fourth is vijnanamayakosha, higher mental or transrational or intuitive cognition, the beginning of actual spiritual insight. The fifth is anandamayakosha, the level of ecstatic illumination-insight. The highest state is *turiya,* or Brahman-Atman itself, although it is not so much one level among other levels but the ground, reality, or suchness of all levels (*tathata,* the Buddhists call it).

Anyway, I undertook an explicitly hermeneutic reading of the world's great traditional psychologies, attempting to analyze and interpret the general structural units of meaning presented in the various classic texts. I practiced Zen Buddhism under various teachers for ten years, so I know at least one tradition "from the inside," via empathetic participation.

The result of this hermeneutical and practical encounter with the traditional psychologies was presented in *The Atman Project,*[101] although in an extremely skeletal fashion and without methodological explanation. The conclusion was that it is indeed plausible that there are higher stages of structural organization and integration, and that these higher stages increasingly display what can only be called a spiritual or transcendental tone. These higher structure-stages I called, largely after Vedanta, the psychic, the subtle, the causal, and the ultimate levels. If we add these higher stages to figure 1, then we arrive at a tentative overall scheme of the developmental and structural spectrum of consciousness (see figure 2; Brahman—or Dharmakaya or Keter or Godhead—is said

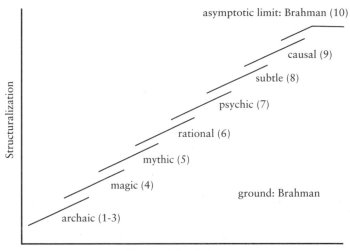

FIGURE 2

to be both the limit-at-infinity of growth, which I have listed as the asymptote, and the ever-present ground of all levels of growth, which can be represented by the paper itself, which I have labeled "ground").

We can also draw this as a circle and then more easily add the three large domains of development—subconscious (prepersonal), self-conscious (personal), and superconscious (transpersonal)—although their precise alignments with the specific structures are, of course, somewhat arbitrary. (See figure 3.)

Let me very briefly describe the higher or transpersonal levels, as disclosed in the various texts themselves. At the same time, I will correlate these levels with the basic types of *esoteric religious practice,* as suggested by such spiritual adepts as Aurobindo[7] and Free John,[22] and the Vajrayana tradition.[101]

The *psychic level** does not necessarily or even usually refer to paranormal events, although some texts say these can more readily or controllably occur here. More specifically, the psychic level can be best understood in reference to the level preceding it, that of formal opera-

---

* In this book I am treating the centauric and the psychic as one domain: as the great transition from personal to transpersonal. Technically, vision-logic is centauric (the "highest" of the personal realms), and vision is psychic (the "lowest" or beginning of the transpersonal realms), but they can, for convenience, be treated together as the transition into the spiritual domains.

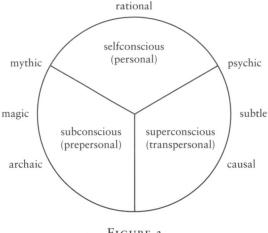

FIGURE 3

tional or propositional reasoning, whose form is "if a, then b." The psychic level simply works with or operates on the results of formal mentation. That is, where the formal mind establishes higher relationships ("if a, *then* b"), psychic cognition establishes *networks* of those relationships. The point is to place each proposition alongside numerous others, so as to be able to see, or "to vision," how the truth or falsity of any one proposition would affect the truth or falsity of the others. Such panoramic or *vision-logic* (the technical term I use to describe the cognitive operations of this level) apprehends a mass network of ideas, how they influence each other, what their relationships are. It is thus the beginning of truly higher-order synthesizing capacity, of making connections, relating truths, coordinating ideas, integrating concepts. It culminates in what Aurobindo called the "higher mind." It "can freely express itself in single ideas, but its most characteristic movement is a mass ideation, a system or totality of truth-seeing at a single view; the relations of idea with idea, of truth with truth, self-seen in the integral whole."

This is obviously a highly *integrative* structure. Although it might be thought of as the first and lowest of the transpersonal levels [psychic], it might also be described as the last and highest of the personal structures [centauric], beyond which lie more transcendental occasions. This highly integrated, highest personal structure is, in my opinion, generally correlated with Loevinger's integrated and autonomous stages, Maslow's self-actualization needs, Broughton's integrated stage, and so forth. (In Eastern systems, this is the sixth chakra, the beginning of manas and vijnanamayakosha, Tiferet, etc.)

Many orthodox psychologists have already suggested that there are probably one or more cognitive stages beyond formal operational. Bruner, for instance, believes that some adults may progress from being intelligent (formal operational) to being intelligent about intelligence (or operating on formal operations). The structure we are proposing here— vision-logic—seems to fit that bill exactly, with the added advantage that it meshes explicitly with various Eastern systems (as expressly stated by, for example, Aurobindo, as the above quote makes clear).

Owing to the intense panoramic awareness offered at this level—or rather, at its most mature and highly developed state*—the individual might begin to experience intense insight and even illumination, illumination that seems to go beyond thought into a type of vision, noetic, numinous, inspiring, often enstatic, occasionally ecstatic.[7,22] This can also result in a type of nature cosmic consciousness, or merging of self with the naturic universe (not to be confused with theistic or monistic mystical experiences, as we will see).[7] Those adepts mastering such states, via body manipulation and mental concentration, are generally known as *yogis*.

This does not mean that all who call themselves "yogis" actually attain this level. Nor does it mean that those who call themselves yogis never proceed higher than this level. It is just that the traditions that specifically describe themselves as *yogic* more often than not embody and express an understanding that most centrally reflects the psychic level, as clearly explained by Free John.[22] In the terms of chakra psychology, classic yogic discipline (hatha, kundalini, and ashtanga yoga) most centrally deals with those energies and insights leading from the first or root chakra, at the base of the spine, up through the sixth or ajna chakra, the "blue pearl," the "third eye," between and behind the brows. The ajna chakra is the embodiment of the psychic structure as here described. Beyond that point, consciousness leaves the psychic and enters the subtle.

The subtle level is said to be the seat of actual archetypes, of Platonic forms, of subtle sounds and audible illuminations *(nada, shabd),* of transcendent insight and absorption.[22,85,86,105] Some traditions, such as Hinduism and Gnostic Christianity, claim that, according to direct phenomenological apprehension, this level is the home of personal deity-

---

* In other words, the difference between centauric vision-logic and psychic vision.

form (*ishtadeva,* demiurge, *yidam*), cognized in a stage known as *savikalpa samadhi* in Hinduism.[26,86,117] Overall, this is the level of the "illumined mind" (Aurobindo); the culmination of manas and vijnamayakosha; a truly transrational structure (not prerational and not antirational); intuition in its highest and most sober sense (gnosis, jnana, prajna), not emotionalism or merely bodily felt meaning or vegetative-pranic-privatistic "hunch"; home of archangelic forms or ideas; bijamantra, vasanas; beginning of seventh chakra (the *sahasrara*); and, of course, the start of Maslow's *self-transcendence needs.*

Those adepts who master these subtle realms of halos of truth and light, revelations of subtle sound, and direct soul-God-communion are generally known as *saints.* Again, this does not mean that all who call themselves saints have reached this level, nor that some authentic saints do not surpass this level. It means only that the disciplines, practices, and insights of the saintly traditions tend most centrally to reflect the subtle level of structural organization. In the terms of shabd chakra psychology, the subtle region begins at the sixth or ajna chakra, continues into the seventh or sahasrara, and then discloses several more levels of subtler and subtler hierarchic structures secreted within and beyond the sahasrara itself. Those adepts who master such subtle structures—nicely symbolized (both East and West) by halos of light at the crown of the head (sahasrara)—are generically referred to as saints. Beyond these saintly revelations, however, lies the causal/ultimate ground itself, or radical and transcendental Consciousness as Such.

The *causal level* is said to be the unmanifest source or transcendental ground of all the lesser structures, what Aurobindo called the "overmind." It is realized in a stage of consciousness known variously as *nirvikalpa samadhi* (Hinduism), *nirodh* (Theravada Buddhism), *jnana samadhi* (Vedanta), the eighth of the ten ox-herding pictures (of Zen). This is the anandamayakosha (Vedanta), the *alayavijnana* (Mahayana), Keter, and so forth. Passing fully through the state of cessation or unmanifest absorption, consciousness is said finally to reawaken to its absolutely prior and eternal abode as spirit, radiant and all-pervading, one and many, only and all. This is classical, *sahaj samadhi,* the state-condition of *turiya,* transcendental and unqualifiable consciousness as such, Aurobindo's "supermind," Zen's "One Mind," Brahman-Atman itself, Ein Sof, the Svabhavikakaya, and such. Throughout this book I will, for convenience, treat the causal and ultimate "levels" as one—spirit in the highest sense, not as a Big Person but as the "Ground of Being" (Tillich), "Eternal Substance" (Spinoza), "Geist" (Hegel), the ground *and* the goal of development-revolution itself.

The causal/ultimate level does not involve any particular experience but rather the dissolution or transcendence of the experiencer itself, the death of the watcher principle. That is, the subject-object duality is radically transcended, so that the soul no longer contemplates Divinity, it becomes Divinity, a release the Sufi calls the Supreme Identity. If the subtle is the home of God and God-communion, the causal/ultimate is the home of Godhead and Godhead Identity.[7,22,26,81,86,101,117]

At that stage, asymptotic at infinity, one becomes radically egoless, or free of the separate self sense, thus assuming an absolute identity with all manifestation, high or low, sacred or profane. And yet, in being one with everything, only and all, there is nothing other to this state, and so it appears perfectly, radically, paradoxically *ordinary,* as in the famous Zen saying, "How marvelous, how transcendental this! I draw water, I carry fuel." The adepts who realize this adaptation are generally known as *sages.*

As an example of the distinction between subtle saints and causal sages, we may take the Mosaic and Christic epiphanies.[105] The Mosaic revelation on Mount Sinai has all the standard features of a subtle level apprehension: a numinous Other that is Light, Fire, Insight, and Sound (shabd). Nowhere, however, does Moses claim to be one with or identical with that Being. In India, at roughly the same time, a similar level of religious insight was expressed in the Vedas. Christ, on the other hand, does claim that "I and the Father are one," a perfect Atmic or causal level apprehension. In India, also at about the same time, a similar understanding was being set down in the Upanishads, where we find such causal/ultimate and Christic-equivalent statements as "Thou art That," "This Atman is Brahman," "I am Brahman," and such, with the proviso that *anyone* can potentially attain this supreme identity, a tenet that was retained in Gnostic Christianity but lost/denied in exoteric-mythic Christianity, where Christ got "kicked upstairs," taking the supreme identity with him. Anyway, the difference between subtle saints and causal sages, or between the Mosaic-Vedic and Christic-Upanishadic revelations, is essentially the difference between savikalpa and nirvakalpa samadhi: in the former, one sees Being, in the latter, one becomes Being.

The point is that not only is there a variety of religious experience, there is a *hierarchy* of religious experience, with each successive stage—psychic, subtle, causal—being higher (by developmental, structural, and integrative standards) than its predecessor, and each correlative practice—yogic, saintly, and sagely—being likewise more ultimately revelatory.[105] This schema and its impact on the sociology of religion will be explored in chapters 6 and 7. For the moment, let us simply note that this scheme enters decisively into the debate started by Zaehner and still raging among scholars of religion.

Zaehner[134] began by clearly and correctly pointing out that "what goes by the name of mysticism, so far from being an identical expression of the selfsame Universal Spirit, falls into three distinct categories," which are panenhenic or nature mysticism (e.g., Rimbaud, Wordsworth), monistic mysticism (e.g., Vedanta, Zen), and theistic mysticism (e.g., Christianity). Zaehner then used this scheme in an attempt to give theistic mysticism a higher status than panenhenic and monistic mysticism. Ninian Smart,[134] on the other hand, wants to champion the nondualist schools of religion (Vedanta, Mahayana, etc.) as being, if not higher than, then at least not inferior to theistic mysticism, and so consequently attempts to defuse Zaehner's position by denying the distinction between theistic and monistic mysticism, although he does accept the clear distinction between them and panenhenic mysticism.

To my mind, both are partially right. There *is* a distinction between panenhenic, theistic, and monistic mystical experience; they correspond almost precisely to the levels of structural organization we have termed psychic, subtle, and causal. But we turn the structural tables on Zaehner and side with Smart: theistic religion is not higher than monistic; in fact, the opposite: saintly communion with spirit is transcended by sagely identity with spirit. Thus, for example, when Watts[94] argues that monistic mysticism includes theistic mysticism, but not vice versa, he intuitively invokes the principle of hierarchization that adjudicates degrees of comprehensive validity.

Such, then, is one (simplified) version of a nested hierarchy of structural organization, one that includes prepersonal or subconscious components, personal or self-conscious components, and transpersonal or superconscious components. Whether or not that scheme is valid—indeed, the overall methodology of verifying (or rejecting) such schemes—will be explicitly dealt with in chapter 9. In the meantime, we may *hypothetically* or provisionally accept it as valid.* We will simply *assume* it is more or less the case and see if acting on this assumption helps clarify the psychology and sociology of religion. In the next two chapters, we will fill in a few more details of this overall model or hypothesis. Then, in chapter 5, we will indeed begin acting on it.

---

* [See *Integral Psychology* for extensive cross-cultural comparisons of this spectrum of consciousness.]

3

The Compound Individual as a Link between Psychology and Sociology

STRUCTURES ARE STRUCTURES *OF* RELATIONAL EXCHANGE

WHAT MAKES THE ABOVE SCHEME—the ten or so levels of structural organization—not merely of relevance to sociology but somehow fused with sociology is the nature of each level itself. Namely, as *Up from Eden* tried to demonstrate, each level is a *process of exchange* with *corresponding* levels of structural organization in the world process at large, and that makes its psychology always also social psychology, as this chapter will now suggest.

For convenience's sake, I will reduce the number of levels of structural organization to five and use the names most familiar to Westerners: matter (1), body (2–3), mind (4–6), soul (7–8), and spirit (9–10). Now, since each of these levels of structural organization *transcends but includes* its predecessors, each structure of development enfolds, envelops, comprehends, or *compounds* the previous structures, much as the neocortex envelops the mammalian limbic system, which in turn envelops the reptilian stem.[100] Again, a nested hierarchy, a development that is envelopment.

For this reason, and in an explicit attempt to connect developmental

54

psychology and evolution theory with the philosophical groundwork of Whitehead[97] and Hartshorne,[44] we say that the human being is a *compound individual*—compounded of all the past levels of development and capped by the present level itself. Potentially, then, the human being is *compounded* of matter, prana, mind, soul, and spirit. The material body is exercised in labor with the physical-natural environment; the pranic (emotional) body is exercised in breath, sex, and feeling with other pranic bodies; the mind is exercised in linguistic communication with other minds; the soul, in psychic and subtle relationships; the spirit, in absolute relation to and as Godhead (or God-communion and God-identity). That is, *each level of the compound human individual is exercised in a complex system of ideally unobstructed relationships with the corresponding levels of structural organization in the world process at large.*[105]

Furthermore, humanity actually and literally reproduces itself on each level by an appropriate *exchange* of the elements of that level (with corresponding levels in the world at large). Humanity reproduces itself physically through the exchange of food secured by labor from the natural environment. It reproduces itself bodily (or biologically) via exchange of breath and sex. It reproduces itself mentally via education and communicative exchange. It reproduces itself spiritually (soul and spirit) via living exchange-transmission from adept to disciple.[105]

It thus appears that each level is intrinsically part of a sliding chain of relational exchanges and therefore *is itself* most fundamentally a *society* of exchanges, or social relationship. Even the material body, the very lowest level, is a *process* of food intake, assimilation, and release, and thus is always bound not to but as the community of its exchange partners. Sexual reproduction is obviously relational exchange. As for the mental level, Lévi-Strauss (among many others) has clearly established that "in mathematics, in logic, or in life, a symbol must be exchanged with another person; in the act of exchange the symbol creates and maintains a relationship. Thus, the word *symbol* refers us back to the original Greek meaning: pact, bond, covenant, intercourse, or link."[107] And spiritual levels are not only exchanges with divinity, or communion-identity, but with divinity embodied as the spiritual master *and* the community of contemplative partners. Each level is a society of relationships or exchange occasions, with the human *compound* individual being an integral of those societies, hopelessly interlocked with other humans in societies of *those*.[105]

The notion of relational exchange is sometimes expressed (redundantly) in the concept of "drives" or "needs." Since each level in the human being *is* a process of relational exchange with a corresponding environment, the human being has drives that express the need for those various environments: physical needs (food, water, air, shelter), emotional needs (feeling, touch-contact, sex), mental-egoic needs (interpersonal communication, reflexive self-esteem, meaning), spiritual needs (God-communion, depth), and so on. It is as if there were levels of "food" or "mana"—physical food, emotional food, mental food, spiritual food. Growth and development is simply the process of adapting to, and learning to digest, subtler and subtler levels of food, with each stage of growth marked by a phase-specific adaptation to a particular type of food. (We will return to the concept of phase-specific mana in the next chapter.)

The point is simply that, because each structure-level *is* a process of relational exchange (or food-needs), it is *necessarily* wedded to the objects that "satisfy" those needs. "Structure," "need," and "object-relations" are simply three aspects of the single exchange process that is each level. Take away the need-objects or food of the structure, and one takes away the structure itself. Take away gross food, and the physical body begins to wither; take away vital food, feeling or warmth, and the emotional body begins to wither; take away "food for thought," intersubjective communication or symbolic exchange, and the mind begins to wither; take away transcendental food, spiritual relationship or grace-faith, and the soul begins to wither. In short, the notion of need or drive expresses nothing but the necessity for a structure to engage its corresponding object-relations or perish.

THE DISTORTION OF RELATIONAL EXCHANGE

The developmental nature of these levels of structural organization and relational exchange (or food-needs) should be emphasized, however, because all of these levels are not *manifest* in individual humans from birth. Rather, the human individual apparently begins its growth and development by adjusting to the physical world (and its food), then to the emotional world (and its food), then the verbal-mental, then the transcendental, and so on (until growth stops in its own case). While these developments often parallel or overlap one another, nonetheless each level is built upon, and rests upon, the foundation afforded by its immediately junior level. However, and in my opinion this cannot be overemphasized, while the higher level "rests on" the lower, the higher is not caused by or constituted by the lower. The higher is in part *emergent,* discontinuous, milestone, revolutionary. The higher emerges *by way of* the lower; it comes *through* the lower, so to speak, but not *from* it, much as a baby chick comes through its eggshell but is not made of eggshells. For example, mind comes *through* libido, not *from* it.[105]

As the higher begins to emerge, it has to pass through the lower for the simple reason that the lower is *already* there, it already exists. As the higher appears on the scene, the scene *is* the lower or immediately junior dimension itself, and the higher is thus initially fused and confused with that lower—it is initially *undifferentiated* from it. Growth of the higher level is in part the process of vertical transcendence or *differentiation* from (and then integration of) the lower level through which it passed on its own emergence.[101]

Thus, for example, prior to age 1½ or so, the infant cannot clearly differentiate the bodyself from the physical environment; it lives in a state of protoplasmic indissociation (Piaget: "the self is here material, so to speak")[70]; bodyself and material world are largely undifferentiated. Between the ages of 1½ to 3 or so, the infant learns to differentiate the bodyself from the objective physical world, thus allowing the body to transcend that primitive-material fusion state.[50] As the symbolic mind begins to emerge (around 24 months or so), it is then initially undifferentiated from the body itself—mind and body are fused and confused (thinking is physiognomic, as Werner put it, or contaminated with sensorimotor categories, according to Piaget).[95,70] It is not until around age 7 or so that mind and body are first differentiated, and not until age 11–15 that they are clearly differentiated and mind finally transcends (but subsumes) the body itself.[57,70] Likewise, when (and if) the soul eventually emerges, it is initially fused and confused with the mind (it is clothed in mental forms and thoughts, not yet its own intrinsic visions and illuminations), and so on. The point is that in each case the higher emerges through, or by way of, the lower, only transcending the lower when it finally differentiates from it. This process of separation-individuation, or transcendence-and-integration, marks each major stage of growth or emergence.[101] But we repeat: although the higher comes through the lower, it does not come *from* the lower, its essence being in part emergent.

Nonetheless, this emergence *through* the lower can have fateful consequences, because a distorted lower can *incline* the higher to subsequently reproduce the distortion on its own domain, much as a tough or brittle eggshell can damage the chick in its emergence. Perhaps a better metaphor here is a skyscraper: because the higher both comes through and then rests upon the foundation of the lower, a "tilt" in the first floor tends to cause a similar tilt in the second, and so on. Physical trauma can lead to emotional disturbances; emotional disturbances can generate mental instabilities, and so on.

But this is not an absolute causality; not only is the lower distortion only partially passed on, but *the higher level, by virtue of its emergent freedom, can often redress the imbalance.* We say, then, that a distortion in the lower *predisposes* (but does not cause) the higher to reproduce similar if dampened distortions in its own domain.

On the other side of the fence, the higher, because it does partially transcend the lower, can *repress* the lower. For example, sex cannot easily repress sex, but mind can repress sex, simply because mind is higher in structural organization than sex and can thus "come down on" sex.

Repression, as I use the term, is fundamentally an *internal* affair; it is instigated by the separate self in order to defend its own precarious sense of existence in the face of prior and always apprehended mortality. Repression is not caused by others or instigated by others, and it will occur, to various degrees, in even the most idyllic surroundings, simply because no setting is free of the skull that, as James said, will soon grin in at the banquet. Any aspect of the self-system—sensation, perception, emotion, cognition—that becomes too threatening, too laden with death-guilt, too charged with taboo, will be split from the system, outlawed, banished. Such repression does not actually destroy the "shadow," however, but merely sends it underground, where it registers its existence by sending up cryptic symbols (the hidden text) and disturbing symptoms.[101,105]

Although one individual cannot directly repress another, one individual can *oppress* another. This oppression has several consequences, two of which are (1) the oppression can disrupt and distort the exchange processes and capacities of any and all levels of the compound individual (as Marx found out for *material* exchange, Freud for *emotional-sexual* exchange, Socrates for *mental* communicative exchange, and Christ for *spiritual* exchange); and (2) the separate self, as it endures in (and attempts to adapt and adjust to) the atmosphere of such oppression, can and will *internalize* the originally external oppression, and *internalized oppression* then leads to *surplus repression,* repression over and above that which the self would induce on its own.[105]

Here are our generalizations so far: (1) the higher comes *through* the lower but not *from* the lower; (2) a distorted lower *inclines* the higher to reproduce similar distortions in its own sphere but (3) does not absolutely *cause* the higher to reproduce the distortions (the higher can to some degree dampen, reverse, amend, compensate, etc.); (4) the individual can defensively *repress* or internally distort, to one degree or another, any or all of his own levels of exchange (physical, emotional, mental, spiritual); (5) an external (powerful) other can *oppress* and distort an individual's levels of exchange; and (6) internalized oppression is surplus repression.

THE BACKBONE OF A COMPREHENSIVE CRITICAL THEORY IN SOCIOLOGY

I have elsewhere suggested how these generalizations can help us to reconstruct the essentials of such theorists as Marx and Freud without their reductionistic tendencies.[105] For, as we look at the levels of structural organization and relational exchange of the compound individual, it becomes obvious that many theorists have taken *one* level and tried to make it paradigmatic. If they take a higher level, as idealists do, they tend to elevate the lower levels to an exalted status they simply do not possess, or they tend to ignore the lower levels altogether. Reading history according to Hegel, for instance, one always gets the impression that the material world might at any moment evaporate. This apparently annoyed Marx so much that he took the opposite but perfectly standard reductionistic approach: take a lower level, call it "the only really real" level, then reduce all higher levels to it, or at least explain all higher levels in terms of the lower. I need not tell you that Marx made the material level and its exchanges paradigmatic for *all* forms of existence. Freud did *exactly* the same thing for the next level up; emotional-sexual energies are *the* reality, and all else—culture, ego, mind, religion—is just a sneaky twisting of libido. At the next level up, we often find theorists who admirably refuse to reduce mental consciousness to sexual offsprings or material modes of production and, instead, accord mind its own rightful and higher place in development, but they tend to deny validity to realms higher than mind, realms that they then subject to standard reductionism—such "spiritual realities" are, at best, merely functional symbols without *real* referents. Communication becomes paradigmatic for such theorists (e.g., Habermas), and direct spiritual awareness is accorded something of a derivative status at best.

But you can see where such theorists *have* made absolutely crucial—if absolutely partial—contributions. Marx, for instance, compellingly demonstrated that when the material-economic exchange process is oppressed and distorted, then upon that distorted base tends to emerge alienated thoughts and feelings, or "false consciousness," and that the higher cultural productions of art, philosophy, and religion are thereby pressed as ideology into mere servants of oppression, each becoming, in its own way, an "opiate of the masses." Similarly, Freud demonstrated that emotional-sexual distortions tilted mental consciousness toward symptomatic sclerosis, blocked the free flow of mental ideas, and generally set up another type of false consciousness in the form of a façade or pseudo-self alienated from aspects of its own being (because it is alienated from aspects of relational exchanges *with others,* hence the modern emphasis on object-relations theory).

Now we want to take all of those essentials with us, but without their reductionism. For both Marx and Freud went from saying, "A distorted lower predisposes the higher to similar distortions" (correct), to saying, "The distortions in the higher stem almost entirely from the distortions in the lower" (incorrect; they stem partially from them, but they can also be distorted for reasons purely their own), to saying, "The higher itself must therefore come from a distortion or frustration of the lower" (even more incorrect; that amounts to making the dynamics of repression/oppression paradigmatic for the whole of development), to saying, "If there were no frustration of the lower, there would be *no* higher" (patently absurd, but the reductionism is here completed). Hence the orthodox Marxist position that when material exchanges are finally communalized, there will be *no need for* philosophy, art, religion, and so forth; and the precisely correlative Freudian notion that without frustration of instinctual urges, the mind would never emerge and develop. Thus we utilize the valid insights of such theorists with the second generalization; we counteract their reductionism with the first and third generalizations.

My point is that a comprehensive, unified, critical sociological theory might best be constructed around a detailed, multidisciplinary analysis of the developmental-logic and hierarchic levels of relational (psychosocial) exchanges that constitute the human compound individual. The theory would be *critical* in two important ways: (1) adjudicative of each *higher* level of structural organization and critical of the comparative partiality of each lower level, and (2) critical of the *distortions* in exchange when and if they occur on any particular level. The latter is a criticism *within* a level and demands as its corrective a self-reflection on the historical formations that led to the distortion in the particular realm, economic, emotional, communicative, or spiritual. The former is a criticism *between* levels and demands as its corrective a *growth* to higher levels. The one is a horizontal emancipation, the other, a vertical emancipation. Neither can be dispensed with—growth to a higher level does not ensure the healthy normalization of a lower level, and healing a lower level does not in and of itself produce a higher level. (We will return to this topic in chapter 8.)

At a minimum, then, our levels of analysis would include (1) the physical level of material exchange, whose paradigm is food consumption and food extraction from the natural environment, whose sphere is that of manual (technic) labor, and whose archetypal analyst is Marx; (2) the emotional level of pranic (vital) exchange, whose paradigm is breath and sex, whose sphere is that of emotional intercourse, from feeling to sex to power, and whose archetypal analyst is Freud; (3) the mental level of symbolic exchange, whose paradigm is discourse (language), whose sphere is that of communication, and whose archetypal analyst is Socrates; (4) the psychic level of intuitive exchange, whose paradigm is siddhi (or psychic insight and vision in general), whose sphere is yogic kundalini, and whose archetypal analyst is Patanjali; (5) the subtle level of God-Light exchange, whose paradigm is shabd-revelation and subtle illumination (savikalpa samadhi), whose sphere is saintly "heaven" (Brahma-Loka, the higher structural potentials of one's own compound individuality), and whose archetypal analyst is Moses/Saint Paul/Kirpal Singh; and (6) the causal level of infinite exchange, whose paradigm is radical absorption in and as the Uncreate (nirvikalpa/sahaj samadhi), whose sphere is sagely Godhead, and whose archetypal analyst is Buddha/Krishna/Christ.[105]

4

Translation, Transformation, Transcription

GENERAL DEFINITIONS

B EFORE WE FINALLY APPLY this general theory to such specifics as
the sociology of religion, new religions, cults, and such, we need a
few technical definitions. If we simplistically think of the various levels
of structural organization as so many floors in a tall building (in this
case, ten stories, with tenth being Brahman as highest level and asymptotic limit of growth, and the building itself being Brahman as the
ground of all levels of growth), then (1) each floor itself is a *deep structure,* while (2) the variable components on each floor—its actual furniture, so to speak—are *surface structures;* (3) the movement of surface
structures we call *translation;* (4) the movement of deep structures we
call *transformation;* and (5) the relation between a deep structure and its
surface structures we call *transcription.* Translation is moving furniture
around on one floor; transformation is moving to a different floor; transcription is the relation of the furniture to each floor.

As a more accurate example, take a game such as checkers or chess.
The surface structures are the various pieces and the various moves they
make in a given game. The deep structure is the *rules* of the game, the
patterns that define the *internal relations* of the various pieces to each
other. The rules holistically unite each piece to each other via patterned
relations. The deep structure *defines the game*—you can alter the surface

structures, make the pieces out of clay, plastic, or wood, and you still have the same basic game. You can even use rocks; all you have to do is transcribe the pieces according to the basic rules, that is, show how each piece fits into the rules of the deep structure. That relation of deep to surface structures is *transcription*. Finally, actually moving the pieces around on the board, or executing a play, is *translation*.

Now if we change the deep structure, we change the basic rules of the game, and then obviously it is no longer the same game. We have *transformed* it into something else—perhaps another good game, perhaps a mess. Sometimes people will take checkers pieces and a checkerboard (if they do not want to buy a chess set) and transform them into chess by first changing the rules, or transforming the deep structure to that of chess; then transcribing the checkers according to their functions in chess, which means marking them as a rook, king, pawn, and so forth; and then finally translating these new surface structures according to the deep rules of chess.

Notice, even in this simple example, that the deep structures do not themselves change during the course of a game, nor are they influenced by the particular moves of a particular game. They are "a-historical." The surface structures do change, however, for each sequence of moves is different from game to game. What determines the particular course of moves is the sum of previous moves in the game so far. That is, the next move I make in a particular game will occur *within* the rules of the deep structure, but it is determined specifically by all the preceding moves (plus my present judgment about those previous moves). Those surface structures, in other words, are *historically conditioned*—not totally caused, but definitely molded to some degree, by past surface structures.

That is a small example of an overall postulate that refers to the basic levels of structural organization themselves: insofar as they have emerged, the deep structures of consciousness (e.g., as presented in figure 2) are relatively a-historical, collective, invariant, and cross-cultural, whereas their surface structures are everywhere variable, historically conditioned, and culturally molded.[105] Thus, for example, the deep structure of the formal operational mind is, as far as we know, identical wherever it emerges, but the actual surface forms of that mind—its particular belief systems, ideologies, languages, customs, and so forth—are everywhere different, molded largely by the culture in which that mind itself develops.[70] This postulate (or rather, experimental conclusion) is similar to Chomsky's universal-grammar/specific-cultural-semantics,[24] except that it is not confined to the mental/linguistic levels but refers to all levels of basic structural organization (e.g., the deep structure of the physical body is everywhere identical—208 bones, 2 kidneys, 4 limbs, 1 heart, etc.—but the surface activities of that body—the acceptable forms of play, work, sports, etc.—differ from culture to culture; and so on with emotional, subtle, causal, and other levels of structural organization). The idea itself took its initial impetus from Jung's work on archetypes as "forms devoid of content"[53] (although see Wilber[102]), but was bolstered by the cross-cultural investigations related to the work of Piaget, Kohlberg, Werner, and others. That this conclusion also and expressly applies to the deep and surface structures of the three stages of religious-mystical experience (psychic, subtle, causal) should especially be noted, for we will be drawing on this point in chapter 7.

THE FUNCTION OF TRANSLATION: MANA AND TABOO

Development or growth, then, seems to occur in two primary dimensions: horizontal-evolutionary-historical and vertical-revolutionary-transcendental, or, in short, translative and transformative. Horizontal or translative growth is a process of transcribing, filling in, or "fleshing out" the surface structures of a given level; that is, assuming responsibility for the relational exchange of surface structures that constitutes the very lifeline or "food" of that level, a process that must occur if that level and the society of its reciprocal exchange partners are to reproduce themselves both moment to moment (or individually) and generation to generation (or collectively). Transformation, on the other hand, is a vertical shift, a revolutionary reorganization of past elements and emergence of new ones. It is synonymous with *transcendence,* although notice that transcendence is then not confined to the upper levels of consciousness (although it occurs there royally), but rather refers to the fact that *each* successive level transcends or goes beyond its predecessor(s): myth transcends magic, reason transcends myth, soul transcends reason, spirit transcends soul.[101]

Translation apparently has one major function: to integrate, stabilize, and equilibrate its given level; transformation apparently has one major function: to go beyond its given level. This dialectic of tensions seems to constitute much of the dynamic of development.[95,102] In this section, we key on its translative dimension.

Translation's major function—to integrate, stabilize, and equilibrate its given level—seems to have two basic facets, which we call *mana* and *taboo*.[105] Mana refers to the "food" of each level: for example, physical food, emotional food (love, belongingness), mental food (symbol, truth), spiritual food (illumination, insight). Translation is involved in securing the mana-food of its particular level via, of course, the processes of relational exchange (reception, assimilation, and release), for mana-food is exactly what *is* exchanged in those processes. Further, it seems that mana-translation, by virtue of this *necessary* relationship in and as a society of exchange partners, establishes and constitutes, in all of its phase-specific forms, the "glue" that binds the particular society in which the exchanges occur. With that in mind, and on any given level, we define "good mana" as that which is integrative, healthy, legitimate, and intrinsically binding, both within the boundaries of the particular individual and between the boundaries of individuals in the exchange process at large. "Bad mana," conversely, is less integrative or even disintegrative for the particular level.

We also suggest that, besides good and bad mana within a level, there are higher and lower forms of mana between levels. That is, each progressively higher level of structural organization seems to have access to a progressively higher mana, or higher truth-food. This does not, however, deny the relative and *phase-specific validity* of the lower truths. Nor does it, in and by itself, guarantee integrative stability for the higher level, since the bad mana of a higher level is often less integrative than the good mana of a lower one. But the potential for higher truth and integration is most definitely present, and so on balance we say that, for example, science is more truthful than myth just as saintly illumination is truer than science, but all serve their necessary and phase-specific functions and deliver themselves of appropriate-enough truths. Vertical growth is a series of phase-specific adaptations to increasingly higher levels of food, mana, truth, while horizontal growth is a process of learning to digest (intake, assimilation, release) that food on its own level.

For the taboo facet of translation, I have explicitly tied my arguments into those of Rank,[74] Becker,[10] and Brown,[19] although again I have tried to avoid what I feel are reductionistic elements in their theories. Their position is basically existential; it deals with the impact of death-apprehension on the individual psyche and the resultant attempts to deal with, or deny, the terror of mortality.

For *death*, they maintain, is *the* fundamental taboo, the fundamental terror, and to the extent the separate self awakens to its own existence, then to that extent terror-angst is *inherent* in the self. ("The essential, basic arch-anxiety is innate to all isolated, individual forms of human existence. In the basic anxiety human existence is afraid *of* as well as anxious *about* its 'being-in-the-world.' ") Thus, there is simply but absolutely no way to avoid that terror except by repression or some other defensive or compensatory mechanism. Angst is not something the self suffers; it is something the self *is*.

Now the traditional psychologies—Hinduism and Buddhism, for example—agree perfectly and explicitly with that assessment (Buddha is regarded by many scholars, myself included, as having given *the* existential statement and analysis of the human predicament: anicca, anatta, dukkha—fleeting, selfless, pain). Wherever there is self, there is trembling; wherever there is other, there is fear. However—and this is where the traditions transcend mere existentialism—these psychologies maintain that one can go beyond fear and trembling by going beyond self and other; that is, by transcending subject and object in satori, moksha, the supreme identity.

But those traditions also maintain that the great liberation finally takes place only at the sagely level of causal/ultimate adaptation.[22,28,105] All lesser stages, no matter how occasionally ecstatic or visionary, are still beset with the primal mood of ego, which is sickness unto death. Even the saint, according to the sages, has yet to finally surrender his or her soul, or separate-self sense, and this prevents the saint from attaining absolute identity with and as Godhead.[22] Since the separate-self sense forms very early in development—a primitive series of ego nuclei arise within months of birth[17]—and since it does not finally uncoil until the sagely level of structural adaptation, it follows that all levels of development, short of the great liberation, are marked by the separate self. And the separate self *is* a contraction of angst; specifically, a fear of its own death or nonbeing.

It was Otto Rank[73,74] who supplied the necessary psychodynamic characteristic of this state of affairs. The separate self, he said, faced with the fundamental taboo that is mortality, is forced, in order to attain a modicum of stability (translative equilibrium), to close its eyes to its own possible nonbeing. Put simply, it represses death ("Consciousness of death is the primary repression, not sexuality," as Becker[10] put it). One of the results of doing this, or one of the actual ways of doing this, said Rank, is by creating a series of *immortality symbols,* which, in their *promise* to transcend death, assuage the paralyzing cold that would otherwise freeze the self's operations.

If this is so, then translation deals not only with mana but with taboo, the basic taboo that is death, but a taboo that takes different and phase-specific forms on each level. From this angle, psycho-cultural productions could be seen (in part) to be *codified systems of death-denial* (I say "in part" because in my opinion that is half the truth; the other half is mana accumulation). It was Rank's genius to see that not only magic and myth but *rational* productions and purely logical beliefs were likewise immortality projects. They were productions that, in aspiring to some degree of truth, aspired to some degree of durability, and in aspiring to durability claimed hoped-for immortality ("My ideas will live on. . . ."). From that angle, culture—even rational culture—is what a separate self does with death: the self that is doomed only to die, and knows it, and spends its entire life (consciously or unconsciously) trying to deny it, both by manipulating its own subjective life and by erecting "permanent" and "timeless" cultural objects and conceptual principles as outward and visible signs of an inward and hoped-for immortality.

I will not repeat the entire argument of Rank, Becker, or Brown or my reformulation of its essentials. Take, instead, a simple summary by Becker: "Man from the very beginning could not live with the prospect of death. . . . Man erected cultural symbols which do not age or decay to quiet his fear of his ultimate end. This way of looking at the doings of man gives a direct key to the unlocking of history. We can see that what people want in any epoch is a way of transcending their physical fate, they want to guarantee some kind of indefinite duration, and culture provides them with the necessary immortality symbols or ideologies; societies can be seen as structures of immortality power."

In *Up from Eden,* I tried to show some of the phase-specific forms of such death-denial. It can be the immortality promised by magic ritual: "Where there is magic, there is no death,"[23] as Campbell summarized paleolithic religion. It can be the immortality promised by myth: "To be a favorite of the gods, to be an immortal," as Becker[11] would summarize classic mythic religion. It can be the immortality promised by reason: "The god of his own thought," said L. L. Whyte,[98] "which as recompense promises immortality." There even seems to be a very subtle form of immortality project in the soul realms: the last remnant of the separate self intuits timeless Being and then mistakes that timelessness for an *everlasting duration* or *permanent* self sense ("your immortal soul," which is no such thing; the Mahayana texts are always warning practitioners not to mistake the causal-alaya for a permanent soul).[88] The point is that, until there is final liberation—if such, indeed, exists—there remains some form of immortality project. Those projects become less and less compensatory at each higher level of structural organization, but they are never fully uprooted until the separate-self sense is itself uprooted. Prior to that time, life remains a battle of mana versus taboo.

In summary, the function of translation is to integrate, stabilize, and equilibrate its present level by securing mana and avoiding taboo in the process of relational exchange. This function obviously takes on different forms on different levels, but the function itself is present on all levels (functional invariant, Piaget calls it). Along with the basic deep structures, and the transformative functional invariant, this capacity seems to be part of the *native apparatus* of the self-system (cf. Hartmann's "inborn apparatus").[42]

TRANSFORMATION: DEATH AND REBIRTH ON EACH LEVEL

As we now turn to transformative or vertical development, it is a little more obvious what is involved: in order for an individual to transform to the next higher level, he or she has, in effect, to accept the *death* of the present level of adaptation, that is, to cease an *exclusive* identity with that level. Thus, for example, to progress to operational myth, the child has to give up or die to an exclusive allegiance to magical wishes; to progress to rational science, the adolescent has to give up an exclusive attachment to mythic outcomes; to progress to yogic adaptation, the adult has to surrender and release isolated-linear rationality into a larger intuitive vision, and so on.[101]

In each case, it is only when the self is *strong enough to die to that level* that it can *transcend* that level, that is, transform to the next higher level of phase-specific truth, food, mana. As the self identifies with the new level and begins to adapt to its food-mana, it *then* faces the fear of dying on and to *that* level, and its translative processes swing into gear to screen out the new version of always mortality that otherwise would freeze still the movement of self. The *new* self adapts to *new* truth-mana, faces *new* other, therefore suffers new death-seizure, therefore instigates new defense measures, and therefore, among other things, erects new immortality projects.[105]

Development, in this sense, is a series of progressively shedding immortality projects by progressively shedding the layers of self these projects were designed to protect, thereby simultaneously rising to new levels of phase-specific food, truth, mana. *Each* transformation is a process of death and rebirth: death to the old level, and transformation to and rebirth on the newly emergent level. And, according to the sages, when all layers of self have been transcended—when all deaths have been died—the result is only God in final Truth, and a new Destiny beyond destiny is resurrected from the stream of consciousness.

5

Some Usages of the Word "Religion"

O NE OF THE GREAT DIFFICULTIES in discussing religion—its sociology, its possible universality, its "civil" dimensions—is that it is
not an "it." In my opinion, "it" has at least a dozen different, major,
largely exclusive meanings, and unfortunately these are not always, not
even usually, distinguished in the literature. Let me point out some of
the ways we can (and do) use the word "religion," and what I believe is
actually behind each usage. My point will be that each of these usages is
legitimate enough—we are free to define religion any way we wish—but
we *must specify that meaning.* For what we will find is that many scholars have several implicit but often very different definitions in mind, and
they slip between these usages in a way that generates pseudo-conclu-
sions. I will number these religious definitions and subsequently refer to
them as rd-1, rd-2, and so on.

1. *Religion as nonrational engagement.* This has both positive and
negative connotations. To theologians, it means that religion deals with
valid but nonrational aspects of existence, such as faith, grace, transcendence, satori, and such. To positivists, it means religion is nonvalid
knowledge; it might be "meaningful" to humans in an emotional way,
but it is not real cognition.

This usage is often reflected in common sense. Most people would
intuitively say that magic-voodoo is a type of religion, however primitive, and that mythic gods and goddesses are definitely religious, although maybe not very "serious." They would also say that what yogis,
saints, and sages do is certainly religious. But science-rationality? *That*

is not religious. This overall usage says that religion is not so much something done on all levels but rather on particular levels, and specifically, those that are not rational-scientific per se. If you are pro-religion, then this definition implies that religion is something you can grow into; if con, something you hope to outgrow. In either case, it is nonrational; it belongs to or at least originates in a dimension that is other to reason.

2. *Religion as extremely meaningful or integrative engagement.* This usage says religion is not something that occurs on specific nonrational dimensions or levels but is a particular functional activity on any given level, an activity of seeking meaning, integration, etc. In my opinion, this usage actually reflects each level's search for mana—the search for meaning, truth, integrity, stability, and subject-object relationship (exchange). Since mana-translation, as we have seen, must occur on each level of structural organization, then whether that level appears "religious" or "secular" does not matter; it is religious, or mana-searching, by this definition.

This usage is also reflected in common sense. Thus, even the typical individual who initially says that myths, saints, sages, and such are religious but science is *not,* will usually understand exactly what you mean if you say, "Science was Einstein's religion." *Star Trek* fans say, "Logic is Spock's religion." Here, even purely rational endeavors are said to be religious, because they are, like all levels, in search of their phase-specific mana, and this mana-search—on *whatever* level, high or low, sacred or secular—is natively understood as religion.

Notice that, although both rd-1 and rd-2 are acceptable usages, they are nonetheless quite different, almost contradictory, and unless we specify which we mean, certain paradoxes and spurious conclusions will result. For instance, rd-1 denies secular religion, rd-2 demands it; rd-1 denies science is religion, rd-2 says it is (or can be). Both are acceptable, as long as we understand that behind the one word "religion" there are different functions. Oftentimes common sense will use both of these meanings without specifying them, thus producing a pseudo-paradox. The person might say, "Mr. Jones doesn't go to church; he doesn't believe in religion—money is his religion."

3. *Religion as an immortality project.* This is using the technical term we earlier introduced, but the actual term itself need not be invoked. The idea is simply that religion is fundamentally a wishful, defensive, compensatory belief, created in order to assuage insecurity/anxiety. This meaning is often applied to theology, but it is also used for rational and

secular endeavors, as when Becker says that Marxism is Soviet religion, meaning not just mana-search (rd-2) but death-denial. This can occur, as we have seen, on any level, and simply reflects that level's inherent taboo avoidance. In this particular function, science does *for* the rational ego exactly what *myth* does for the childish ego and *magic* does for the infantile ego—helps to veil the apprehension of ultimate and inescapable mortality by providing a belief system to "hang on to." This seems especially true of "scienticians," that is, scientists whose rd-2 religion (mana religion) happens to be science itself. I have found that, when push comes to shove, they will guard their exclusively Rational World View with a quivering passion every bit as charged with hoped-for immortality as that of a shrieking fundamentalist preacher. The point is simply that each level (short of the ultimate) tends to erect some sort of immortality project as part of its necessary defense structures, and this usage of religion simply keys on this particular function (although, typically, most of those who use this definition deny that there is any other).

4. *Religion as evolutionary growth*. This is a sophisticated concept maintaining that all evolution and history is a process of increasing self-realization, or the overcoming of alienation via the return *of* spirit *to* spirit *as* spirit. Hegel, for instance, or Aurobindo. In this sense, religion is actually a term for the transformative drive in general. The religious impulse here means, not searching for meaning, integration, mana or value *on* a given level (which is rd-2), but dying to that level altogether so as to find increasingly *higher* structures of mana-truth, eventuating in God Realized Adaptation itself.

5. *Religion as fixation/regression*. We already discussed this usage; the only thing we need say here is that this meaning differs from rd-1 only in being more specific and always derogatory. Religion is not nonrational, it is prerational, and that exhausts the alternatives. This is standard primitivization theory: religion is childish illusion, magic, myth.

6. *Exoteric religion*. This generally refers to the lower, outward, and/or preparatory aspects of any religion that has higher, inward, and/or advanced aspects of teaching and practice. It is usually a form of *belief* system used to invoke or support *faith*, both being preparatory to esoteric *experience* and *adaptation* (see chapter 6 for those definitions). If a religion lacks an esoteric dimension altogether, then that religion on the whole is referred to as exoteric (the point of comparison being the esoteric dimensions of other religions).

7. *Esoteric religion.* This refers to the higher, inward, and/or advanced aspects of religious practise, with the proviso that such practices culminate in, or at least have as goal, mystical experience.

(For the next two definitions, we need a preliminary explanation. Once an author defines religion, he or she has automatically established some sort of criteria for "more valid" or "less valid" religion, simply because once the function of religion is actually specified, there are always better and worse cases. Now the nature of this "better or worse" depends upon the prior, basic definition the author gives to religion. If rd-1 is used—religion as a nonrational dimension or realm, and in this case it means higher realm—then valid religion, or more valid religion, comes implicitly or explicitly to mean actually contacting those authentic, higher realms or levels. On the other hand, if rd-2 is used—religion as search for mana on *any* level—then valid or more valid religion does not mean experiencing a particular level but finding legitimate mana on one's present level. These are obviously two entirely different meanings of "valid," and it presents a chronic semantic difficulty rarely acknowledged in the literature. I therefore have no choice but to use two different words—"authentic" and "legitimate"—to specify these two meanings of valid.)

8. *Legitimate religion.* This is religion that primarily *validates translation;* usually by providing "good mana" and helping avoid taboo, that is, providing units of meaning on the one hand and immortality symbols on the other. If an author (implicitly or explicitly) defines religion as meaningful integration of a given worldview or level (rd-2), then *the more integrative* religion (within that worldview or level) is implied or defined by the author to be the more valid. In these cases, since we refer to rd-2 as mana religion in general, we refer to its more valid forms as legitimate or "good mana" religion.

A *crisis in legitimacy* occurs whenever the prevailing mana and immortality symbols fail their integrative and defensive functions. This can occur on the lower levels of mythic-exoteric religion (for example, the Pope's encyclicals on human reproduction, based as they are on Thomistic/Aristotelian biological notions, long outmoded, have lost legitimacy with many people), on the middle levels of rational-secular religion (e.g., the Newtonian paradigm as a world view has lost legitimation), and on the upper levels of mystical religion (e.g., Mahayana Buddhism eventually lost legitimation in India, its place being taken by Shankara's Vedanta). In each case, the religion in its rd-2 function simply fails to provide enough meaningful integration, on the one hand, or enough immortality power, on the other, and thus loses its legitimacy, or its capacity to validate translation.

Corollary: "Degree of legitimacy" refers to the relative degree of integration, meaning-value, good mana, ease of functioning, avoidance of taboo, and so forth within any given level. This is a *horizontal scale;* "more legitimate" means more integrative-meaningful within that level.

9. *Authentic religion.* This is religion that primarily *validates transformation* to a particular dimension-level deemed to be most centrally religious. When an author (implicitly or explicitly) defines religion as a particular dimension-level of existence (rd-1), then the religion that more completely or accurately *contacts* that dimension-level is implied or defined by the author to be the more valid. In those cases, I use the word "authentic" or "more authentic" to indicate "more valid."

A *crisis in authenticity* occurs whenever a prevailing worldview (or religion) is faced with challenges from a *higher-level* view. This can occur at any level, whenever a new and higher (or senior) level begins to emerge and itself gain legitimacy. The new world view embodies a new and higher transformative power and thus challenges the old view, not merely as to its legitimacy but as to its very authenticity.

Corollary: "Degree of authenticity" refers to the relative degree of actual transformation delivered by a given religion (or worldview). This is a *vertical scale;* "more authentic" means more capable of reaching a higher level (and not merely integrating the present level).

An author is, of course, free to specify the nature of the centrally religious or higher realm. For myself, it is the psychic, subtle, causal, and ultimate levels of structural organization and relational exchange. It follows that, for myself, authentic religion is any practice leading to a genuine emergence of, and eventual adaptation to, those transpersonal realms (with the further understanding that causal religion is more authentic than subtle, which is more authentic than psychic). I will occasionally use the corollary "degree of authenticity" in a looser sense, as meaning the degree of developmental structuralization *in general* (e.g., myth is more authentic than magic, reason is more authentic than myth, vision is more authentic than reason, etc.). However, when I refer to authentic religions per se, they are ones that have reached a degree of structuralization at or beyond the superconscient border (i.e., psychic or higher). Thus, magic, myth, and reason can be (and often are) *legitimate* religions, and they can occasionally *express* authentic religious insight via peak experience (see chapter 6). But in neither case are they the source of *authentic* religious insight, which, for me, is always and expressly *trans*rational, not merely rational, and certainly not prerational.

Notice that, in very general terms, any religion (or world view) can be judged in its degree of validity on two different, independently variable scales: its degree of *legitimacy* (horizontal scale; degree of *translative* smoothness and integrity, measured against the potential capacity of the given level itself) and its degree of *authenticity* (vertical scale; degree of *transformative* power, measured by the degree of hierarchical structuralization delivered by the transformation). Thus, for example, there are situations where magic, at its *full* potential (say, in some paleolithic societies) was just as *legitimate* as myth at its full potential (say, in some Bronze Age societies), but myth was more *authentic* (embodying a higher level of structural organization). If our scale of legitimacy is 1 to 10 (degree of using the integrative-mana potential of the given level) and our scale of authenticity is 1 to 10 (representing the ten levels of structuralization given in figure 2), then in that example, the ratings would be (10, 4) and (10, 5), respectively. Here are some other examples, more commonplace:

Chinese Maoism has (or rather had) a fairly high degree of legitimacy but a very mediocre degree of authenticity. It was a *legitimate* religion (or worldview) in that it apparently integrated large blocks of peoples, provided social solidarity and a measure of meaning-value, and avoided a good deal of taboo by providing the immortality ideology of an unending, never-dying people's revolution (a legitimacy rating of, say, 8–9). It was not very *authentic,* however, because it offered adaptation only to or at the mythic-rational realms (5–6); say what you will, Maoism did not produce superconscient realization of, and adaptation to, only God. Thus: Maoism (8–9, 5–6). (Notice that today Maoism has lost some of its legitimacy in China; the "cultural revolution" and its subsequent events were exactly a *legitimacy crisis* as defined above.) Soviet Marxism/Leninism, on the other hand, is as inauthentic as was Maoism (5–6), for the same reasons (it does not produce psychic, subtle, or causal transformation), but it also appears to be of a much lower degree of legitimacy (say, 4–5) than Maoism in its heyday, because its mana and its immortality symbols apparently have to be backed by rather large sticks.[3] So there we have examples of relatively legitimate/inauthentic (8–9, 5–6) and illegitimate/inauthentic (4–5, 5–6). (Lest my judgment seem biased toward American-Protestant capitalism, I will quickly add that, in my opinion, the American "civil religion"—a mixture of exo-

teric, Protestant, biblical myths and nationalistic immortality symbols—
possesses essentially the same legitimacy and authenticity ratings as did
Maoism. That this civil religion faced a *legitimacy crisis* during the
1960s will be discussed in chapter 7.)

As for the authentic but illegitimate, examples abound: when Mahayana Buddhism died in India, it was not because its tenets were per se
inauthentic, for they still embodied causal level practice (9–10), but because Vedanta Hinduism, regenerating itself via Shankara and claiming
a more historical rootedness, became more legitimate with practitioners.
Likewise, Vedanta is a perfectly causal-authentic religion, but it seems it
will never achieve widespread legitimacy in America, its rating there thus
being something like (1–2, 9–10). In the West, in fact, most esoteric
spiritual tenets, no matter how authentic, never gained much legitimacy
(witness Eckhart, al-Hallaj, Giordano Bruno, Christ's esoteric-causal
message itself).

As for religions that have been both legitimate and authentic, we may
take Ch'an (Zen) Buddhism during T'ang China, Vedanta Hinduism in
India from the time of Gaudapada and Shankara to the British intensi-
fied occupation, or Vajrayana in Tibet from Padmasambhava to Mao
Tse-tung, all of which seemed somewhere around (8–9, 9–10).

Each of the preceding nine (or more) usages of the word "religion"
has its appropriate place—some "religious" expressions *are* fixation/re-
gressions, some are immortality projects, some are mana generators,
some are legitimate, some are authentic. But we must be careful to express precisely which usage we mean. Otherwise, statements such as
"The religious impulse is universal," "All religions are true," "Religion
is transcendental," "All religions are one at some deep level," and so on
are at best strictly meaningless, at worst profoundly misleading.

6

Belief, Faith, Experience, and Adaptation

I N THIS CHAPTER I wish to distinguish religious *belief*, religious *faith*, religious (mystical or peak) *experience*, and religious structural *adaptation* (or actual adaptation to authentic-religious levels of development). For again, if they are all "religious," they are religious to differing degrees. The series itself shows increasing religious involvement: it seems you can have belief without faith, faith without experience, and experience without permanent adaptation.

BELIEF

Belief is the lowest form of religious involvement, and, in fact, it often seems to operate with no authentic religious connection whatsoever.[105] The "true believer"—one who has no literal faith, let alone actual experience—embraces a more-or-less codified belief system that appears to act most basically as a fund of immortality symbols.[10] This can be mythic-exoteric religion (e.g., fundamentalist Protestantism, lay Shintoism, pop Hinduism, etc.), rational-scientism, Maoism, civil religion, and so on. What they all have in common, when thus made a matter of "true belief," is that an ideological nexus is wedded to one's qualifications for immortality.

I believe this generates a peculiar, secondary psychodynamic: since

77

one's immortality prospects hang on the veracity of the ideological nexus, the nexus as a whole can be critically examined only with the greatest of difficulty. Thus, when the normal and unavoidable moments of uncertainty or disbelief occur (magic: is this dance really causing rain? mythic: was the world *really* created in six days? scientistic: what happened *before* the big bang? etc.), the questioning impulses are not long allowed to remain in the self-system (they are threats to one's immortality qualifications). As a result, the disbelieving impulse tends to be *projected* onto others and then attacked "out there" with an obsessive endurance. The true believer is forever on the make, looking for converts and battling disbelievers, for, on the one hand, the mere existence of a disbeliever is one token less in the immortality account, and, on the other, if the true believer can persuade others to embrace his ideology, it helps to quiet his own disbelieving impulses. If mythic-religious, he crusades against sinners, burns witches, hangs heretics; if Marxist, he lives for the revolution that will crush disbelievers (and in the meantime jails "witches," psychiatrizes "heretics"); if scientistic, he often begins a concerted diatribe on rival (heretic) worldviews, even or especially those that are otherwise ridiculously insignificant (e.g., astrology, UFO, Uri Geller, Velikovsky, etc.). It is not the rightness or wrongness of the opposing view but the peculiar passion with which it is opposed that belies its origin: what one is trying to convert is one's own disbelieving self.

On the more benign side, belief *can* serve as the appropriate conceptual expression and codification of a religious involvement of any higher degree (faith, experience, adaptation). Here, belief system acts as a rational clarification of transrational truths, as well as the introductory, *exoteric,* preparatory "reading material" for initiates.[114] When belief systems are thus linked to actual higher (authentic) religiousness, they can be called, not because of themselves but because of association, authentic belief systems.

FAITH

Faith goes beyond belief but not as far as actual religious experience. The true believer can usually give you all the reasons he is "right," and if you genuinely question his reasons he tends to take it very personally (because you have, in fact, just questioned his qualifications for immortality). His belief system is a politics of durability. The person of faith, on the other hand, will usually have a series of beliefs, but the religious involvement of this person does not seem to be generated solely or even predominantly by the beliefs. Frequently, in fact, the person cannot say exactly why he is "right" (has faith), and should you criticize what reasons he does give, he generally takes it all rather philosophically. In my opinion this is because belief, in these cases, is not the actual source of the religious involvement; rather, the person somehow intuits very God as being immanent in (as well as transcendent to) this world and this life. Beliefs become somewhat secondary, since the same intuition can be put in any number of apparently equivalent ways ("They call Him many who is really One"). The person of faith tends to shun literalism, dogmatism, evangelicalism, fundamentalism, which define almost solely the true believer.[13]

Paradoxically, the person of faith is often in great and agonizing religious *doubt,* which the true believer rarely experiences. The true believer has projected his doubts onto others and is too busy trying to convert them to pay attention to his own inner status. The person of faith, however, begins to transcend mere consoling beliefs and thus is open to intense doubt, which the person frequently takes to be a sign of *lack* of faith, which worries him sorely. But that is not usually the case.

Here is what seems to occur: The person of faith intuits, although in a preliminary and somewhat vague fashion, the existence of very God. On the one hand, this confers a measure of peace, inner stability, and a release from mere belief. On the other hand, precisely because that is so, the person yearns for a greater closeness to this Divinity, a more complete knowledge-union with God. Since the person does not yet have this greater closeness, it throws his present state, by comparison, into *doubt* (and yearning). In fact, *the greater the faith-intuition, the greater the doubt.* Zen has a profound saying on this:

> Great doubt, great enlightenment;
> Small doubt, small enlightenment;
> No doubt, no enlightenment.

How different that is from the literal and dogmatic certainty of the true believer.

There seem to be only two ways fundamentally to alleviate this doubt and yearning. One is to revert to mere belief and clothe the doubt in more rigid and external forms (i.e., immortality symbols). The other is to act on the yearning and advance to experience.

EXPERIENCE

Experience goes beyond faith into actual encounter and literal cognition, however brief. Experience, as I am using it, means *peak experience*,[61] a temporary insight into (and influx from) one of the *authentic* transpersonal realms (psychic, subtle, causal). In my opinion, authentic religious experience must be differentiated from mere emotional frenzy, from magical trances, and from mythic mass-enthusiasms, all of which result in a temporary suspension of reason via regression to *pre*-rational adaptations, a slide that is altogether different from *trans*-rational epiphany. Pre-rational frenzies are usually chthonic in mood, emotionally laden, body-bound, and noninsightful[105]—an emotional short-circuit that sparks and sizzles with unconscious orgiastic current. Trans-rational epiphany can be blissful, but it is also numinous, noetic, illuminative, and—most importantly—it carries a great deal of insight or understanding.[6,7]

Temporary peak experiences of the transpersonal realms can occur at almost any stage of development. Actual faith seems conducive to experience; belief systems seem to inhibit it (although none of these correlations are highly positive; peak experiences are notorious for hitting just about anybody with no apparent reason).[61] When they occur to a person who previously rejected religious involvement, such experiences might effect a "conversion," with the individual subsequently adopting a particular religious belief system in order to make sense of "what hit him" (e.g., Saint Paul).

If an authentic peak experience occurs to a mythic-religious true believer, it often has the awkward effect of energizing his or her mythic immortality symbols. The result is a "born-again" believer, a particularly explosive affair. To begin with, analytic experience[29,36] has consistently disclosed that the mythic true believer often possesses a particularly harsh superego (internalized aggression)—an *excessive* guilt, a *surplus* repression, often forged in the atmosphere of overly oppressive/puritanical parents. One of the reasons the mythic true believer might have become a true believer in the first place is to attempt to redress surplus guilt by establishing relations with a fictive-mythic parent who this time around would forgive the guilty transgressions (emotional-sexual impulses). At the same time, the unacceptable and guilty impulses can be projected as a world of *dirty* sinners out there. (I believe that is why a "sinner," in such cases, is usually two things: a disbeliever, or threat to the immortality account, and a "dirty" disbeliever, or contaminated with emotional-sexual guilt.)

When that type of belief system is hit with an authentic peak experience, the system *translates* it into the terms of its own immortality symbols. The whole ideology thus appears to receive a jolting sanctification; this allows the harsh superego to be extroverted, even more than usual, into a moralizing and proselytizing fury; and the true believer, now with the absolute approval of God Almighty Himself, sets out to remake the world in his own image. A *vertical* insight, usually yogic/saintly, is turned into a *horizontal* pitch forward, because the level of structural adaptation is incapable of containing and sustaining the cognitive flood.

On the other hand, but more rarely, an authentic peak experience might jolt a true believer into a person of faith, with subsequent diminution of particular-belief passion and opening of more universal tolerance.

The peak experience itself apparently can *originate* in any of the three higher realms of the person's as yet unrealized structural potentials—psychic, subtle, causal—with the precise nature of the experience differing in each case (panenhenic, theistic, monistic). It is also important to determine "into" which level of present structural adaptation the influx is "poured," since *that* seems to determine the form of its eventual expression—magical, mythical, rational.

Notice, then, that even with our simple scheme we have suggested nine substantially different varieties of authentic peak experience: psychic, subtle, or causal influx poured into magical, mythical, or rational structures. I believe I can produce ample *structural evidence* for each of these nine epiphanies, with the proviso that the more extreme pairings (e.g., magic with causal) are so structurally difficult to achieve that for all practical purposes they are nonexistent. Aside from that exception, examples from the other eight pairings are rather abundant. Typical shamanism, for instance, seems to be panenhenic magic, or psychic intuition poured into magic structures.[105] Beyond that, Joseph Campbell[23] has presented evidence that the *most advanced* and esoteric shamans understood that there was indeed one being behind the polyforms of naturic or panenhenic epiphanies—an example of theistic magic. Moses' Mount Sinai experience seems to have been theistic mythic, or subtle realm revelation flooding a mythic adaptation.[105] A modern-day Zen student's first major satori is monistic rational, or a causal-identity insight breaking into and through a rational adaptation.[88] Bertrand Russell's famous mystical experience appeared largely theistic rational, or subtle-realm illumination flooding logic. On the other hand, the most common form of religious/mystical experience today seems to be yogic or panenhenic rational. The individual at a rational level of adaptation gets a "peek" experience into the psychic dimension; this is often behind everything from the "aha" or "Eureka!" experience of rational scholars to the more mundane flights of ecstatic happiness that occasionally interrupt one's purposive-rational translations.[7]

Finally, there is an esoteric or highly advanced meaning of peak experience: a person already *on* the psychic level can peak experience the subtle or causal; a person on the subtle can peak the causal. This sometimes makes it very difficult to distinguish yogic, saintly, and sagely religions, because occasionally all three will claim that all things are mere modifications of a radiant One Reality, but only the latter claims it as matter of enduring structural adaptation, the others basing the claim on mere peak experience.[7,22,105] We will now investigate that distinction.

STRUCTURAL ADAPTATION

A peak experience, however authentic, is nonetheless merely a glimpse into those transpersonal realms that can be actually and permanently realized via higher *transformative growth* and actual structural adaptation.[101] We will, in this section, examine the implications of that view.

Prior to the modern-day influx of Eastern religions to the West, most religious scholars, psychologists, and sociologists tended to look at religion solely in terms of belief and/or faith. Largely through the influence of Eastern religion, but also due to an increased interest in Christian mysticism, Neoplatonism, and so on, the idea of *actual religious experience* (usually mystical) was added to belief and faith.

In some ways the psychologists led the field in this exploration. William James's *Varieties* was a classic investigation that concluded that the fundamental wellspring of religion was neither belief nor faith but direct experience. After all, he noted, all world religions *began* as an experience in some prophet/seer and only later were codified into belief systems that demanded faith. Carl Jung directed his investigations to the possible archetypal wellsprings of such experience, and then—relatively recently—Maslow's studies made *peak experience* the fundamental paradigm of authentic religiosity.

It has been a mixed blessing. However appropriate and necessary the peak paradigm was in helping scholars see beyond belief and faith to direct experience, the paradigm itself has blinded us to the fact that actual adaptation to these higher realms is a permanent and stable possibility and not merely a fleeting experience. A person can evolve to, for example, the saintly level of structural adaptation with the same eventual stability and continuous functioning that a person can now operate at the linguistic level.[101] We do not speak of such stable adaptations as "experiences," just as we do not say, of the typical person, "He's having a linguistic experience"—he is *at* the linguistic level, *as* that level, more or less continuously.

Once we see that, beyond mere transitory experience, authentic religiosity might actually involve concrete developmental transformation and structural adaptation, then we introduce a revolution in the cognitive validity of spiritual knowledge and truth-claims. For mere belief cannot be cognitively verified, since it has no manifest referent; nor can faith, since it has no necessary content. Consequently, when psychologists and theologians introduced mystical *experience,* they thought they finally had a way to verify or cognitively ground religious claims, because experience is at least concrete. Unfortunately, it is also transitory, fleeting, impossible to replicate, privatistic, and altogether too brief to establish any claim to cognitive validity, as philosophers were very happy (and very correct) to explain.

On the other hand, if we understand that yogic, saintly, and sagely knowledge-claims are based, *not* on belief, faith, or transitory experience, but on actual levels of structuralization, cognition, and development, then the deep structures of their truth-claims assume a perfectly appropriate, verifiable, and replicable status. In fact, they would assume precisely the same *type* of status as, for example, Piaget's levels and Kohlberg's stages and could be clearly demonstrated so in the same basic way: via stage-structural analyses in any correspondingly adapted community of adequately evolved practitioners. (We will return to this topic in chapter 9.)

I realize that the theologians are just now moving from belief and faith to experience, a move that is generating much excitement, enthusiasm, and controversy.* While all of that is a step in the right direction, I feel that its severe limitations should be kept in mind and that we should move on, as quickly as possible, from the paradigm of peak experience to the paradigm of structural adaptation.

---

* Witness Peter Berger's *The Heretical Imperative.*

7

Present-Day Sociology of Religion

W ITH THE ABOVE as background, we can quickly make a few schematic comments on various theories and topics now at the forefront of the sociology of religion.

INCREASING RATIONALISM

Sociologists since Weber have been interested in the increasing trend toward secularization, individualism, and rationalism. In the face of the increasingly purposive-rational worldviews, the older mythological worldviews, based primarily on exoteric mythic-membership and traditional conformity, began slowly but inevitably to lose their cogency, and the very process of legitimation began to shift, in every sector, to rational adjudication and humanistic-secular appropriation. This process is far from complete, and most cultures have yet a way to go before the integrative-stabilizing forces inherent in the rational level of adaptation and organization achieve anything resembling their structural potential. But I am convinced that the mythic-membership structure has reached the inherent limit of its integrative and truth-disclosing capacities. It first emerged c. 9000 B.C. in certain mythic farming cultures, where it slowly replaced the paleolithic magic of the great hunt; it matured in the high civilizations of classic mythology (Egypt, Shang China, Indus Valley India); and it peaked in medieval Europe under mythic-exoteric Christianity.[105] It began to die in seventeenth-century Europe; each succeeding decade has been largely defined by those persons and events that disclosed the mythic inadequacy and made plain its obsolescence: Copernicus, Newton, Locke, Nietzsche, Comte, Darwin, Freud, and so on. There are and will certainly continue to be repressions/fixations to this mode, both in individuals and societies at large, but in my opinion its force as a cogent and legitimating *translator of reality* is defunct. It can no longer provide mana of a high enough degree, and few educated individuals *can* believe its mythic immortality symbols. Like all levels of structural adaptation, it is phase-specific. Its leading-edge phase has passed (which does not prevent it from being dominant in prerational pockets of culture here and abroad).

Thus, I agree with sociologists in general that the central course of modern development is marked by increasing rationalization. However, my major point is that the overall trend of rationalization only covers the *first half* of our proposed developmental scheme: archaic to magic to mythic to rational. But the scheme *continues* from rational to psychic to subtle to causal to ultimate, and thus what perhaps distinguishes my viewpoint from other spiritually sympathetic theorists is that I believe the trend of rationalization per se is necessary, desirable, appropriate, phase-specific, and evolutionary. In fact, I believe it is therefore perfectly religious, *in and by itself* (no matter how apparently secular), in sense rd-4: an expression of increasingly advanced consciousness and articulated awareness that has as its final aim, and itself contributes to, the resurrection of Spirit.

I also believe rational adaptation is perfectly religious in sense rd-2: capable of providing a legitimate, cogent, integrative, and meaningful worldview, or good mana (rd-8). Now, it cannot provide us with a Total Worldview—only causal/ultimate impact, according to the sages, can achieve absolutization.[7] But it can, I believe, provide a worldview every bit as coherent and meaningful as archaic magic or syncretic myth— more so, in my opinion, for reasons we will soon investigate.

But the form of rational-individual integration is so different from that of mythic-conformity that it sometimes confuses scholars. Mythic-membership is marked by an intermediate degree of perspectivism: greater than magic, which has almost none, but not as developed as rational-reflexive, which is the first major structure to display easy and continuous perspectivism. Perspectivism itself is simply the capacity to *take the role of others,* to cognitively project oneself into a mental perspective and viewpoint other than one's own. Psychologists from Werner to Piaget have demonstrated how and why increasing perspectivism, or conversely, decreasing egocentricism, is a primary indicator of development.[57,70,95] Mythic-membership ranks intermediate; it is aware of others, and can begin to take the role of others, but because it is something of a learner's stage in perspectivism, it tends to become trapped in those roles, defined by those roles, bound to them. It is thus captured by a conformist, conventional, or traditional attitude: the culture's codes are its codes, the society's norms are its norms, what they want is what I want. This is exactly Kohlberg's conventional and Loevinger's conformist stages.

With the rise of rational level, however, the person moves into a more self-and-other reflexive, or perspectivist, position. The person can, for the first time, critically distance himself from society's norms and thus adjudicate them for himself. He can norm the norms. He might find them unworthy and reject them; he might find them honorable and embrace them, but in either case he does so out of potentially reasonable and perspectivist considerations, and no longer out of blind conformity. This, of course, is Kohlberg's postconventional and Loevinger's conscientious-individualistic stages.

The paradigm of mythic-membership unity seems to be "Everybody has to think the same thing, share the same symbols, and have the same father-god-king in common." The paradigm of rational-individual unity seems to be "Let's do different things together, share different symbols, exchange different perspectives." That is still a perfectly *legitimate* form of integration or social stability; it simply does not cater to the conformity-traditional paradigm, which many sociologists seem to take as sacred. Its stability does not depend upon mythic mana, or exchange of conformity units, but on rational mana, or exchange of self-reflexive units. Mythic-membership achieves unity via shared belongingness needs; rational-individual, via shared self-esteem needs (to use Maslow's needs hierarchy). In many ways, it is potentially *more* stabilizing than mythic-membership translation because it is more resilient, more *differentiated* and *therefore* more potentially integrated. For developmental theorists, differentiation and integration are not opposites, they are complements, as when Werner summarizes: "Wherever development occurs it proceeds from a state of relative globality and lack of differentiation to a state of increasing differentiation, articulation, and hierarchical integration." Rational-individuation stands in just that relationship to the globality of mythic-membership, and it is that fact that allows scholars such as Fenn[30] and Bell[12] to point out that modern society can potentially achieve adequate stabilization without recourse to fused traditionalistic units of mana. Ogilvy's *Many Dimensional Man* presents a persuasive (although very phase-specific) argument for perspectivist integrity, or unity *via* diversity, which he contrasts with the older but once appropriate integrity of one-god, one-king, one-party mentality.

If individuals at the rational level of structural adaptation choose then to pursue an *authentic* religion, as opposed to the merely *legitimate* religion of secular-rationalism, they almost invariably carry their perspectivism with them and acknowledge that there are different but equally valid approaches to authentic religion—so unlike the mythic-membership believer, who, lacking sophisticated perspectivism, usually claims that his father-god-king is the only possible one and that if you want to get saved, you "got to get" membership.*

At the same time, I do not want to glorify the rational-individual level of adaptation. It is merely phase-specific. I believe it too will pass, eventually to be subsumed in a truly yogic worldview. We may further suppose that, like any level, it can translate its world sanely or morbidly, provide good mana or bad. There seems to be "good" and "bad" reason just as there is "good" and "bad" mythology. But in my opinion we should not take the worst of reason, compare it with the best of mythology, and then claim reason itself, or the level of differentiated-individuated rational adaptation, is a degenerate structure in contrast to yesterday's "really religious," Garden-of-Eden, mythic-conformity modes.

My point is that religious scholars have often seen the trend toward rationalization and concluded that it is an anti-religious trend, whereas for me it is a *pro-authentic-religious* trend by virtue of being transmythic or post-mythic and *on its way to* yogic and higher levels of structural adaptation. If indeed rationality is the great divide between subconscient magic and myth and superconscient subtle and causal, then its major purpose in the overall scheme of evolution might be to strip Spirit of its infantile and childish associations, parental fixations, wish fulfillments, dependency yearnings, and symbiotic gratifications. When Spirit is thus de-mythologized, it can be approached *as* Spirit, in its Absolute Suchness (*tathata*), and not as a Cosmic Parent.

When asked to explain the religious worldview that rationalization is supposedly "destroying," such scholars almost always point to magic or mythic symbologies, thereby elevating prerational structures to a trans-

---

*For an excellent discussion of modern sociological pluralism/perspectivism, see Berger's *The Heretical Imperative*.

rational status. Since development *does* move from prerational myth to rational discourse to transrational epiphany,[102] then if one confuses authentic religion with myth, naturally rationalization *appears* anti-religious. If, however, authentic religion is seen to be transrational, then the phase-specific moment of rational-individuation is not only a step in the right direction, it is an absolutely necessary prerequisite.

ROBERT BELLAH

In my opinion, the greatest contribution of Bellah's work, other than being marked at every turn by immense clarity and perception, is his rigorous demonstration that in some sense religion should be treated as religious, that is, nonreductionistically. This started a minor revolution in modern sociology. Beyond that, however, I have a few reservations.*

1. In treating all religious expressions "nonreductionistically," Bellah tends to lose any serious critical capacity (see chapter 1, section C, Phenomenological-Hermeneutics). Indeed, when he says "religion is true," he abandons the position of *profound* developmental possibilities and overlooks the hierarchy of truth capacities. One might as well say "morality is true" and then overlook the extraordinary differences—including the increasingly *higher* nature—of the half-dozen or so stages of moralization discovered by modern developmental psychology.

This lack of vertical critical dimension, under what often seems to me a questionable use of "nonreductionism," not only overlooks the possible hierarchy of authentic religious adaptation—yogic, saintly, sagely—it takes at close to face value any apparently religious symbol ("symbolic realism") and thus accords eminent status to what might simply be childish fixations. Reductionism, in my opinion, rightly refers to trying to explain *higher* domains by *lower* ones (mind by instinct, subtle by mind, etc.), and that is indeed deplorable. Bellah, however, does not systematically distinguish higher and lower; reductionism thus comes to mean saying anything about a domain other than what it wishes to say about itself. Especially, Bellah does not distinguish prerational religion from transrational religion and thus, in trying to protect the latter from reductionism, he often must glorify the former.

---

* [See *Sex, Ecology, Spirituality* for a discussion of Bellah's important contributions in elucidating the evolutionary-structural stages of religion. See also "Sociocultural Evolution," in volume 4 of the *Collected Works,* for a discussion of other aspects of Bellah's works.]

2. Bellah's background definition of religion is that which serves the holistic interrelation of subject and object in a meaningful way. This is basically rd-2: religion as the relational exchange of mana (on whatever level). It is with this definition that Bellah can (correctly) say that all societies are religious, even secular ones, and that all religions (in that sense) are true. And because he is generally working with rd-2, his criteria of "more valid" religion is rd-8: a more integrative religion is a more valid, useful, or meaningful one. The criterion here is that of *legitimacy*. For example, the American "civil religion" (a mixture of mythic Protestant ethic and American nationalistic immortality symbols) is or was a legitimate religion, according to Bellah, because it provided adequate integrative-meaning, moral restraint, and social cohesion. I agree that that is so. The civil religion was a good mana generator and taboo avoider; it was a legitimate religion (in the rd-8 sense).

However, because of his noncritical ("nonreductionistic") stance, Bellah fails to distinguish systematically between such merely legitimate religions and *authentic* religions. Thus, he will say things like, "The civil religion at its best is a *genuine apprehension of universal and transcendental reality. . . .*"[13] Now, say what you will, civil religion per se, even at its best, did not produce anything resembling real satori, moksha, or *genuine apprehension* of very Spirit. This obfuscation occurs, in my opinion, because Bellah confuses legitimate mana religion—what should happen on all levels of structural adaptation—with authentic-transcendent religion, which happens only on the upper levels of structural adaptation.

3. On occasion, however, Bellah will also use religion as rd-1; for various reasons, he has a specific dimension-realm in mind when he says "religion," and that realm, whatever else it is, is not scientific-rational. Thus he will say, "It is in this sense religious, not scientific."[13] That is a perfectly acceptable usage of religion, as we have seen; it is rd-1.

In my opinion, Bellah is here attempting to refer not merely to a *legitimate* religion, which even secular-rational society can be, but also to an *authentic* religion, which is beyond or trans to rational-individuation (and which, therefore, Bellah is understandably reluctant to grant to scientific-secular societies; in my view, they may be legitimate but are not authentic). But in failing systematically to distinguish between trans-rational and prerational domains, Bellah extends *authenticity* to prerational, mythic engagements and civil religions, whereas they possessed at most a sturdy *legitimacy*. Now scientific-rational society is, for a variety of reasons, today facing various sorts of legitimation crises itself, and these are an important topic of investigation and criticism. But I believe that Bellah confuses the present-day loss of legitimation, which civil and mythic religions had, with a loss of *authenticity* that they *never* possessed. He thus laments: "So-called postreligious man, the cool, self-confident secular man that even some theologians have recently celebrated, is trapped in a literal and circumscribed reality that is classically described in religious terms as the world of death and sin, the fallen world, the world of illusion. Postreligious man is trapped in hell."[13]

What Bellah calls "postreligious" is simply postmythic and postconventional. And, as we suggested in the last section, postmythic men and women are not post-authentic-religious, but preauthentic-religious, poised at the rational level of structural adaptation, ready for the next overall step in collective development and the *first* step in authentic, collective, spiritual experience—that of widespread yogic adaptation. Trapped in hell? Most definitely, as are *all* stages short of superconscient resurrection. But the point is that the previous mythic-religious men and women were equally trapped in hell—in fact, more so; they simply had not the high degree of rational-reflexive awareness necessary to thoroughly realize their plight, and thus suffered their misery in relative innocence, allowing what qualms as might surface to be suckled by a mythic cosmic parent. *That* covenant needed to be broken.

They are indeed still trapped in hell, as were their predecessors, but postmythic men and women have at least, and finally, thrown off their childish images of deity as a protective parent sniveling over their every move, listening to their every wish-fulfillment, catering to their every immortality project, dancing to their prayers of magic. Postmythic men and women did not get thrown out of Eden; they grew up and walked out, and, in now assuming rational and personal responsibility for a measure of their own lives, stand preparatory for the next great transformation: the God within, not the Father without.

4. Finally, Bellah maintains that religion, unlike science, has no verifiable (testable) cognitive truth-claim. I disagree with this strongly, for reasons suggested in chapter 6 and discussed again in chapter 9.

ANTHONY AND ROBBINS

Dick Anthony and Thomas Robbins have recently moved to correct what they see as some of the weaknesses and contradictions in Bellah's theories, principally by replacing (or supplementing) symbolic realism with structuralism, and specifically a structuralism modeled on Chomsky's deep and surface patterns.

I am obviously in sympathy with the main thrust of their work, and I can recommend its general features with enthusiasm. Here, I would simply like to suggest a few minor amendments to their presentations in light of our discussion thus far.

1. Anthony and Robbins[3] begin by suggesting that Bellah's approach to religion, which sees it as a universal and nonreducible *factum* of human existence, is a start toward a long-sought formulation of "universal structural principles intrinsic to religion," that is, "Symbolic realism seems to imply a fundamental unity of all religions at a deep level." They point out, however, that Bellah fails to carefully distinguish between the deep structures of such universal religion, which would be largely invariant and ahistorical, and the surface structures of religion, which would be mostly variable and contingent. Consequently, they note, "Bellah's recent work has emphasized two trends that, on the face of it, seem contradictory. In his metatheoretical papers, he has stressed the underlying uniformity of seemingly diverse religious traditions and epochs. However, in his actual description of concrete religious systems, Bellah has emphasized the necessity of religious change [and] religious evolution. . . ." Anthony and Robbins then argue that

> the apparent contradictions between these positions arise because Bellah has not made explicit the distinction between the surface structure and deep structure of religions. When he emphasizes the similarities in religions of different cultures and epochs, he is focusing upon what should properly be called the deep structure of religion. When he focuses upon the changes in religion relative to changing psychological, sociological, and economic conditions, he is describing surface structures.

As cogent as that argument for deep and surface structure is (we will return to it in a moment), the failure to make that distinction is not primarily the cause of "the apparent contradictions" in Bellah's work. Bellah does not, it is true, explicitly make that important distinction, but *prior* to that omission, in my opinion, is the more fundamental lack of distinction between legitimate and authentic religions, *each* class of which has representative deep and surface features. For example, there is the deep structure of magic religion (marked by confusion of symbol and thing symbolized, condensation, diplacement, etc.), and there are actual surface manifestations of magic religion (voodoo here, naturic animism there, Bon religion here, and so on). There is the deep structure of causal religion (marked by unmanifest absorption, identity of self and absolute ground, etc.), and there are actual surface manifestations of causal religion (Zen, Vedanta, Eckhart, etc.). And so with each class. If these levels of structural realization are not first distinguished, then any merely legitimate religion may be confused with genuinely authentic religion, and the *dynamics* of legitimacy may be likewise confused with the *dynamics* of authenticity. That is, what happens at each level of the spectrum of existence (universal or ever-present need for mana, meaning) might be confused with what specifically defines the *higher* levels of the spectrum (actual universal mysticism), with the result that what we mean by "deep" and "surface" structures is skewed from the start, most often by having "deep" mean authentic (or mystical) and "surface" mean legitimate, instead of seeing that authentic religions have deep and surface structures, legitimate religions have deep and surface structures, and the two do not necessarily overlap.

Let me give as a correlative example Maslow's work on the hierarchy of needs, which are: physiological needs (material), safety needs (magic-body protective), belongingness needs (mythic-membership), self-esteem needs (rational-reflexive), self-actualization needs (centaur/psychic), and the self-transcendence needs (subtle/causal).[61] Now we can say *need is universal,* or ever-present, which of course it is, because it occurs on *all* levels. But that "need-as-universal" is not to be confused with *the* need for universal-mystical self-transcendence, which occurs on the *highest* levels. Just so, if we define religion as meaning-need (rd-2), then of course it is universal and occurs on all levels, as mana search, and we can further investigate what constitutes *good* mana on all levels (rd-8), so as to trace out the actual *dynamics* and possible functional invariants, cross-level, of legitimation itself. But if by religion we *also* wish somehow to convey, as Anthony and Robbins appropriately do, a meaning of authentic or universal-mystical union (and *philosophia perennis*), then only the highest and transcendent levels are directly involved.

Those are two completely different (but equally important) forms of "universal religiousness" or "universal structural principles intrinsic to religion," principally because they reflect two quite different forms of religion (rd-2 and rd-1) and correlative validity scales (rd-8 and rd-9, or legitimacy and authenticity). The former is a universality of all good-mana religion at some deep level, "deep level" here meaning the functional similarities and dynamics of all legitimately integrative-horizontal translations. The latter is a "transcendental unity" reached and shared only by those rather rare sub-sects of certain religions that actually embrace an authentically mystical or *esoteric* level, or the superconscient realm in general, which is what scholars of the *philosophia perennis* mean by the phrase "transcendent unity of religions." Bellah's work deals basically with the former, or legitimate mana and taboo-avoidance (or accumulation of immortality symbols, which is why I think he speaks so highly of Norman O. Brown's works). Anthony and Robbins wish to make more explicit room for the latter, or authentic mystical religion, but—in failing to explicitly distinguish legitimate and authentic—they generally try to make the former a surface structure of the latter as deep structure. They consequently overlook the possibility that mysticism per se (panenhenic, theistic, or monistic) is the deep structure of which *only* the authentic religions (yogic, saintly, or sagely) are surface structures. For, in my opinion, actual mysticism is no more the deep structure of, for example, civil religion, than the self-transcendence need is the deep structure of, for example, the safety needs.

In other words, Anthony and Robbins significantly improve Bellah's ideas by introducing deep and surface structures to his formulations, but they tend to simply reproduce his confusion of legitimate and authentic religions, the confusion of legitimate mana on any level with authentic mana on the mystical levels, the confusion of universal functional invariants of good integration with universal mystical integration. They then take the deep structure of authentic mysticism (or divine immanence) and instead of assigning it its own *authentic* surface structures, assign it any merely *legitimate* surface structures from any lower level, no matter how otherwise completely lacking in authenticity they might be. It is in this vein that they say, for example, "Maoism shares certain universal features of traditional religions (and thus *is* a religion in our sense), whereas Russian communism does not. . . ."[3] These features, which Maoism supposedly possesses, Anthony and Robbins wish explicitly to connect to the deep structure of "an inner experience of ultimate reality."[3] In other words, the deep structure of authentic mysticism is supposed to underlie the surface structure of legitimate Maoism. Again, I think it is obvious that the experience of Maoism and the experience of samadhi are not related as surface and deep structures but as two different levels of structuralization altogether. Better to say that Maoism is a *legitimate* religion (surface structure) at the mythic-to-rational level (deep structure), whereas Russian communism is still struggling for similar legitimacy at the same level, but *neither* are *authentic* religions, as are, for example, Vedanta and Zen, which are two different but more or less legitimate surface structures (in India and Japan, respectively) of the *same* causal-level deep structure.

At the same time, one can compare all types of *legitimate* religions, whether also authentic or not—say, Maoism, American civil religion, Vajrayana in precommunistic Tibet, exoteric Shi'ite Islam—in order to determine what they have in common ("deep structure" in an entirely different sense) as good integrators of societies, and thus discover and formulate the dynamics and basic functional invariants of "healthy" religion. I have already suggested that such dynamics would include good mana production and taboo avoidance (via meaning-units and immortality symbols). Such "deep structures," in their potential form, would also probably be native, as explained for translative potentials in chapter 4. Lack of authenticity would then be related to lack of *transformative* symbology; lack of legitimacy, to lack of adequate *translative* symbology, itself related in part to a failure of transcription, or adequate read-out of the potentials available to the particular level.

In summary, if the distinction deep/surface is made without the prior distinction of authentic/legitimate, then one of the results is that *authentic* mysticism may appear to be the deep structure of which all lower and merely *legitimate* religions are supposed to be surface structures, instead of seeing that each level has its own deep and surface structures, that the surface structures can function legitimately or illegitimately on every level, that only on the highest levels does authentic mystical union manifest itself, and that the deep structures of those mystical levels—psychic, subtle, causal—have as surface structures only the religions evoking them—yogic, saintly, sagely.

2. Anthony, in an important paper ("A Phenomenological-Structuralist Approach to the Scientific Study of Religion"),[2] the merits of which I will emphasize in a moment, again suggests "convergence of lines of evidence pointing toward *universal mysticism* as the data base for the deep structure component of . . . a two-level [deep/surface] structuralist theory of religion." Now we have already suggested that universal mysticism is *not* the deep structure of lower-level legitimate religions, such as magic-voodoo, exoteric mythic religion, Maoism, or civil religion, for they take as deep structure the intrinsic rules and patterns that define and govern the particular (lower) level of structural adaptation on which their existence is grounded.

But what I wish specifically to emphasize in this section is that even when we understand that actual mysticism is the deep structure of only authentic religious experience-adaptation, we still have to be careful to differentiate the hierarchical *types* of mystical union. There are at least three or four types, as we have seen, and each has a *deep structure* (psychic, subtle, causal, or ultimate) that underlies various *surface structures* of authentic religious symbology (e.g. and respectively, Tundra Shamanism, Mosaic Judaism, Vedanta Hinduism, Maha Ati Vajrayana), authentic religious practice (e.g. and respectively, hatha-yoga arousal, shabd or interior prayer-contemplation, jnana-insight or radical absorption in the Heart, and sahaja or ultimate-spontaneous Identity), and authentic mystical unions (panenhenic, theistic, monistic, nondual).

My own feeling is that even this four-level hierarchy will soon be replaced with a much more complex one, containing up to a dozen discrete developmental structures. But in any event, the old notion that there are only two types or levels of religion—exoteric, which is everywhere different, and esoteric, which is everywhere identical—is about as precise as saying there are two forms of mental cognition, primary and secondary. That early Freudian division is acceptable enough, but we can be much more precise: for example, Piaget's description of four structure-stages, which is, of course, exactly the type of refinement I believe will happen with both exoteric *and* esoteric religions.

But the real reason I mention Anthony's paper is that, aside from these small amendments, I believe it is packed with all the right insights and suggestions for a general structural approach to religion. There is no need of my merely repeating his contributions here; I suggest the reader consult the paper itself, for the essentials of his suggestions are surely ones we will want to include in a well-rounded approach to religion.

3. The refinements I have suggested might also allow us to tease apart the idea that only surface structures change in religious history while deep structures remain everywhere monolithic. Now it is true that a deep structure in itself is a-historical, but it *emerges* in the course of history, and we can trace those revolutionary emergences. On the other hand, when it is thought that there is only *one* basic deep structure of religion, then naturally that deep structure must also be assumed to have been present from the earliest religious expression, and so all religious history is pictured as a mere shuffling of various surface structures around this "single," "universal" deep structure. But once we see that there might be four or more major deep structures of authentic religion

(not to mention exoteric religions), then it becomes more than probable that the history of religion involves not only evolution of surface structures but also revolution in deep structures.

Stated differently, most religions, in the course of their histories, seem to face various *legitimation crises*, usually prompted by various rival surface structures. But occasionally a particular religion might face what amounts to an *authentication crisis*: it either fails to provide the actual *transformation* that it promised, or it is faced with a religion that delivers higher-level transformation altogether. For example, at least two such significant transformations in the West seem to have occurred:[105] (1) The transformation from a somewhat crude yogic-shamanistic and panenhenic worship to a truly subtle and saintly involvement, epitomized perhaps by Moses, who, according to legend, descended from Mount Sinai to directly challenge such "nature worship"; and (2) the transformation from Mosaic saintly worship to causal identity, epitomized by Christ and al-Hallaj, both of whom were murdered "because you, being a man, make yourself out God."

These religion-transformational crises and conflicts are, I believe, simply a subset of what happens at every level of development as a new and higher structure emerges to replace or subsume the prior and lower. My point is simply that, in the study of religious development (as a subset of general developmental principles), we might be sensitive to the differences in historico-dynamics between surface structure rivalries and deep structure revolutions, between legitimation crises and authentication crises.

The New Religions

There is an abundance of literature dealing with the new religious movements in America; they seem to be the acid test of a sociological theory. In this section I will apply the theory of transcendental sociology in outline form.

1. We can again begin with Bellah's work, for I think his analysis of American civil religion is cogent. I disagree that it was an authentic religion, but it seemed most definitely a legitimate religion: it served good mana on a mythic-membership level and it offered an easy abundance of taboo-avoidance and immortality symbols. According to Bellah (and others), the American civil religion fatally hemorrhaged in the 1960s,

and the new religions, in various forms, are in large measure the result. What follows—the rest of section 1—is my *opinion* of what happened.

The old civil-religious, traditional-membership covenant was already under strain due to increasing rationalization and consequent (healthy) de-mythologizing; what legitimation it had left was finally broken under the combined onslaught of radical student politics, post-conventional rationality, Vietnam, alternative (Eastern) spiritual epiphanies, economic doubts, and a general debunking of American nationalism. As the old translation-covenant finally disintegrated, it left in its wake *three separate lines of development,* lines that were already in existence to some degree but now stood naked in their form and accelerated in their pace.

a. The sector of ongoing secular-rationalization, which has now dominated the universities, the media, most central political-technical steering decisions, the intelligentsia, and the worldview of most educated, liberal individuals.

b. A very small sector that, already brought up in an atmosphere of increasing rational-secularism and more or less adapted to it, began to search for, or actually develop to, transrational and transpersonal structuralization. Interest in Eastern yogic and meditative disciplines, Christian and Jewish mysticism, and certain new forms of intensive psychotherapy, were evidence of a thirst for such transrational saturation. *However,* not all, not even most, individuals interested in the "new religions" were authentically ready for actual transrational and yogic adaptation, because . . .

c. The broken covenant found a large sector of the population unready and unable to transform to responsible, postmythic, rational individuality (let alone transrational yogic discipline). This was exacerbated by the uncontested fact that the (horizontal) developmental course of rational-individuation was not itself operating up to its integrative potential: it was not providing the good mana it is structurally capable of. Thus, for various reasons, a significant number of individuals were alienated from the rational-individual society that was rapidly if precariously emerging. In search of some sort of legitimate mana (integrative truth), some of these individuals took regressive consolation in various prerational immortality symbols and mythological ideologies. These were largely of two sorts.

(1) Fundamentalistic mythic religion: a new surge in exoteric Protestant mythology, complete with proselytizing fury, evangelical non-

perspectivism, saved-by-the-father (Oedipal) immortality symbols, patriarchal sexism, and authoritarian obedience. Largely composed of true believers, this sector, basically, wanted to put the broken covenant back together again.

(2) Cultic new age religions: such as the Moonies, Hare Kirshna, Jesus freaks, and so forth; these are essentially *identical* in deep structure with the fundamentalist mythic religion of the evangelicals, but their drastically different surface structures have the all-important advantage of allowing one, in such cults, to express disaffection with both rational society *and* one's parents, should one's parents already be expressing disaffection with rationality via mythic revivals. Dressing up like a Hindu can both scream disapproval of society at large and really get to your own fundamentalist Christian parents; even better, dress up like Jesus Christ.

My point is simply that "the" new religions really involve at least two drastically different structural celebrations: transrational, on the one hand, and prerational, on the other. The former is primarily (but not solely) a manifestation of ongoing postrational development, vertical transformation, and higher structuralization, whereas the latter is largely (but not solely) a product of failure at rational-individuation (exposed when the covenant broke) and a regression/fixation to prerational, mythic, and even archaic-magical (narcissistic) structural disadvantages, which define much of the "new age" movements.[102]

2. There remains the possible role that the authentic mystical sector (*b* above) might have in actual large-scale societal transformation. For our general paradigm of revolutionary (not merely evolutionary) change is as follows: the present translation begins to fail its soothing, phase-specific integrative tasks, that is, its units of meaning no longer command common sense; too many of its immortality symbols have shockingly suffered damage (death); structural tension begins to increase, driving the system into various turmoils and perturbations; the structure eventually begins to loosen and break; if there are no viable seed crystals in the old translative repertoire, the system either regresses to lower forms or completely disintegrates; if there are viable seed crystals, then the structural tensions are absorbed and channeled through those crystals, and the system as a whole escapes its conflicts into a higher level of structural organization and integration. The old translation dies; transformation ensues; new and higher translations are born.

So where do we look for these seed crystals? Where are the enclaves and harbingers of future transformation? By definition-paradigm, they are most likely in those sectors now deemed "out-law" by the laws and in-laws of the present translation. Robbins and Anthony[77] quote Tiryakian:

> If we accept the notion that social revolutions essentially involve a fundamental re-ordering of the social structure, and if we accept the supposition that the social order is essentially viewed as a moral phenomenon by the members of the collectivity, then there must be a new source of morality involved in societal change, one that both desacralizes the present system and paves the way for the acceptance of a new order. (This is the death and rebirth aspect of social revolutions [we have already examined this death/rebirth aspect of all forms of transformation; see chapter 4, "Transformation"].) Since established religion represents a compromise with the ongoing secular institutions, the only other possible host of revolutionary thought, however unwittingly, is the noninstitutionalized religious sector. . . .

Thus, concludes Tiryakian, "important ideational components of change (i.e., changes in the social consciousness of reality) may often originate in the noninstitutionalized ["out-law"] groups or sectors of society whose paradigms of reality may, in certain historical moments, become those which replace institutionalized paradigms and become in turn new social blueprints."

I believe such statements are true, but it would help if we could be more specific. For notice that although all future truths are now contained in out-laws (by definition), not all out-laws are truthful (just as in science only the theories that today seem absurd *can* be the truths of tomorrow, but not all absurd theories are therefore true—most are, in fact, absurd, today and tomorrow). Just so with social "absurdities": in the class of general out-laws in any society, there are prelaws, counterlaws, and translaws, and apparently their influences on social revolutions are completely different.

Pre-laws are those individuals who, for various reasons, are not able or do not wish to rise to the average expectable level of structural adaptation of a given society. They often end up in jails (as blatant antilaws) or mental institutions, although frequently their preconventional structuralization is benign enough and simply adds, for want of a better metaphor, salt to societal stew. But it should be noted that *most* of the teachings and practices that call themselves "esoteric" or "occult" are, in my opinion, prelaw; they are thinly rationalized magic, *not* psychic and *not* saintly. Astrology, tarot, "magick," voodoo, festival ritual, and such largely follow exactly the deep structure of magical/primary process cognition, and they—along with other forms of prelaw, preconventional consciousness—are *not* seed crystals of the future, unless that future spells regression.

Counter-laws make up the largest portion of what is loosely called "counterculture." Neither prelaw nor translaw, counter-law is the precise mirror image of the present law. It is largely composed of adolescent-like mentality, which, in a phase-specifically appropriate enough fashion, attempts to establish individual identities by taking each facet of present law and either acting out its precise *converse* (e.g., short-hair society produces long-hair counterculture) or its precise *caricature* (prove mastery of it and thus independence from it by "hamming it up," although this is initially an unconscious posturing and thus is performed with monumental seriousness; e.g., Mom and Dad drink, I'll be a drunk). If either of these tendencies is overblown, the counter-law becomes an anti-law (and is usually jailed). In general, however, "Counterculture may be described," says Marin, "as the tribalized, ritualized, mirror of national culture."[59]

Notice in particular that when authentic yogic-saintly religions are introduced to counter-laws, those disciplines are merely *translated* into the terms of the struggle for adaptation at adolescent rationality (i.e., counter-rationality). Such otherwise authentic disciplines thus end up embodying, via caricature, all of the predominant values of the present laws and translations of society. In this particular case, "New spiritual patterns, like the sixties counterculture, do not really challenge or antithesize dominant cultural patterns, but rather reflect and elaborate those patterns, including consumerism, individualism, spiritual privitism, and a fetishism of 'techniques.' "[77] Counter-laws can take authentic spiritual practices and turn them into caricatured thrills, "so self-centered," says Bellah, "that they begin to approximate the consumer cafeteria model."[78]

This is not to say these counter-law movements are therefore trivial; they are not transformative, but they do seem to serve a useful function for *present* society: they help forward and stabilize the given translations of the society by allowing its members, especially adolescent-phasers, to embrace its dominant values while pretending not to, thus accomplishing necessary socialization and individuation at once. In allowing its counter-laws to stand out in theory, it tucks them in in fact. Failure to grasp that elemental point has led more than one scholar to mistake counter-laws for translaws and proclaim the greening of America, the aquarian new age, and so on.

So far, we have discussed prelaws and counter-laws (and possible anti-laws): The prelaws are a relatively regressive sector, either trapped in or exploiting levels of structural organization lower than the present, average expectable level of societal translation. Their effect is per se disintegrative; however, in small numbers, and especially in their more benign modes, they may contribute to the overall translative integration of society by forming sub-societies that answer their own needs and thus spare society the disruption. Should this sector assume significant proportions, however, it generally becomes a source (or a symptom) of what can only be called "decadence," and if society at large finds its own higher-level translations burdensome, a truly disintegrative-regressive trend can result. The classic example, apparently, is Rome.

The counter-laws, on the other hand, usually serve the overall translative integration of society by embracing its fundamental values via a converse-caricatured rehearsal that simultaneously allows the necessary process of individuation and post-conformist moralization. This seems to be the basis of the swing in styles with each generation; Eisenhower parents produced student radicals who now, as parents, are giving birth to little Republicans. What occasionally can result within this counter-swing is a more benign re-arrangement of the present translations; for example, student protests sometimes *are* legitimate protests.

The point is that neither prelaws nor counter-laws seem to be significant sectors of actual social *transformation*—not on the emergent scale we are now discussing. (All sorts of "translative revolutions" are also possible, of course, especially in material modes of production, technological innovations, etc. These, however, do not necessarily involve actual transformations in structures of consciousness.) If actual social transformations do generally come from some sort of presently outlawed sector, the only one left to consider is that of the translaws. It would be helpful, then, if we could specify more precisely the type of seed crystals that might give birth to the eventual transformation, because merely being a translaw, however authentic, does not ensure being the eventual *legitimate* catalyst of a given transformation.

Perhaps we can surmise where we will find the major future catalysts by looking at the structure-stage they will replace. For, in my strongest opinion, before a true collective transpersonal (e.g., psychic) transformation can occur, rational-individual society will first have to reach its full potential and provide the phase-specific truths, values, and substructures for which it is designed and upon which future transformations will depend, such as appropriate technology, a sophisticated medical base, telecommunications as global bonding via global perspectivism, computer interfacing as an extension of mind, and especially a de-mythologizing of reality, divinity, and consciousness.

It follows that, in my opinion, the first *large-scale* transformative trends will come through those who have already adequately mastered that rational-individuated operative base. For transrational insight comes *through* and then out of the realm of reason, not around it or away from it or against it. They will come from within, these yogis. They might have first flirted with yogic (spiritual, transpersonal, panenhenic) philosophy during their adolescent counter-law phase, but they will have subsequently come to terms with the law itself and therefore will be in a firm position to consciously move beyond it and not merely unconsciously react to it.

Whether esoteric, mystical, nonfundamentalist Christianity will be able to carry out this transformation, or whether it can even survive the prior, necessary demythologizing and dismantling of its exoteric, patriarchal, mythical accouterments, I do not know. (For a superb account of what this new/renewed Christianity would have to look like, see Jacob Needleman's *Lost Christianity*.) But I am fairly convinced that one of the keys to the specific *type* of future transformation lies in *surface structure compatibility,* that is, in a compatibility of the old and new translations, a *bequeathing of legitimacy* (the old and new have to be different enough to constitute an actual transformation, but similar enough to encourage people to jump, as it were). Therefore, the new yogic (shamanic, panenhenic) translations will likely have certain surface structures that are compatible with (and perhaps occasionally direct continuations of) past surface structure symbolizations. For example, the modern phase of rational-individuation, however otherwise different from its mythic-Christian predecessor, retains an emphasis on personhood and individuality, which is clearly Judeo-Christian in origin and nature (God loves and protects individual souls; the individual person is cherished in the eyes of the Lord; God Himself is a big person, so is His Son, etc.).

Because of this general necessity for surface structure compatibility, I do not believe that Eastern religions will serve as large-scale models for Western transformation, however otherwise significant they might have proven to be in terms of being provocateurs. Their influence will be considerable, to be sure, but in a way that is finally translated and assimilated in the new Western panenhenic worldview, and not merely transplanted *en bloc*. Therefore, if the panenhenic transformation is not esoterically Christian, it would not surprise me if a new and specifically Western mysticism arose, although it would be compatible in surface terms with Christian symbology *and* rational technology. (To give a silly example, but one I have already heard elsewhere: yogic meditation is called "a psychotechnology of contemplative love." In the same vein, notice three phenomena whose deep structure is often that of mystical impulse but whose surface structures are such that they could initially have arisen almost nowhere but in America: biofeedback, widespread LSD use, and *A Course in Miracles*. Those are in some ways authentic yogic-saintly endeavors that became very popular because of *surface structure compatibility* with, respectively, American technology, American drug-oriented medicine/culture, and American fundamentalistic-Protestant belief in magic prayer.) My point is simply that the new Western panenhenic consciousness will say all the right things, use all the right symbols, cater to all the old desires, and it will begin to remake the Western world.

3. The three great domains of human development—childish subconsciousness, adolescent self-consciousness, and mature superconsciousness—are each marked by a dominant psychological attitude: passive dependence, active independence, and actively passive surrender (they stand in the relationship thesis, antithesis, synthesis).[101,93] The point of this section is that the first and last attitudes are often confused by scholars, a confusion that results in certain mistaken conclusions on the nature of spiritual community.[102]

Passive dependence is the disposition of the infant-child self-system, simply because it is not yet developed enough to assume responsibility for the relational exchanges of its basic mana-needs (physiological, safety, belongingness). It depends for its very existence on specific relational exchanges with specific partners: mother, father, significant others. Due to its fledgling boundaries, it is especially open to traumatic displacements, splitting, fragmentation, dissociation. These distortions are particularly significant for future development, because (as outlined in chapter 3, "The Distortion of Relational Exchange"), they tend to reproduce themselves on the higher levels of structural organization as the latter emerge and consolidate. Like a grain of sand caught in the early layers of a pearl, each successive layer is crinkled and weakened at a stress point that keeps reproducing itself. Such stress points for the young self-system especially concern its relation to disciplinary or authority figures, since for the most part this actually represents the relation between its own lower and preverbal structures, especially emotional-sexual and aggressive impulses, and its fledgling symbolic-verbal and mental structures, one of whose jobs will be to subdue and transform the emotional-vital components into higher expressions. That is, the interpersonal relation between child and parent is also the intrapersonal relation between the child's own body and mind. Neither relationship can the child yet master, and thus both basically highlight the child's fundamental mood of passive dependence.

All of which changes, or can change, with the emergence in adolescence of the critical, self-reflexive, self-conscious mentality.[54,66,101] The adolescent rebellion against the parents is largely an outward symptom of the inner (and healthy) fight to differentiate from or transcend childish dependence and magic-mythic subconsciousness. The prelaw of the child gives way to the counter-law of the adolescent. There is a corresponding swing in mood from general passive dependence to active independence (again, this *can* go too far, from counter-law to anti-law, but by and large it is nothing but a healthy differentiation and transformation).

The adolescent mood of active independence is a phase-specific form of transcendence—the transcendence from subconscious dependence to self-conscious responsibility.[101] But if it persists beyond its phase-specific moment—which in most Western cultures it does—it acts merely to *prevent* the emergence of the mature disposition of an actively passive surrender of isolated individuality to its own higher and prior nature, or radical superconsciousness, in and as the entire world process at large. This is a *surrender,* in that adolescent swaggering has to be released—died to—in order to make room for rebirth on the superconscient levels. It is *passive,* in that the center of squirming impatience known as ego must eventually relax its chronic contraction in the face of a wider awareness. And it is *actively* passive because it is no mere trancelike submission, but entails an effort of keenest concentration, perception, and will to cut through the obsessive rationalization and stream of contracted thought that constitutes the ego. In the gesture of actively passive surrender, the higher centers of superconscient potential are *actively* engaged, the ego is rendered open and *passive,* and consequently the egoic self-sense can relax into, and *surrender* as, the wider currents of being and awareness that constitute the goal and ground of its own develop-ment—a surrender that marks the end of its own self-alienation.[7,22,45,105]

Now the only reason I bring all this up is that the discipline of actively passive surrender, especially under the guidance of an acknowledged spiritual master, is always being confused with childish passive depen-dence.[93,102] By "always" I mean, specifically, that the vast majority of orthodox psychologists and sociologists do not wish, or are not able, to tell the difference between prepersonal helplessness and dependence on a paternal authority figure, and transpersonal surrender and submission via a spiritual adept. For those scholars, apparently, the adolescent stance of active independence and fierce isolation is held to be, not a phase-specific moment in the greater arc of development, but the goal and highest stage of development itself, whereupon any stance other than that is viewed with ghoulish academic fascination.

Now, it is certainly true that many of the "new religions," or at least the new cults, are based on the dynamics of prepersonal regression/fixa-tion, with consequent obedience to a father figure/totem master, with self-clan fusion and indissociation (participation mystique), with group ritual, magic incantations, mythic apocrypha. The members of the clan-cult often show borderline neurotic or borderline psychotic disposi-tions; that is, low ego-strength, concrete immersion in experience with difficulty holding abstract locations, narcissistic involvement, low self-esteem, with correlative difficulty handling moral ambiguity, contradic-tions, or choice structures.[4,56,59] The clan-cult is magnetic for such per-sonalities, because it (and usually its totem master) offers and fosters an atmosphere of passive dependence to authoritarianism, which re-creates the child-specific mood in which such personalities are still psychologi-cally trapped. Cults do not have to "brainwash" such members; all they have to do is show up and smile.

Because it caters to the child-specific mood of passive dependence, the one thing *not* allowed in the clan-cult is the exercise of active adolescent independence, especially the exercise of rational self-reflection, critical appraisal, logical discourse, and systematic study of alternative philoso-phies. This, coupled with the allegiance to totem master, or the magical "father" of the entire clan, constitutes much of the psychosocial founda-tion of the cult.

To the untutored eye, a community of transpersonal contemplatives—what the Buddhists call a *sangha*—often appears similar or even identi-cal to the clan-cult, principally because, I suppose, it is usually rather close-knit and often organized around a spiritual adept held in various degrees of reverence or at least profound respect. This community is also interested in nullifying adolescent active independence, but in an entirely different direction—its transcendence, not its prohibition. In fact, because each higher stage transcends but *includes* its predecessors, the true sangha always *retains access to,* and retains an appropriate place for, rational inquiry, logical reflection, systematic study of other philosophical frameworks, and critical appraisal of its own teachings in light of related areas. Historically, in fact, the mystical centers of contemplation have often been the great centers of education and learning—Nalanda in India, for instance, or the T'ien T'ai Buddhist centers in China. Needham[64] has already demonstrated that mysticism and scientific inquiry have usually been historically linked, simply because both have always rejected dogmatic belief and insisted on open experience.

The point is that what one is attempting to "destroy" in contemplation *is not the mind but an exclusive identity of consciousness with the mind.*[101,102] The infant-child is identified more or less exclusively with the body; as the adolescent mind emerges, it destroys the exclusive identity with the body but does not destroy the body itself; it subsumes the body in its own larger mental identity. Just so, as spirit emerges, it destroys the exclusive identity with mind (and subsumed body) but does not destroy the mind itself; it subsumes the mind to its own larger supreme identity.[102] The mind itself is perfectly valued, as is its free and critical inquiry into any theoretical area.

The adolescent separate-self sense, however, which is an exclusive identification with mind in a stance of rebellious independence, is not so highly valued; therefore, many preliminary exercises in contemplative communities are specifically designed to remind the ego of its phase-specific and intermediate place in overall development. Exercises such as simple bowing in Zen, the prostrations in Vajrayana, or mandatory community service-dharma in monastic sects are outward and visible signs of an inward and actively passive surrender to a state of selfless being more panoramic than ego. The eventual aim of such practices is to keep the mind but transcend the egoic self-sense by discovering a larger self in the spiritual dimension of creation at large.

Now, that is radically different from the clan-cult strategy of *reducing* the self to prepersonal and passive dependence by restricting and prohibiting the free engagement of critical reflection. The aim of sangha is to keep mind but transcend ego; the aim of the cult is to prohibit both.

I realize that in practice it is not always easy to determine whether a particular community is a cult or a sangha—like most life situations, there is something of a continuum between ideal limits. But I feel that the above criteria at least offer a plausible basis for the psychodynamic distinction between these groups (for an expansion of these criteria, see note 106). There is obviously much research to be done in this area, but speaking both personally and as a transpersonal psychologist, I think orthodox psychologists and sociologists could show a little more imagination when it comes to reporting on the psychodynamics of a communal occasion; they have all but made Jonestown a paradigm of "spiritual" get-togethers. I would only like to suggest that an honest effort be made to distinguish child-specific passive dependence from mature actively passive surrender, with a correlative distinction between prepersonal cults and transpersonal sanghas.

4. I have, throughout this book, been emphasizing what sociology might gain from an infusion of psychology (and transpersonal psychology in particular). I should like to emphasize, however, that this is a two-way street, and that psychology (and transpersonal psychology in particular) has much to gain from a study of modern sociology, and especially the sociology of religions. Accordingly, I should like to end this chapter by reprinting my review of *In Gods We Trust: New Patterns of Religious Pluralism in America* (Robbins and Anthony, eds.), which was published in *Journal of Transpersonal Psychology*. That book is representative of the type of serious, disciplined sociological inquiry that is now occurring with regard to various new religious movements in America (though we could almost say, with certain surface modifications, the Western world at large). Other such volumes are, at this moment, being compiled. No question: this is good news—for psychology, sociology, *and* religion.

My comments on this book, while not nearly as detailed as what has gone above, may nonetheless serve as a general summary of our discussion thus far, and as an indication of the type of interdisciplinary dialogue upon which the future of this field depends.

> Assuming that psychology is always also social psychology, a study of the "new religions" from a decidedly sociological perspective would be of great significance to psychology in general and to transpersonal psychology/therapy in particular; even more so given the fact that a "transpersonal sociology" is a discipline desperately awaiting birth. *In Gods We Trust* is, I believe, the first rigorously sociological treatment of the new religious

movements; as such, it possesses all of the strengths of a truly pioneering effort, and some of the unavoidable weaknesses; in any event, its simple appearance is monumental.

The anthology has as its starting point (and in many ways its central theme) Robert Bellah's immensely influential concept of "civil religion" and its recent disintegration. The idea, briefly, is that, whatever else the function of religion, it serves centrally as a way to meaningfully integrate and legitimate a world view [rd-2 and rd-8]. According to Bellah, American civil religion is (or was) a blend of Biblical symbolism and American nationalism ("One nation, under God. . . ."), a "religion" which adequately served social integration, ethic, and purpose for the better part of American history. However, in recent decades, according to Bellah and others, the American civil religion began to disintegrate, or, technically, to lose its legitimacy (what Bellah calls "the broken covenant"). Assuming (as these theorists do) that religion as integrative function [rd-2] is a universal necessity or impulse, it follows that *something* would have to take the place of the old civil religion; hence, the new religions of the last few decades: "The appeal of oriental mysticism and quasi-mystical therapy groups can best be understood in relation to the needs created by this decline [in civil religion]."

From that point, the anthology moves progressively into various sociological theories, research, and data, arranged in six sections. The subtitles tell the story: Religious Ferment and Cultural Transformation; Disenchantment and Renewal in Mainline Traditions; Civil Religion Sects, Oriental Mysticism and Therapy Groups; The Brainwashing Explanation (since I won't discuss this topic in the rest of this review, let me point out here that this book stands as a sound indictment of the "brainwashing" theory wherever it appears; the data simply doesn't support such an explanatory theory, even with such problematic groups as the Moonies); New Religions; and the Decline of Community. Some highlights:

Robert Wuthnow's "Political Aspects of the Quietistic Revival" is almost humorously titled (re: "quietistic"), because it effectively challenges the longstanding prejudice (found in researchers from Weber to Freud) that there is a " 'hydraulic relation' between experiential religion and political commitment, that the more mystical a person is, the less involved in [social or] political activity he is likely to be." On the basis of empirical data, Wuthnow demonstrates that not only are those attracted to mysticism *not* less socially committed, they consistently ranked higher in most social commitment categories (e.g., value of social improvement, equal rights for women, solving social problems, etc.). Related is Donald Stone's "Social Consciousness in the Human Potential Movement." Based on systematically collected data, Stone suggests that at least some (not all) of the human potential movements tend to increase social responsibility by *lessening,* not increasing, narcissistic withdrawal, *contra* Lasch and other critics (although this by no means invalidates all of Lasch's arguments, which apparently do apply to some "new age" movements, the differential remaining unspecified [a differential I have suggested as prelaw versus translaw]).

Robert Bellah's chapter is a clarification of his concept of "civil religion," as well as a cogent argument that, in effect, the American constitution implicitly but fatally assumed moral discipline (or purpose) would always be effected by the Church, so that, as the Church now declines, there is no obvious national moral replacement; some of the new religions then offer, not a legitimate replacement for fractured moral bonding, but a privatistic escape ("so self-centered that they begin to approximate the consumer cafeteria model").

Robbins and Anthony's own contribution includes a superb introduction—perhaps the best single chapter in the anthology; a complete and devastating critique of the brainwashing model; and an insightful report on the Meher Baba community. The latter is especially important, because it demonstrates that sophisticated sociological analysis (largely Parsonian) can be performed on a spiritual community without reductionistically denigrating the community or its teachings. (In so doing, it everywhere transcends, however subtly, strict Parsonianism.)

Finally, as a general statement, the empirical sociological data presented in the volume is both interesting and significant, demonstrating the considerable power of sociological methodology.

Because psychologists tend to study trees and not forests, and because sociologists tend to study forests and not trees, these disciplines seem always to need balancing via interdisciplinary dialogue. This seems especially true for the psychology and sociology of religion. For instance, a transpersonal psychologist might wish to point out that a few of the book's chapters contain subtle reductionistic tendencies. For example, if the "new religions" are basically the result of the disintegration of American civil religion, is that *all* they are? Is what Zen Buddhism offers *essentially* the same as what civil religion offered? Many sociologists say yes; a transpersonal psychologist would probably say no. The latter religion offered an integration of egos, the former, their transcendence—a fact that sociology as sociology tends to miss. (Although I must mention that the editors of this volume are, in their own writings, acutely attuned to this distinction.) A transpersonal psychologist might therefore acknowledge the sociological perspective by saying that the breakdown of the old civil religion was necessary but *not sufficient* for the recent interest in authentic mystical religions. *Necessary,* in that if there were no disharmony at all in orthodox religions, one would not seek elsewhere; *not sufficient,* in that the new authentically mystical traditions offer something *never* officially offered by civil or orthodox religions: actual transcendence (and not merely communal immersion).

For the same reasons, a transpersonal psychologist might point out that there seems to be a stark difference between *transpersonal* growth and *prepersonal* regression; that some of the so-called new religions or new therapies are actually prepersonal, not transpersonal; that these prepersonal movements are indeed often narcissistic, cultic, authoritarian, anti-rational, and self-centered (although via the "group self" [i.e., mythic-membership]); and that these cultic movements—Jonestown, Synanon, Children of God—cannot believably be equated with authentic transpersonal sanghas, or contemplative communities—such as, perhaps, various genuine Buddhist centers (Zen, Vajrayana, Theravada), Christian mystical enclaves, some Yoga centers, etc. But again, sociology *as* sociology [or functionalism bereft of hierarchic structuralism] tends to miss these types of distinctions, since it sees only what these forests have in common: they are all different from mainstream, orthodox religions.

But if those are the types of things sociology might learn from transpersonal psychology, *In Gods We Trust* is an extraordinary compendium of what transpersonal psychologists can learn from modern sociology. I mean explicitly to include psychologists in general, but transpersonal psychologists and therapists in particular. For, as we said, if such theories are not sufficient for transpersonalists, they nevertheless remain absolutely necessary. Just as psychoanalysis of productions "on the couch" can't tell you about the sanity of society at large, so the study of the productions "on the zazen mat" can't tell you about larger and equally significant societal currents. In my opinion, many of the recalcitrant theoretical problems faced by transpersonal psychology have already been substantially answered by the sociology of religion, and *In Gods We Trust* is exactly a compendium of such answers.

This anthology is all the more significant given the commitment of its editors. Dick Anthony, for instance, is acutely aware of the difference between regressive, prepersonal, and prerational movements and progressive, transpersonal, and transrational concerns. His work is permeated with a genuine sensitivity to nonreductionistic interpretations of spiritual endeavors. Moreover, he is, in conjunction with Jacob Needleman, Thomas Robbins, and others, almost singlehandedly initiating the dialogue between orthodox sociologists and transpersonal psychologists. *In Gods We Trust* is not that dialogue—it is (and was appropriately intended to be) a genuinely sociological anthology, with little psychology, transpersonal or otherwise. But beyond that stated aim, which it thoroughly achieves, it is an invitation to a future dialogue with transpersonal psychologists, an invitation whose significance cannot be overestimated, and an invitation to which I trust psychologists in general, and transpersonal psychologists in particular, will enthusiastically respond.

8

Knowledge and Human Interests

I N THIS CHAPTER I would like to take Habermas's work on knowledge and cognitive interests as a starting base for extending sociology, and especially a critical sociology, into a more truly comprehensive formulation, one capable of adequately embracing authentically spiritual or actually transcendental *knowledge* and *interest*. Since I wish only to suggest certain possibilities, the discussion will be conducted on a more than usually generalized and preliminary level.

Habermas[38] distinguishes three principal modes of knowledge-inquiry: the empirical-analytic, which deals with objectifiable processes; the historical-hermeneutic, which aims at interpretive understanding of symbolic configurations; and the critical-reflective, which apprehends (past) cognitive operations and thus subjects them to a measure of insight.

The especially intriguing part of Habermas's theory is that each mode is intrinsically linked to a type of human *interest*, for knowledge as knowledge is always moved and moving. To get an idea of what Habermas means by cognitive interests, if every time you wanted to know something you asked yourself, "*Why* do I want to know this?" and then removed all the purely personal-idiosyncratic motives, you would have the *general cognitive interest* that guides the particular process of inquiry.

According to Habermas,[38] "The approach of the empirical-analytic sciences incorporates a *technical* cognitive interest; that of the historic-hermeneutic sciences incorporates a *practical* one; and the approach of critically oriented sciences incorporates the *emancipatory* cognitive interest." *Technical* interest is interest in predicting and controlling events in the objectifiable environment. *Practical* interest is interest in understanding and sharing the mutualities of life, morality, purpose, goals, values, and such. *Emancipatory* interest is interest in releasing the distortions and constraints of labor, language, or communication that result from their nontransparency, or their not being looked at steadily with critical awareness. (At this point, I remind the reader that we have earlier distinguished between horizontal emancipation, which aims at redressing the distortions within any given level, and vertical emancipation, which aims at moving to a higher level altogether. Habermas treats only the former, and therefore I will always refer to his as horizontal-emancipatory interest.)

I am now going to take two shortcuts. First, I am going to use only our three general domains of the sub, self, and superconscient, by the names of physical-sensorimotor, mental-rational, and spiritual-transcendental, or body, mind, and spirit for short. Body possesses a degree of *pre*-symbolic or sensory knowledge; mind works with symbolic knowledge; and spirit deals with *trans*-symbolic knowledge or gnosis. Notice that mind, being *the* symbolic mode, can form symbols *of* each of the three domains: the material world, the mental world itself, and the spiritual world. Those three modes of symbolic knowledge, when added to transsymbolic gnosis and presymbolic awareness, give us five general modes of cognition. Figure 4 indicates these modes.

Number 1 is spiritual gnosis, or spirit's direct and nonmediated knowledge *of* spirit *as* spirit. Number 2a is what has been called paradoxical or mandalic reason, because it is mind's attempt to put into

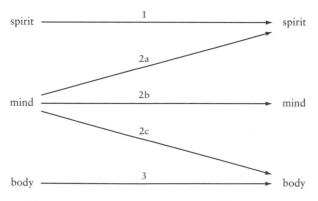

FIGURE 4. Five General Modes of Cognition.

mental symbols that which is finally transmental, and the result is always eventually paradoxical. Number 2b is mind's knowledge of other minds, or a symbol's awareness of other symbols, as when you are reading this. Number 2c is the mind's awareness of the physical and sensory world, or the symbol-models used to picture the *pre*-symbolic world. Number 3 is the sensorimotor apprehension of the sensorimotor world, or the presymbolic grasp of the presymbolic world.*

In my opinion, those forms of knowledge are *grounded* in the levels of *structural organization* themselves. The deep structures of developmental or self-forming consciousness dictate the very *forms* of those cognitions; to that extent they are largely invariant, deep-rooted, native, and collective (although, of course, their surface structures are in large measure culturally molded and conditioned).

My second shortcut is to identify Habermas's empirical-analytic mode with number 2c, or mind's awareness of the empirical-sensory world; and his historical-hermeneutic mode with number 2b, or mind's interaction with other minds. This is a shortcut because the distinctions are not precise; for example, insofar as a hermeneutic occasion has an empirically objective component, that component can become object to empirical-analytic inquiry; likewise, insofar as a sensory-objective occasion comes under interpretive understanding, it can become object to historical-hermeneutic inquiry. Nonetheless, it is my opinion that the central form, the very paradigm, of empirical-analytic inquiry is symbolic mind reflecting presymbolic world, and the paradigm of historical-hermeneutic inquiry is symbolic mind interacting with symbolic mind. To put it crudely, the former is mind reflecting matter; the latter, mind reflecting mind. As a generalization, then, we use number 2b as historical-hermeneutic and number 2c as empirical-analytic, and we assign them their respective cognitive interests, practical-moral and technical-predictive, which are all listed in figure 5 (page 118).

What, then, are we to make of Habermas's horizontal-emancipatory interest, the interest in "clearing up" the distortions in relational exchange on each major level? If knowledge and human interests are really grounded in *structures,* we should be able to point to a central structure as paradigmatic for this emancipatory interest (as we pointed to number 2c for empirical-technical, etc.). And yet, for reasons that will become clearer as we proceed, none of the five cognitive modes quite fits the bill. For one thing, horizontal-emancipatory interest apparently can operate

---

* See *Eye to Eye* for a fuller discussion of these modes.

on all or almost all levels. For another, it is not *necessarily* operative, but comes into existence only if there have, in fact, been distortions that demand clarification. As Habermas[38] puts it:

> Compared with the technical and practical interests in knowledge, which are both grounded in deeply rooted (invariant? [i.e., deep?]) structures of action and experience . . . , the [horizontal-] *emancipatory interest in knowledge* has a derivative status. It guarantees the connection between theoretical knowledge and an "object domain" of practical life which comes into existence as a result of systematically distorted communication and thinly legitimated repression.

The horizontal-emancipatory interest, in other words, is rooted not so much in specific structures per se, for it then would be continually active, but rather in structural *tension* caused by structural distortion, and its aim is to remove the source of the tension. Once the distortions are gone, the horizontal-emancipatory interest loses its juice. It is therefore not surprising that the only two major instances of such horizontal-emancipatory concerns given by Habermas (other than his own work) are Freudian psychoanalysis and Marxist materialist critique.

To put it simplistically, the need for psychoanalysis arises only when something "goes wrong" in psychological development. Psychological distortions—repressions and oppressions—give rise to psychological tensions; these tensions can be resolved only by a critical reflection on, or analysis of, "what went wrong" itself, and this critical-reflective knowledge has as its *interest* the *emancipation* from those distortions, obstructions, and repressions. Marxist material-economic critique operates in a similar fashion—past (historical) economic oppressions give rise to societal tensions. These tensions (class struggle, false consciousness, alienated labor, opaque ideology) can be resolved only by a critical analysis of their historical (development) genesis, with an interest in the emancipation from such oppressive economic distortions. And what Habermas himself is doing, with his philosophy of communicative ethics, is using critical-reflective inquiry and horizontal-emancipatory interest in an attempt to illumine and then correct the distortions and restraints placed upon what should otherwise be free and open *communicative exchange*. The oppression of communication and intersubjective exchange gives rise to distortions in discourse (and truth) itself—propaganda being the simplest example. Such "systematically distorted communication and thinly legitimated repression" generates both the possibility and the necessity for critical-reflective inquiry into such distortions with an interest in the emancipation from such opaque communication. *In all three cases,* once the distortions are cleared, the need for analysis and the interest in emancipation both tend to wane, since they have served their purpose by dissolving their own source.

I would simply add that, in my opinion, the fact that Freud and Marx were both aware of the importance of communicative exchange in their various fields should not conceal the fact that material-economic obstruction (which most but not solely interested Marx), emotional-sexual obstruction (which most but not solely interested Freud), and communicative obstruction (which most but not solely interests Habermas) refer to quite different structural levels of relational exchange and potential distortion. *The horizontal-emancipatory interest can swing into play with regard to each,* but the actual dynamics are slightly different in each case because the object domain of each has a different structure. To put it simply, "clearing up" matter, clearing up sex, and clearing up communication are all forms of horizontal-emancipation, but the concrete dynamics differ in each case because the dynamics of matter, emotions, and thoughts are themselves different. After all, the murder of Socrates, for example, was not a result of economic-material distortion nor emotional-sexual repression, but communicative oppression. These various distortions, like the levels they infect, are hierarchic. And in that hierarchy of disease, what Marx did *primarily* for the material sphere, and Freud did *primarily* for the emotional sphere, Habermas is now doing primarily for the communicative (mental) sphere. Those three theorists stand as exemplars of the horizontal-emancipatory interest on those levels. (We are still awaiting the analyst who as brilliantly studies the distortions and oppressions of spirituality, the repression of transcendence, the politics of Tao, the denial of Being by beings.)

We can now fill out figure 5 by adding the other forms of knowledge and their respective interests. I tentatively suggest the following: the interest of mode number 3, or bodily knowledge of the sensory world, is *instinctual*; the schemata of sensorimotor cognition are grounded in instinctual survival. The interest of mode number 2a, or the mind's attempt to reason about spirit, is *soteriological*—interest in salvation; an attempt to comprehend spirit in mental terms so as either to orient oneself toward the pull of a transcendental intuition or to help "picture" the spiritual realm for those minds not yet so *interested*. (The picture is always eventually paradoxical, as both Kant and Nagarjuna explained, but this neither hampers the human interest in the divine nor restricts the usefulness of mandalic reason; e.g., there is some sort of useful information carried in the paradoxical-mandalic statement that spirit is both perfectly transcendent and perfectly immanent.) The interest of gnosis, mode number 1, or spirit's knowledge of spirit as spirit, is *liberational*—interest in radical liberation (satori, moksha, wu, release). Where soteriological interest wishes to present to the self a higher knowledge, liberational interest aims at dissolving the self into higher knowledge *as* that knowledge, that is, as spirit's knowledge of and as spirit. The former wishes, as self, to be saved by spirit; the latter wishes, as spirit, to transcend self.

It remains to comment on the vertical-emancipatory interest. Like its cousin the horizontal-emancipatory interest, it is generated not so much by a specific structure as by a structural *tension,* and its interest is to remove the source of the tension. But here the source is not a tension *within* a particular level but a tension *between* levels; specifically, the tension of *emergence,* the tension of a coming transformation, or vertical shift in levels of structural organization. The aim of this vertical-emancipatory interest is to free awareness, not from a distortion that might or might not happen within a level, but from the relatively limited perspective offered by that level even at its best—and to do so by opening awareness to the next higher level of structural organization. This interest cannot be allayed by clearing up the distortions within a level but only by the emergence of the next higher level. We may suppose that the interest then temporarily wanes, until (and if) the inherent limitations of the next level begin increasingly to display themselves, and emancipation *from,* not *within,* that level increasingly exerts itself. Barring arrest, such vertical-emancipatory interest will continue periodically until final emancipation, that is, until satori. At that point, the last form of vertical-emancipatory interest coincides precisely with liberational interest; that is, the two are the same at the asymptotic limit of growth. All in all, the interest of horizontal-emancipation is to clear up translation; the interest of vertical-emancipation is to promote transformation.

Figure 5 lists all of these modes of knowledge and their interests.

My point, then, introductory as it may be, is that when we add these various modes and interests of human knowledge to the various levels of structural organization and relational exchange of the human compound individual, with all the corollaries and psychosocial displays suggested in the other chapters, we have the outlines of a fairly comprehensive (though far from completed) cultural theory: a skeleton, as it were. We have most of the bones here, even if we do not know yet

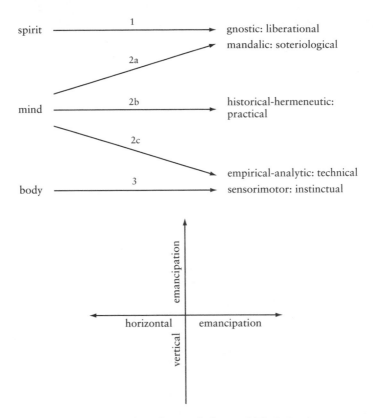

FIGURE 5. Modes of Knowledge and Their Interests.

everything to hang on them. But at least we make perfect and appropriate room for the prepersonal, the personal, and the transpersonal dimensions of existence—their levels, their development, their social exchange nature, their possible repressive (psychological) and oppressive (social) distortions, their modes of knowing and interest, their structural organization, their functional relations. And it is a truly *critical* and *normative* sociological theory, by virtue of the two emancipatory interests that rear their heads wherever structural nonfreedom and nontransparency arise. This critical (what went wrong) and normative (what should go right) dimension, especially in its vertical form, is not based *on* ideological preference, dogmatic inclination, or theoretical conjecture, but *in* the observable, verifiable, inherently preferred direction of structural development and evolution, a direction that discloses itself in successive hierarchic emancipations that *themselves* pass judgments on their less transcendental predecessors.

9

Methodology, Summary, and Conclusion

I WOULD LIKE TO summarize and conclude this outline by giving an example of proposed methodology in a sociological investigation of a religious group, with specific emphasis on any psychotherapeutic counseling that might be requested (not that such therapy is necessary, but the topic always seems to come up with regard to "religious groups," and so I will take the opportunity to comment in general). This will be merely a specialized example of the overall sociological methodology implicit in the model we have presented throughout this book.

STRUCTURAL ANALYSIS (DETERMINATION OF AUTHENTICITY)

1. Whenever sociologists are met with an apparently religious expression, they may, in addition to other methodological approaches (described below), perform a *structural* analysis on the *form* of the expressions, symbologies, psychosocial exchanges, and so forth. The aim of such standard structural analysis is, by means of increasingly subtracting/abstracting the surface structures, to arrive at the deep structure underlying and governing the operations (i.e., translations) of the surface structures themselves.[5,70,101] This analysis aims, in effect, to assign all surface structures to their appropriate deep structure by demon-

strating that they obey the transcriptive rules of the particular deep structure (or that they can, via transcription, be resolved into the deep structure).

Such structural analyses might include any of the tests devised by, for example, Kohlberg; Loevinger; Broughton; Sullivan, Grant, and Grant; Isaacs; Peck; Bull; Selman; and Graves. That these various formulations are all *roughly* correlative has been demonstrated by Loevinger;[57] in any event, they suffice perfectly to give us a first approximation of the degree of general structural organization reached by the central belief systems embraced by the group. We are not so much interested in the scores of any *particular* members, although those can certainly be ascertained (and should be ascertained for any member specifically seeking counseling). Rather, we wish structurally to analyze the central belief systems by which the group *defines itself*. One way of determining this is to structurally analyze the occasion that *defines membership in the group*; that is, What interaction, series of interactions, or belief structures must be internalized by a person in order to be socially *recognized* as a member of this group? What has to be "in" a person before the person is officially "in" the group? What level of "food" has to be digested by initiates in order to be "family"? For it is *that* occasion, embodying *that* mana, which marks the central-level or base-level of structural organization by which the group defines its self-identity and around which the group as group inevitably revolves. If there are levels of initiation/belief, analysis is applied at each level. (As for structural tests for the higher-authentic levels, see below, item 3 on page 121)

2. Once an approximate determination of central-level deep structure has been made, its relative location on the developmental hierarchy of structuralization can be determined. For example, is this "religious involvement" archaic, magical, mythical, rational, centauric, psychic, subtle, causal, nondual? (Or, for example, Loevinger: symbiotic, impulsive, self-protective, conformist, conscientious, individualistic, autonomous, integrated? and so on.)

This determination—or something like it—is especially important for counseling purposes, because in psychotherapeutic service (and social work) it is a great advantage, as psychoanalytic ego psychology has clearly demonstrated, to know the degree of structuralization reached by the self-system in question.[17] Are there archaic fusion elements (self-group indissociation, archaic-uroboric "oneness," oral-cannibalistic trends)? Is there borderline structure present (magical-psychotic, animistic, totem confusion, delusional reference systems)? Is there extreme mythic-membership conformity (with terror of individuality, surrender of self-will and determination, yearning for belongingness and cultic association, passive dependence on authority figures)? Is there rational structure but with possible complicating side-issues (merely and more or less healthy counter-law tendencies, or actual neurotic splitting, symptomology, and identity crisis)? Is there actual psychic, subtle, or causal structure, but with consequent alienation from mainstream mythic or rational consensus (communication viscosity, social isolation, possible depression)?

I cannot emphasize too strongly the importance of such structural diagnosis; without it, any therapeutic intervention can be disastrous.[102] As only a simple example, take the differences between prerational and transrational engagements. A prerational, borderline individual, who needs desperately to create rational structure and ego strength, should not be introduced to the more strenuous transrational meditative-yogic disciplines, because they are designed to *loosen* the rational structure temporarily and thus will simply dismantle what little structure the borderline has left. Likewise, such clients, in my opinion, should not be exposed to "experiential" therapies, since they already live too much in the experience and not enough in the mind.[17] Conversely, someone beginning or undergoing a true transformation to psychic-subtle realms will find no help from an orthodox psychiatrist, who tends to see all transrational development as prerational regression, and who, in helping to re-entrench exclusive rational structure in this person, will deliver his or her spiritual consciousness stillborn. Such a person should be referred to a qualified spiritual master, Jungian therapist, transpersonal psychologist, or some other authentically oriented service.

In short, the aim of structural analysis is to determine the *type,* and consequently the *degree,* of developmental structuralization and organization, and correlatively, if the situation claims religiosity, its degree of authenticity.

3. The above analysis, of course, will eventually hinge on a more refined developmental-structural hierarchy than we have presented here. The refinement and sophistication of this hierarchy will occur through the continued structural-developmental-stage research in psychological cognition, identity, perception, normalization, natural epistemology, and so on. This refinement is already occurring—has been occurring for quite some time—on the subconscient and self-conscient realms of structuralization, under the names of psychoanalytic developmental psychology, cognitive psychology, genetic epistemology, developmental ego psychology, and so on. As interest and research increasingly extend to

the superconscient realms, we will naturally (I assume) witness a refinement-sophistication of the developmental-structural hierarchies with regard to the higher and contemplative levels. The initial phases of this research seem likely to follow two stages.

a. *Hermeneutical reading of authentic texts:* In order to map out research design and strategy, it is necessary to have some sort of working hypotheses, and one of the best sources of such working sets seems to be the experimental-maps of superconscious stages offered by the traditional texts. A careful and systematic hermeneutical reading of the various (esoteric) religious texts will help provide us with a fund of working hypotheses-maps around which to frame actual research and against which to judge initial progress. *The Atman Project* is a basic but very general attempt in this direction, drawing on *cross-cultural parallels* to suggest some basic deep structures of the higher stage-levels (centauric, low-subtle, high-subtle, low-causal, high-causal, and ultimate, which I have condensed in this book to psychic, subtle, causal, and ultimate). Daniel Brown[20] has presented a hermeneutical reading of one particular stage-conception of higher meditative states, that of Mahamudra, which is the type of detailed hermeneutics we will need in each esoteric tradition so that we can draw more precisely our cross-cultural parallels and conclusions. The works of Pascal Kaplan,[55] Daniel Goleman,[35] Huston Smith,[86] Fritjof Schuon,[81] and René Guénon[37] are important guides in this endeavor.

b. *Direct investigation:* In order to test our refined hypothetical maps, we will need actual data accumulation from populations of those genuinely engaged in superconscient development and adaptation. This topic itself demands no less than book-length treatment, and instead of even trying to mention all the pertinent points (and problems), I will only say that, using the hermeneutical working maps, we will be able to design proposed characterologies of the higher structure-stages, construct adequate tests to register and measure the emergence and degree of these traits, and eventually subject the results to standard structural analyses à la Piaget, Kohlberg, Loevinger, and others. These will be repeated wherever possible in cross-cultural conditions (Japan, India, Burma, etc., have very large contemplative sectors, as does now the United States). Initial work is being done in this area by Maliszewski, Twemlow, Brown, Engler, Gabbard, Jones, and others.[21,58,92]

I feel this field is especially ripe for sociologists, since almost all research to date has overlooked the intersubjective patterns of relational exchange that constitute the higher as well as lower levels of structural adaptation. Psychologists interested only in perceptual changes, cognitive shifts, affect reinterpretation, or impulse control of meditators tend to overlook the psycho*social* nature of their artificially isolated data, just as psychoanalysts tended to overlook the fact that analysis of productions "on the couch" cannot tell you that the society at large might itself be sick, and adaptation to a sick society is a poor criterion of "mental health." Just as analysis of social patterns at large cannot be conducted on the couch, so identification of the fundamental psychosocial relationships constitutive of the contemplative realms cannot be conducted on the zazen mat. Transpersonal psychology will eventually have to find itself in transpersonal sociology.

As for the direct investigation of the superconscient realms, as opposed to indirect psychological or sociological data accumulation, see below, "The Methodology of Direct Gnostic Verification" (page 128).

FUNCTIONAL ANALYSIS (DETERMINATION OF LEGITIMACY)

1. Once the degree of authenticity of the religious expression is determined via structural analysis, the degree of legitimacy can be determined via standard functionalist (systems theory) approaches. The point is simply to determine how well the particular religious engagement is serving stability and integration *within* the group itself (content legitimacy) and *between* the group and its broader societal background (context legitimacy). Here all the standard functional analyses and more or less empirical-analytic determinations swing into play—tension management, pattern maintenance, boundary determinations, content and context analyses, latent and manifest functions, and so forth[62,69]—but with a refined understanding as to hierarchic levels of structural interaction. For example, if the particular group is determined (via previous structural analysis) to be prelaw, that fact will set a boundary with relation to law that is not merely between two systems but between two different levels of systems, a fact that functionalism itself cannot detect (lacking normative hierarchy). We have to use developmental structuralism to impose this boundary condition, or else the functional analyses tend to slide over (and then collapse into) each other.

With regard to legitimacy/illegitimacy, here are what seem to be some common content and context patterns. Frequently, prelaw sectors (or individuals) are found to be both content *and* context illegitimate, which means that their symbologies and relational exchanges provide little or no internal mana/integration and little or no larger societal co-existence (in which case they are always on the verge of anti-law engagement). However, it is not uncommon to find content and context legitimate prelaw sectors (e.g., stereotypical gypsies, although in America they are supposedly always on the verge of context illegitimacy, i.e., anti-law) or "part-time" prelaw sectors (i.e., serve societal law-translations "by day" and benign but ritual prelaw celebrations "by night," e.g., witches' covens). Perhaps most common, however, are prelaw groups that no matter how possibly content legitimate are context illegitimate (i.e., anti-law; e.g., Hell's Angels).

At the other end of the spectrum, it is not uncommon to find an *authentic* religious expression that is having context legitimation difficulties *because* it is trans-law. Such translaws, therefore, for functional pattern maintenance and tension management, tend to form microcommunities of like-minded practitioners (sanghas), which is simply another way of saying that, since each level of structural adaptation *is* a level of relational exchange, communities of exchange partners are inevitable, and it is within that community that one measure of legitimation is sought (content legitimation). But also we want to watch the boundary phenomena *between* translaw groups and the law-society at large (context legitimation), and, for particular individuals, how they handle (integrate) the structural tensions of living in both sectors.

2. All in all, then, the overall patterns of social interrelation seem to be determined in part by (a) the degree of authenticity and (b) the degree of legitimacy, evidenced (c) within and (d) across each boundary situation. Thus, the *internal content* of a given group will be among the set: (prelaw, counter-law, law, anti-law, translaw) × (legitimate, illegitimate). Likewise, *between* each group and its larger societal background (context) there are the same ten possibilities (although one of them—anti-law context legitimacy—is for all practical purposes an impossibility). The overall result is a display of twenty (or nineteen) different possible cells into which any psychosocial exchange in general, and any religious expression in particular, will fall.

Now by no means am I implying that that analysis is complete or even adequate, and I certainly do not wish to exclude other typologies. My only point is that by adding a basic structural-hierarchical analysis to the standard functional ones, we achieve a vertical (authenticity) scale in addition to a horizontal (legitimacy) scale, and it is this combination that gives us four compass points by which to navigate our sociological investigations.

The Hermeneutical Moment

1. If the structural and functional analyses form the methodological backbone of this approach, they by no means exhaust the necessary approaches. Deep structural analysis *cannot* determine specific surface structure contents and values, just as the rules of chess cannot tell you which moves a particular player will actually make. Nor is overall functionalism helpful here, because it sees forests and not trees. So, for specific understandings of specific individual values, meanings, and expressions, we always rely on phenomenological-hermeneutics. In this task we are helped by our prior structural and functional analyses, for they provide, respectively, the proper narrative foil (i.e., developmental hierarchy) and proper narrative context (i.e., the relation of the individual text to society at large). But in the last analysis, we are face to face with a living person who reads us while we read him or her, and this co-production is a human sharing in which both sides are correspondingly enriched or diminished.

For this general phenomenological-hermeneutics, we have the important works of, for example, Gadamer, Schutz, Berger and Luckmann, Garfinkle, Taylor, Ricoeur.

2. For specific therapeutic service, the hermeneutic procedure involves a conscious *interpretation* of symptoms deemed problematic by the client, with the eventual aim of re-constructing the possible developmental miscarriages that splintered or fragmented the ongoing sweep of structuralization. When this fragmentation occurs, aspects of consciousness are split off and thus become opaque in their meaning. They are "hidden texts," alienated facets of self, dissociated *symbols* that show up as *symptoms*. By *interpreting* the symbol-symptoms—the hidden texts and subtexts—the therapist helps the client to re-own those facets of self by *re-authoring* them and thus re-authorizing them, that is, consciously assuming responsibility for their existence.[105]

This is where a general knowledge of development as ongoing hierarchical structuralization is so essential, because the historical-hermeneutic procedure is not merely digging into past developments on the present level, but into past and *less structured* levels, whose meanings are very difficult to *translate* without a knowledge of past *transforma-tions*. The therapist, for instance, might find that, within the client's rational, linguistic, conscious communication of a particular message or series of messages, there is a hidden meaning, a subtext. Now this opaque subtext might indeed be a fairly rational message itself, but one the client wishes not to acknowledge (taboo for the moment); therapy here involves not much more than the therapist's providing a *context* for the acknowledgment of the rational subtext. However, on occasion the hidden message, the opaque communication, the subtext, is written in *mythic* syntax, which itself might have a core of *magical* wish-fulfill-ments (which *in turn* are often informed or subtexted by archaic *instinc-tual* or emotional-sexual interests).[35,101,105]

In such cases, apparently, at some point in the course of early develop-ment, a magical (and/or emotional) subtext was deemed taboo and de-fensively split off (repressed, dissociated) from the ongoing march of structuralization. Since structures are always structures *of* relational ex-change, this also involves a *privatization* of what otherwise could form a unit in intersubjective exchange. That is, the alienation from self *is* an alienation from others. Once cut off from personal understanding and removed likewise from all possibility of consensual interpretation, it be-comes an illegitimate subtext isolated from the narrative of ongoing de-velopment. Thus alienated from immediate narration, isolated and privatized, it tends to draw around itself any other subsequently out-lawed elements. Thus gathering layer after layer of *mistranslation* (dis-torted relational exchange), it finally protrudes into awareness as a baffling symptom. And baffling it is, because, as a doubly secret text, hidden to both self and others, it has no referent for interpretation; it remains clothed in opaque symbols and nontransparent urges. Ask the client why he or she is producing such symptoms or what they mean, and the client replies, "I have no idea; that's why I'm here. Why is this happening? Why won't it stop?" The very fact that the client usually refers to a symptom as "it," instead of "I" or "me" (e.g., "*I* move my hand, but the symptom, *it* happens against my will") mirrors exactly the dissociated, alienated, and foreign state into which the now hidden impulse or subtext or shadow-message has fallen. Indeed, when Freud summarized the goal of therapy as "Where it was, there I shall become" (poorly translated as "Where it was, there ego shall be"), he must have had essentially this crucial point in mind.

Part of the therapeutic procedure, therefore, is to use this knowledge of structural development (archaic to magic to mythic to rational) as a narrative foil against which to interpret the hidden meanings of the various subtexts, until those meanings once again become transparent to the client (i.e., nonrepressed). At that point, the symptom tends to wane because its symbolic content has been released from its privatized alienation to rejoin the community of relational exchange, and its bioenergetic component (should it have one) is released for bodily participation in emotional-sexual sharing, and its overall meaning-message has rejoined the individual's ongoing narrative unfoldment. In this overall procedure, developmental structuralism gives us the external narrative foil, and hermeneutics gives us the various internal-personal meanings of the various subtexts as they unfold against (and because of) the narrative foil itself.

3. There is, as we mentioned earlier, the role of hermeneutics in suggesting initial working maps of the higher realms (via textual analysis of the world's esoteric traditions). Here I would only like to issue a caveat: as researchers such as Daniel Brown have suggested, a hermeneutic reading of esoteric texts discloses hierarchic stages of contemplative development. It is important to remember, however, that the hierarchy or stage-conception itself is *not* a hermeneutical disclosure. The stages are disclosed via developmental-logic—the narrative foil—in actual practice and evolution. These successive *emergent* occasions everywhere surprise narrative; however, when the overall results are simply entered in a text, it may deceptively appear that they are created by the text and therefore discoverable solely by hermeneutics, which is not the whole case, as I tried to suggest in chapter 1, "Phenomenological-Hermeneutics."

Emancipatory Moments

Without belaboring the point, I will take it as obvious that overall therapy involves a critical self-reflection on past translations and possible mistranslations (hidden texts). I believe this is true for individuals as well as for societies at large (although obviously the specifics vary). Such reflection is driven by the *horizontal-emancipatory interest*—a desire to "clear up" past mistranslations (hidden subtexts, repressions, oppressions, dissociations). These distortions, secretly lodged in the hierarchy of the compound individual, generate structural tensions and irritations that drive the emancipatory interest. When such fixations/repressions are re-membered, re-authored, and re-integrated, then those aspects of individual consciousness (or groups of people) formerly trapped in a lower level of structuralization become liberated, or capable of transformation-upward, thus surrendering their symptomatic complaints and rejoining the average higher mode of structuralization now characteristic of the central self (or society at large). Such transformative advance is driven by the *vertical-emancipatory interest* inherent in development and evolution itself.

THE METHODOLOGY OF DIRECT GNOSTIC VERIFICATION

There is, finally, the methodological problem of the *direct* (as opposed to textual) investigation of the higher (superconscient) levels themselves, and here we draw on our last two major modes of inquiry: gnosis/jnana for direct apprehension of these levels, and mandalic-logic to communicate them, however paradoxically, in linguistic symbols. For spiritual knowledge itself is *not* symbolic; it involves direct, nonmediated, transsymbolic intuition of and identity with spirit.[7,22,88] As I have tried to suggest elsewhere,[99] this spiritual knowledge, *like all other forms of valid cognitive knowledge,* is experimental, repeatable, and publicly verifiable, because, like all other valid modes, it consists of three strands:

1. *Injunction:* always of the form, "If you want to know this, *do* this."
2. *Apprehension:* a cognitive apprehension-illumination of the "object domain" addressed by the injunction.
3. *Communal confirmation:* a checking of results with others who have adequately completed the injunctive and illuminative strands.

I shall give an example of all three strands in, say, empirical-analytic sciences. If you want to know whether a cell really contains a nucleus, then you must (1) learn to operate a microscope, learn to take histological sections, learn to stain cells, and so forth (injunctions), then (2) look and see (apprehension), then (3) compare your apprehensions with those of others, especially a qualified teacher if you are just beginning, or a community of like-minded scientific adepts if you are professionally continuing a career (communal confirmation).

Bad injunctive theories (no. 1) will be rebuffed by noncongruent apprehensions (no. 2) and subsequently rejected by the community of investigators (no. 3), and it is this potential rebuff that constitutes the nonverifiability principle of Popper.

Just so with authentic spiritual knowledge. For example, we will take Zen, vis-à-vis the three strands. It has an injunctive strand, which requires years of specialized training and critical discipline: the practice of meditation, or zazen, which is the injunctive tool for possible cognitive disclosure. Not surprisingly, then, it is always of the form "If you want to know whether there is Buddha-nature, you must first do this." That is *experimental* and *experiential* injunction.

After that strand is mastered, the investigator is opened to the second strand, that of apprehension-illumination; in this case, satori. Satori is a "direct seeing into one's nature"—as perfectly direct as looking into the microscope to see the cell nucleus, with the important proviso in each case: only a trained eye need look.

The third strand is careful confirmation, by both a Zen Master and the community of participant meditators. This is no merely automatic pat on the back and mutual-agreement society; it is a vigorous *test,* and it constitutes a potentially powerful rebuff and *nonverification* of any particular apprehension suffered in strand number 2. Both in private, intense interaction with the Zen Master (dokusan) and in exacting public participation in rigorous tests of authenticity (shosan), *all* apprehensions are struck against the community of those whose cognitive eyes are adequate to the transcendent, and such apprehensions are soundly nonverified if they do not match the facts of transcendence as disclosed by the community of like-spirited (and this includes past apprehensions once judged, by the standards of the times, to be true but now subrated or found to be partial by more sophisticated experience).[99]

It is with gnosis, then, verifiable gnosis, that our methodological repertoire is completed. And it is with gnosis that I end my informal sketch of a transpersonal sociology. For the final contribution that transpersonal psychology can make to sociology is, if you want to know about the actually transcendent realms themselves, then take up a contemplative-meditative practice (injunction) and find out for yourself (illumination), at which point the all-inclusive community of transcendence may disclose itself in your case and be tested in the fire of the like-spirited (confirmation). At that point, God ceases to be a mere symbol in your awareness but becomes the crowning level of your own compound individuality and structural adaptation, the integral of all possible societies, which you now recognize as your own true self. And when God is thus seen as the integral of all possible societies, the study of sociology takes on a new and unexpected meaning, and we all find ourselves immersed in a sociable God, formed and forming, liberated and liberating—a God that, as Other, demands participation, and that, as Self, demands identity.

References

The following is by no means a comprehensive or even representative bibliography. It is merely a list of those works directly mentioned or quoted in the text. I have included a short list of recommended reading in transpersonal psychology for those who might be unfamiliar with its basic tenets.

1. *A Course in miracles.* 3 vols. New York: Foundation for Inner Peace, 1977.
2. Anthony, D. "A phenomenological-structuralist approach to the scientific study of religion," chap. 8, *On religion and social science.* D. Anthony et al., eds., University of California, forthcoming.
3. Anthony, D., and Robbins, T. "From symbolic realism to structuralism." *Journ. Sc. Study Rel.,* vol. 14, no. 4, 1975.
4. Anthony, D., and Robbins, T. "A typology of nontraditional religions in modern America." Paper, A.A.A.S., 1977.
5. Arieti, S. *The intra-psychic self.* New York: Basic Books, 1967.
6. Assagioli, R. *Psychosynthesis.* New York: Viking, 1965.
7. Aurobindo. *The life divine, and the synthesis of yoga,* vols. 18–21. Pondicherry: Centenary Library, n.d.
8. Baldwin, J. *Thought and things.* New York: Arno, 1975.
9. Bateson, G. *Steps to an ecology of mind.* New York: Ballantine, 1972.
10. Becker, E. *The denial of death.* New York: Free Press, 1973.
11. ———. *Escape from evil.* New York: Free Press, 1975.
12. Bell, D. *The end of ideology.* Glencoe: Free Press, 1960.
13. Bellah, R. *Beyond belief.* New York: Harper, 1970.
14. ———. *The broken covenant.* New York: Seabury, 1975.
15. Berdyaev, N. *The destiny of man.* New York: Harper, 1960.
16. Berger, P., and Luckmann, T. *The social construction of reality.* New York: Doubleday, 1972.
17. Blanck, G., and Blanck, R. *Ego psychology: theory and practice.* New York: Columbia Univ. Press, 1974.

18. Broughton, J. "The development of natural epistemology in adolescence and early adulthood." Doctoral dissertation, Harvard, 1975.

19. Brown, N. *Life against death*. Middletown: Wesleyan, 1959.

20. Brown, D., "A model for the levels of concentrative meditation." *Int. J. Clin. Exp. Hypnosis,* vol. 25, 1977.

21. Brown, D., and Engler, J. "A Rorschach study of the stages of mindfulness meditation." *J. Transp. Psych.,* 1980.

22. Bubba (Da) Free John. *The paradox of instruction*. San Francisco: Dawn Horse, 1977.

23. Campbell, J. *The masks of God: primitive mythology*. New York: Viking, 1959.

24. Chomsky, N. *Problems of knowledge and freedom*. London: Barrie and Jenkins, 1972.

25. Clark, G., and Piggott, S. *Prehistoric societies*. New York: Knopf, 1965.

26. Deutsch, E. *Advaita Vedanta*. Honolulu: East-West Center Press, 1969.

27. Eliade, M. *Shamanism*. New York: Pantheon, 1964.

28. Fairbairn, W. *An object-relations theory of the personality*. New York: Basic Books, 1954.

29. Fenichel, O. *The psychoanalytic theory of neurosis*. New York: Norton, 1945.

30. Fenn, R. "Towards a new sociology of religion." *J. Sc. Study Rel.,* vol. 11, no. 1, 1972.

31. Freud, S. *The future of an illusion*. New York: Norton, 1971.

32. Gadamer, H. *Philosophical hermeneutics*. Berkeley: Univ. Cal. Press, 1976.

33. Garfinkel, H. *Studies in ethnomethodology*. Englewood Cliffs: Prentice-Hall, 1967.

34. Geertz, C. *The interpretation of cultures*. New York: Basic Books, 1973.

35. Goleman, D. *The varieties of the meditative experience*. New York: Dutton, 1977.

36. Greenson, R. *The technique and practice of psychoanalysis*. New York: Int. Univ. Press, 1976.

37. Guénon, R. *Man and his becoming according to the Vedanta*. London: Luzac, 1945.

38. Habermas, J. *Knowledge and human interests*. Boston: Beacon, 1971.

39. ———. *Legitimation crisis*. Boston: Beacon, 1975.

40. ———. *Theory and practice*. Boston: Beacon, 1973.

41. ———. *Communication and the evolution of society*. Boston: Beacon, 1976.

42. Hartmann, H. *Ego psychology and the problem of adaptation*. New York: Int. Univ. Press, 1958.

43. Hartshorne, C. *The logic of perfection*. La Salle: Open Court, 1973.

44. ———. *Whitehead's philosophy*. Lincoln: Univ. Nebr. Press, 1972.

45. Hegel, G. *The phenomenology of mind*. Baillie, J., trans. New York: Humanities Press, 1977.

46. ———. *Science of logic*. Johnston and Struthers, 2 vols., London: Allen & Unwin, 1951.

47. Horkheimer, M. *Critical theory.* New York: Seabury, 1972.
48. Hume, R., trans. *The thirteen principal Upanishads.* London: Oxford Univ. Press, 1974.
49. Ihde, D. *Hermeneutic phenomenology: The philosophy of Paul Ricoeur.* Evanston: Northwestern, 1971.
50. Jacobson, E. *The self and the object world.* New York: Int. Univ. Press, 1964.
51. James, W. *The varieties of religious experience.* New York: Collier, 1961.
52. Jonas, H. *The gnostic religion.* Boston: Beacon, 1963.
53. Jung, C. G. *The basic writings of C. G. Jung.* DeLaszlo (ed.). New York: Modern Library, 1959.
54. Kohlberg, L., and Gilligan, C. "The adolescent as philosopher." In Harrison, S., and McDermott, J. (eds.), *New directions in childhood psychopathology.* New York: Int. Univ. Press, 1980.
55. Kaplan, P. "An excursion into the 'undiscovered country.'" In Garfield, C. (ed.), *Rediscovery of the body.* New York: Dell, 1977.
56. Lasch, C. *The culture of narcissism.* New York: Norton, 1979.
57. Loevinger, J. *Ego development.* San Francisco: Jossey-Bass, 1976.
58. Maliszewski, M., *et al.* "A phenomenological typology of intensive meditation." *ReVision,* vol. 4, no. 2, 1981.
59. Marin, P. "The new narcissism." *Harpers,* Oct. 1975.
60. Marx, K. *Selected writings.* Bottomore, T. (ed.). London, 1956.
61. Maslow, A. *The farther reaches of human nature.* New York: Viking, 1971.
62. Merton, R. *Social theory and social structure.* Glencoe: Free Press, 1957.
63. Mishra, R. *Yoga sutras.* Garden City, N.Y.: Anchor, 1973.
64. Needham, J. *Science and civilization in China.* vol. 2, London: Cambridge, 1956.
65. Needleman, J. *Lost Christianity.* New York: Doubleday, 1980.
66. Neumann, E. *The origins and history of consciousness.* Princeton: Princeton Univ. Pres, 1973.
67. Ogilvy, J. *Many-dimensional man.* New York: Oxford Univ. Press, 1977.
68. Palmer, R. *Hermeneutics.* Evanston, 1969.
69. Parsons, T. *The social system.* Glencoe, 1951.
70. Piaget, J. *The essential Piaget.* Gruber, H., and Voneche, J. (eds.). New York: Basic Books, 1977.
71. Polanyi, M. *Personal knowledge.* Chicago: Univ. of Chic. Press, 1958.
72. Radin, P. *The world of primitive man.* New York: Grove, 1960.
73. Rank, O. *Psychology and the soul.* New York: Perpetua, 1961.
74. ———. *Beyond psychology.* New York: Dover, 1958.
75. Rapaport, D. *Organization and pathology of thought.* New York: Columbia, 1951.
76. Rapaport, D., and Gill, M. "The points of views and assumptions of metapsychology." *Int. J. Psychoanal.,* vol. 40, 1959.
77. Robbins, T., and Anthony, D. "New religious movements and the social system." *Ann. Rev. Soc. Sc. Rel.* 2, 1978.

78. ———. *In gods we trust*. San Francisco: Transaction Books, 1981.
79. Ricoeur, P. *Freud and philosophy*. New Haven: Yale, 1970.
80. Roheim, G. *Magic and schizophrenia*. New York, I.U.P. 1955.
81. Schuon, F. *Logic and transcendence*. New York: Harper, 1975.
82. Schutz, A. *The phenomenology of the social world*. Evanston: Northwestern, 1967.
83. Schutz, A., and Luckmann, T. *The structures of the life-world*. Evanston: Northwestern, 1973.
84. Selman, R. "The relation of role-taking to the development of moral judgement in children." *Child Development*, 42, 1971.
85. Singh, K. *Surat shabd yoga*. Berkeley: Images Press, 1975.
86. Smith, H. *Forgotten truth*. New York: Harper, 1976.
87. Sullivan, H. *The interpersonal theory of psychiatry*. New York: Norton, 1953.
88. Suzuki, D. T. *Studies in the Lankavatara Sutra*. London: Routledge and Kegan Paul, 1968.
89. Taimni, I. *The science of yoga*. Wheaton: Quest, 1975.
90. Takakusu, J. *The essentials of Buddhist philosophy*. Honolulu: Univ. of Hawaii, 1956.
91. Teilhard de Chardin, P. *The future of man*. New York: Harper, 1964.
92. Twemlow, S., et al. "The out-of-body experience." Submitted *Am. J. Psych.*
93. Washburn, M. "The bimodal and tri-phasic structures of human experience." *ReVision*, vol. 3, no. 2, 1980.
94. Watts, A. *Beyond theology*. Cleveland: Meridian, 1975.
95. Werner, H. *Comparative psychology of mental development*. New York: Int. Univ. Press, 1957.
96. ———. "The concept of development from a comparative and organismic point of view." In Harris (ed.), *The concept of development*. Minneapolis: Univ. of Minnesota, 1957.
97. Whitehead, A. *Process and reality*. New York: Free Press, 1969.
98. Whyte, L. L. *The next development in man*. New York: Mentor, 1950.
99. Wilber, K. "Eye to eye." *Revision*, vol. 2, no. 1, 1979.
100. ———. "Physics, mysticism, and the new holographic paradigm." *ReVision*, vol. 2, no. 2, 1979.
101. ———. *The Atman project*. Wheaton: Quest, 1980.
102. ———. "The pre/trans fallacy." *ReVision*, vol. 3, no. 2, 1980.
103. ———. "Ontogenetic development—two fundamental patterns." *Journal of Transpersonal Psychology*, vol. 13, no. 1, 1981.
104. ———. "Reflections on the new age paradigm." *ReVision*, vol. 4, no. 1, 1981.
105. ———. *Up from Eden*. New York: Anchor/Doubleday, 1981.
106. ———. "Legitimacy, authenticity, and authority in the new religions." Privately circulated ms.
107. Wilden, A. "Libido as language." *Psychology Today*. May 1972.
108. Zilboorg, G. "Fear of death." *Psychoanal. Quart.* vol. 12, 1943.

Recommended Reading: An Introduction to Transpersonal Psychology

109. Assagioli, R. *Psychosynthesis.* New York: Viking, 1965.
110. Benoit, H. *The supreme doctrine.* New York: Viking, 1959.
111. Campbell, J. *The masks of God.* 4 vols. New York: Viking, 1959–1968.
112. Fadiman, J., and Frager, R. *Personality and personal growth.* New York: Harper, 1976.
113. Goleman, D. *The varieties of the meditative experience.* New York: Dutton, 1977.
114. Govinda, L. *Foundations of Tibetan mysticism.* New York: Weiser, 1969.
115. Green, E., and Green, A. *Beyond biofeedback.* New York: Delacorte, 1977.
116. Grof, S. *Realms of the human unconscious.* New York: Viking, 1975.
117. Hixon, L. *Coming home.* New York: Anchor, 1978.
118. Huxley, A. *The perennial philosophy.* New York: Harper, 1944.
119. James, W. *The varieties of religious experience.* New York: Collier, 1961.
120. Jung, C. G. *Memories, dreams, reflections.* New York: Vintage, 1965.
121. Kornfield, J. *Living Buddhist masters.* Santa Cruz: Unity, 1977.
122. LeShan, L. *Alternate Realities.* New York: Ballantine, 1977.
123. Maslow, A. *The farther reaches of human nature.* New York: Viking, 1977.
124. Needleman, J. *Lost Christianity.* New York: Doubleday, 1980.
125. Neumann, E. *The origins and history of consciousness.* Princeton: Princeton Univ. Press, 1973.
126. Roberts, T. (ed.). *Four psychologies applied to education.* Cambridge: Schenkman, 1974.
127. Schumacher, E. *A guide for the perplexed.* New York: Harper, 1977.
128. Smith, H. *Forgotten truth.* New York: Harper, 1976.
129. Tart, C. *States of consciousness.* New York: Dutton, 1975.
130. Walsh, R., and Vaughan, F. *Beyond ego.* Los Angeles: Tarcher, 1980.
131. White, J. *The highest state of consciousness.* New York: Doubleday, 1973.
132. Wilber, K. *The Atman project.* Wheaton: Quest, 1980.
133. ———. *Up from Eden.* New York: Anchor/Doubleday, 1981.
134. Woods, R. (ed.). *Understanding mysticism.* New York: Image, 1981.

EYE TO EYE

*The Quest for the
New Paradigm*

Preface to the Third Edition

T HE VAST MAJORITY of the great philosophers of the West have maintained that there does indeed exist some sort of Absolute, from the Good to God to Geist. That has never seriously been doubted by the vast majority. The burning question, rather, has always been this: What is the relation of the absolute One to the world of the relative Many?

This crucial question has, like many of the most profound questions in Western philosophy, generated a series of utterly intractable difficulties, paradoxes, absurdities. Like the mind/body problem and the question of free will versus determinism, the absolute/relative issue has been a bloody thorn in the side of the Western tradition, a thorn that has refused to either go away or have the good sense to be solved.

And, more intriguingly, all of these central issues—mind/body, mind/ brain, free will/fate, absolute/relative, noumenon/phenomena—are, we will see, precisely the same problem.

And they all have precisely the same answer.

Aristotle gave the classic statement of a God that has nothing substantial to do with the relative world. Aristotle's God is a God of pure Perfection, and for such a God to dirty its hands with the relative world—to be involved with relative and finite creatures—would surely indicate a lack of fullness, a lack of completeness, and thus a lack of self-contained perfection. Since God requires nothing, there is certainly no reason for God to produce or create a relative world. In fact, if God actually created the relative world, that would indicate that God lacked something in its own being, which obviously is not possible (you don't get to be God by lacking something!). Thus, God is "in" the relative world only as final cause: the Good toward which all relative creatures strive but never, never reach.

Aspects of Plato's writing could certainly be interpreted to support Aristotle's notion of an untouchable, uninvolved, totally self-contained God. This world, after all, could be seen as nothing but the fleeting and shadowy reflection of the real world, a world utterly transcendent to the relative world of sense and confused opinion.

But that is only half of Plato, so to speak. The other (and less noted) half confirms in the strongest way that the entire relative world is a production, an emanation, a mark of the Plenitude of the Good. Thus, in the *Timaeus*—arguably the most influential book of Western cosmology—an Absolute that cannot create a world is described as decidedly inferior to an Absolute that can. Contrary to Aristotle's conclusion—that God must be totally self-contained to be perfect—the conclusion of the *Timaeus* is that a God that cannot create is no God at all. (It is even implied that a God who cannot create is envious of a God who can!) Thus, through the Absolute's *creative outflowing,* the entire manifest realm issues forth, so that all things are essentially the Plenitude of the Good. Therefore this very earth Plato describes as a "visible, sensible God."

Thus would begin this version of the West's most intractable dualism: the Absolute versus the relative, and what exactly is their relation?

The great difficulty with Aristotle's position is that it simply leaves the dualism as it finds it. Aristotle's God creates nothing; all things are driven by their desire to reach up to that God, but none of them make it. And however "clean" this might be logically, it leaves the Kosmos with a divisive wedge driven violently into its heart. God over there, us over here, and the two meet only in perpetually unrequited love.

And yet the other side of the attempted solution—God is present in the world as Plenitude—also had its own grave difficulties, at least as it was usually presented. Namely, if we intellectually picture the Absolute as substantially creating the relative world, then how do we account for the existence of evil? If God has his, her, or its hand in this world, then doesn't God get blamed for Auschwitz? If so, what kind of grotesque monster is that God?

This dualism between the Absolute and the relative—and their relation, if any—would split the entire tradition of Western philosophy and theology into two warring and largely irreconcilable camps: those who saw God strongly (or even totally) in this world versus those who saw God strongly (or even totally) out of this world: this-worldly versus otherworldly, the Descenders versus the Ascenders, the immanentists versus the transcendentalists, empiricists versus rationalists, one flavor or another.

The Aristotelian tradition simply stood back from the commotion of the relative world, and refused to have its God dirty its fingers. God is a self-contained and unitary perfection, and thus that God has no need to create the world or anything else. How could anything so utterly Perfect do anything further without falling away from Perfection? To create implies that something is lacking now, and God lacks nothing; hence God does not create. Where the world came from, and why, is thus left literally hanging, though buried deep in the relative world's heart is the burning desire to reach the state of God-perfection, which would actually mean, for this autistic God, to simply be done with all its neighbors and disappear into its own self-contained absoluteness, basking in the wonders of its unending specialness.

But the alternative intellectual position—that the Perfect One nonetheless got itself involved with imperfect creatures—is scarcely more attractive. If the Perfect One steps down into imperfect evil, something has gone terribly wrong somewhere, and the blame for that can only rest with the One itself.

Christian theologians would, for the most part, maintain that God's Will creates the world, and since freedom is a good component of that world, God allows, but does not create, evil. The Gnostics headed in the other direction: this world is so obviously evil (as in the famous Gnostic line, "What kind of God is this?") that they maintained the entire world was created, not by the real Absolute, but by a Demiurge, an evil or at least inferior spirit. This tricky attempt to keep God out of the world! Because if we let God into the world, something has gone horribly, wretchedly wrong.

Approaching the dualism in this intellectual fashion does little to ameliorate it. If, as the Gnostics maintain, this world is phenomenal, illusory, evil, the product of the Demiurge and not of the real Godhead, then the Demiurge itself comes perilously close to absolute status, and indeed some Gnostics would simply claim that the Demiurge itself creates but is not created, and that is in fact a definition of the Absolute. So now we have two absolutes: an absolute Good, and an absolute Evil, and we have reintroduced exactly the dualism we set out to overcome.

This intractable dualism, I maintain, is the central dualism in the Western tradition, and it would appear and reappear in numerous disguises: it would show up as the dualism between noumenon and phenomena, between mind and body, between free will and determinism, morals and nature, transcendent and immanent, ascending and descending. That these are essentially the same dualism is a theme I carefully pursued in *Sex, Ecology, Spirituality* (and its popular version, *A Brief History of Everything*), and the interested reader might consult those sources for a much more detailed look.

But what I would like to emphasize here is simply that, buried in the Western tradition—and in the Eastern—is a *radical and compelling solution to these massive dualisms,* a literal solution to the West's most intractable philosophical problems, from the absolute/relative to the mind/body dilemma. But this solution—appropriately known as "nondualism"—has an unbelievably awkward characteristic: namely, its compelling answer cannot be captured in words, a type of metaphysical catch-22 that absolutely guarantees to solve all your problems as long as you don't ask it to.

And that is where *Eye to Eye* comes in.

The premise of *Eye to Eye* is that there is a great spectrum of human consciousness; and this means that men and women have available to them a *spectrum of different modes of knowing,* each of which discloses a different type of world (a different worldspace, with different objects, different subjects, different modes of spacetime, different motivations, and so on).

Put in its simplest form, there, at the very least, is the eye of flesh, the eye of mind, and the eye of spirit (or the eye of contemplation). An exclusive or predominant reliance on one of these modes produces, for example, empiricism, rationalism, and mysticism.

The claim of *Eye to Eye* is that each of these modes of knowing has its own specific and quite valid set of referents: *sensibilia, intelligibilia,* and *transcendelia.* Thus, all three of these modes of knowing can be validated with similar degrees of confidence; and thus all three modes are perfectly valid types of knowledge. Accordingly, any attempt at a comprehensive and graceful understanding of the Kosmos will most definitely include all three types of knowing; and anything less comprehensive than that is gravely suspect on its own merits.

Once we allow that the Kosmos is an altogether big and wondrous thing, and once we allow that at least these three types of knowing are necessary to get a decent taste of this miracle of existence, then we very well might find that some of our most recalcitrant philosophical problems are not so recalcitrant after all. And that includes, yes, the most aggravating dualism of all—the absolute and the relative—and its dozen or so bastard offspring, from the mind/body problem to fate and free will to consciousness and brain.

In order to see the moons of Jupiter, you need a telescope. In order to understand *Hamlet,* you need to learn to read. In order to vote on the truth of the Pythagorean theorem, you must learn geometry. In other words, valid forms of knowledge have, as one of their significant components, an *injunction*—if you want to *know* this, you must *do* this. (This, for example, is the actual meaning of Kuhn's term "paradigm" or "exemplar"—a type of practice or injunction that brings forth a particular domain.)

As you will see outlined in the following pages, the injunctive strand of all valid knowledge leads to an *apprehension* or an *illumination,* a direct disclosing of the data or referents in the worldspace brought forth by the injunction, and this illumination is then *checked* (confirmed or refuted) by all those who have adequately performed the injunction and thus disclosed the data.

In short, all valid forms of knowledge have an *injunction,* an *illumination,* and a *confirmation;* and this is true whether we are looking at the moons of Jupiter, the Pythagorean theorem, or . . . the nature of the Absolute.

And where the moons of Jupiter can be disclosed by the eye of flesh (by the senses or their extensions—sensibilia), and the Pythagorean theorem can be disclosed by the eye of mind and its inward apprehensions (intelligibilia), the nature of the Absolute can only be disclosed by the *eye of contemplation* and its directly disclosed referents—its transcendelia, its spiritual data, the brought-forth facts of the spiritual worldspace.

But in order to gain access to any of these valid modes of knowing, I must be *adequate* to the injunction—I must successfully complete the injunctive strand. This is true in the physical sciences, the mental sciences, and the spiritual sciences. If we want to *know* this, we must *do* this. And where the exemplar in physical sciences might be a telescope, and in the human sciences might be linguistic interpretation, in the spiritual sciences the exemplar, the injunction, the paradigm, the practice is: meditation or contemplation. It too has its injunctions, its illuminations, and its confirmations, all of which are generally repeatable, verifiable or falsifiable—and all of which therefore constitute a perfectly valid mode of knowledge acquisition.

But in all cases, we must engage the injunction. We must take up the exemplary practice, and this is certainly true for the spiritual sciences as well. If we do not take up the injunctive practice, then we will not have a genuine paradigm, and therefore we will never see the data of the spiritual worldspace. We will in effect be no different from the Churchmen who refused to follow Galileo's injunction and look through the telescope itself.

And that is where the catch-22 comes in.

As I will argue in the following pages, *we cannot solve the absolute/ relative problem using the eye of flesh or the eye of mind.* This deepest of problems and mysteries directly yields its resolution only to the eye of contemplation. And, as both Kant and Nagarjuna forcefully demonstrated, if you try to state this solution in intellectual or rational terms, you will generate nothing but antinomies, paradox, contradiction.

In other words, we cannot solve the absolute/relative problem empirically, using the eye of flesh and its sensibilia; nor can we solve it rationally, using the eye of mind and its intelligibilia. The solution, rather, involves the direct apprehension of transcendelia, which are disclosed only by the eye of contemplation and are most definitely verifiable or falsifiable in that domain, using what are in fact quite *public* procedures—public, that is, to all who have completed the injunction and disclosed the illumination.

And likewise again with fate and free will, the one and the many, mind and brain, noumenon and phenomena. *Eye to Eye* argues that only with the higher stages of the spectrum of consciousness development— part and parcel of the meditative or contemplative unfolding—does the solution to these dilemmas become obvious. But that is not an empirical discovery nor a rational deduction; it is a contemplative apprehension.

To the question, what is the relation of mind and body—or mind and brain—typical Western answers include the *identity thesis* (they are two different aspects of the same thing), *dualism* (they are two different things), *interactionism* (they are different but mutually causal), *parallelism* (two different things that never speak to each other), *epiphenomenalism* (one is the byproduct of the other). And, despite what their adherents all claim, not one of those positions has been able to carry the day, simply because they are all basically flawed in one way or another.

The reason they are inadequate, a more integral philosophy would maintain, is that the mind/body problem cannot be satisfactorily solved with the eye of flesh or the eye of mind, since those are exactly the two modes that need to be integrated, something neither of them could accomplish on its own.

Thus, the only acceptable response to the question, What is the relation of the mind and body?, is to *carefully explain the actual contemplative injunctions*—the contemplative practices or paradigms or exemplars—and invite the questioners to take up the practice and see for themselves. If you want to *know* this, you must *do* this. Although both the empiricist and the rationalist will not find this answer satisfactory—they wish only to engage their own paradigms and exemplars—nonetheless this is the only acceptable answer and course of action.

Both the rationalist and the empiricist press us: they want us to state our contemplative conclusions and let them check these conclusions *against their own injunctions.* That is, they want our words without our injunctions. They want to try to follow our words without the pain of having to follow our exemplars. And so we must remind them: Words without injunctions are meaningless. That is, words without injunctions have no means of verification whatsoever. Our conclusions can indeed be carefully justified—verified or rejected—but only if the injunctions are engaged.

And so when the empiricist and the rationalist demand our conclusions without the injunctions, they have guaranteed a *meaningless* answer—and they blame us for the meaninglessness! Our data cannot be generated by their particular paradigms and exemplars, and so they scratch their heads. They will *not* do this, and therefore they will *not* know this. They circle in the orbit of their self-imposed blindness, and they call this blindness reality.

In the East, Zen would handle the problem of the One and the Many in the following way. The question might be, as a famous Zen *koan* has it, "If all things return to the One, to what does the One return?" This is, of course, that intractable dilemma: what is the relation of the absolute and the relative, the One and the Many, Emptiness and Form?

But Zen, of course, will reject every intellectual response. A clever student might respond, "To the Many!," which is a perfectly good intellectual answer, yet it will earn only a sharp blow from the Master. Any intellectual response will be radically rejected, no matter what its content!

Rather, the student must take up an *injunction*, a paradigm, an exemplar, a practice, which in this case is *zazen*, sitting meditation. And—to make a very long and complex story brutally short—after an average of five or six years of this exemplary training, the student may begin to have a series of profound illuminations. And you will simply have to trust me that no one would go through this extended hell in order to be rewarded only with an epileptic fit, a schizophrenic hallucination, or a socially induced illusion.

No, this is Ph.D. training in the realm of transcendelia. And once this injunctive training begins to bear fruit, a series of illuminations— commonly called *kensho* or *satori*—begins to flash forth into direct and immediate awareness, and this data is then checked (confirmed or refuted) by the community of those who have completed the injunctive and the illuminative strands. At this point, the answer to the question "To what does the One return?" will become extremely clear and straightforward—and I will give that answer in a moment.

But the point is, the *answer* to the question, What is the relation of the One and the Many, the absolute and the relative, free will and fate, consciousness and form, mind and body?—the technically correct and precise answer is: satori. The technically correct answer is: take up the injunction, perform the experiment, gather the data (the experiences), and check them with a community of the similarly adequate.

We can't *state* what the answer is other than that, because if we did, we would have merely words without injunctions, and they would indeed be utterly meaningless. It's very like baking a pie: you follow the recipe (the injunctions), you bake the pie, and then you actually taste it. To the question "What does the pie taste like?" we can only give the person the recipe, and let them make it and taste it themselves. We *cannot* theoretically or verbally or philosophically or rationally describe the answer in any other satisfactory fashion: if you want to *know* this, you must *do* this.

And thus: take up the injunction or paradigm of meditation; practice and polish that cognitive tool until awareness learns to discern the incredibly subtle phenomena of transcendelia; check your observations with others who have done so, much as mathematicians will check their proofs with others who have completed the injunctions; and thus confirm or reject your results. And in the verification of that transcendelia, the relation of the One and the Many will become perfectly clear—at least as clear as rocks are to the eye of flesh and geometry is to the eye of mind—and thus will that most intractable of dualisms quite literally come unglued.

The answer to the relation of the Absolute and the relative is therefore most definitely *not*: the Absolute created the world. It most definitely is *not*: the world is illusory and the Absolute alone is real. It is *not*: we perceive only the phenomenal reflection of a noumenal reality. It is *not*:

fate and free will are two aspects of one and the same process. It is *not*: all things and events are different aspects of a single interwoven web-of-life. It is *not*: the body alone is real and the mind is a reflection of that only reality. It is *not*: mind and body are two different aspects of the total organism. It is *not*: mind emerges from hierarchical brain structure. In fact, it is not even: noumenon and phenomena are not-two and non-dual.

Those are all merely *intellectual symbols* that purport to give the answer, but the real answer does not lie in sensibilia or intelligibilia, it lies in transcendelia, and that domain only discloses itself after the meditative exemplar is engaged, whereupon every single one of those intellectual answers is seen to be inadequate and off the mark; each generates nothing but more unsolvable and insuperable difficulties, dilemmas, and contradictions. The answer is not more talk; the answer is satori, by whatever name we wish to use to convey valid contemplative awareness.

And, much more to the point, even if this answer could be stated in words—and in fact, the answer can be stated in words, because Zen Masters talk about it all the time!—nonetheless, it would make no sense to anybody who had not also performed the injunction, just as mathematical symbols can be seen by anybody but understood only by those who have completed the training.

But open the eye of contemplation, and the answer is as obvious, as perfect, as unmistakable as the play of sunlight on a crystal clear pond, early on a cool spring morning.

You see, that was the answer.

In subsequent books, particularly *Sex, Ecology, Spirituality,* I have elaborated on themes first presented in *Eye to Eye.* But looking back on the almost fifteen years since I wrote this book, subsequent theory and research have convinced me more than ever of the basic fruitfulness and soundness of the book's approach. I have engaged in a certain fine-tuning and refinement of some of the central issues, but they basically remain as presented here, I trust in a clear and concise fashion.

The first two chapters—"Eye to Eye" and "The Problem of Proof"—set forth the general notion of the three eyes of knowing, and prepare the ground for all that follows. Chapter 3, "A Mandalic Map of Consciousness," is perhaps noteworthy in that it was something of a historical first: critics agreed that it was the first presentation of a genuinely "full-spectrum" model of human growth and development, a model that plausibly integrated both Eastern and Western approaches to psychology and spirituality (an approach that was fleshed out in *The Atman Project* and *Transformations of Consciousness*). This model is further explored in chapter 4, "Development, Meditation, and the Unconscious," and in chapter 9, "Structure, Stage, and Self."*

Chapters 5 and 6 take a critical look at various "new age" paradigms. The whole new age movement is unfortunately often shot through with regressive and antirational prejudices, and thus any genuinely "integral paradigm" should include a critical stance to those approaches that claim to be transrational but are in fact prerational, antiprogressive, antiliberal, and all too often retrograde.

Chapter 7, "The Pre/Trans Fallacy," has received perhaps more attention than any of the other essays in this volume. It has been reprinted in numerous languages around the world, and has become something of a standard reference in the field—both for those who agree with it and those who don't. The essence of the pre/trans fallacy is simple and straightforward: since prerational and transrational are both nonrational, then they appear similar or even identical to the untutored eye. And if they are confused—if prepersonal is confused with transpersonal, if preverbal is confused with transverbal, if subconscious is confused with superconscious—then one of two things happen: the trans states are reduced to pre states (and thus explained away), or the pre states are elevated to trans glory (thus elevating nonsense to God). These twin problems—reductionism and elevationism—are the topics of this essay.

Chapter 8, "Legitimacy, Authenticity, and Authority in the New Religions," takes a careful look at various new religious movements, both those deemed generally benign or even beneficial (Zen, Vedanta, Taoism), and those deemed disastrous (Jonestown, the Moonies, cults in general). This chapter suggests a set of criteria that have, in the cases tested so far, spotted those movements that are potentially dangerous.

The last chapter, chapter 10, is called "The Ultimate State of Consciousness," and it is about exactly that. What is the ultimate state? Does that even make any sense? I believe it does, and this chapter attempts to explain why. It is really a statement of the "Always Already" schools of truth, such as Dzogchen, Zen, and Vedanta. It contains a set of "pointing out instructions" for the location of Spirit in the midst of one's ordinary and present state of consciousness. As such, it is an altogether appropriate way to end this volume.

And as for the answer to the great Western dualism? The final answer

---

* [See *Integral Psychology* for the most comprehensive treatment of this model.]

to the mind/body problem? To the One and the Many? God and creation? Was God at Auschwitz? Are we fated or free willed? It's all the
same question, you see, so here is another perfectly complete answer:

This slowly drifting cloud is pitiful!
What dreamwalkers we all are!
Awakened, the one great truth:
Black rain on the temple roof.

In the following pages I will attempt to explain exactly why that is
so.

Boulder, Colo.
February 1996

Preface to the Second Edition

THIS IS A BOOK about an overall or "comprehensive" knowledge quest—not with a view toward any sort of *finality* in knowledge, but with a view toward some sort of *balance* in the quest itself. It is about empirical science, philosophy, psychology, and transcendental religion; about sensory knowledge, symbolic knowledge, and spiritual knowledge; and about how they might all fit together. It discusses what a "comprehensive" paradigm might eventually look like, and—just as important or perhaps more important—it attempts to expose and unravel some of the major obstacles to the emergence of such a paradigm.

Each chapter is meant to be something of a self-contained unit; indeed, most were originally written and circulated as independent presentations. Nonetheless, each chapter builds upon its predecessor to drive home the point of the book as a whole: A new and comprehensive paradigm is *possible;* this is what aspects of it might look like; and here are some of the greatest obstacles now preventing its emergence.

In looking over this book for its new release, I remain more convinced than ever of the truth and cogency of its central points. In fact, the existing orthodox *and* new age paradigms have both severely narrowed and distorted the full range of human knowing and being. Both approaches have fallen considerably short of offering a new and comprehensive paradigm, because both have consistently failed to take a *full-spectrum* view of the human condition in its secular as well as divine possibilities. The orthodox tend to deny the higher reaches of the human spirit, while the new-agers, equally blind but in the other eye, ignore or underestimate the lower and primitive roots of the human animal. Both are terribly half-sighted.

This is a book about what a new and comprehensive paradigm might look like if a full-spectrum approach is taken, an approach that attempts to restore vision to the many eyes of the human spirit.

Boulder, Colo.
December 1989

1

Eye to Eye

W E HEAR A LOT TODAY about "paradigms," and especially about "new and higher" paradigms—"supertheories" that would include, beyond the physical sciences, the higher knowledge claims of philosophy-psychology *and* of transcendental-mystical religion—a type of truly unified world view. The vision itself is fascinating: finally, an overall paradigm or theory that would unite science, philosophy-psychology, and religion-mysticism; finally, a truly "unified field theory"; finally, a comprehensive overview. Some very skilled, very sober, very gifted scholars, from all sorts of different fields, are today talking exactly that. Extraordinary.

The precise implications and meanings of all this will become, I believe, more obvious as we proceed; for the moment, let us simply call any such paradigm, however tentative or fledgling (and assuming it is even possible), an "integral paradigm," meaning an *overall* knowledge quest that would include not only the "hard ware" of physical sciences but also the "soft ware" of philosophy and psychology and the "transcendental ware" of mystical-spiritual religion. If this type of new, higher, and comprehensive paradigm is indeed starting to emerge—and I think it is—then it is probably true that the single greatest issue it must face—an issue it has *not* yet adequately treated—is its relation to *empirical science*. For, the argument goes, if any sort of "new and higher" paradigm is not an empirical science, then it has no valid epistemology—no valid means of acquiring knowledge—and thus anything it says or proclaims, no matter how otherwise comforting, must therefore be invalid, nonsensical, and meaningless. There is no use trying to figure out the range or scope or methods of knowledge of the "new and higher" paradigm, which wishes to include philosophy and mysticism, until you can demonstrate that you *have* actual knowledge of any sort to begin with. Make no mistake about it:

> We do not deny *a priori* that the mystic is able to discover truths by his own special methods. We wait to hear what are the propositions which embody his discoveries, in order to see whether they are verified or confuted by our empirical observations. But the mystic, so far from producing propositions which are empirically verified, is unable to produce any intelligible propositions at all.[3]

The statement is from A. J. Ayer, the noted philosopher, and he concludes that the fact that the mystic "cannot reveal what he 'knows' or even himself devise an empirical test to validate his 'knowledge' shows that his state of mystical intuition is not a genuinely cognitive state."[3]

Would a new integral paradigm be an empirical science? If not, could it claim genuine cognition and knowledge? Or, for that matter—and this is really the whole point of our discussion—can any sort of higher philosophical or spiritual truths be adequately "validated"? There has been an immense amount written on these subjects, but I personally find that most of it just slides off the main issues, like greasy hands chasing soap. In this chapter and the next, then, I would like to examine briefly the nature of empirical science, the meaning of philosophical knowledge, and the essence of transcendental or spiritual knowledge, as well as the relationships between them—and that might help us more easily envision the nature of a new and truly comprehensive paradigm, if such, indeed, exists.

THREE EYES OF THE SOUL

St. Bonaventure, the great *Doctor Seraphicus* of the Church and a favorite philosopher of Western mystics, taught that men and women have at least three modes of attaining knowledge—"three eyes," as he put it (following Hugh of St. Victor, another famous mystic): the *eye of flesh,* by which we perceive the external world of space, time, and objects; the *eye of reason,* by which we attain a knowledge of philosophy, logic, and the mind itself; and the *eye of contemplation*, by which we rise to a knowledge of transcendent realities.

Further, said St. Bonaventure, all knowledge is a type of *illumination*. There is exterior and inferior illumination *(lumen exterius* and *lumen inferius)*, which lights the eye of flesh and gives us knowledge of sense objects. There is *lumen interius*, which lights the eye of reason and gives us knowledge of philosophical truths. And there is *lumen superius*, the light of transcendent Being which illumines the eye of contemplation and reveals salutary truth, "truth which is unto liberation."

In the external world, said St. Bonaventure, we find a *vestigium* or "vestige of God"—and the eye of flesh perceives this vestige (which appears as separate objects in space and time). In ourselves, in our psyches—especially in the "threefold activity of the soul" (memory, reason, and will)—we find an *imago* of God, revealed by the mental eye. And ultimately, through the eye of contemplation, lighted by the *lumen superius*, we find the whole transcendent realm itself, beyond sense and reason—the Divine Ultimate itself.

All of this fits precisely with Hugh of St. Victor (first of the great Victorine mystics), who distinguished between *cogitatio, meditatio,* and *contemplatio. Cogitatio,* or simple empirical cognition, is a seeking for the facts of the material world using the eye of flesh. *Meditatio* is a seeking for the truths within the psyche itself (the *imago* of God) using the mind's eye. *Contemplatio* is the knowledge whereby the psyche or soul is united instantly with Godhead in transcendent insight (revealed by the eye of contemplation).

Now that particular wording—eye of flesh, mind, and contemplation—is Christian; but similar ideas can be found in every major school of traditional psychology, philosophy, and religion. The "three eyes" of a human being correspond, in fact, to the three major realms of being described by the perennial philosophy, which are the gross (flesh and material), the subtle (mental and animic), and the causal (transcendent and contemplative). These realms have been described extensively elsewhere, and I wish here only to point to their unanimity among traditional psychologists and philosophers.[107,110,137]

To extend St. Bonaventure's insights, we moderns might say that the eye of flesh—the *cogitatio,* the *lumen inferius/exterius*—participates in a select world of shared sensory experience, which it partially creates and partially discloses. This is the "gross realm," the realm of space, time, and matter (the subconscient). It is the realm *shared* by all those possessing a similar eye of flesh. Thus humans can even share this realm, to some degree, with other higher animals (especially mammals), because the eyes of flesh are quite similar. If a human holds a piece of meat in front of a dog, the dog will respond—a rock or plant will not. (The meat does not exist for the organism lacking the necessary mode of knowledge and perception, the necessary eye of flesh.) In the gross realm, an object is never *A* and not-*A;* it is either *A* or not-*A*. A rock is never a tree, a tree is never a mountain, one rock is not another rock, and so on. This is basic sensorimotor intelligence—object constancy—the eye of flesh. It is the *empirical eye,* the eye of sensory experience. (It should be said, at the start, that I am using the term "empirical" as it is employed in philosophy: capable of detection by the five human senses or their extensions. When empiricists like Locke concluded that all knowledge is experiential, they meant that all knowledge in the mind is first in the five senses. When Buddhists say that "meditation is experiential," they do *not* mean the same thing as Locke; they are rather using the term "experience" to mean "directly conscious, not mediated by forms or symbols." We will return to this topic in the next chapter; in the meantime, I will use "empirical" as the empiricists use it: "sensory experience.")

The eye of reason, or more generally, the eye of mind—the *meditatio,* the *lumen interius*—participates in a world of ideas, images, logic, and concepts. This is the subtle realm (or more precisely, the lower portion of the subtle, but the only one I will discuss here). Because so much of modern thought is based solely on the empirical eye, the eye of flesh, it is important to remember that the mental eye *cannot* be reduced to the fleshy eye. The mental field includes but transcends the sensory field. While not excluding it, the mind's eye rises far above the eye of flesh: in imagination, it can *picture* sensory objects not immediately present, and thus transcend the flesh's imprisonment in the simply present world; in logic, it can internally operate upon sensorimotor objects, and so transcend actual motor sequences; in will, it can delay the flesh's instinctual and impulsive discharges and thus transcend the merely animal and subhuman aspects of the organism.

Although the eye of mind relies upon the eye of flesh for much of its information, not all mental knowledge comes strictly from fleshy knowledge, nor does it deal solely with the objects of the flesh. Our knowledge is *not* entirely empirical and fleshy. "According to the sensationalists [that is, empiricists]," says Schuon, "all knowledge originates in sensorial experience [the eye of flesh]. They go so far as to maintain that human knowledge can have no access to any suprasensory knowledge and are unaware of the fact that the suprasensible can be the object of a genuine perception and hence of a concrete experience [notice that Schuon correctly refuses to equate empirical and experiential, since there are supraempirical or suprasensory experiences]. Thus, it is upon an intellectual infirmity that these thinkers build their systems, without their appearing to be in the least impressed by the fact that countless men as intelligent as themselves have thought otherwise than they do."[106]

The point is precisely as Schumacher said: "In short, we 'see' not simply with our eyes but with a great part of our mental equipment as well [the eye of mind]. . . . With the light of the intellect [the *lumen interius*] we can see things which are invisible to our bodily senses. . . . The truth of ideas cannot be seen by the senses."[105] For example, mathematics is a nonempirical knowledge or a supraempirical knowledge. It is discovered, illuminated, and implemented by the eye of reason, not by the eye of flesh.

Even introductory philosophy texts are quite certain on that point: "Whether these [mathematical] expressions are to be understood as referring to anything physical is not his concern but that of the physicist. For the mathematician, statements are viewed as statements of logical relationships; he is not interested in their empirical or factual meaning [if they have any]."[96] Thus, no one has ever seen, with the eye of flesh, the square root of a negative one. That is a transempirical entity, and can only be seen by the mind's eye. Most of mathematics, as Whitehead says, is transempirical and even *a priori* (in the Pythagorean sense).

Likewise with logic. The truth of a logical deduction is based on internal consistency—it is not based upon its relation to sensory objects. Thus, a valid logical syllogism might say, "All unicorns are mortal. Tarnac is a unicorn. Therefore Tarnac is mortal." Logically that is valid; empirically it is meaningless (not sound), for the simple reason that no one has ever seen a unicorn in the first place. Logic is transempirical. Thus many philosophers, such as Whitehead, have held that the abstract (or mental) sphere is necessary and *a priori* for the manifestation of the natural/sensory realm, and this is approximately what the Eastern traditions mean when they say that the gross arises from the subtle (which arises from the causal).

In mathematics, in logic—and more: in imagination, in conceptual understanding, in psychologic insight, in creativity—we *see* things with the mind's eye which are not fully present to the eye of flesh. Thus we say that the mental field includes but greatly transcends the fleshy field.

The eye of contemplation is to the eye of reason as the eye of reason is to the eye of flesh. Just as reason transcends flesh, so contemplation transcends reason. Just as reason cannot be reduced to, nor derived solely from, fleshy knowledge, so contemplation cannot be reduced to nor derived from reason. Where the eye of reason is transempirical, the eye of contemplation is transrational, translogical, and transmental. "Gnosis [the eye of contemplation, the *lumen superius*] transcends the mental realm and *a fortiori* the realm of the sentiments [the sensory realm]. This transcendence results from the 'supernaturally natural' function of [gnosis], namely the contemplation of the Immutable, of the Self which is Reality, Consciousness, and Bliss. The quest of philosophers, therefore, has nothing in common with that of contemplatives, since its basic principle of exhaustive verbal adequacy is opposed to any liberating finality, to any transcending of the sphere of words."[106]

We will be returning to these three different fields of knowledge throughout this chapter. In the meantime, let us simply assume that all men and women possess an eye of flesh, an eye of reason, and an eye of contemplation; that each eye has its own objects of knowledge (sensory, mental, and transcendental); that a higher eye cannot be reduced to nor explained solely in terms of a lower eye; that each eye is valid and useful in its own field, but commits a fallacy when it attempts, by itself, to fully grasp higher or lower realms.

Within that context, I will try to demonstrate that while an integral or truly comprehensive paradigm will draw freely on the eye of flesh and the eye of mind, it must also draw significantly on the eye of contemplation. This means that a new and integral paradigm—if such is ever to exist—would be in the extremely favorable position of being able to use and integrate all three eyes—gross, subtle, and causal. I will also argue that, by and large, empiric-analytic science belongs to the eye of flesh, phenomenological philosophy and psychology to the eye of mind, and religion/meditation to the eye of contemplation. Thus a new and integral paradigm would ideally and ultimately be a synthesis and integration of empiricism, rationalism, and transcendentalism (whether this overall endeavor can or should be called a "higher science" will be dealt with in the next chapter; in this chapter, "science" will refer to classical empiric-analytic science).

But there is one major difficulty and one major hazard which is first to be overcome, and that is the tendency toward *category error*, which is the attempt of one eye to usurp the roles of the other two. I will point out some of the major category errors committed by religion, by philosophy, and by science, and then—as one example—I will discuss the historical category errors that led to the rise of modern scientism. I do not mean to pick on science in this regard—religion and philosophy have been just as guilty, as we will see. However, historically speaking, the most recent and most pervasive category error has concerned the role of empirical science, and it is important to try to understand that error as carefully as we can, not only because, of all the category errors, it has probably had the most impact, but also because in many subtle ways it is still with us.

Following those assumptions, we can begin with an examination of the rise and meaning of empirical science.

THE RISE OF SCIENCE

It is not generally realized that science—by which I mean, for the moment, what Kepler, Galileo, and Newton did—was *not* a rationalistic system, but an empirical one. As we have seen, these two are not at all the same: rationalism lays stress on the eye of reason; empiricism, the eye of flesh. Science, in fact, began as an *anti*rationalism, as a direct revolt against the rational systems of the scholastic age. As Whitehead put it: "Galileo keeps harping on how things happen, whereas his [rationally minded] adversaries had a complete theory as to why things happen. Unfortunately the two theories did not bring out the same results. Galileo insists upon 'irreducible and stubborn facts,' and Simplicius, his opponent, brings forward *reasons.*"[130]

Notice that the clash between Galileo, with his "irreducible and stubborn facts," and Simplicius, with his "satisfactory reasons," is precisely a clash between the eye of flesh and the eye of reason—between empiricism and rationalism. Whitehead is very insistent on that point: "It is a great mistake to conceive this historical revolt [of science] as an appeal to reason. On the contrary, it was through and through an anti-intellectualist movement. It was a return to the contemplation of brute fact [the eye of flesh; empiricism]; and it was based on a recoil from the inflexible rationality of medieval thought."[130] Again and again Whitehead drives home that crucial point: "We cannot too carefully realize that science started with the organization of ordinary [sense] experiences. It was in this way that it coalesced so readily with the antirationalistic bias of the historical revolt."[130] Science was, as Bertrand Russell remarked, nothing more than consistent *common sense,* which actually means: based on the most commonsense organ we all possess: the eye of flesh.

It is very easy to see why science began as a revolt against rationalism. Recall that logic, in and by itself, so transcends the subhuman eye of flesh that at times it seems almost disembodied, totally unrelated to the world of fleshy objects. This in itself does not constitute a flaw in logic, as so many romantics seem to think, but rather constitutes its very strength: to reason about an activity means not to have to actually perform that activity with the flesh. The very power of logic lies in its transcendence of sensory objects (as Piaget has demonstrated, formal operational thinking or rational logic operates *upon,* and thus transcends, concrete and sensorimotor experience).

But logic—or in general, the entire eye of mind—can be severely misused. The only final test of "correct reasoning" is whether the train of logical thought is itself internally consistent, and whether it has violated any canons of logic in the process. If it meets these criteria, then it is, in its own realm, quite valid. It starts with an initial premise, and through subtle processes of abstract (or formal operational) reasoning, draws out all of the implications and deductions enfolded in that premise.

The premise itself—the initial starting proposition—can originate in any of the three realms: fleshy, mental, or contemplative. If the initial starting point originates in the realm of the eye of flesh, and is itself valid, we speak of "indubitable facts" (Russell) or Galileo's "irreducible and stubborn facts" or simply empiric-analytic facts. If the initial starting point originates in the realm of the eye of mind, we speak of "indubitable principles of reference" (Russell) or of "intuitively self-evident truths" (Descartes) or of "direct phenomenological apprehensions" (Husserl), which can be either philosophical or psychological. If the proposition is influenced by the higher eye of contemplation, we speak broadly of revelation or mandalic reasoning (as we will explain). At any rate, let us note the three starting points for reasoning: irreducible facts (flesh), self-evident or axiomatic truths (mind), and revelatory insights (spirit).

Now we mentioned that logic can be put to a grave misuse, and it is this: In the *selection of the initial premises* for reasoning, all sorts of errors and even frauds can be committed. Outstanding among these is the "category error," which occurs when one of the three realms is made to wholly substitute for another realm—or, we might say, when things (flesh) are confused with thoughts (mind) are confused with transcendental insights (contemplation). For once that occurs, then facts try to replace principles and principles try to replace God.

For example, a true rationalist is one who claims all valid knowledge comes only from the eye of reason and dismisses the eye of flesh (not to mention contemplation) as being wholly unreliable. Descartes was such a philosopher. "We should never allow ourselves to be persuaded excepting by the evidence of our Reason," he said, and by that he explicitly meant evidence "of our Reason and not of our senses." For Descartes, reason—and reason alone—could discover ultimately self-evident truths, an apprehension Descartes called intuition (rational intuition, not spiritual intuition):

> By *intuition* I understand not the fluctuating testimony of the senses, but the conception which an unclouded and attentive mind gives us so readily and distinctly that we are wholly freed from doubt about that which we understand. Or, what comes to the same thing, *intuition* springs from the light of reason alone. . . .[96]

"Intuition springs from the light of reason alone. . . ." And rational-intuition alone could discover self-evident truths. Once we have arrived at self-evident truths, then, according to Descartes, we may deduce from those truths a whole series of secondary truths. And, he says, "These two methods [the initial rational truth and deduction] are the most certain routes to knowledge, and the mind should admit no others. All the rest should be rejected as suspect of error and dangerous."[96]

There is the statement of a pure rationalist, one who believes only in the eye of reason, and discards the eye of flesh and the eye of contemplation. But what a severe limitation! For now the eye of reason is forced to try to disclose empirical truths as well as contemplative truths, a task it simply is not equipped to do, and a task that therefore leads inexorably to category errors. It is quite obvious that the eye of reason cannot adequately disclose the realm of contemplation; and it soon became obvious that the eye of reason could not itself, by itself, disclose the truths lying in the realm of the objective and sensory world. As we will soon see, it was the role of modern science to show precisely why reasoning alone could not disclose empirical facts. The truth in the domain of the eye of flesh can be checked only with the eye of flesh.

The only point I wish to emphasize here is that when one eye tries to usurp the role of any of the other eyes, a category error occurs. And it can occur in any direction: the eye of contemplation is as ill-equipped to disclose the facts of the eye of flesh as the eye of flesh is incapable of grasping the truths of the eye of contemplation. Sensation, reason, and contemplation disclose their own truths in their own realms, and any-time one eye tries to see for another eye, blurred vision results.

Now that type of category error has been *the* great problem for al-most every major religion: the great sages of Hinduism, Buddhism, Christianity, Islam, and so on all opened, to one degree or another, the eye of contemplation—the third eye. But that does not mean, at all, that they then automatically became experts in the realms of the first and second eyes. Enlightenment, for instance, does not carry the information that water is composed of two hydrogen and one oxygen atoms. If it did, then that fact would appear in at least one religious text, whereas in fact it is in none.

Unfortunately, the Revelation—given by the eye of contemplation—is then taken as the supreme arbiter of truth for the eye of flesh and the eye of reason. The Book of Genesis, for instance, is a Revelation of the evolution of the manifest realm from the Unmanifest, which occurs in seven major stages (seven days). It is a translation of a *supramental* in-sight into the poetic images of the mind's eye. Alas, those whose own eye of contemplation remains closed take the Revelation as both an *em-pirical fact* and a *rational truth*. And that is a category error. And science discovered that error—with a vengeance.

Thus, for example, in A.D. 535, the Christian monk Cosmas wrote a book called *Christian Topography*. Based entirely upon a literal reading of the Bible, Cosmas demonstrated once and for all that the earth had neither North nor South Pole, but was a flat parallelogram whose length is double its width. Dogmatic theology abounds with that type of howl-ing error—and that is true of both Eastern and Western religions. The Hindus and Buddhists, for instance, believed that the earth, because it must be supported, was sitting on an elephant which, because it must also be supported, was sitting on a turtle (and to the question, "Upon what, then, rests the turtle," the answer was given, "Let us now change the subject").

The point is that Buddhism and Christianity and other genuine reli-gions contained, at their summit, ultimate insights into ultimate reality, but these transverbal insights were invariably all mixed up with rational truths and empirical facts. Humanity had not, as it were, yet learned to differentiate and separate the eyes of flesh, reason, and contemplation. And because Revelation was confused with logic and with empirical fact, and all three were presented as *one truth,* then two things hap-pened: the philosophers came in and destroyed the rational side of reli-gion, and science came in and destroyed the empirical side. I will argue that that was as it should be. However, theology—which in the West had a somewhat weak eye of contemplation anyway—was so heavily dependent upon its rationalism and its empirical "facts" (the sun circles the earth as the Bible says), that when these two eyes were taken away by philosophy and science, Western spirituality all but went blind. It did not fall back on its eye of contemplation—but merely fell apart and spent its time in futile argument with the philosophers and scientists. From that point on, spirituality in the West was dismantled, and only philosophy and science seriously remained.

Within a century, however, philosophy as a rational system—a system based on the eye of mind—was in its own turn decimated, and decimated by the new scientific empiricism. At that point, human knowledge was *reduced* to only the eye of flesh. Gone was the contemplative eye; gone the mental eye—and human beings had enough collective low self-esteem to restrict their means of valid knowledge to the eye of flesh—the eye we share with animals. Knowing became, in source and referent, essentially subhuman.

THE NEW SCIENCE

Understand that this dismal restriction of human knowledge was not the fault of science. Empiric-analytic science is simply the organized body of verifiable knowledge *grounded* by the eye of flesh. To say we should not have that knowledge nor rely on it is to say we shouldn't have flesh. Something else—almost sinister—occurred, which converted science into scientism, and that is what will concern us.

But first the rise of science itself. By historical account, we are now reaching the year A.D. 1600. Prior to that time human knowledge was dominated by the Church—by a dogma which confused and combined the eyes of contemplation, of reason, and of sense. If the Bible said the earth was created in six days, so be it; if the dogma said an object ten times heavier than another object falls to earth ten times faster, so be it. In this confused state, nobody bothered to carefully exercise the eye of flesh and *simply look at the natural world*. In fact, did a heavier object fall faster than a light object, as the Church said? Why not test it out?

If civilized men and women have been on the face of the earth for, say, ten thousand years, then it took ten thousand years for someone to think of that simple idea and actually carry it through. But then, around the year 1600, one Galileo Galilei stood on the Pisa Tower and dropped two objects—one heavy, one light—and they hit the ground at the same time. The world has never, but never, been the same.

The scientific method was invented independently and simultaneously by Galileo and Kepler about A.D. 1600. It would not be too far wrong to say that they simply used the eye of flesh to *look* at the realm of flesh, for that is essentially what happened. "Prior to the time of Kepler and Galileo," says L. L. Whyte, "the only developed systems of thought had been religious [the eye of contemplation] or philosphic [the eye of reason] organizations of subjective experience, while such objective observations of nature as had been collected had remained relatively unorganized. Medieval rationalism was subjective; there was as yet no rational philosophy of nature [no empiric-analytic thought] of comparable complexity or precision."[131]

But what Kepler and Galileo did was actually much more brilliant than just using the eye of flesh carefully and precisely. Many before them had looked carefully and steadily at nature (e.g., Aristotle), but none before them had invented the scientific method. Please mark that point well, because everybody seems to miss that fact: If the term "scientific method" has any historical meaning whatsoever, then it can be said to have been invented and practiced by Kepler and Galileo.

For Kepler and Galileo used the eye of flesh not just to look at nature, but to look at nature in a particular way, and that particular way constituted a new discovery: the scientific method, modern science, real empirical science. It is popular today to say that science just means "knowledge," or that it is basically "good observation," but that is not true. As Whyte points out: "For two thousand years man had been observing, comparing, and seeking to classify his observations, but as yet there was no system of thought concerning nature which provided any method which might be systematically used for facilitating the process of discovery. . . ."[131] Science was not just good observation, which had been around for thousands of years; it was a peculiar type of observation.

Before I describe the heart of that particular type of observation, let me set forth a few of its auxiliary characteristics. First of all, the new scientific method was empirical-experimental. Suppose we have a question: "Does an object twice as heavy as another fall twice as fast?" A medieval rationalist might proceed as follows: "We know in all respects that as a natural object increases in one physical quantity it increases in all others proportionately. For instance, a wooden rod twice as long as another weighs twice as much. Weight is a physical quantity, and so is speed. Therefore any object twice as heavy as another must fall twice as fast." Galileo, on the other hand, simply went out and tried it.

Notice that the logic of the rationalist was valid. Starting from initial premises, it deduced correctly a set of conclusions. Problem is, the initial premises were wrong. Deduction is a sound mode of knowledge, provided one's initial premises are sound. Some initial premises are indeed self-evident and true; as the history of philosophy has shown, however, some are self-evident and false. What Galileo and Kepler needed was a way to decide, as regards the sensory realm, whether an initial proposition was true or false. *Not a rational way*—because there is none—but a sensory way, an empirical way. And that way, in short, was the empirical experiment: Devise a situation such that all variables are held constant except one. Run the experiment several times, each time changing that one variable, then look at the results.

For Galileo it meant gathering several objects—all the *same* size, dropped from the *same* height, at the *same* time. But consisting of *different* weights. If the objects fall at different speeds, then the weight of the objects is the likely reason. If they fall at the same speed (actually, acceleration), then the weight is unimportant. As it turns out, they fell at the same speed; therefore, the proposition that "heavier objects fall faster" is disproved. All objects (in a vacuum) fall at the same rate of acceleration—and there is an initial premise you may *now* use in deductive logic.

This scientific proof is empirical and inductive; it is not rational and deductive (although, obviously, science uses logic and deduction, only it makes them subservient to empirical induction). Induction—systematically proposed by Francis Bacon—is the formation of general laws on the basis of numerous specific instances (the opposite of deduction). For instance, after Galileo tried his experiment on metallic objects, he might try it on wooden ones, then clay ones, then paper ones, and so on and see if he got the same results. That is induction: the suggested proposition is tested in all sorts of new circumstances; if it is *not disproved* in those circumstances, it is to that extent confirmed. The proposition itself is generally called a *hypothesis*. A hypothesis not yet disproved (without extenuating circumstances) is generally called a *theory*. And a theory that looks like it may in fact never be disproved (supplemented, perhaps, but not fundamentally invalidated in its own realm) is generally called a *law*. Galileo discovered two laws of earthly motion; Kepler discovered three laws of planetary motion; and the genius Newton put these laws *together* to join the forces of heaven with those of earth: he showed that an apple falls to earth (Galileo) for the same reason that the planets circle the sun (Kepler)—namely, gravity.

The point is that the classic scientific method was empirical and inductive, not rational and deductive. What Bacon and Kepler and Galileo did was simply promise to yoke the eye of reason to the eye of flesh when the proposition in question concerns the domain of flesh. Odd as it sounds today, that was a stroke of genius: let the eye of flesh itself check facts in the domain of flesh, and thus avoid the category errors of confusing flesh with reason and contemplation. I am going to suggest that not only was that a great benefit to science, but also a potentially great benefit to religion, because it acts to strip religion of its nonessential and pseudoscientific dross, which has contaminated every major religion bar none.

But there is one other point in regard to Galileo and Kepler, and the most important point at that, the very heart of the matter. We saw that others before them had carefully used the eye of flesh; and others before them had, in a crude sense, used a type of induction, trying to validate their theories in several circumstances. But Galileo and Kepler hit upon the real and essential secret of empirical-inductive proof: in a scientific experiment, one desires to see if a particular event occurs; if it does, something changed. In the physical world, change necessarily involves some sort of displacement in space-time; displacement can be *measured*. Conversely, if an event cannot be measured, it cannot be the object of an empiric-scientific experiment; and, as far as *that* science is concerned, it does not exist.

Thus, it is only a slight exaggeration to say that empiric-analytic science is measurement. Measurement, and virtually measurement alone, gives the data of scientific experiments. Galileo measured. Kepler measured. Newton measured. *There* was the real genius of Kepler and Galileo. The reason modern science was not discovered before Kepler and Galileo was that nobody really measured before Kepler and Galileo. "We have here reached a moment of great significance," says L. L. Whyte. "About 1600 Kepler and Galileo simultaneously and independently formulated the principle that the laws of nature are to be discovered by measurement, and applied this principle in their own work. Where Aristotle had classified, Kepler and Galileo sought to measure."[131] Whyte is at pains to emphasize: "The process of measurement was the one objectively reliable approach to the structure of nature and the numbers so obtained were the key to the order of nature. After 1600 mankind was thus in possession of a systematic method of research into those aspects of nature which were accessible to measurement. The centuries since 1600 may well be regarded as the age of quantity. Never before had such a technique been available. . . ."[131]

Whitehead is just as certain: Aristotle, he said, tended to mislead the physicists because "in effect, these doctrines said to the physicist *classify* when they should have said *measure.*" For, says Whitehead, "if only the schoolmen had measured instead of classifying, how much they might have learnt!"[130] Whitehead summarizes the essence of the new empiric-analytic method: "Search for *measurable* elements among your phenomena, and then search for relations between these measures of physical quantities." That, he says, is a "rule of science."[130]

I am not going to make a drawn-out argument for this, but take it as obvious that "the scientific gauge is quantity: space, size, and strength of forces can all be reckoned numerically. . . . A number is a number, and number is the language of science."[110] Psychology is considered an empirical science only if it offers *measurable* patterns, which is why behaviorism is an empirical science and psychoanalysis is not. (Notice I did not say that behaviorism is therefore valid and psychoanalysis is not; they are two sets of data gathered through two different eyes, both of which are valid, one of which is empirical, and one of which is mental-phenomenological.) Even psychoanalysis realized this right off. As the pioneering analyst Melanie Klein put it:

> It has to be kept in mind that the evidence which the analyst can present differs essentially from that which is required in physical sciences, because the whole nature of psychoanalysis is different. In my view, endeavors to provide comparable exact data result in a pseudoscientific approach, because the workings of the un- conscious mind, and the response of the psychoanalyst to them, cannot be submitted to measurement. . . .[73]

In summary, we have this: The ingenious and enduring contribution of Galileo and Kepler was the demonstration that, as regards the physical or sensorimotor world, the eye of reason can and must be linked to and grounded in the eye of flesh by inductive experimentation, whose very heart is repeatable measurement (number). Let the eye of flesh speak for the eye of flesh—and empirical science was invented for just that purpose.

Kant and the Beyond

The epitome of fleshy truth is empirical fact; the epitome of mental truth is philosophic and psychologic insight; and the epitome of contemplative truth is spiritual wisdom. We saw that prior to the modern era men and women had not sufficiently differentiated the eyes of flesh, reason, and contemplation, and thus tended to confuse them. Religion *tried* to be scientific, philosophy tried to be religious, science tried to be philosophic—and all were, to just that extent, wrong. They were guilty of category errors.

Thus, Galileo and Kepler, in delineating the true nature of empiric-scientific truth, actually did religion and philosophy a great service. They actually separated out the eye of flesh from its confusion with the eyes of mind and contemplation. Science, by performing its duty faithfully and honestly, could liberate both philosophy and religion from trying to be pseudoscience. The monk Cosmas would not have to spend his time trying to figure out the shape of the earth; the science of geology could do that and free Cosmas for the pursuit of contemplation. By showing us precisely what truth is in the realm of the eye of flesh, it would eventually, by subtraction, help us rediscover the mind's eye and the contemplative eye.

Now what Galileo and Kepler did for the eye of flesh, vis-à-vis religion, Kant did for the eye of reason. That is to say, as Galileo and Kepler helped to strip religion of its nonessential "scientific" dross, Kant helped strip it of its nonessential rationalizing. And that was to have extraordinary, if almost wholly misunderstood, repercussions.

Prior to Kant, the philosophers were not only trying to *deduce* scientific facts—which we saw was impossible—they were also trying to *deduce* contemplative or spiritual truths, which is just as impossible but twice as dangerous. Both secular and religious philosophers were making all sorts of rational statements which they claimed were about ultimate realities and ultimate truths. Thus, Thomas Aquinas had put forth rational "proofs" for the existence of God; so had Descartes—and Aristotle and Anselm and others. Their common mistake lay in trying to prove with the eye of reason that which can only be seen with the eye of contemplation. And somebody, sooner or later, was bound to find it out.

This was Kant's brilliance. He himself did indeed believe in God, in a Transcendent Ultimate, in noumenon. And he correctly believed that it was transempirical, transsensory. But he demonstrated that anytime we attempt to *reason* about this transempirical reality, we find that *we can create arguments for either of two completely contradictory views with equal plausibility*—and that plainly shows that such reasoning is futile (or, at any rate, does not carry near the weight it had so generously given itself under the title of "metaphysics"). But here were all these philosophers and theologians cranking out rational statements about God (or Buddha or Tao) and about ultimate reality as if they were speaking directly and actually of the Real itself, whereas in fact, as Kant demonstrated, they were speaking nonsense. Pure reason is simply incapable of grasping transcendent realities, and when it tries, it finds that its contradictory can be put with equal plausibility. (This insight was by no means confined to the West. Almost fifteen hundred years before Kant, the Buddhist genius Nagarjuna—founder of Madhyamika Buddhism—arrived at virtually the same conclusion, a conclusion echoed and amplified in succeeding generations by every major school of Eastern philosophy and psychology: Reason cannot grasp the essence of absolute reality, and when it tries, it generates only dualistic incompatibilities.)

One of the reasons for this—if I may speak poetically—is that, as disclosed by contemplation, the Ultimate is a "coincidence of opposites" (Nicholas de Cusa) or as Hinduism and Buddhism put it, *advaita* or *advaya,* which means "nondual" or "not-two," a fact that *cannot* be pictured in logic. You cannot, for instance, picture a thing being itself *and* not being itself *at the same time.* You *cannot* see it raining and not raining at the same time in the same spot. You cannot picture nor reason accurately about nonduality, about ultimate reality. If you attempt to translate nondual Reality into dualistic reason, then you will create two opposites where there are in fact none, and therefore each of these opposites can be rationally argued with absolutely equal plausibility—and that, to return to Kant, shows why reason only generates paradox when it tries to grasp God or the Absolute. To indulge in metaphysical speculation (solely with the eye of pure reason) is thus to indulge in nonsense. To say "Reality is absolute subject" is not false, it is nonsensical, it is meaningless, it is neither true nor false but empty, because its opposite can be put with equal force: "Reality is absolute object." In the East, the same nonsense would exist ("Reality is Atman" versus "Reality is Anatman") until totally dismantled by Nagarjuna in precisely the same way followed by Kant.

What Kant demonstrated was that—as Wittgenstein would later put it—most metaphysical problems are not false, they are nonsensical. Not that the answer is bad, but that the question is silly. . . . It is supported by a category error: The eye of pure reason is trying to see into Heaven. Now I don't mean to imply that Kant was enlightened (i.e., that his eye of contemplation was fully opened). Clearly, he was not. An excellent way to grasp Kant's position is by studying the aforementioned Buddhist genius, Nagarjuna, because Nagarjuna applies the same critical philosophy to reason, but he does so not just to show the limitations of reason but to push further and help open the eye of contemplation *(prajna)*, which knows the Ultimate directly, nonconceptually, and immediately. Kant doesn't really know about *prajna* or contemplation, but since he *does* know that God is beyond sense and reason, he thinks God is therefore forever hidden to direct awareness. Soon Schopenhauer would point out just that shortcoming in Kant.

But the only point I want to stress is that Kant correctly demonstrated that the eye of pure reason *cannot,* by its very nature, see into the realm of spirit. Philosophy, that is, cannot reach God—at most it can posit God morally (practically). This demonstration actually stripped religion of the burden to rationalize God, just as Galileo and Kepler relieved religion of the necessity to putter around with molecules. As McPherson put it:

> Perhaps positivistic philosophy has done a service to religion. By showing, in their own way, the absurdity of what theologians try to utter, positivists have helped to suggest that religion belongs to the sphere of the unutterable. . . . Positivists may be the enemies of theology, but the friends of religion.[85]

Thus, both scientific fact and rational philosophy—besides being correct and excellent uses of their own respective eyes of flesh and reason—were potentially quite beneficial to religion in that they could help to strip spirituality of its nonessentials, and clarify its own role in human knowledge and illumination. For what we learn, if we put Galileo and Kepler and Kant and Christ together, is that sensorimotor intelligence is not philosophic insight is not spiritual wisdom—neither can be reduced to the others, neither can be dispensed with.

But within mere decades of Kant, the eye of flesh, blinded by Newton's light, thought that it, and it alone, was worthy of knowledge. For empirical science, spurred on by the likes of Auguste Comte, became scientism. It did not just speak for the eye of flesh, but for the eye of mind and for the eye of contemplation as well. In so doing, it fell prey to precisely the same category errors that it discovered in dogmatic theology, and for which it made religion dearly pay. The scienticians tried to force *empirical* science, with its eye of flesh, to work for all three eyes. And that is a category error. And for that the world, not science, has paid dearly.

THE NEW SCIENTISM

Empiric-analytic science is one aspect of the knowledge to be gained in the realm of the eye of flesh (not all sensory knowledge is scientific: aesthetic impact, for instance). Of course, empiric-analytic science does indeed use the eye of reason, and I believe it even uses the eye of contemplation for creative insight, but all are made subservient to, or grounded in, the eye of flesh and its data. And from being thus one aspect of the lowest eye, it came in the hands of the scienticians to claim all aspects of all three. What happened?

There are many ways to state the fallacy of scientism. It went from saying, "That which cannot be seen by the eye of flesh cannot be empirically verified" to "That which cannot be seen by the eye of flesh does not exist." It went from saying, "There is an excellent method for gaining knowledge in the realm of the five senses" to "Thus the knowledge gained by mind and contemplation is invalid." As Smith put it: "With science there can be no quarrel. Scientism is another matter. Whereas science is positive, contenting itself with reporting what it discovers, scientism is negative. It goes beyond the actual findings of science to deny that other approaches to knowledge are valid and other truths true."[110] Or, more to the point: "The triumphs of modern science went to man's head in something of the way rum does, causing him to grow loose in his logic. He came to think that what science discovers somehow casts doubt on things it does not discover; that the success it realizes in its own domain throws into question the reality of domains its devices cannot touch."[110]

Recall that the extraordinary significance of Kepler and Galileo lay in the discovery of a method to settle once and for all the truth-value of a sensory-empirical proposition. "Does a heavy object fall faster than a light one" is *not* to be thought about with the *lumen interius* of reason, it is *not* to be contemplated with the *lumen superius* in *contemplatio*—it is to be *tested* with the eye of flesh. Prior to that time there simply was no accepted method of settling such disputes, there was no method whereby one could demonstrate empirically that an opponent's ideas were wrong. But now, with Galileo and Kepler, there was a means to decide such empirical disputes—propositions could be shown to be true or false, and shown in such a way that all reasonable men and women would acknowledge agreement.

And with that, the impact of science began to floor theologians and philosophers (God is not a verifiable proposition, but the ground of all propositions, and thus God cannot pass the scientific quiz). *The* test had arrived, and philosophers, religionists, theologians, mystics, and poets were flunking it by the thousands. In fact, they should have refused to take the test—they should have realized that transcendent values are not empiric facts revealed to the eye of flesh but contemplative and nonverbal insights revealed by the *lumen superius* in the cave of the Heart. As it was, they simply began a long series of undignified retreats, trying to think of ways to prove that God was an object, like a rock, or a proposition, like $F = ma$. The work of Galileo and Kepler culminated in Newton's great *Principia,* which in many ways represents (to this day) the pinnacle of the empiric-scientific method. The *Principia* is full of "stubborn and irreducible facts," and such logical laws as conform to those facts. It was an overwhelming achievement for the eye of flesh.

Newton's impact on philosophy was naturally immense. The philosophers, quite simply, wanted in on a good thing. Given the disastrous years of unchecked rationalism and unused contemplation, the philosophers simply swung over their allegiance to the eye of flesh and its greatest proponent, Newton. Even Kant, for all his brilliance, fell prey to this Newtonian religion. It is well known that Kant wanted to be a physicist if he weren't a philosopher, and his critical philosophy, aside from its importance in delineating the sphere of pure reason, is otherwise wrecked with its physicalism. As Gilson so precisely points out: "Kant was not shifting from mathematics to philosophy, but from mathematics to physics. As Kant himself immediately concluded: 'The true method of metaphysics is fundamentally the same as that which Newton has introduced into natural science, and which has there yielded such fruitful results. . . .' " In a sentence, Gilson concludes that Kant's *"Critique of Pure Reason* is a masterly description of what the structure of the human mind should be, in order to account for the existence of a Newtonian conception of Nature."[53]

In other words, what began to occur is that all three eyes of knowledge were reduced to the lowest: they were all modeled on and collapsed to the Newtonian eye of flesh. On the one hand, the philosophers were envious of Newtonian success: Adam could name the stars, Pythagoras could count them, but Newton could tell you how much they weighed to the nearest pound. On the other hand, the more science advanced and the more individuals trained the eye of flesh, the less relevant the mental and contemplative eyes seemed. Science viewed the world largely as quantitative and objective, and that left little room for contemplative or even properly mental interventions. As Whyte put it, the empiric-scientific view of nature, since it was quantitative and objective, "drew attention away from the organizing aspects of personality which are known subjectively [that is, via the *lumen interius* or mental eye], and this encouraged the decline of confidence in the powers of the subjective mind. . . . Instead of the subject being dominant to the object, the object now dominated the subject, though in the new picture of objective nature there was no element corresponding to the constructive mental processes of the subject."[131] In plain language, the eye of mind was closed out, as the eye of contemplation before it. Scientism was not only relieving humanity from God, it was relieving it from the responsibility of thinking.

Thus, in effect, the sole criterion of truth came to be the empiric criterion—that is to say, a sensorimotor test by the eye of flesh (or its extensions) usually based on measurement. The empirical verification principle came to apply not only to the eye of flesh, which was valid, but to the eye of mind and the eye of contemplation as well, which was, as William James himself put it, pure bosh. In the words of Thomas McPherson, "Because the scientist's observation statements are empirically verifiable, the test for sense becomes 'amenability to verification by sense experience,' and whatever is not so verifiable accordingly is nonsense."[85] Understand at once that *this does not mean verifiable by direct experience in general; it means verifiable by sense experience.* That is, empirically verifiable. The scientific philosophers disallow the direct experiences of the mystic/meditator, because these are not capable of detection by the five senses, however otherwise direct the mystic claims them to be. (This is a point we will return to.)

In the meantime, we simply note that nonfleshy came to mean unreal, and on that the new crop of scientific philosophers perched. "Anyone who in practise or theory disregarded them was denounced with unsparing vigor,"[130] says Whitehead. And yet here is the real point: "This position on the part of the scientists was pure bluff, if one may credit them with [actually] believing their own statements."[130] Science was becoming scientism, known also as positivism, known also as scientific materialism, and *that* was a bluff of the part playing the whole. "Thereby," Whitehead concludes, "modern philosophy has been ruined."[130]

It has been ruined because it has been reduced, just as spirituality before it. Bad enough the eye of contemplation was closed, but so was the eye of proper philosophical speculation, synthesis, and criticism. Whitehead is perfectly explicit on that point. So is J. J. Van der Leeuw: "Mutual contempt of philosophy and science is as harmful as it is unfounded, but we must ever be on our guard against asking of one a question belonging to the domain of the other [category error]. A scientific answer to a philosophical question will necessarily be unsatisfactory and beside the point, just as a philosophical solution to a scientific question would be empty of meaning and scientifically valueless. We honour both best by understanding their respective spheres of knowledge and by coordinating them to their greatest benefit, never by confusing their respective tasks."[121]

But that coordination is what the eye of flesh refused to do. Instead it came to say, what it can't see does not exist; whereas what it should have said was, what it can't see it can't see. Kant did *not* say God doesn't exist—he said that sense and scientific reason cannot grasp the Absolute. As Wittgenstein would put it, "Whereof one cannot speak, thereof one must be silent," which the scienticians perverted into, "That of which one cannot speak, is not there."

For example: Recall that one of Kant's contributions was the clear demonstration that anytime you try to reason about the Absolute, you can always reason in two contradictory but equally plausible directions. This is not, as later positivists thought, a sufficient proof that Godhead doesn't exist, but a demonstration that It transcends reason.

Whenever higher dimensions are represented on lower ones, they necessarily lose something in the translation. As a simple example, whenever a three-dimensional sphere is reduced on a two-dimensional surface, it becomes a circle. The sphere, as it were, is cut in half so as to fit on the paper. And notice that the sphere can be cut in two totally different directions—say, from east to west and from west to east—*and it still appears as the same circle*. We would say, then, that whenever a circle tries to think about a sphere, it can manufacture two totally contradictory statements with equal plausibility, because—to the circle—*both* are indeed correct. It is the same with reason and spirit.

The positivists think that this means the sphere doesn't exist—and all it means is that spheres can't be grasped by circles.

Kant firmly believed in the Transcendent, although he knew it couldn't be grasped by sense or scientific reason. But his half-follow-ers—Comte, Mach, and down to today, Ayer, Flew, Quine, and all—had not even that good sense. Upset by the role of proper speculative philos-ophy, and totally blind to the eye of contemplation, the scienticians gave all knowledge over to the lowly eye of flesh, and *no* knowledge other than that was henceforth deemed respectable.

There was the new empirical scientism—it simply said, as it says today, that only the eye of flesh and its number quantities are real. All else, the mind's eye, the eye of contemplation, God, Buddha, Brahman, and Tao—all of that is meaningless because none of that appears as an object "out there." Because scientism could not get a ruler on God, it proclaimed Spirit nonsensical and meaningless. Christ was therefore de-luded, Buddha was schizophrenic, Krishna was hallucinating, Lao Tzu was psychotic.

And so there, just there, was the perverted legacy of Galileo and Kepler. From them to Newton, from Newton to Kant, from Kant to Comte and Mach and Ayer and down to Willard Quine. "The best way to characterize Quine's world view is to say that . . . there is fundamen-tally only one kind of entity in the world, and that is the kind studied by natural scientists—physical objects; and second, that there is only one kind of knowledge in the world, and it is the kind that natural scientists have."[110]

And Willard Quine? "Willard Quine is the most influential American philosopher of the last twenty years."[110]

THE NATURE OF SCIENTISM

"However you disguise it," says Whitehead, "this is the practical out-come of the characteristic scientific philosophy which closed the seven-teenth century." Viewed through the scientific eye, he says, "Nature is a dull affair, soundless, scentless, colourless; merely the hurrying of mate-rial, endlessly, meaninglessly."[130] That's all there is, and all there is worth knowing.

But worse:

> We must note its astounding efficiency as a system of concepts for the organization of scientific research. In this respect, it is fully worthy of the genius of the century which produced it. It has held its own as the guiding principle of scientific studies ever

since. It is still reigning. Every university in the world organizes itself in accordance with it. No alternative system of organizing the pursuit of scientific truth has been suggested. It is not only reigning, but it is without a rival. And yet—it is quite unbelievable.[130]

There is Whitehead's famous judgment of the scientific world view. Others have been even less charitable: "The issue is not the conscious structure of science, but the unconscious strata of the scientific ego, in the scientific character-structure. Whitehead called the modern scientific point of view 'quite unbelievable.' Psychoanalysis adds the crucial point: it is insane."[26] As the psychiatrist Karl Stern put it: "Such a view is crazy. And I do not at all mean crazy in the sense of slangy invective but rather in the technical meaning of psychotic. Indeed such a view has much in common with certain aspects of schizophrenic thinking."[105]

Scientists aren't totally mad, but only because they don't totally believe the empiric-scientific world view. Or, if they do believe it, they genuinely *value* science; or they are appropriately *proud* of it; or they find science *meaningful, enjoyable, purposeful*. But every one of those italicized words are nonempiric entities, being subjective values and intentions. That is to say, a sane scientist is nonscientific as regards his or her person.

We will, however, leave the insanity of the scientistic world view to the psychiatrists, and concentrate instead on Whitehead's point of unbelievability. And the empiric-scientific world view is unbelievable because it is partial, and in pretending to be total, it lands itself in incredulity. For, among other things, the empiric-scientific method is virtually incapable of dealing with *quality*. "Science is primarily quantitative," says Whitehead, and one is not thinking scientifically if one "is thinking qualitatively and not quantitatively." For science is "a search for quantitives."[130] That is, *numbers*.

Now the problem with numbers is that, whereas one quality can be better than another, one number cannot. Love is *intrinsically* better than hate, but three is not intrinsically better than five. And thus, once you have translated the world into empiric measurement and numbers, you have a world without quality, guaranteed. Which is to say, without *value* or *meaning*. All that is left, says Whitehead, is "bare valuelessness," which "has directed attention to *things* as opposed to *values*."[130] Bertrand Russell, who probably ought to know, agrees: "The sphere of values lies outside science."[103] According to Huston Smith, science tends to miss values because "quality itself is unmeasurable. . . . Inability to deal with the qualitatively unmeasurable leads science to work with what Lewis Mumford calls a 'disqualified universe.' " In short, says Smith, "values, life meanings, purposes, and qualities slip through science like sea slips through the nets of fishermen."[110]

Empiric-analytic science cannot easily operate without measurement; measurement is essentially quantity; quantity is number; number is per se outside of values. Quality never gets in and cannot get in. L. L. Whyte nailed it: "All magnitudes have equal status before the laws of elementary arithmetic, whose operators recognize no distinction between one value and another."[131]

Notice I am not condemning empiric-analytic science for this; I am simply trying to delineate its role, so that when it steps outside of its proper sphere and tries to become a complete world view, we will be in a better position to criticize this overreach, this category error, known as empirical positivism or exclusively empirical verification, or scientific materialism.

Now the traditional view of reality had maintained that existence is hierarchically graded, that the contemplative realm is more real and more valuable than the mental realm, which in turn is more real and more valuable than the fleshy realm. All three realms were to be appreciated and used, but let there be no mistake as to their relative worth: the causal is higher than the subtle is higher than the gross—and, as Smith says, the higher is *more real* than the lower because it is more fully saturated with Being.

But as all knowledge came to be reduced to fleshy, empiric knowledge, and since the arbiter of fleshy knowledge is number, and since number is quantity without quality or value, then when science looked carefully for the great value Chain of Being, an extraordinary translation occurred, perhaps the most significant ever to appear in history. *Everything* science could see was viewed numerically, and since no number is intrinsically better than another, the whole hierarchy of value collapsed—it was reduced to simple, valueless place setters, there to take its rightful spot in the rest of nature, to become part of that dull affair, soundless, scentless, colorless; merely the hurrying of material, endlessly, meaninglessly.

The old hierarchy of value and being was thereby ditched in favor of a hierarchy of number. Certain realms could no longer be said to be *higher* or *more real* or *better* than others—they could only be said to be bigger or smaller than others. We might say that *levels of significance* were replaced by *levels of magnification*. We no longer recognized realms which were higher and more significant and more real than the ordinary—such as the contemplative heaven—we only recognized realms *bigger* than the ordinary—such as astronomical distances. And in place of lower, less significant, and less real realms than the ordinary—the subhuman, fleshy, materialistic—we found only realms *smaller* than the ordinary—such as the subatomic. Better and worse were converted into bigger and smaller, and subsequently dropped altogether.

But what could one expect from an animal that had renounced the mind's eye and the contemplative eye? The only eye left was fleshy and physical, and as it searched around, the only differences it could locate were differences in size. As the eyes of reason and contemplation closed, the eye of flesh leveled its gaze unflinchingly at the material world, and began to click off its litany of claims: 1, 2, 3, 4, 5. . . .

THE CONTRADICTION OF SCIENTISM

Now if scientism were merely unbelievable, we all might be tempted to let it go at that. But it is not merely unbelievable—nor merely insane in its quantifying madness—it is, as a world view, a formal self-contradiction.

There are many ways to approach this topic. Perhaps we might first note that scientism maintains that contemplative knowledge of the Absolute is impossible—the only knowledge admissible is fleshy knowledge, which is by all accounts *relative* knowledge. Now if the positivist simply said, "We will limit ourselves to the study of relative knowledge," then that would be quite acceptable. But he goes beyond that and says, "Only relative knowledge is valid." And that is an *absolute* statement: it says, "It is absolutely true that there is no absolute truth." As Schuon puts it: "Relativism sets out to reduce every element of absoluteness to a relativity, while making a quite illogical exception in favor of this reduction itself." He continues:

> In effect, relativism consists in declaring it to be true that there is no such thing as truth, or in declaring it to be absolutely true that nothing but the relatively true exists; one might just as well say that language does not exist, or write that there is no such thing as writing.[106]

In other words, the scientistic claim is "disproved by the very existence of the postulate itself."[106]

In a similar vein the scientician does not merely say, "The empiric proof is the best method of gaining facts in the sense realm," but goes on to say, "Only those propositions that can be empirically verified are true." Unfortunately, *that* proposition itself cannot be empirically verified. There is no empirical proof that empirical proof alone is real. Thus, as Smith says, "The contention that there are no truths save those of science is not itself a scientific truth, and thus in affirming it scientism contradicts itself."[110]

One of the other fashions of scientism is the notion that evolution by *natural selection* (mutation plus statistical-probability) is the sole explanatory agent for all of creation. Now we are not discussing whether evolution occurred; it most apparently did. We are discussing its cause or agent, in this case, chance. For it is asserted that everything, in no matter what domain, is equally a product of chance evolution. Jacques Monod, whose *Chance and Necessity* is the bible of such views, explains: "Evolution . . . the product of an enormous lottery presided over by natural selection, blindly picking the rare winners from among numbers drawn at utter random. . . . This conception alone is compatible with the facts." He is saying that, as far as we know, the concept of evolution as chance selection is *truer* than its rival theories.

But if it were true, there would be no way whatsoever to find out. If all phenomena are equally the product of blind chance, there can be no question of one thing being truer than another. A frog and an ape are equally products of statistical evolution, and we cannot say a frog is truer than an ape. Likewise, since all phenomena are results of statistical chance, *ideas* too are such products—thus it is impossible for one idea to be truer than another, for all are equally chance productions. If everything is a product of statistical necessity, then so is the idea of statistical necessity, in which case it carries no more authority than any other production.

In psychology, this type of scientism appears as the statement—almost uncontested in orthodoxy—that (to use Tart's wording of it, although he himself does not believe it) "All human experience is ultimately reducible to patterns of electrical and chemical activity within the nervous system and body."[118] But if all human activity is reducible to biochemical activity, then so is that human statement itself. So, in fact, are *all* statements equally biochemical fireworks. But there could then be no question of a true statement versus a false statement, because *all* thoughts are *equally* biochemistry. There cannot be true thoughts versus false thoughts, there can only be thoughts. If thoughts are indeed ultimately reducible to electrons firing in the nervous system, then there cannot be true thoughts and false thoughts for the simple reason that there are no true electrons versus false electrons. And so, if that statement is true then it cannot be true.

In short, as Schuon, Smith, and so many others have pointed out, the very existence of the idea of scientism proves that scientism is fundamentally incorrect.

Now it is frequently said today that scientism is dead, and so in the preceding sections I might seem to be resurrecting not only a straw man, but a very dead straw man at that. It is certainly true that the scientistic-positivistic worldview has lost some of its overt persuasiveness; but I believe that it is not only still with us but also, in many ways, extending its influence. Nobody would overtly claim to be a "scientician"—the word itself sounds like a disease. But the *empiric*-scientific enterprise all too often implicitly or explicitly rejects other approaches as not equally valid. My point is that while few would claim to be scienticians, in fact, many are in effect. "Empirical verification" still rules the day in mainstream philosophy and psychology, and that means "verification by the senses or their extensions." In principle, not much else is accepted. How else explain the fact that just a few years ago, Jürgen Habermas—considered by many (myself included) the world's greatest living philosopher—had to devote an entire book to once again refuting and beating back positivism? (A book whose first paragraph contains the stinging comment, "That we disavow reflection [the mind's eye] *is* positivism.") If empirical-positivism is dead, it is a decidedly frisky corpse.

But the basic reason for examining scientism and its contradictions is simply to use it as an example of pervasive category error, so that what is involved in that fallacy can be more easily grasped. My eventual conclusion will be that an overall integral paradigm—or any comprehensive investigative paradigm—should use and integrate all three eyes, and so it is necessary, at the start, to delineate the respective roles of each. If they are not delineated, then our "comprehensive paradigm" can be opened to scientism, to mentalism, or to spiritualism, each based on category error, each deadly in effect.

BUT CAN IT BE VERIFIED?

To escape from scientism or exclusive empiricism is simply to realize that empiric knowledge is not the only form of knowledge; there exists beyond it mental-rational knowledge and contemplative-spiritual knowledge. But if that is so, then how can these "higher" forms of knowledge be verified? If there is no empirical proof, what is left?

This seems to be a problem because we do not see that all valid knowledge is essentially similar in structure, and thus can be similarly verified (or rejected). That is, all valid knowledge—in whatever realm—consists of three basic components, which we will call injunction, illumination, and confirmation. But this topic itself is so intricate and so complex that we will actually devote an entire chapter—the next chapter—solely to it. What I would like to do here is simply introduce and outline the essentials of our argument, so we will be better prepared for the details. In essence, we will simply suggest that all *valid knowledge*—in whatever realm—consists most fundamentally of these basic components:

1. *An instrumental or injunctive strand.* This is a set of instructions, simple or complex, internal or external. All have the form: "If you want to know this, do this."

2. *An illuminative or apprehensive strand.* This is an illuminative *seeing* by the particular eye of knowledge evoked by the injunctive strand. Besides being self-illuminative, it leads to the possibility of:

3. *A communal strand.* This is the actual sharing of the illuminative seeing with others who are using the same eye. If the shared-vision is agreed upon by others, this constitutes a communal or consensual proof of *true seeing*.

Those are the basic strands of any type of true knowledge using any eye. Knowledge does become more complicated when one eye tries to match its knowledge with a higher or lower eye, but these basic strands underlie even that complication (as we will see in the next chapter).

Starting with the eye of flesh, let me give some examples. The injunctive strand, we said, is of the form, "If you want to see this, do this." In the eye of flesh, which is the simplest knowledge, injunctions can be as prosaic as, "If you don't believe it's raining outside, go look." The person looks, and there is his or her illumination, his or her knowledge (strand #2). If others repeat the same instruction ("Go look out the window"), and all see the same thing, there is the communal strand (#3), and we can say, "It is true that it is raining," and so on.

Even in the eye of flesh, however, the injunctions can be quite complex. In empirical science, for instance, we usually find highly difficult and technical instructions, such as: "If you want to see a cell nucleus, then learn how to take histological sections, learn how to use a microscope, learn how to stain tissues, learn how to differentiate cell components one from the other, and *then* look." In other words, the injunctive strand *demands* that, for whatever type of knowledge, the *appropriate eye must be trained until it can be adequate to its illumination.* This is true in art, in science, in philosophy, in contemplation. It is true, in fact, for all valid forms of knowledge.

Now if a person refuses to train a particular eye (flesh, mental, contemplative), then it is equivalent to refusing to look, and we are justified in disregarding this person's opinions and excluding him or her from our vote as to communal proof. Someone who refuses to learn geometry cannot be allowed to vote on the truth of the Pythagorean theorem; someone who refuses to learn contemplation cannot be allowed to vote on the truth of Buddha Nature or Spirit. In other words, if an individual will not take up strand #1 of knowledge, he or she will be excluded from strands #2 and #3. We say that person's knowledge is inadequate to the task. The Churchmen who *refused* to look through Galileo's telescope were *inadequate* in the eye of flesh, and their opinions can be disregarded in that realm.

Moving up to the next eye, the mind's eye, we find that the injunctive strand can be even more complex and more difficult to share. But you and I are hopefully doing so now—we are seeing eye to eye using the mind (although we might not totally agree on what we see); if not, you wouldn't be able to understand one word written. But in order to *see* the meaning of any of these words, we all had to follow certain instructions, foremost among which is, "Learn to read." And that ushered us all into a world which is *not* given to the eye of flesh all by itself. E. F. Schumacher put it nicely: "With the light of the intellect [*lumen interius*] we can see things which are invisible to our bodily senses. No one denies that mathematical and geometrical truths are 'seen' this way [i.e., with the eye of mind, not the eye of flesh]. To *prove* a proposition means to give it a form, by analysis, simplification, transformation, or dissection [the injunctive strand], through which the truth can be *seen* [the illuminative strand]; beyond this seeing there is neither the possibility nor the need for any further proof [except, I might add, *sharing* this proof with others to establish communal proof, the third strand]."[105]

One can train the mind's eye for outward philosophic seeing or for inward psychologic seeing. To the extent the mind's eye refuses to rise above the eye of flesh, it produces in philosophy nothing but positivism and in psychology nothing but behaviorism. On the other hand, to the extent the mind's eye rises to its own occasion, it produces phenomenology, linguistics, proper speculative philosophy (critical, analytical, and synthesizing), and intersubjective psychology (as we will explain in the next chapter).

Proof in this area shares the same form, the same three strands, as in the other areas: train the mental eye, personally look, and then communally compare and confirm. The communal wing of this knowledge is, of course, harder to come by than it is with fleshy knowledge, because everybody is given the same eye of flesh but different mental outlooks. This is certainly not a drawback in the mind's eye, but simply an indication of its richness.

Knowledge in the transcendent realm is gained in precisely the same way: it has an injunction, an illumination, and a confirmation. In Zen: zazen, satori, and imprimatur. There is no Zen without *all three strands;* there is, in fact, no real esoteric or transcendent knowledge without all three. One first takes up the practice of *contemplatio,* which may be meditation, zazen, mantra, japa, interior prayer, and so on. When the eye of contemplation is fully trained, then *look.* Check this direct illumination with others and, more importantly, with the teacher or master. Checking with the master is just like checking math problems with the teacher when one is first learning geometry.

This final and highest proof is ultimately a proof of God or Buddha Nature or Tao—but it is not an empiric proof, and not a rational-philosophic proof, but a contemplative proof. "Our whole business in this life," said St. Augustine, "is to restore to health the eye of the heart whereby God may be seen." To restore that eye is to train that eye, thereby becoming adequate to the knowledge "which is unto salvation."

It is sometimes said that mystic knowledge is not real knowledge because it is not public knowledge, only "private," and hence it is incapable of consensual validation. That is not quite correct, however. For the secret to consensual validation in all three realms is the same, namely: a *trained eye* is a *public eye,* or it could not be trained in the first place; and a public eye is a communal or *consensual* eye. Mathematical knowledge is public knowledge to trained mathematicians (but not to non-mathematicians); contemplative knowledge is public knowledge to all sages. Even though contemplative knowledge is ineffable, it is *not* private: it is a shared vision. The essence of Zen is: "A special transmission outside the Scriptures [that is, between Master and student]; Not dependent upon words and letters [the eye of mind]; Seeing into one's Nature [with the eye of contemplation] and becoming Buddha." It is a *direct seeing* by the contemplative eye, and it can be *transmitted* from teacher to student because it is directly *public* to that eye. The knowledge of God is as public to the contemplative eye as is geometry to the mental eye and rainfall to the physical eye. And a trained contemplative eye can *prove* the existence of God with exactly the same certainty and the same public nature as the eye of flesh can prove the existence of rocks.

A comprehensive-integral paradigm would draw freely on the eye of flesh and on the eye of reason; but it would also be grounded in the eye of contemplation. That eye embodies a valid mode of knowledge; it can be publicly shared; it can be communally validated. No more is possible, no more is needed.

SCIENCE AND RELIGION

The conflict between empirical-science and religion is, and always has been, a conflict between the pseudoscientific aspects of religion and the pseudoreligious aspects of science. To the extent that science remains science and religion remains religion, no conflict is possible—or rather, any conflict that occurs can always be shown to reduce to a category error: theologians are trying to be scientists or scientists are trying to be theologians. In the past, it was most common for the theologians to try to become scientists, and talk of Christ as a historical fact, creation as an empirical fact, the virgin birth as a biological fact, and so on, in which case they should be prepared to answer scientific questions about all that. The virgin birth as an *empirical* fact means that a person was born without a biological father; as a mental symbol it might signify the birth of one whose Father is in Heaven (i.e., one who realizes the transpersonal Self); as a contemplative insight, it might be a direct realization that one's True Self is virgin-born moment to moment. Now the virgin birth as an empiric fact is probably quite wrong; as a symbol and a realization, it is probably quite valid. The point is that when theologians talk empiric facts, they must be prepared to face scientists; when they talk mental principles, they must face philosophers or psychologists; only when they practice contemplation are they truly at home. And a comprehensive-integral paradigm should be able to embrace, charitably, all three. That makes it different from traditional religion, traditional philosophy/psychology, and traditional science—because it includes and can potentially integrate all of them.

More recently, it is the *empirical* scientists who are trying to become theologians or even prophets. This is also an unflattering stance. But when empiric-scientists attempt to become theologians or religionists, they must be prepared to face the same type of stern questioning, this time coming from the contemplatives. If, for instance, the physicist says, "Modern physics shows us that *all* things are fundamentally One, just like the Tao or Brahman," then he is making a statement, not just about the physical realm, but about all realms, about ultimates and absolutes. The religionist is therefore able to say, "That is simply an *idea* presented by the eye of mind; where is your *method* for opening the eye of contemplation? Describe to me, in injunctive language, what you must *do* in order to *see*—directly see—this Oneness. If you cannot do that, you have committed a category error: you are merely talking about the contemplative/meditative realm using only the eye of mind." Notice the Zen Master can pass that test; we are still awaiting word from the physicist. For the simple fact is that one *can* be a good physicist *without* becoming mystically or transcendentally involved. One *can* master physics without mastering enlightenment. But one *cannot* become a good Zen Master without becoming a mystic. That the in-depth and heartfelt study of physics leads some physicists (perhaps 10 percent or so) to a mystical world view tells us something nice about, not physics per se, but about those sensitive and noble physicists. Those sensitive physicists, however, often then make the category error of claiming that physical data per se prove transcendental states—an understandable but messy confusion, and one clearly refuted by the number of great physicists who are *not* mystics.

Thus, it is my feeling that the most important thing a comprehensive or integral paradigm can do is try to avoid the category errors: confusing the eye of flesh with the eye of mind with the eye of contemplation (or, in the more detailed models, such as the five-level Vedanta, avoid confusing any of the levels). When someone asks "Where is your empirical proof for transcendence?" we need not panic. We explain the instrumental methods of our knowledge and invite him or her to check it out personally. Should that person accept and complete the injunctive strand, then that person is capable of becoming part of the community of those whose eye is adequate to the transcendent realm. Prior to that time, that person is inadequate to form an opinion about transcendental concerns. We are then no more obliged to account to that person than is a physicist to one who refuses to learn mathematics.

We of today are in an extraordinarily favorable position: we can preserve the utterly unique position of possessing and championing a balanced and integrated approach to reality—a "new and higher" paradigm—one that can include the eye of flesh and the eye of reason and the eye of contemplation. And I think that the history of thought will eventually prove that to do more than that is impossible, to do less than that, disastrous.

2

The Problem of Proof

G IVEN EACH OF THE THREE modes of knowing—sensory, symbolic, and spiritual—the question naturally arises, as it certainly did in the history of philosophy, psychology, and religion, how can we be sure that the "knowledge" gained by any of these modes is valid? Or conversely—and more significantly—on what grounds may we reject any "knowledge" as likely being erroneous?

DATA AND KNOWLEDGE

By data I simply mean any *directly apprehended experience* (using "experience" in the broad sense, as prehension or awareness). As William James explained it, using as an example the perception of a piece of paper, "If our own private vision of the paper be considered in abstraction [or bracketed off] from every other event, then the paper seen and the seeing of it are only two names for one indivisible fact which, properly named, is *the datum, the phenomenon, or the experience.*"[67] And I am saying (and will try to demonstrate) that there are legitimate data—*direct apprehensions*—to be found in the realms of flesh, mind, and spirit; that is, real data in these *real* object domains, object domains that we can call *sensibilia, intelligibilia,* and *transcendelia.* It is the existence of these real object domains (sensory, mental, and spiritual) and their real data that *grounds* the knowledge quest and assures its consummation.

Notice that what especially defines a datum, in any realm, is not its simplicity or atomism, but its immediate givenness, its direct apprehension. A datum is not necessarily the smallest bit of experience in any realm, but the immediate display of experience disclosed when one is introduced to that realm. Thus, for example, when James talks about data in the realm of sensibilia, he uses as examples the direct experience of a piece of paper, a tiger, the walls of a room, and so on: whatever is immediately *given* in present sensibilia. Now that sensory data may in fact be very atomistic—the dark-adapted human retina, for instance, can register a *single* photon, and in that immediate register, the photon (or whatever it is) is the sensory datum. But the datum can also be very large and fairly complex—a sunset, the sky at night, the view from a hilltop, and so on. The point is not so much size or complexity; the point is immediateness or givenness in direct experience. (Many philosophers, in fact, refer to this direct apprehension of sensibilia as *intuition*—James and Kant, for example. But this sensory intuition is not to be confused with spiritual intuition, or even mental intuition, as Kant was careful to point out. When I use "intuition" in this broad sense, it simply means direct and immediate apprehension in *any* realm, and that direct apprehension, experience, or intuition is what most defines a datum.)

Exactly the same thing applies to the data of intelligibilia and transcendelia. In the realm of intelligibilia, for instance, one's present, given, immediate mental experience, whatever its nature, is a *datum,* a *mental* datum (or series of them). The datum may be rather brief or atomistic—a simple image, a fleeting thought—or it may be rather complex and sustained—the understanding of the overall meaning of a sentence, the grasp of an idea, a sustained memory. In either case the mental datum is simply the immediate gestaltlike mental experience, whatever its "size" or complexity or duration. Even if you are thinking of some past event or anticipating tomorrow's actions, the thought *itself* is a *present* event immediately perceived and experienced—that is, it is a *datum.*

In the field of language, analysts often speak of the present and direct apprehension of symbols as "linguistic intuition." Once you have mastered a particular language, you simply know (or mentally "intuit") the meaning of its common words. And even when you are learning the language, you still directly experience the symbols *themselves* as and when you think them, even if you don't yet know their meaning. The point is that, either way, you see them with the mind's eye, and that "seeing" per se is direct and immediate. If meaning then follows, the perception of *that* is now the direct and immediate mental datum, and so on. Thus, whether of a letter, a word, a sentence, an idea—in each case the mental datum is simply the *immediate mental experience,* whatever it is.

Likewise, in the realm of transcendelia, a datum may be a single spiritual intuition, a mass illumination, a particular gnostic insight, or overall satori—all such transcendental data are directly perceived or intuited by the eye of contemplation. Here, too, not complexity but immediacy or givenness most defines a datum.

On further analysis or inquiry, of course, we might find that various data contain *other* data or flow into other data. For instance, James's piece of paper, itself a single sensory datum, contains four corners, each of which can become an individual sensory datum (by simply looking at them), and is itself part of a larger experience of paper-desk-room, another sensory datum. Likewise, the mentally perceived symbol "tree," itself a single mental datum, is composed of four letters, each of which can be apprehended as a separate mental datum. But the important point is that, for instance, when I apprehend the meaning, the immediate datum, of the word "tree," I do *not* do so by adding up letters. The mental datum or meaning or linguistic intuition of the word "tree" is not given to me as four fast additions, *t* plus *r* plus *e* plus *e*. The mental datum "tree" is a direct, nonreducible, gestaltlike apprehension, and it is that direct apprehension or intuition, the present, immediate, given experience, whatever it is, in whatever realm, that essentially defines a datum—a sensory datum, a mental datum, a transcendental datum.

THE MEANING OF "EXPERIENCE" AND "EMPIRICISM"

We have said that a datum is any immediate experience in any of the three realms—sensory, mental, or transcendental. But right here we are faced with an extreme semantic and philosophic difficulty, because traditionally it was the empiricists who insisted that all knowledge must be grounded in experience, and they claimed the rationalists as well as the mystics had no such grounding. And further, although empiricism in that stance is very reductionistic, many new schools of humanistic and transpersonal psychology and philosophy dearly wish and loudly claim to be empirical. Obviously, the words "experience" and "empirical" are being used in several different ways, and this has generated certain grave misunderstandings.

The core of the problem is that there is a great ambiguity in the meaning of the word "experience." It can be used to mean only sensory experience (as many empiricists do), but it can also be used to cover virtually all modes of awareness and consciousness. For instance, there is a sense in which I *experience* not only my own sensations and perceptions (sensibilia) but also my own ideas, thoughts, and concepts (intelligibilia)—I see them with the mind's eye, I *experience* my train of thoughts, my personal ideals, my imaginative displays. These are subtler experiences than a clunk on the head, but they are nonetheless experiential, or directly and immediately perceived by the mind's eye. Likewise, there is a sense in which I can *experience* spirit—with the eye of contemplation or *gnosis,* I directly and immediately apprehend and experience spirit *as* spirit, the realm of transcendelia.

In all these broader senses, "experience" is simply synonymous with direct apprehension, immediate givenness, intuition—sensory, mental, and spiritual.

Stated thus, there is indeed a sense in which all knowledge is grounded in experience (as empiricists claim)—but not in *sensory* experience (which they also claim). Thus, various *a priori* or rational truths are those I *experience* in the mental realm but not in the sensory realm (e.g., mathematics). And transcendental truths are those I *experience* in the spiritual realm but not in the mental or sensory realms (e.g., satori). And in that sense, there are all sorts of knowledge outside of sensory experience, but none that is finally outside of *experience* in general. Sensibilia, intelligibilia, and transcendelia can all be open to direct and immediate experiential apprehension or intuition, and those apprehensions constitute the data of the knowledge quest in each of those domains.

Empiricism, then, rightly claims that all valid knowledge must be grounded in experience, but it then reduces the meaning of experience solely to *sensibilia.* Empiricism wishes to derive my experience of reason solely from my experience of sensations—that is, to claim that there is no experience of reason that is not first found in my experience of sensations. And that attempt has a type of strong attraction ("We want *empirical* data!") simply because one can easily but vaguely confuse sensory experience (pure empiricism) with experience *in general.* Empiricism sounds like it's making such good sense, being so pragmatic and all, but only because it confuses two basic propositions; it says all real knowledge must be experiential, which is true enough using experience in the broad sense, but then it can't resist the temptation to say that experience is really or basically *sensory* experience—and that is the great disaster.

Let me repeat that one of the reasons that ambiguity can and does occur is that "experience" can be used in the broad sense ("direct awareness"), but then also given a common and much narrower meaning: *sensory* perceptions. By consciously or unconsciously juxtaposing those meanings, the modern-day empiricist can ridicule the idea of knowledge outside experience (so far, so good), but then *limit* experience to its sensory-empiric modes (reductionistic fallacy, category error, etc.). And to completely confound matters, many of the new humanistic and transpersonal psychologists, working mostly with intelligibilia and transcendelia, and correctly realizing that their data is indeed experiential (in the broad sense), and wishing equal recognition as "real sciences," simply *call* their endeavors and their data "empirical," only to find that strict empirical scientists simply reject their results, sometimes with undisguised mocking.

To avoid these ambiguities, in this chapter I will usually restrict the term "empirical" to its original meaning: knowledge grounded in sensory experience (sensibilia), although the context will tell. Classical empiricism was an attempt to reduce all higher knowledge and experience to sensory knowledge and experience. The emphasis on direct experience (in the broad sense) was the great and enduring contribution of the empiricists; the reduction of experience to sensory experience was their great and enduring crime.

THE VERIFICATION PROCEDURES

Each of the three modes of knowing, then, has access to real (experiential) data in its respective realm—to sensible data, intelligible data, and transcendental data—and the data in each case is marked by its immediate or intuitive apprehension. (The data might indeed be mediated, but the moment of apprehension is itself immediate.) This intuitive immediateness, as James knew, must be the defining characteristic of data and our only *starting* point, or else we end up in an infinite regress.

The problem then becomes, given my immediate apprehension or intuition of any datum, how can I be reasonably sure that the perception itself is not mistaken? And that brings us to the notion of adequate verification (or nonverification) principles for the gathering of data in each of the modes of knowing involved. But two points should be kept equally in mind as we discuss these data-gathering and verification procedures: (1) the *actual methodologies* of data accumulation and verification differ drastically in all three modes, but (2) the *abstract principles* of data accumulation and verification are essentially *identical* in each. Exactly what that means, and the reason I emphasize both, will become increasingly obvious as we proceed.

First, the abstract principles of data accumulation and verification. As we suggested in the last chapter, valid data accumulation in any realm has three basic strands:

1. *Instrumental injunction.* This is always of the form, "If you want to *know* this, *do* this."
2. *Intuitive apprehension.* This is a cognitive grasp, prehension, or immediate *experience* of the object domain (or aspect of the object domain) addressed by the injunction; that is, the immediate *data*-apprehension.
3. *Communal confirmation.* This is a checking of results (apprehensions or data) with others who have adequately completed the injunctive and apprehensive strands.

Science, of course, is often taken as the model of genuine knowledge, and the philosophy of science is now dominated by three major approaches, which are generally viewed as mutually exclusive: that of empiricism, Thomas Kuhn, and Sir Karl Popper. The strength of empiricism, as we have seen, is its demand that all genuine knowledge be grounded in experiential evidence; and if we use evidence and experience in the general sense, this is a grounding that I firmly share. But evidence and data are not simply lying around waiting to be perceived by all and sundry, which is where Kuhn enters the picture.

Thomas Kuhn, in one of the greatly misunderstood ideas of our time, pointed out that normal science proceeds most fundamentally by way of what he called *paradigms* or *exemplars.* A paradigm is not merely a concept, it is an *actual practice,* an injunction, a technique taken as an exemplar for generating data. And Kuhn's point is that genuine scientific knowledge is grounded in paradigms, exemplars, injunctions, which bring forth new data. New injunctions disclose new data, and this is why Kuhn maintained *both* that science is progressive and cumulative *and* that it also shows certain breaks or discontinuities (new injunctions bring forth new data). Kuhn, in other words, is highlighting the importance of strand #1 in the knowledge quest, namely, that data are not simply lying around waiting for anybody to see, but rather are brought forth by valid injunctions.

The knowledge brought forth by valid injunctions is indeed genuine knowledge precisely because paradigms disclose data, they do not merely invent it. And the validity of this data is demonstrated by the fact that bad data can be rebuffed, which is where Popper enters the picture.

Sir Karl Popper's approach emphasizes the importance of falsifiability: genuine knowledge must be open to disproof, or else it is simply dogma in disguise. And, as we will see, the three strands fully acknowledge the falsifiability principle *in every domain,* sensibilia to intelligibilia to transcendelia.

Thus, this integral approach acknowledges and incorporates the moments of truth in each of these important contributions to the human knowledge quest (evidence, Kuhn, and Popper), but without the need to reduce these truths to sensibilia alone, as I will now try to demonstrate.

We can now give some examples of these three strands as they appear in the realms of sensibilia, intelligibilia, and transcendelia. As we do so, I will try to emphasize that although the same three abstract strands operate in each, the actual or concrete methodologies are quite different (owing to the different structures of the data or object domains themselves).

EMPIRIC-ANALYTIC INQUIRY

In the realm of sensibilia—empirical or sensorimotor occasions—if you want to know, for instance, whether the volume of hydrogen gas released by the electrolysis of water is twice that of the volume of oxygen gas, then you must (1) learn to perform electrolysis, build the equipment itself, run the experiment, collect the gases (injunctions, exemplars); (2) look at and measure the volumes of the gases collected (apprehensions); and (3) compare and confirm the data with other researchers. These mundane examples could be repeated indefinitely—the point is simply that every empirical scientist, in doing actual research (i.e., collecting data), follows *injunctions,* apprehends *data* (either directly or via extended-sensory instrumentation), and then *communally* checks his or her results. That is how the very data base of empiric-analytic science is built. And any data that is obedient to *all three strands* is provisionally accepted as valid.

The key point, however, is that those three strands contain a way to *reject* data that are apparently erroneous. For, as Karl Popper has made very clear, if there is no way whatsoever to at least theoretically disprove a datum, then that datum cannot enter cognitive status—if there is no way whatsoever to disprove a point, then there is no way to prove it either. The three strands provide a potential "disproof mechanism," and this is the key to their success.

The problem is this: Although it is the defining nature of data (in any realm) that, when they present themselves to awareness, they do so in an immediate, intuitive, and apparently self-validating fashion, nonetheless that presentation (the apprehension) depends upon a prior *injunction* or *instrument*, and it is sometimes the case that one's cognitive instruments, whether scientific, personal, or spiritual, are occasionally less than perfected. To give a simple example: If I develop cataracts, I might see two moons—the data itself is erroneous because the instrument is blurred. The data is still immediate, direct, and evident—it really looks like two moons—but it is nonetheless misleading. The three strands help correct this. In this example, I turn to friends and say, "Do you see two moons?" My empirical data, my sensibilia, are accordingly rebuffed. Thus, in empirical inquiry, a "bad" fact (such as in a poorly run experiment) will be *rebuffed,* not only by other facts, but by the community of investigators, and it is this *potential rebuff* that constitutes the falsifiability principle of Popper.

Because the same three strands operate in all modes of valid cognitive inquiry—empirical, rational, and transcendental—the same rebuff mechanism is at work in each (as we will see), and it is this rebuff mechanism that prevents the true knowledge quest, *in any domain,* from degenerating into mere dogmatism and blind-faith embrace. In other words, what specifically marks empiric-analytic inquiry is not its "superior methodology" and its supposedly unique "verification/rejection" procedure—for that, we will see, can and should be applied to *all* realms. No, what marks empiric-analytic inquiry is simply that the only *data* with which it operates is *sensibilia*—the eye of flesh or its extensions. Empiric-analytic inquiry, of course, uses mental and rational reflection, but those operations are grounded in, and always subservient to, sensibilia.

It is sometimes objected that empirical sciences, such as physics or biology, often work with objects or events that in fact cannot be experienced by the senses (or their extensions). For example, when Mendel proposed the existence of genes, the genes themselves were never seen. Likewise, the atomic/molecular theory was proposed by Dalton without his ever actually *seeing* molecules. The point, however, is as James said: "Even if science supposed a molecular architecture beneath the smooth whiteness of the paper, that architecture itself could only be defined as the stuff of a farther possible experience, a vision, say, of certain vibrating particles with which our acquaintance with the paper would terminate if it were prolonged by magnifying artifices not yet known."[67] Thus, decades after Mendel proposed the existence of genes, electron microscopes delivered actual pictures of DNA molecules. The "gene substances" were apprehended by an extended sensory eye, and the existence of genetic material became an empirical *datum* (and not just a theory). It is true that the farther we go into submolecular realms, the fuzzier become our apprehensions, but the point is that an empiric-analytic proposition has meaning only insofar as it grounds itself in sensible or potentially sensible data. That, as we saw, was the great contribution of Galileo, Kepler, and Newton, and as far as it goes, that grounding—empiric-analytic inquiry—is just right.

The problem, we have seen, is that empiric-analytic science soured into scientism by refusing to admit as real any data other than sensibilia, and that, indeed, is what is now called "the crime of Galileo" (perhaps unfairly to the man himself, who never seemed to intend such ugly reductionism). And while we certainly must make ample room for empiric-analytic inquiry, we by no means must restrict our cognition to that mode alone. For next up, in the hierarchy of the knowledge quest, is inquiry into *intelligibilia*.

MENTAL-PHENOMENOLOGICAL INQUIRY

The same three abstract strands operate in the gathering of valid linguistic, noetic, or mental-phenomenological *data,* although of course the actual methodology is quite different because the object domain is that of intelligibilia, not mere sensibilia. The "things" we are looking at here are *thoughts*—their structure and their form—as they immediately display themselves to the inward mental eye.

Take, as an initial example, the field of mathematics, for there we find the same three basic strands. As G. Spencer Brown points out: "The primary form of mathematical communication is not description, but injunction [strand #1]. In this respect it is comparable with practical art forms like cookery, in which the taste of a cake, although literally indescribable, can be conveyed to a reader in the form of a set of injunctions called a recipe. . . . Even natural science [i.e., empiric-analytic] appears to be dependent on injunctions. The professional initiation of the man of science consists not so much in reading the proper textbooks [although that is also an injunction], as in obeying injunctions such as 'look down that microscope' [as in the example given in the first chapter]. But it is not out of order for men of [empirical] science, having looked down the microscope [#1], now to describe to each other, and to discuss among themselves [#3], what they have seen [with the eye of flesh; #2], and to write papers and textbooks describing it. Similarly, it is not out of order for mathematicians, each having obeyed a given set of injunctions [e.g., imagine two parallel lines meeting at infinity; picture the cross-section of a trapezoid; take the square of the hypotenuse, etc.; #1], to describe to each other, and to discuss among themselves [#3], what they have seen [with the eye of mind; #2], and to write textbooks describing it. But in each case, the description is dependent upon, and secondary to, the set of injunctions having been obeyed first."[25] The great difference, as noted, is that in the empiric sciences, the data (or their macro effects) can be seen or experienced with the eye of flesh (or its extensions); in rational-phenomenology, including mathematics, the *data* itself is seen or experienced only with the eye of mind. The injunctions address a different object domain, that of intelligibilia, not sensibilia.

The same three strands are operative, to give another example, in classical phenomenology (e.g., Husserl). For one begins phenomenology with an *injunction,* which is to "bracket out" extraneous events and various preconceptions and thus approach a direct, immediate, and intuitive *apprehension* of the object domain of mental phenomena *as* mental phenomena, and these apprehensions are then shared and confirmed (or rebuffed) via interpersonal communication and interpretation.

The starting point for such mental-phenomenology is simply this: What is the very nature of a *mental* act, a *symbolic* occasion, a *linguistic* understanding, as it discloses itself intuitively or immediately to the mind's eye? According to phenomenology, if one directly inquires into a mental act—an image, a symbol, a word, as one actually uses it—one will find that it intrinsically possesses *intentionality* or *meaning;* it has a native form or structure; and it is semiotic or symbolic. For, unlike the objects of sensibilia—rocks, photons, trees, and so on, which do not themselves possess meaning (in the sense that they do not symbolically represent or point to something other than themselves)—the objects of intelligibilia intrinsically possess meaning, value, or intentionality (i.e., a mental symbol or act carries the power to represent or point to some other object or act). And the way you discover such *meaning* is via mental inquiry or interpretation, not sensory impact.

To give a simple example, there is no *empirical*-scientific proof for the meaning of *Hamlet*. It is a mental-symbolic production and can thus be understood or apprehended only by a mental act—sensory evidence is almost entirely worthless. *Hamlet* is not composed of electrons, molecules, wood, or zinc; it is composed of *units of meaning*—mental data—which disclose themselves not as sensibilia but as intelligibilia.

Likewise, phenomenology discloses that intelligibilia are not only meaningful and intentional, they are intrinsically *intersubjective*. For example, if you issue a symbol to me (say, the word *apple*), and I intuitively understand or grasp that symbol, then the symbol—once literally "in" your head or mind—is now also literally *in* my mind: we are directly and intimately linked in an *intersubjective* occasion, an interpersonal exchange. In communication and discourse, many minds may step into the union of shared symbols, entering into each other in a way that greatly transcends mere bodily contact or intercourse. And notice that meaningful communication is no mere chaos or random babbling—it has *structure,* it has *rules,* it follows a *logic* or *form. It is a very real territory with very real data*—but data that are hidden to mere sensory apprehension.

All of that—intentionality, value, meaning, intersubjective structure—is essentially true of any mental phenomena, and *overall mental-phenomenological investigation* is simply concerned with the nature, structure, and meaning of intelligibilia—with language, syntax, communication, discourse, logic, value, intentionality, ideas, meaning, concepts, images, symbols, semiotics—as they appear in psychology, philosophy, sociology, and the "human (i.e., mental) sciences" in general. And all of that, basically, we refer to as "mental-phenomenology."

Thus, via injunctive inquiry in general mental-phenomenology, one discovers those facts or data that apply to the sphere of *intelligibilia,* the mental or subjective realm per se, and in that sense the facts are subjective facts. *But that does not mean mere individual whim,* as empiricists like to claim. First of all, these phenomenological apprehensions are not "mere values" or "just ideas" as *opposed* to "real facts," because in the mental realm, values and ideas *are* the real or immediate facts or data *directly* disclosed. Second, these phenomenological apprehensions can be *tested* by striking them against the community of other minds who have followed the proper injunctions. In that case, a "bad" phenomenological apprehension will simply not mesh with the ground of other phe-nomenological facts, as *embedded and disclosed in intersubjective consensus*. This "bad datum" or "poor apprehension" is thus *rebuffed* by a reality that is very real and very lawful—the domain of intelligibilia and its *intersubjective structures*—just as a bad empiric fact will not mesh with, and is rebuffed by, the ground of other sensible facts.

Let us take, as a simple example, the discovery of Egyptian hiero-glyphics. What we have here is a mysterious language—some form of hidden intelligibilia—inscribed on stone tablets. Now empiric-analytic inquiry can tell us how old the stone is, what it is made of, how much it weighs, and so on. But it is of precisely no use in figuring out the intelligi-bilia of the hieroglyphics themselves, or what they *mean*. In order to determine that, I must follow a set of mental injunctions—I must begin to look for the inner structure of the symbols with my mind's eye; I must experiment, try out, various combinations of symbols to see if the right combination, the right injunction, leads to a meaningful apprehension of their possible meanings. If a certain combination looks correct, I still must check it with other combinations—a promising meaning might ac-tually be rebuffed by other meanings down the line, because language does indeed possess intersymbolic structure or syntax, and a bad linguis-tic apprehension simply will not mesh with the other linguistic appre-hensions. Finally, I must check my overall results with others similarly qualified. (And that, of course, is precisely what Jean-François Champol-lion and Thomas Young did with the Rosetta stone.)

The point is simply that, although we are working with a largely sub-jective production—a language—nonetheless that doesn't mean I can pop out any ole interpretation that suits me, because intelligibilia possess intersymbolic and intersubjective *structures* that will themselves *rebuff* erroneous claims. And that is fundamentally true of the meaning of any intelligibilia—the meaning of language, of psychological goals and drives, of logic and syntax, of intentions and values. Although the truths in these domains are not *empirically* verifiable or even obvious, nonethe-less they are by no means based on wishful thinking, subjective bias, or nonverifiable opinion. In determining the truth or facts of intelligibilia, as Ogilvy so clearly explains, "not just any wild hypothesis will do. Nor will a simple negation [i.e., "there's no way to tell since it can't be empirically determined"]. Only a community of interpreters can gener-ate the intersubjective basis for a set of criteria that might validate the truth claims forming a coherent interpretation. The moment of truth is saved from a subjective relativism that renders the idea of truth absurd.

Only *some* interpretations make sense. Their sensibleness is a function of their satisfying certain rules for good interpretation, rules that in some cases are no different from the rules for good [empirical] science, e.g., elegance and simplicity, freedom from subjective bias [or, as I would put it, obedience to the three strands]."[87]

Empiricists, of course, scoff at the notion of any verification procedures not grounded in sensory evidence. They call all such nonempirical or nonsensory investigations (subjective psychology, idealistic phenomenology, ontology, etc.) by the derisive term "metaphysical," and say they are without reliable, reproducible, and verifiable grounding. But they do so only because they have overlooked the intrinsic structures of *intelligibilia* itself. This is indeed odd, because the fact that empiricists *talk* to each other, and repeatedly *understand* each other, rests precisely on the real existence of a lawful, reproducible, intersubjective realm of intelligibilia. And overall mental-phenomenology (in any of its various branches, philosophical, psychological, linguistic, sociological, etc.) is simply the science of discovering and reproducing those meanings, patterns, structures, and laws. It is indeed meta-physical or meta-empirical, but hardly in a pejorative sense.

And so, when even the empiricists frame their hypotheses, formulate their theories, organize their sensory data, and offer systematic explanations, what exactly is the mode of inquiry that guides *that* particular aspect of their endeavors? Rational-phenomenology, of course. And yet it is that very "meta-physical" mode itself that the empiricist or scientician then numbly uses to claim it has no real existence, to claim it is not "really real," not dependable, not meaningful, not verifiable, and just a bunch of metaphysical nonsense. Might as well write a dozen books claiming there is no such thing as writing.

The point is that there are mental-phenomenological facts, truths, or data, but in order to be recognized as such, they too must observe all three strands—and any apprehension failing that overall test is soundly rebuffed by the very *structure* of the intersubjective realm of intelligibilia (the other mental facts themselves and the community of interpreters). This constitutes, for intelligibilia, an *experimental test*—the accumulation and verification of data—that is just as stringent and just as demanding as the empiric test, because *both* rest on the same three strands. The difference lies not in the abstract methodology, but in the actual *territory* being mapped (sensibilia versus intelligibilia). Of course, the empiric test is considerably easier because it is performed by a subject on an object, whereas mental-phenomenology is performed by a subject (or symbol) on or with other subjects (or symbols)—much more diffi-cult. The object domain here is *of* subjective or intersubjective "objects" (intelligibilia), not merely objective "objects" (sensibilia).

And there we can already see one of the profound differences between empiric-analytic inquiry and mental-phenomenological inquiry. In the empiric-analytic, one is using the symbolic mind to map or mirror the *pre*symbolic world. But in mental-phenomenology, one is using the sym-bolic mind to map or mirror the symbolic mind itself. One is using sym-bols to mirror or reflect other symbols, which themselves can reflect the reflection, and so on in a "hermeneutic circle" of meaning that two minds or symbols co-create whenever they inquire into each other. The most obvious example of this is simple verbal communication; when we talk, I try to grasp your meaning and you mine, and so around we go in the intersubjective circle. When one symbol probes another symbol, the latter can *respond* in a way that presymbolic objects (rocks, electrons, planets) cannot: in a *proactive* and not merely reactive fashion. Thus, mental-phenomenology is not so much a starkly objective affair as it is an intersubjective mesh, and it is that mesh that *grounds* the phenome-nological knowledge quest. An empiric proposition is true if it more or less accurately mirrors the sensory, biomaterial, objective world. But a mental-phenomenological proposition is true, not if it matches any set of sensibilia, but if it meshes with an intersubjective structure of meaning (or, as in mathematics, an intersymbolic logic). Thus, for example, in mathematical theorems (i.e., hypotheses with logical injunctions), we do not look to empirical facts for proof (or disproof); the *facts* here are units of intersymbolic intelligibilia. A theorem is true if it conforms to the consensus of intersymbolic logic, not if it conforms to sensory evi-dence. Not mind on matter but mind on mind!

We can put all of these important differences between empiric-ana-lytic and mental-phenomenological inquiry in several different ways:

1. Empiric-analytic inquiry is performed by a subject on an object; mental-phenomenological inquiry is performed by a subject (or symbol) on or with other subjects (or symbols).

2. In empiric-analytic inquiry, the referent of conceptual knowledge is other than conceptual knowledge; in mental-phenomenology, the ref-erent of conceptual knowledge is the process of conceptual knowledge itself (or the structure of ideas, language, communication, intentions, etc.). More simply:

3. The *facts* (data) of empiric-analytic inquiry are things; the *facts* (data) of mental-phenomenology are thoughts.

4. In empiric-analytic inquiry, the propositions themselves are intentional (symbolic), but the data are nonintentional (presymbolic); in mental-phenomenology, *both* the propositions and the data are intentional and symbolic.

5. Empiric-analytic inquiry works predominantly with things in *nature*; mental-phenomenology works predominantly with symbols in *history*. "Among the most important premises would be the distinction between nature [disclosed in or as sensibilia] and human history [disclosed in or as intelligibilia]. For after all, is not the distinction between voluntary action [mental intention] and mechanical behavior [physical causality] another version of the distinction between human freedom and natural necessity? History is precisely the record of our escape from natural necessity. History is the chronicle of *actions* [not just reactions], intentional plots with beginnings, middles, and ends. The logic of the concepts of space, time, and mass [sensibilia] is significantly different from the logic of concepts like success, honor, and duty [intelligibilia]: their presupposed contexts are *non*natural [i.e., historical]. The inventions of reason transcend the uniform regularities of the natural laws. Where the very phenomena in question have to do not with the articulations achieved by natural evolution but by human history, the language used in formulating the creators' *intentions* plays a constituitive role; they are *historical* terms in the sense that their meanings are not *given* by nature but are instead successively constituted by the ways they are used [i.e., historically]. The criteria for satisfying such intentions are not reducible to ahistorical descriptions of natural phenomena"[87]—as, for example, the historical production of Egyptian hieroglyphics cannot be reduced to its empirical sensibilia.

But perhaps the most important distinction, and certainly one of the easiest to use, is this:

6. Empiric-analytic inquiry is a *monologue*—a symbolizing inquirer looks at a nonsymbolizing occasion; mental-phenomenology, however, is a *dialogue*—a symbolizing inquirer looks at other symbolizing occasions. The paradigm of empiric-analytic inquiry is, "I see the rock"; the paradigm of mental-phenomenological inquiry is, "I talk to you and vice versa." Empiric-analytic inquiry can proceed *without talking* to the object of its investigation—no empirical scientist talks to electrons, plastic, molecules, protozoa, ferns, or whatever, because he is studying preverbal entities. But the very field of mental-phenomenological inquiry is *communicative exchange* or intersubjective and intersymbolic relationships (language and logic), and this mental-phenomenology depends in

large measure on talking to and with the subject of investigation. And any science that *talks to* its subject of investigation is not empirical but phenomenological, not monologic but dialogic.

7. In short, empiric-analytic inquiry accepts as its essential data sensibilia; mental-phenomenology accepts as its essential data intelligibilia.

SOME EXAMPLES IN PSYCHOLOGY

Let me give a few examples of these different methodologies as they operate in the field of psychology. Exclusive empiric-analytic inquiry, when applied to the human being, produces classical behaviorism. In its most typical form (e.g., Skinner), behaviorism accepts as data only sensibilia, or objectively perceived occasions. The mind *as* mind, in fact, is all but dismissed, and the organism is viewed as a rather complex but totally *reactive* mechanism. And, indeed, behaviorism can and does collect all sorts of sensible-objective data—data on reinforcement timetables, conditioned responses, positive and negative reinforcements, and so on. And in its classical form, behaviorism does not even really care to *talk* to the person involved. They do talk, of course, because they are human, but in the model itself there's no ultimate reason to do so; if you want a particular response from the person—regardless of whether the person wants it—you simply start reinforcing the desired reaction. In this model, the person really has no choice but to reactively follow the reinforcement, because in this model, the person has no mind *as* mind, no free will, no pro-action, no choice. Behaviorism, that is, is basically a monologue, or a monological science—it is empiric-analytic. And this model works very well with subhuman animals (and the subhuman levels of the human animal), because animals are indeed largely presymbolic, preintentional, prehistorical, and prevolitional—all occasions that can be perceived and studied empirically.

But, of course, the classical behavioristic model works rather poorly with human beings, because human beings possess, *between* the sensory stimuli and the sensory response, a *mental structure,* and that structure obeys laws whose actions are not of sensibilia but intelligibilia. As classical behaviorism began to even vaguely acknowledge this fact, it tried to accommodate its model by introducing the notion of "intervening variables" (e.g., Hull)—that is, between the sensorimotor stimulus and the sensorimotor response, there exist "intervening" or cognitive variables, such as *expectation* and *value* (Hull, Tolman). While that is true enough, the empiric-analytic methodology of behaviorism was ill-equipped to investigate these intervening variables, because empiric inquiry works with objective data, yet the intervening variables—the intelligibilia—are not so much objective as intersubjective. And the moment one starts investigating intersubjective phenomena, one is immediately ushered into the realm of discourse, dialogue, communication, introspection, hermeneutics, phenomenology, and so on. And trying to handle these mental-phenomenological *data* with empiric-analytic methods—by, for instance, calling them "verbal behavior"—is about as effective as trying to discover the meaning of *War and Peace* by analyzing the objective paper and ink by which it is expressed.

This is in no way whatsoever to deny the limited usefulness of empiric-analytic inquiry in human behavior. Not only should human sensibilia be investigated empirically, but also to the extent that intelligibilia (or transcendelia) alter the objective world, those alterations can and should be investigated empirically. But empiricism alone misses the essence of even these alterations. Let me give perhaps the most difficult example, just to show that the point can be made: an artwork, a painting—say, Goya's *May 3, 1808*. By several of our criteria, the artwork can be studied empirically. For one, the composition of the paint, the date of the canvas, and so on can be empirically analyzed, and the sensibilia of the artwork itself—its colors, lines, surfaces, aesthetics—can be apprehended empirically. For another, the artwork itself is indeed an *objective* entity. And for yet another, I can look at the painting and study it *without talking* to Goya (after all, he's dead).

But if I wish also to know if Goya was trying to tell me something, to speak to me, as it were, to communicate not just sensibilia but intelligibilia, then empirical impact and study no longer avail. The canvas and paint are still "objects out there," but they are *formed* and *informed* by human intelligibilia, by the human creative mind; they embody in objective form the *intentions* of a human *subject,* and those *intentions* are not given empirically or sensorily. Even though the work now *exists* in the objective-sensory world, it cannot be *grasped* by that world.

To ascertain those intentions and meanings, then, I must try, somehow, to enter Goya's mind, to "talk" to him—I must use historic-phenomenology, hermeneutics, dialogic technique. Of course, I can't directly talk to Goya; were he alive, we could talk about the painting's meaning, share in discourse the common sentiments it evokes in the human mind and spirit. That being impossible, I must—as in historic-hermeneutic phenomenology—attempt to recreate, via the rules of good interpretation, Goya's intentions. I must look at the *historical* period and mood in which Goya painted; I must attempt to grasp and interpret his personal-subjective intentions; and I must ground these interpretations in a community of similarly skilled. Otherwise, I will know only *my* intentions as I talk to myself.

Proceeding thus historically, phenomenologically, and dialogically, several of the intelligible and not just aesthetic-sensory meanings of the painting begin unequivocally to emerge. Goya was trying to tell me something. The painting was done during the period of Napoleonic invasions, of civil war, of firing squads, all of which appalled Goya. The painting is brilliant and frenzied in its execution; it constitutes a vivid and vicious indictment of human barbarism and outrage at a world given over to war. Of course, there might be other meanings as well, and each person is free to bring personal reactions to it. But any ole meaning or interpretation will not do—this painting is *not* about the joys of war. We might not be able to determine *all* the legitimate meanings via hermeneutic-phenomenology, but we most certainly can determine some, perhaps most of them. And the empiricist who shuns such knowledge is simply one who, in this realm, would rather know nothing at all than half know much.

The point is that the human mind can indeed form and inform the *objective* world, but those objects then *embody* an *intelligibilia* that is not given to mere *sensibilia*. Thus, if we wish to understand not just sensibilia but intelligibilia, we must have recourse to a dialogic (dialogue) science—a general mental-phenomenology. This is especially so in psychology. And thus, once again, I will give the most difficult example: Freudian psychoanalysis.

In many ways Freud began with an empiric-analytic or merely physiological approach. But, as he would later put it, even if we figured out all the physiological aspects of awareness, "it would at most afford us an exact localization of the processes of consciousness and would give us no help toward understanding them."[46] It was the *meaning* of psychological data—their intentionality and their interpretation (interpretation of dreams, symptoms, etc.)—that Freud most wanted to study. That is, his approach, and his territory, was almost entirely mental-phenomenological, hermeneutical, and historical—the *history* here simply being the history and development of the person's own self-system (past fixations, traumas, repressions, etc.). Psychoanalytic consciousness is *historical* consciousness, a reconstruction and remembrance of personal history so as to understand its present influence. And, most importantly, psychoanalysis was a *dialogue*—it demanded *intersubjective discourse*—"the talking cure."

Further—and this, too, is central—Freud's major discovery was not a theory, but an *injunction* (an exemplar, a paradigm). The injunction was free association, which disclosed an object domain (data) hitherto largely ignored (unconscious primary processes). Free association surpassed Bernheim and Charcot's injunction, which was simple hypnosis. So important was the free association injunction that to this day it is called the "basic rule of psychoanalysis" ("Say whatever comes into your mind"). By using this injunction, Freud began to collect *data* on this new object domain, the unconscious primary process. And these data could be *checked* by anyone willing to follow the three strands: (1) take up the injunction to free associate; (2) note the resultant apprehensions or data; and (3) compare and contrast these data in a community of the similarly adequate.

Of course, one may disagree with some of Freud's interpretations and theories *about* the data (a distinction we will return to shortly), but the data itself was as generally sound as the injunctions allowed. Even Jung, who disagreed with Freud's overall theory, generally acknowledged his data. But a mental-phenomenological proposition, to be recognized as sound, must not only account for data, it must do so in a fashion capable of withstanding the fire of unrestrained communication and intersubjective discourse. The circle of subjectivity will eventually but soundly rebuff and dislodge those hypothetical forms that do not mesh with its intersubjective structures. Thus, some of Freud's theories have generally passed that test: the existence of unconscious processes, defensive or repressive mechanisms, narcissism, the importance of development, the existence of different types of psychological structures—these concepts are accepted by virtually all schools of modern psychology, regardless of the emphasis placed on them. Other of his theories have not meshed with informed intersubjective consensus and have thus dropped from the ongoing development of psychological theory—derivation of ego from id, overemphasis on sexual etiology, certain anthropological speculations, phallocentrism, and the exact nature of dreams. The same, of course, can be said for Jung, Wundt, Rank, Adler, and all the dialogical-phenomenological psychologists. Their data are not as gross (dense) as those of the empiricists or behaviorists, but neither are they "mere subjectivism," because there is an external corrective to undue subjective bias: the data *and* their discourse must be grounded in the intersubjective mesh of communicative intelligibilia.

The point is that such dialogical-phenomenological psychology, in its various forms, has today culminated in a most impressive body of sound data and sturdy theory. Among the most recent of such researchers, Piaget may especially be noted, because, again, what immediately distinguishes his system is the introduction of a new *injunction,* in this case, the "method clinique." This method is, of course, dialogical (Piaget despises mere empiricism), a method of investigating intersubjective exchange and discourse. The method clinique is basically a highly refined question-and-answer format, applied to individuals of various age groups (although it is of course altered for the preverbal age, from birth to two years, the period where the child lives mostly in the realm of sensibilia, not intelligibilia). Through this and other injunctive techniques, Piaget has accumulated a massive amount of mental-phenomenological *data,* which he has then subjected to a structural and developmental analysis. The results have largely been reproduced by others and in cross-cultural settings. Essentially the same type of dialogic approach has been used by Kohlberg, Loevinger, Broughton, Maslow, and others.

As for Freud's legacy, psychoanalysis itself has given way to psychoanalytic ego psychology, which is basically structural, developmental, and object-relations oriented (i.e., intersubjective), and *that* now meshes to a surprising degree with the general structural-developmental and cognitive schools of psychology, as many have clearly pointed out, including Piaget himself.

New injunctive techniques—projective techniques (Rorschach), thematic apperception (Murray), method clinique (Piaget), sentence completion (Loevinger), word association (Jung), moral dilemma (Kohlberg), and others—have produced a tremendous fund of phenomenological data, and there has been a marked acceleration of unrestrained communication and open discourse between different branches of psychology. The upshot of all this is that we have been steadily producing a decently coherent and fairly unified view of human psychological growth and development (at least in its personal stages), a view that is structural, developmental, phenomenological, interpersonal, and systems-functional. This view is, of course, far from complete, far from absolutely agreed upon in all details, far from proven in all aspects. The point, however, is that in a very impressive number of areas, there is a decent intersubjective consensus on fact, theory, and practice; a general and ongoing intersubjective movement of *intelligibilia* that not only produces repeatable data but rebuffs incongruent apprehensions and dislodges them from the ongoing sweep of the knowledge quest. This potential rebuff eloquently speaks for a real object domain (intelligibilia) that grounds inquiry and prevents the truths of the subjective realm from becoming merely subjective.

TRANSCENDENTAL INQUIRY

Let us now briefly return to the example of Zen and see how the three strands apply to the accumulation and verification of transcendental data or apprehensions.

At the very heart and foundation of Zen is not a theory, a dogma, a belief, or a proposition, but, as in any true knowledge quest, an *injunction,* an exemplar. This injunctive strand—zazen or contemplation—requires years of specialized training and critical discipline (a certified *roshi* or Zen teacher has to undergo from ten to twenty years of training). Zazen is simply the injunctive tool for possible cognitive disclosure, and a person must be *developmentally adequate* to that disclosure or there is, in fact, no disclosure, just as if you never learn to read you will never grasp *Macbeth.* We might say that meditative awareness or contemplation is to transcendelia as linguistic awareness or ratiocination is to intelligibilia—both the tool and the territory of cognitive disclosure. Not surprisingly, then, the zazen injunction is always of the form, "If you want to know whether there is Buddha Nature, you must first do this." That is *experimental* and *experiential* injunction.

After that strand is mastered, the investigator is opened to the second strand, that of intuitive apprehension of the object domain disclosed by the injunction, in this case, the *data* of the transcendental sphere. This intuitive apprehension—an immediate experiential impact or perception—is known in Zen as satori or *kensho,* both meaning, in essence, a "direct seeing into one's spiritual nature"—as perfectly direct as looking into the microscope to see the cell nucleus, with the all-important proviso in each case: only a trained eye need look.

Of course, the *referent* of transcendental perception, its very data, cannot be perceived with the mental or sensory eyes. Satori takes as its referent, not sensory objects out there and not mental subjects in here, but nondual spirit as such, a direct apprehension *of* spirit, *by* spirit, *as* spirit, an apprehension that unites subject and object by disclosing that which is prior to both, and an apprehension that therefore is quite beyond the capacities of objective-empirical or subjective-phenomenal cognition. As Hegel put it, this is "Spirit's return to itself on a higher plane, a level at which subjectivity and objectivity are united in one infinite act." This transcendental apperception arises when "I am aware, not simply of myself as a finite individual standing over against other finite persons [subjects] and things [objects], but rather of the Absolute as the ultimate and all-embracing reality. My knowledge, if I attain it, of Nature as the objective manifestation of the Absolute [sensibilia; Bonaventure's *vestigium* of God] and the Absolute as returning to itself as subjectivity in the *form* of Spirit [intelligibilia; Bonaventure's *imago* of God], existing in and through the spiritual life of man in history, is a movement in absolute consciousness [transcendelia], that is, in the self-knowledge of Being or the Absolute."[31]

This direct, immediate, intuitive apprehension of Being—not by the eye of flesh, and not by the eye of mind, but by the eye of contemplation—is satori, and it is simply the second strand in the knowledge quest of Zen. (Of course, at its summit, the eye of contemplation does not reveal data, plural, but datum, singular: The Datum, as it were, which is One Spirit as One Spirit. But there are all sorts of stages and sublevels of contemplation leading up to that summit, and all sorts of real but less than ultimate apprehensions along the way, as we will see throughout this book—and for all of those reasons, we speak generally of the eye of contemplation as disclosing the facts or data, plural, of the transcendental realm.)

But, of course, any particular individual's apprehensions of the transcendental object domain may be less than sound or initially mistaken, and therefore Zen, at every stage, has recourse to the third strand, which is careful confirmation by both the Zen Master and the community of participant meditators. This is no merely automatic pat on the back and mutual agreement society; it is a vigorous *test,* and it constitutes a potentially powerful rebuff and *nonverification* of any particular apprehension suffered in strand #2. Both in private, intense interaction with the Zen Master *(dokusan)* and in exacting public participation in rigorous tests of authenticity *(shosan), all* apprehensions are struck against the community of those whose cognitive eyes are adequate to the transcendent, and such apprehensions are soundly nonverified if they do not match the facts of transcendence as disclosed by the community of like-spirited (and this includes past apprehensions once judged, by the standards of the times, to be true but now subrated or found to be partial by more sophisticated experience). It is this explicit and conscientious adherence to *all three strands* of data accumulation and verification that makes Zen—and all similarly sophisticated contemplative inquiries—a sound and valid transcendental methodology.

PROOF OF GOD'S EXISTENCE

At its summit such transcendental methodology constitutes an experimental, verifiable, repeatable proof for the existence of Godhead, *as a fact*, as a penultimate Datum, but that proof is not—indeed, could not be—merely rational or logical (let alone empirical), a truth persistently overlooked by most theologians and religious philosophers from Aristotle to Anselm to Aquinas to Descartes to Leibniz (and down to today with Mortimer Adler, Ronald Green, Alvin Plantinga, Ross et al.)—although *never* overlooked by mystics and sages, from Plotinus ("You ask, how can we know the Infinite? I answer, not by reason") to Pascal ("The heart has its reasons, which reason cannot know") to Nagarjuna (whose dialectic remains the most powerful demonstration of reason's inadequacy in the face of the Divine).

The problem with all these rational "proofs" of God's existence—the cosmological, the teleological, the ontological, the moral, and so on—is that the circle is trying to prove the sphere, the tail is trying to wag the dog, and the results in all cases are rather less than convincing, as philosophers from Russell to Mackie (not to mention Nagarjuna et al.) have amply demonstrated. I will not bore the reader with a point-by-point critique of all these rational "proofs"—able philosophers have already done so. I will simply say that, as one who does believe Spirit exists, as one *already* predisposed, I find the *rational* proofs for such, especially considering the stakes, to be anemic in the extreme (and that includes Ross's supposedly "invincible" update of Anselm-Scotus's ontic "proof"), and I think it quite true, as many philosophers have labored to show, that such arguments can be adequately shredded. The basic problem with them all is simply that they are based on a profound category error—an attempt to prove the transrational realm with merely rational operations.

Of course, reason can and does *attempt* to think about Spirit, however inadequately, and reason is perfectly free to offer various types of *plausibility arguments* for the existence of Spirit. These are by no means *proofs* but rather hints, and I have no quarrel with all that. In fact, I find them vaguely healthy and certainly engaging, and I would definitely prefer to see the (impossible) attempt to rationally prove Spirit than the (equally impossible) attempt to rationally disprove Spirit. But even the most sophisticated of such arguments have concluded, by their authors' own admissions, nothing much more substantial than, "Well, there must be some sort of a transcendental something somewhere," a conclusion that, when placed next to the direct, immediate, in-depth realization offered by the eye of contemplation, appears a pathetically lame performance.

My point is simply that, by offering solely rational "proofs" for the Absolute—proofs that can at least be as easily defeated as defended—then when that poor proof goes, that poor god goes with it. Such category errors then simply delay the realization that there *is* an instrumental proof for the existence of God, but the instrument is contemplation, not reason, and the proof is direct, not mediate. As a *supplement* to *gnosis,* such rational discussions are very useful; as a replacement for *gnosis,* they are profoundly misleading.

But Is It "Science"?

If such endeavors as Zen, Yoga, Gnostic Christianity, Vajrayana Buddhism, Vedanta, and others do in fact follow the three strands of valid data accumulation and verification (or rejection), can they legitimately be called "sciences"?

The answer, of course, depends upon what one means by "science." If by "science" one means the three strands of knowledge accumulation in any realm, then indeed the purer schools of Zen, Yoga, and so on can be called scientific. They are injunctive, instrumental, experimental, experiential, and consensual. That being so, then we could legitimately speak of "spiritual sciences" just as we now speak of social sciences, hermeneutical sciences, psychological sciences, and physical sciences (the latter being empirical, the others being phenomenological or transcendental). Many of the meditation masters themselves like to refer to the science of Yoga, the science of Being, or the science of meditation.

But there are, indeed, some problems with that, because if by "science" we mean sensory-empirical science—and that, in fact, is what is usually meant—then not only are meditative-contemplative-spiritual disciplines *not* science, neither are hermeneutics, phenomenology, introspective psychology, mathematics, psychoanalysis, interpretive sociology, and so on. Empiric-analytic inquiry cannot, as we have seen, even adequately deal with the realm of intelligibilia, and how much less so with that of transcendelia!

Thus, in the past I have been most reluctant, even harsh, in accepting the notion of a "higher science," simply because most advocates of a "higher science" have in fact implicitly attempted to expand the definition of science *without relinquishing the exclusively empiric-analytic mode.* Most of today's psychological, philosophical, and sociological theorists have long ago relinquished mere empiricism (Piaget, Whitehead, Lacan, Habermas, Gadamer, Ricoeur, Bateson, etc.), and the transcendental disciplines, for even more compelling reasons, must surely follow suit (transcending but including empiricism). And yet here were so many theorists claiming that the "new and higher" science— transpersonal, transcendental, spiritual—would be a purely *empirical discipline,* without apparently being very clear about just what they meant by "empiricism." Of course, by "empirical" they often meant experimental and experiential (in the broad sense), but they often also meant, equally and at the same time, objective-sensory data, and this ambiguity has caused much unnecessary confusion.

Let me give a few examples of the messy results that have occurred when purely empirical evidence was advanced as "proof" of higher or transpersonal or transcendental states. Begin with brain-physiological monitoring of "altered states of consciousness." Various researchers have taken advanced meditators, yogis or swamis, who claim to be able to enter a "higher state of consciousness," and, to check out this claim, have plugged them into an empiric-scientific machine, the EEG. The yogi enters his "higher state" *(samadhi)* and, sure enough, a totally unprecedented EEG pattern is produced. Which proves?

Which proves that this yogi is capable of altering his brain patterns and thus the EEG machine. It offers no proof whatsoever of a *higher* state of consciousness, only of a *different* state of consciousness. That state, in fact, might be a new form of psychosis or a new breed of catatonic schizophrenia or *whatever.* Nothing from the EEG can prove this is a *transcendent* state. To the utter contrary, *it is the yogi, using his inward contemplative eye, who alone pronounces this to be a transcendent state.* Not the EEG machine, which is an extended eye of flesh, but only the yogi, using his eye of contemplation, can even talk of higher states. That a higher state might always be correlated with a particular brain-wave pattern would be an important bit of data, but it is *proven* to be *higher* by the yogi (and the community of like-spirited contemplatives), not the machine. The *proof* is contemplative, not empiric. The empiric data is *useful;* it is just not *central.*

But the real problem is even worse than that. As we have often said, the higher leaves its footprints in the lower, and those footprints are a legitimate, if limited, field of investigation (you get the footprints, but never the beast itself). The real problem is that those who advanced empirical brain physiology as "proof" of a transcendent state soon found that the argument quickly turned on them, offering powerful evidence, in fact, of just the opposite. If these "higher states" can indeed be reckoned most fundamentally by brain physiology, then the correct conclusion is that these "higher" or "transpersonal" states are really and merely events occurring in the *personal* brain itself—they aren't really transpersonal or transcendental at all.

As soon as the transpersonal researcher (e.g., Ornstein) comes back with, "No, what's happening is that this new physiological brain state is simply allowing the brain to attune itself with higher and transpersonal energies and realms," then the empiricist merely says, "Show me the empirical evidence of these transpersonal realms." The transpersonalist cannot now point again to brain physiology, because he has just said—in order to escape the first criticism—that physiology is merely allowing *higher* realms to be perceived, and so these higher realms cannot be the same as physiology. But as for these higher realms *themselves,* he has, empirically, precisely nothing, and the empiricist knows it. The transpersonalist is now right back where he started, with the added disadvantage that the empiricist now has new ammunition: The purely empirical data, far from proving a transcendental, transindividual, transpersonal occasion, simply prove—taken in and by themselves—that the mystic is perceiving not Spirit but merely his or her own brain structure. And since the cosmos has been in existence for perhaps 15 billion years, and the human brain for only a pitiful 6 million, then *that* brain "god" is clearly not an infinite, eternal, all-pervading, and transcendental essence, but a simple neurological spark in a purely personal brain. In short, the brain physiology argument, *exactly* by trying to be empirical, now constitutes one of the greatest obstacles to an acceptance of genuinely transpersonal states.

Part of the problem, again, is that such transpersonal researchers have thoughtlessly tried to jump from empirical-sensory data straight to transcendental-contemplative data, without realizing that empiric-analytic inquiry doesn't even adequately cover the intermediate ground of intelligibilia. No amount of EEG sophistication, for instance, no amount of physiological data, can help you decide the meaning of *Macbeth,* the appropriateness of supply-side economics, the geopolitics of the Middle East situation, or the meaning of Egyptian hieroglyphics. All such *intel-*

ligibilia, while certainly leaving their registerable footprints in the brain's physiology, nonetheless have their essence, their referent, their ground, and their *fundamental* existence in the *intersubjective* circle of mental phenomenology. Empiric-physiological studies are not useless in the understanding of intelligibilia, they are simply extremely secondary—and thus, when it comes to transcendelia, they are, one might say, extremely tertiary. Attempting to ground transcendental truth claims in brain physiology is about as useful as hooking Einstein to an EEG in order to find out if E really does equal mc^2.

My point is simply that when it comes to intelligibilia and transcendelia, empiric-analytic studies are of extremely limited and extremely secondary importance. And worse: when it is claimed that there is empiric-scientific proof for any of these states, the researcher has simply but implicitly *accepted the positivistic-reductionistic standards,* and has thus unwittingly played into the hands of the very opponents of such states, thereby hurting the advancement not only of valid rational-phenomenology but also of genuine transcendental inquiry.

Now I am not saying that the word "science" cannot be legitimately applied to phenomenological and transcendental concerns; I am not saying there can be no science of intelligibilia and transcendelia. I am saying that the methodology of monological or empiric-analytic science *cannot* be applied to those higher realms. If we are to speak of a "higher science"—and I think we can—then we must be much more cautious than past advocates of such have generally been. And there is one last caution that—although somewhat technical—cannot be overlooked. It is to that point we now turn.

THEORY AND HYPOTHESIS

We have seen that each of the three general modes of knowing—sensory, mental, and spiritual—has access to direct, immediate, and intuitive apprehensions or data (sensibilia, intelligibilia, and transcendelia). Notice, however, that the very data of the *mental mode*—its words and symbols and concepts—simply because they are indeed symbolic, intentional, reflective, and referential can be used to *point* to, or *represent, other* data, from any other realm: sensibilia, intelligibilia itself, or transcendelia. We can indicate all these epistemological relationships as on page 214.

Mode #5 is simple sensorimotor cognition, the eye of flesh, the presymbolic grasp of the presymbolic world (sensibilia). Mode #4 is em-

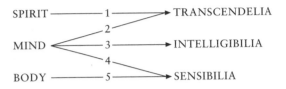

piric-analytic thought; it is mind (intelligibilia) reflecting on and grounding itself *in* the world of sensibilia. Mode #3 is mental-phenomenological thought; it is mind (intelligibilia) reflecting on and grounding itself in the world of intelligibilia itself. Mode #2 can be called mandalic or paradoxical thinking; it is mind (intelligibilia) attempting to reason about spirit or transcendelia. And mode #1 is *gnosis,* the eye of contemplation, the transsymbolic grasp of the transsymbolic world, spirit's direct knowledge of spirit, the immediate intuition of transcendelia.

But notice: Whereas the *data* in *any* realm are themselves immediate and direct (by definition), the *pointing* by *mental* data to *other* data (sensory, mental, or transcendental) is a mediate or intermediate process—it is a *mapping, modeling,* or *matching* procedure. And this mapping procedure—the use of mental data (symbols and concepts) to explain or map *other* data (sensory, mental, or transcendental)—simply results in what is known as *theoretical knowledge.*

We come, then, to a crucial point. Neither the sensorimotor realms per se, nor the spiritual realms per se, form theories. They can be the *object* of theories, but do not themselves produce theories. The one is presymbolic, the other, transsymbolic, and theories are, above all else, symbolic or mental productions. There is valid experience, valid knowledge, valid apprehension in the spiritual and sensible realms but not symbolic or theoretical experience. We will return to this important point shortly; for the moment, let us look more closely at the nature of *mental theories* themselves, because they are crucial in deciding on what we mean by the word "science."

A theory or hypothesis is basically a set of *directly apprehended mental data* used to intermediately map, explain, or organize *other directly apprehended data.* For example, take the empirical hypothesis, "The back side of the moon is made of green cheese." Regardless of the truth or falsity of the proposition, notice that you nevertheless directly understand the *meaning* of that proposition itself, because the proposition per se is a *mental datum,* a direct and immediate apprehension of intelligibilia by the mind's eye. The question *then* arises, does the *mental* datum accurately model or represent the *physical* datum about the moon? In order to find out once and for all, we send a person (or instruments) to the moon and we *look*—that gives us the *direct* and immediate physical datum, and then we discover that the *intermediate* or mapping proposition is false.

Now I emphasize the apparently trivial point that the hypothesis *itself* is a directly apprehended *mental datum,* because without that understanding the status of the mind itself, in the hands of the empiricists, is in great jeopardy. For mind then starts to look like "nothing but" a gross or physical-reflecting entity, "nothing but" an "arid abstraction" that somehow isn't as real as the "concrete territory" of good ole sensibilia, overlooking the fact that the mind itself—the realm of intelligibilia—is an *experiential territory* every bit as (or more) real than sensibilia. Even William James fell into this pernicious reductionism. "There are two ways of knowing things," he says, "knowing them immediately or intuitively [data], and knowing them conceptually or representatively [which would include map-theory]. Although such things as the white paper before our eyes can be known intuitively [he doesn't mean spiritually, he means directly and immediately], most of the things we know, the tigers now in India, for example [i.e., objects outside our present sensory awareness], are known only representatively or symbolically."[67] And, according to James, the symbol-map, such as the image or concept "tiger," mediates or points to the real tiger, but it is *only* the *sensory experience* of the real tiger that constitutes direct and immediate knowledge. Incredibly, James overlooks the fact that the symbol per se, the word-image "tiger," is itself, by itself, directly and immediately experienced or apprehended by the mind's eye, *just as* the physical tiger can be directly apprehended by the eye of flesh. And, indeed, the mental-phenomenological sciences—linguistics, for instance—take as their *concrete territory* the native and intuitive experience and grasp of mental symbols and words themselves! Thus, in no sense does "real territory" mean just physical sensibilia; there is sensory territory, mental territory, and spiritual territory—*all* being real and experiential object domains. And in no sense does "map" take on the derogatory epithet, "just a mere abstraction," for the abstraction per se is itself part of a very real territory, the territory of intelligibilia.

A theory or hypothesis, then, is an *immediately* apprehended mental datum (or gestalt of data) used to *mediately* point to, map, or logically systematize other *immediately* apprehended data (sensory, mental, spiritual). But if a theory is a mental map, nonetheless the map may be wrong, and what distinguishes a theory or hypothesis from a merely dogmatic formulation is its call to experiential or data-based verification. A hypothesis is not just a formulation of present data; it is a formulation of present data in an attempt to create a map that will not be surprised by future data. And the only way to see if a map is surprised by future data is to actually gather future data.

And we have already seen the means for doing so: the three strands of data accumulation and verification—injunction, apprehension, and confirmation. With hypotheses, there is simply the *extra step* of *intermediate mapping*: the readjustment (or sometimes total rejection) of the hypothesis or map in light of the newly acquired data. A hypothesis, then, is a tentative map *plus* suggested injunctions.

Thus, for example, Freud gathered his data—various images, symbols, dream displays, free associations, abreactions, and so on; he formed various theories; then checked the theories against new data; then reformulated his theories, and so on. The same applies whenever we are discussing not just *direct experiential apprehension* (data in any realm) but the systematic *mental mapping* of that data (from any realm)—that is, it applies (or can apply) to empiric-analytic inquiry (#4), to mental-phenomenological inquiry (#3), and to mandalic inquiry (#2; e.g., mental cartographies, however limited, of the higher and transmental realms).

I think most of this is fairly self-evident. I am simply emphasizing the fact that the maps, theories, or hypotheses *themselves,* regardless of their referents (sensory, mental, or transcendental), and regardless of their eventual truth or falsity, are still themselves part of the realm of *mental data:* produced by mind and directly apprehended by mind.

But this makes a "spiritual science" or genuinely "transcendental science" doubly difficult. For unlike sensibilia or intelligibilia, transcendelia cannot be easily or adequately described in mental terms or maps. Spiritual *data* themselves are transmental and transconceptual, and thus they resist, even defy, conceptual, rational, theoretical mapping and codification. We saw, in fact, that when the *mind* attempts to look at or think about spirit, it produces paradoxical results. The mind can adequately look at and map sensibilia because it transcends sensibilia; it can adequately look at and map intelligibilia because that is its own backyard; but it cannot adequately look at or map spirit because spirit transcends *it.* And when spirit *is* described in mental terms, it is not in the nice, commonsensical, down-to-earth categories of empiric-analytic thought or even in the subtler symbolic logic; it is in the slippery, paradoxical, poetical terms of mandalic reason. Understand that spiritual knowledge itself—*gnosis, #1*—is the most direct, clearcut, impactful knowledge imaginable—it simply transcends conceptualization and therefore resists neat hypothetical categorizations and mental mappings.

The point is that one of the standard definitions of any sort of science is "theoretical consistency." Even Charles Tart accepts that as a criterion of a "spiritual," "state specific," or "higher science." But it is useless to demand theoretical consistency from transtheoretical states. Of course, Hinduism, Buddhism, and others can speak logically and consistently, it is just a great mistake to think that their hearts can be poured into concepts. As Watts put it: "Zen does not attempt to be intelligible, that is to say, capable of being understood by the intellect." Yogananda put it thus: "Reason is powerless to understand transcendental truth. Man's highest faculty is not reason but intuition [*gnosis*]: apprehension of knowledge derived immediately and spontaneously from the soul, not from the fallible agency of the senses or of reason." As Kaplan explains: "Esotericists see the theory-building activity of the mind as a lower-state-specific function—one which is left behind with the attainment of those altogether different but [valid] cognitive functions of the mind, which result in esoteric [spiritual] knowledge. Esotericists insist that esoteric knowledge per se is not a matter of theory, which means that this [criterion of science] has no applicability to esoteric knowledge."[69]

So What Do We Mean by "Science"?

And so, for all the above-mentioned reasons, I have in the past been very reluctant to speak of a "higher science"—a science not just of sensibilia but of intelligibilia and transcendelia. But there is, admittedly, something of a "political" or perhaps "public relations" problem with saying that a discipline is "not scientific," no matter how carefully the definitions are arranged, because "not scientific" has come to mean, for reasons good and bad, "not verifiable," "not really real," or "not cognitively valid."

Accordingly, if by "not scientific" we mean "not amenable to direct observation and verification," then by "scientific" we must mean the opposite: open to direct experiential observation and consensual validation. If that is so, then by science we cannot mean merely empirical verification (or rejection), because then everything from mathematics on up is "not scientific." By science, then, we must mean, in the most general sense, any discipline that openly, honestly, and conscientiously opens its knowledge claims to three strands of valid data accumulation and verification. And, similarly, those knowledge claims would not have to be *just* theoretical (or mental); they could also be *transmental* claims or gnostic-awareness claims, as long as they were conscientiously obedient to the three strands themselves. That being so, then we could legitimately speak, not only of the science of sensibilia—physics, chemistry, biology, astronomy, geology—but also the science of intelligibilia—linguistics, mathematics, experimental phenomenology, introspective and interpersonal psychology, historic-hermeneutics, logic, interpretive sociology, communicative philosophy—*and* the science of transcendelia—openly experimental and contemplative disciplines, such as Zen, Vedanta, Vajrayana, mystical Christianity and Judaism, and so on.

But, indeed, if we want to speak of a "higher science," we must be very careful not to mean a higher "sensory-empirical" science. For if the general honesty and openness of the scientific enterprise can be expanded to the higher realms of intelligibilia and transcendelia, the narrowly empiric-analytic methodology *cannot*. Therefore, if we wish to speak of such higher sciences or, indeed, of science in general, much confusion can be avoided if we observe the following general suggestions (however they may finally be worded):

1. By "science," let us explicitly mean any discipline that conscientiously follows the three strands of data accumulation and verification, whether in the realm of sensibilia, intelligibilia, or transcendelia.

2. When the data comes from, or is grounded in, the object domain of sensibilia, let us speak of empiric-analytic or monological (monologue) sciences; based on mode #4.

3. When the data comes from, or is grounded in, the object domain of intelligibilia, let us speak of mental-phenomenological, rational, hermeneutical, semiotic, or dialogical (dialogue) sciences; based on mode #3.

4. When the data comes from, or is grounded in, the object domain of transcendelia, let us speak of translogical, transcendental, transpersonal, or contemplative sciences. And let us carefully and decisively divide these into two classes:

   a. Mandalic sciences—the attempt by the mind to arrange or categorize, however inadequately, the data of transcendelia; based on mode #2 (this would include mental cartographies of the transmental realms; rational "plausibility arguments" for spirit; verbal discussions of Godhead; and so on, as long as the relative inadequacy and paradoxicality of this mode is firmly understood).

b. Noumenological or gnostic sciences—the methodologies and injunctions for the *direct* apprehension of transcendelia as transcendelia; direct and intuitive apprehension of spirit, noumenon, *dharmakaya;* based on mode #1.

(Let us also tentatively but charitably include the possibility of the *parasciences,* the sciences of the investigation of paranormal events. A discussion of this complex topic is quite beyond the scope of this presentation, and so let us simply note: (1) the parasciences are *not* the same as the transcendental sciences per se, simply because, in virtually all psychic events, the mind and senses are *not vertically transcended,* they are simply *horizontally extended,* by mechanism[s] as yet unclear. They work with parasensibilia and paraintelligibilia, so to speak, but not with completely transmental transcendelia. (2) Whereas the realms of sensibilia, intelligibilia, and transcendelia are normal, natural, and necessary structures that *invariably* unfold in all humans who complete the overall growth cycle, psychic occasions seem more often than not to be events that may or may not occur at various stages of growth [although some texts suggest they *more easily* occur at the transition from mental to spiritual spheres]. Even so, they do not seem to be universally *necessary* structures of growth, but exceptional or paranormal structures of growth. (3) This, of course, makes their data accumulation and verification very difficult—much more difficult than even that of transcendelia, because the realm of transcendelia, as a higher but *natural* stage of growth and structure of consciousness, can be repeatedly demonstrated by those who attain it, whereas psychic events, like creativity, seem to come and go.)

SOME EXAMPLES

Let us, as an example of all four major sciences (monological, dialogical, mandalic, and noumenological), use Maslow's works on the hierarchy of human needs: the physiological needs, the safety needs, the belongingness needs, the self-esteem needs, the self-actualization needs, and the self-transcendence needs. It is sometimes said that Maslow's works were empirical science—Maslow himself claimed as much—but from what we have seen thus far, we needn't fall into that semantic and philosophic trap. Here is a more accurate breakdown:

The physiological needs, and to some extent the safety needs, can be essentially investigated by empirical-monological sciences. Physiology, biochemistry, nutrition sciences, and so on are just such sciences. Their essential data is that of sensibilia, and they can be largely conducted in a monological fashion.

By the time we get to the belongingness and self-esteem needs, however, empiric and monological sciences no longer suffice; monologues no longer disclose the data. We are now in the realm of intelligibilia, whose data disclose themselves only in dialogues, intersubjective discourse, interpretations, communicative exchange, role-taking, and so on. At this point, Maslow was no longer doing just empirical science; he was doing phenomenological and dialogical science.

He found, however, that in certain of his most developed or most advanced subjects, certain needs and certain states of consciousness began to emerge that were clearly transcendental—they seemed to transcend space, time, separate self, and, of course, language and verbalization. Maslow categorized this overall realm, in general, as a perception-identity with absolute Being (transcendelia). At their peak, in other words, these people were perceiving, not so much phenomena but noumenon—Being itself—and thus phenomenology as phenomenology is no longer a decently adequate methodology. Of course, we can loosely speak of the "phenomenology" of transcendental states, of meditation, of religious experiences, but the point is that the experiences themselves become less and less phenomenal and more and more noumenal, and accordingly phenomenological methodology—questionnaires, verbal reports, intentionality accounts, interpretive-thematics, and so on— become less and less adequate.

Not that they shouldn't be used! It's just that we ought to acknowledge, as these subjects themselves do, that the *data,* the actual apprehensions, are no longer in the realm of intelligibilia but transcendelia, and accordingly, when the data of transcendelia are put into verbal or phenomenological form, not only is the essence of the apprehension obscured or even lost, it tends to degenerate into contradictory or paradoxical statements. And right there we are dealing, not so much with phenomenological-dialogical sciences, but with *mandalic* sciences. Of course, we still talk to these people, and of course we still ask them questions and collect verbal reports, but the point is that we are trying to put into mental forms and concepts that which is finally transconceptual and transmental. And we ought to *acknowledge* this by explicitly using a different terminology, such as, I have tentatively suggested, paradoxical, translogical, or mandalic sciences.

This is all the more important because, philosophically, we are going to have to face and acknowledge the fact that rational-mental statements about Spirit or Being always eventually degenerate in contradictions or paradoxes, for reasons pointed out by Kant, Stace, Nagarjuna, and others (and summarized in the first chapter). And so what, indeed, did Maslow find at the heart of the self-transcendent experience? These people, he says, can only be described as "simultaneously selfish and unselfish, Dionysian and Apollonian, individual and social, rational and irrational, fused with others and detached from others, and so on . . . the simultaneous existence and perception of inconsistencies, of oppositions, and of flat contradictions. What I had thought to be straight-line continua, whose extremes were polar and as far apart as possible, turned out to be rather like circles or spirals, in which the polar extremes came together into a fused unity," and this fused unity "characterizes Being-perception."[83]

You can already see the problems of trying to "phenomenologically describe" these highest states in mental-verbal forms. But it's even worse than Maslow himself imagined, for a more accomplished dialectician (e.g., Nagarjuna) would point out that Being described as "fused unity" is *still* a *dualistic* notion, because unity is the *opposite* of diversity. And we do precisely no better if we then say the absolute is unity *and* diversity, because those two terms, taken together, now constitute a class that itself has an opposite (neither unity nor diversity), and so on ad infinitum. Even the term "Being" is dualistic, taking as its opposite "Nothingness," and so on. But you get the point: mandalic science will always be based, in whole or part, on paradoxes, and we had better face that fact right up front or our mandalic science will simply be called self-contradictory and dismissed by "real scientists." Spirit as Spirit is not paradoxical; it is not characterizable at all in mental terms—but when *put* into mental terms, the result is paradoxical. And since part of the higher and translogical sciences *will* be discussing transcendelia in mental and conceptual terms, *that* part will be what we have called paradoxic-mandalic, and *that* we must acknowledge up front.

We have seen, then, that Maslow performed empirical science, phenomenological science, and mandalic science. In each case he presented and explained his *injunctions* or methodologies (questionnaires, biographical interpretation, direct verbal reports, etc.); he gathered *data;* he had others check, repeat, and confirm his studies (all three strands). He left a way, in other words, for others to reach the same or similar data and understanding that he himself discovered and possessed. Beyond that, however, did he do *noumenological science?*

The answer is no. Maslow studied some of those who had noumenal experience; he himself also seems to have had several noumenal experiences. But he did not present, in a careful way, a systematic series of *injunctions* that would lead to the *apprehension* of Being which could then be *communally* confirmed. Unlike all his other scientific studies, he did not here leave us the three strands; he left us no path, no way, to reach and replicate this ultimate apprehension itself.

Who, then, does perform noumenological science? The answer is: Zen Masters, Theravadin teachers, Vajrayana adepts, Christian contemplatives, Vedantin masters, and so on—any genuine discipline that conscientiously and openly displays and contains transcendental (contemplative) injunctions, apprehensions, and communal confirmations. Now most of these gnostic sciences also perform *mandalic* sciences— they translate the higher realms (downward) into mental maps, cartographies, and so on, mostly for the use of beginners or outsiders, but they are very explicit about the limited functions of such mandalic maps— they are simply pictures of reality, not reality itself. (Or, as Zen graphically puts it, they are like a menu and the real meal, and the problem is not to eat the menu instead of the meal.)

Today, we are seeing the emergence of a new type of scientist, one who has already studied and mastered one or more empirical and phenomenological sciences, and who now has or is mastering a noumenological science. And this, in general, is the domain of overall transpersonal studies—by whatever name one prefers: noetics (Mitchell, Harman), metapsychiatry (Dean), transpersonal psychology (Sutich, Maslow), transcendental or perennial philosophy (Leibniz, Huxley), and others. This endeavor and its overall or "integral paradigm," by whatever name, attempts to use and integrate the eye of flesh, the eye of reason, and the eye of contemplation, and thus to do justice to the full spectrum of human and, indeed, divine possibilities.

What about Measurement in the New Sciences?

We saw that one of the defining characteristics of the classic empiric-scientific method was its use of *measurement* to generate data. That, indeed, was the genius of Kepler and Galileo. If we have agreed that the scientific enterprise—meaning the three strands—can be expanded to all the higher realms, the question remains: Can *measurement* be likewise expanded?

Begin with the distinction between physical sensibilia and mental intelligibilia. As Descartes himself eloquently explained, one of the great differences between these two general realms is that the physical world is marked by *extension,* the mental world, by *intention.* This physical page, for instance, clearly has extension—it is about six inches by nine inches, it is distinct from the other physical objects surrounding it, and so on—it is part of the gross-matter realm, the realm of physical extension, physical space, physical time. For all those reasons, physical objects—sensibilia—are ideally suited to *measurement*—I can measure their length, width, height, and weight.

But what about hope, envy, pride, joy, understanding? What is the length of a concept? How much does insight weigh? What is the width of an idea? For what characterizes intelligibilia is not so much their *extension* as their *intention*—their meaning, their value, their intersubjective understanding. Physical space-time no longer quite applies to them, and thus *physical* measurement and quantification are of rather limited use.

This is not to say, however, that some types of measurement or quantification are not applicable to intelligibilia; nor is it to deny that intelligibilia have their own subtler forms of space-time. For the mental realm does indeed have a form of time, but it is not merely natural time or seasonal time—it is *historical time* or history: the mode of time marked not just by its extension but also and mostly by its *intention.* It is *narrative* time, the time that marks the history of one's own life story or self, the time that carries and creates hopes and ideals, plans and ambitions, goals and visions; the *subtle* time that can speed up or slow down, expand or collapse, transcend or concentrate, according to its *interest,* whereas poor ole physical time just clicks along, stuck in the passing present, mindlessly, monotonously, causally.

In other words, historical time *transcends* physical time: not stuck in the simple moment-to-moment time of sensibilia, historical time can span and scan the past and future, anticipate and remember, reminisce and envision, and thus allow mind to escape its bondage to the merely passing present of bodily sensations and perceptions and thereby enter the larger span of consciousness called historical perspective. Thus, this *subtler* form of time is also a more encompassing and transcendent mode of time. As you are now reading these words, following my intentions, grasping my symbolic points, your body is existing in physical time, clicking away in the present, but your mind is moving in historical time, speeding up, slowing down, looking forward, looking backward—the time that is the movement not of things but of thoughts, the time that stretches beyond the naive present and marks *its* pace with vision and intention.

Likewise, the realm of intelligibilia has a *subtle* form of space, exactly the space that today's jargon calls "psychological space." It is the space of self-identity; also the space of imagination, the space of dreams, the space of vision, the inward space created by mind in its formal operations. It is a *narrative* space, the space of stories and intentions and choices, not merely the physical space of extensions and collisions and causalities. This space, being *subtler* than physical space, can transcend physical space. My "psychological space" can expand to include, in the very circle of myself, my friends, my family, even my country. I can do all this without even moving in physical space. This mode of mental space, and its *correlative* mode of time (history), characterize intelligibilia and its dynamics.

Look now at transcendelia: for here, space-time has become so subtle, so transcendent, so expansive, so all-encompassing that we can either say (paradoxically!) that time and space cease to exist entirely, or that all time and space exist simultaneously, now, in the eternal moment (what the mystics call the *nunc stans,* which they are very careful to point out should not be confused with the *nunc fluens,* the simple passing present of mere sensibilia). We are here in the realm of the Timeless that is All Time, the Spaceless that is All Space.

And so here is the point about *measurement:* It is not that space and time exist *only* in the gross realm of sensibilia. It is that in the physical realm, space and time are the densest, the grossest, the most head-knockingly concrete. As we move up the spectrum of consciousness, space and time become subtler and subtler (and therefore more encompassing or transcendent), but, accordingly, measurement becomes subtler and thus infinitely more difficult to perform, until it becomes, finally, completely meaningless.

Measurement, then, most easily and most essentially characterizes the gross realm of sensibilia. In the realm of intelligibilia, measurement, if used, switches from a gauge of extension to a gauge of intention. We speak, for instance, of the *intensity* of a value, *how much* we love someone, the *degree* of ambition, and the *measure* of intelligence. And we can also use number-measures as a marker of *relative* values (as, for instance, a person does when he or she subjectively judges a member of the opposite sex on the scale of "one to ten"). In the field of social phenomenology itself, there has been much work done on the quantification of mental intention (not extension). And even in transcendelia, there is a sense in speaking of the *degree* of spiritual progress and understanding (the ten stages of enlightenment, for example).

All of which is fine; measurement, in the broadest sense, simply means "more" or "less" of a datum, and *all* realms have their data. But we ought to be very careful not to confuse what we mean by measurement of *extension* with measurement of *intention* with measurement of *transcension* (or degree of specific transcendence). And *the* problem with empirical scientism was that, by measurement, it meant the easiest and most objective form of measurement: measurement of extensive gross-realm sensibilia. Since it is much harder to measure subjective intelligibilia (let alone spiritual transcendelia), the scienticians simply dismissed data that could not be forced into physical measurement dimensions—and that was the horrendous crime that led to the "disqualified universe." All of this can be avoided if we simply remember that measurement in the monological sciences is primarily of extension; measurement in the dialogical sciences is primarily of intention; and measurement in the gnostic sciences is primarily of transcension.

SUMMARY AND CONCLUSION:
THE GEIST-SCIENCES

The Germans have a beautiful concept for our larger science: *Geisteswissenschaften*. *Geist* itself is a fortunate word because it means both mind and spirit, and simply signifies all realms not merely physical or empirical. Wilhelm Dilthey, who first introduced the idea, simply pointed out that alongside the *natural sciences* there has grown up the *Geisteswissenschaften*, the mental and spiritual sciences, which include "history, national economy, the sciences of law and the state, the science of religion, the study of literature and poetry, of art and music, of philosophical world views, systems, and finally psychology."[31]

It was Dilthey's genius to point out that although the natural sciences deal with the purely objective, natural world, and the geist-sciences with the cultural, historical, and spiritual world, nonetheless *Geist* itself—the human mind and spirit—can and does form and inform, mold and alter, the objective world of material sensibilia. We already gave an example of this with Goya's painting, or sensibilia formed and informed by intelligibilia. But of course the same is true of transcendelia—it can form and inform its junior levels: intelligibilia (as mandalic reason, mystical poetry, etc.) and sensibilia (as art, sculpture, temples, etc.). *Geist* (mind and spirit) everywhere *objectifies* itself, and part of Geist-science is *not only dealing with the higher realms in and as themselves* but also in grasping and understanding the meaning and intent of their particular *objectifications* in their junior realms, the intermediate realms of culture and history, and the lower realms of nature and physical material.

According to Dilthey, there are two essential ingredients necessary for "decoding" these objectifications of *Geist*. The first he called *Erlebnisse*, which means my own personal and *lived experience* in the realm which issued the objectification. This is similar to the notion of *adequatio*—if I am to grasp any objectification of mind or spirit, I must, in my own personal lived experience, my own *Erlebnisse*, be *adequate* to the realm that produced the objectification, or else, as the biblical wisdom has it, we are casting pearls before swine.

Using *Erlebnisse* as a base, I must then attempt to understand (*verstehen*), or grasp from within, the mind or spirit that formed and informed the objectification of itself. "And to understand a phase of objective spirit means relating its phenomena to an inner structure which finds expression in these phenomena."[31] That is, where the original objectification or expression was a movement from the inside to the outside, my *understanding* of it is the reverse: a movement from the outside to the inside, an attempt to re-create its inner life and meaning. Thus, the Geist-sciences " 'rest on the relation of *lived experience, expression, and understanding.*' Expression is required because the underlying spiritual structure is grasped only in and through its external expressions. Understanding is a movement from the outside to the inside. And in the process of understanding a spiritual object rises before our vision . . . ,"[31] a vision-insight given only by the mental and/or contemplative eye.

The point is that the higher realms everywhere leave their footprints in the lower. The higher realms form and inform, create and mold, produce and alter, all manner of forms in the lower realms. But those productions cannot be grasped *by* the lower realms nor reduced *to* them. And it is that double understanding—the higher *as* higher and the higher as objectified, expressed, and embodied in the lower—that will announce the new and truly higher sciences.

3

A Mandalic Map of Consciousness

W E HAVE SEEN THE NEED for a comprehensive paradigm to include monological, dialogical, and translogical sciences. When
applied to psychology, such an integral approach would produce a
broad-spectrum map or model of consciousness on the whole—its development, its structures, its levels—stretching from material and sensory
stages to mental and verbal stages to transcendental and spiritual stages.
In this chapter we will examine one such possible model.

THE NATURE OF DEVELOPMENT

Everywhere we look in nature, said the philospher Jan Smuts,[111] we see
nothing but *wholes*. And not just simple wholes but hierarchical ones:
each whole is a part of a larger whole which is itself part of a larger
whole. Fields within fields within fields, stretching through the cosmos,
interlacing each and every thing with each and every other.

Further, said Smuts, the universe is not a thoughtlessly static and inert
whole—the cosmos is not lazy but energetically dynamic and even creative. It tends to produce higher- and higher-level wholes, ever more
inclusive and organized. This overall cosmic process, as it unfolds in
time, is nothing other than evolution. And the drive to ever higher unities, Smuts called *holism*.

If we continued this line of thinking, we might say that because the
human mind or psyche is an aspect of the cosmos, we would expect to

find, in the psyche itself, the same hierarchical arrangement of wholes within wholes, reaching from the simplest and most rudimentary to the most complex and inclusive. In general, such is exactly the discovery of modern psychology. As Werner put it, "Wherever [psychological] development occurs it proceeds from a state of relative globality and lack of differentiation to a state of increasing differentiation, articulation, and hierarchical integration."[127] Jakobson speaks of "those stratified phenomena which modern psychology uncovers in the different areas of the realm of the mind,"[64] where each stratified layer is more integrated and more encompassing than its predecessor. Bateson points out that even learning itself is hierarchical, involving several major levels, each of which is "meta-" to its predecessor. As a general approximation, then, we may conclude that the psyche—like the cosmos at large—is many-layered ("pluridimensional"), composed of successively higher-order wholes and unities and integrations.

Now the holistic evolution of nature—which produces everywhere higher and higher wholes—shows up in the human psyche as development or growth. The same force that produced humans from amoebas produces adults from infants. That is, a person's growth, from infancy to adulthood, is simply a miniature version of cosmic evolution. Or, we might say, psychological growth or development in humans is simply a microcosmic reflection of universal growth on the whole and has the same goal: the unfolding of ever higher-order unities and integrations. And that is one of the major reasons that the psyche is, indeed, stratified. Very like the geological formation of the earth, psychological development proceeds stratum by stratum, level by level, stage by stage, with each successive level superimposed upon its predecessor in such a way that it transcends but includes it ("envelopes it," as Werner put it).

Now in psychological development, the whole of any level becomes merely a part of the whole of the next level, which in turn becomes a part of the next whole, and so on throughout the evolution of consciousness (what Koestler nicely called a "holon"—an entity which, looking down, is whole, looking up, is part). Take, as but one example, the development of language: The child first learns babbling sounds, then wider vowel and consonant sounds, then simple words, then small phrases, then simple sentences, and then extended sentences. At each stage, simple parts (e.g., words) are integrated into higher wholes (e.g., sentences), and as Jakobson points out, "new additions are superimposed on earlier ones and dissolution begins with the higher strata."[64]

Modern developmental psychology has, on the whole, simply devoted itself to the exploration and explanation of the various levels, stages, and strata of the human constitution—mind, personality, psychosexuality, character, consciousness, and object-relations. The cognitive studies of Piaget and Werner, the works of Loevinger and Arieti and Maslow and Jakobson, the moral development studies of Kohlberg—all subscribe to the concept of stratified stages of increasing complexity, integration, and unity.

Having said that much, we are at once entitled to ask, "What, then, is the *highest* stage of unity to which one may aspire?" Or perhaps we should not phrase the question in such ultimate terms, but simply ask instead, "What is the nature of some of the higher and highest stages of development? What forms of unity are disclosed in the most developed souls of the human species?"

We all know what the "lower" stages and levels of the psyche are like (I am speaking in simple, general terms): they are instinctual, impulsive, libidinous, id-ish, animal, apelike. And we all know what some of the "middle" stages are like: socially adapted, mentally adjusted, egically integrated, syntactically organized, conceptually advanced. But are there no "higher" stages? Is an "integrated ego" or "autonomous individual" the highest reach of consciousness in human beings? The individual ego is a marvelously high-order unity, but compared with the Unity of the cosmos at large, it is a pitiful slice of holistic reality. Has nature labored these billions of years just to bring forth this egoic mouse?

The problem with that type of question lies in finding examples of truly higher-order personalities—and in deciding exactly *what* constitutes a higher-order personality in the first place. My own feeling is that as humanity continues its collective evolution, this will become very easy to decide, because more and more "enlightened" personalities will show up in data populations, and psychologists will be forced, by their statistical analyses, to include higher-order profiles in their developmental stages. In the meantime, one's idea of "higher-order" or "highly developed" remains rather philosophic. Nonetheless, those few gifted souls who have bothered to look at this problem have suggested that the world's great mystics and sages represent some of the very highest, if not the highest, of all stages of human development. Bergson said exactly that; and so did Toynbee and Tolstoy and James and Schopenhauer and Nietzsche and Maslow and Hegel.

The point is that we *might* have an excellent population of extremely evolved and developed personalities in the form of the world's great mystic-sages (a point which is supported by Maslow's studies). Let us, then, simply assume that the authentic mystic-sage represents some of the very highest stages of human development—as far beyond normal-and-average humanity as it itself is beyond apes. This, in effect, would give us a sample which approximates the "highest state of consciousness," a type of "super-conscious" state. Furthermore, most of the mystic-sages have left rather detailed records of the stages and substages of their own transformations into the upper reaches of consciousness. That is, they tell us not only of the highest level of consciousness and super-consciousness but also of all the intermediate levels leading up to it. If we take these higher stages and add them to the lower and middle stages and levels which have been so carefully described and studied by Western psychology, we would then arrive at a fairly well-balanced and comprehensive model of the spectrum of consciousness. I have attempted this type of synthesis in a series of books.[133, 137, 139] As a very general and simplistic outline, here is what we find:

THE LOWER REALMS

It is generally agreed, by Eastern and Western psychology alike, that the lowest levels of development involve simple material and biological functions and processes. That is, the lowest levels involve somatic processes, instincts, simple sensations and perceptions, and emotional-sexual impulses. In Piaget's system, these are the sensorimotor realms; Arieti refers to them as instinctual, exoceptual, and protoemotional; Loevinger calls them presocial, symbiotic, and impulsive. In Vedanta, this is the realm of the *annamayakosha* and *pranamayakosha,* the levels of food, hunger, and emotional sexuality. The Buddhist calls them the lower five *vijnanas* or the realm of the five senses. The Yoga *chakra* psychology refers to them as the lower three *chakras:* the *muladhara* or root material and pleromatic level; the *svadhisthana* or emotional-sexual level; and *manipura* or aggressive-power level. This is also the lower three *skandhas* in the Theravadin Buddhist system of psychology: the physical body, perception-sensation, and emotion-impulse. And it is Maslow's lowest two needs, the physiological and safety needs. All of this simply goes to point up one of Freud's major ideas: "The ego," he said, "is first and foremost a body-ego."[44]

Now the body-ego or body-self tends to develop in the following way: It is generally agreed, by virtually all schools of modern psychology, that the infant initially cannot distinguish self from not-self, subject from object, body from environment. That is, the self at this earliest of stages (the first four to eight months of life) is largely one with or confused with the physical world. As Piaget put it, "During the early stages the world and the self are one; neither term is distinguished from the other. . . . The self is still material, so to speak."[93] That initial stage of *material oneness*, which Piaget called "protoplasmic," Neumann calls "pleromatic" and "uroboric." "Pleromatic" is an old gnostic term meaning the material universe—the *materia prima* and *virgo mater*. "Uroboros" is a mythic symbol of a serpent eating its own tail, and signifies "wholly self-absorbed" and "not able to recognize an other" (autistic and narcissistic); it also refers to alimentary-reptilian drives and the crudest forms of sensations and rudimentary perceptions.

It is out of this primordial fusion state that the separate self emerges, and as Freud said, the self emerges first as a body, a body-self. The infant bites a blanket, and it does not hurt; he bites his thumb, and it hurts. There is a difference, he learns, between the body and the not-body, and he gradually learns to focus his awareness *from* the pleroma *to* the body. Thus, out of primitive material unity emerges the first real self sense: the body-ego. The infant *identifies* with the newly emergent body, with its sensations and emotions, and gradually learns to differentiate them from the material world at large.

Notice that the body-ego, by differentiating itself from the material environment, actually *transcends* that primitive state of fusion and embeddedness. The body-ego transcends the material environment, and thus can perform physical operations upon that environment. Toward the end of the sensorimotor period (around age two), the child has differentiated the body-self and the material environment to such a degree that he has a fairly stable image of "object constancy," and so he can muscularly coordinate physical operations on those objects. He can coordinate a physical movement of various objects in the environment, something he could not easily do as long as he could not differentiate himself *from* those objects.

Let us note that triad: by *differentiating* the self from an object, the self *transcends* that object and thus can *operate* upon it (using *as tools* the *structures* of the self at that level—at this stage, the sensorimotor body).

At this body-self stage(s), then, the self is no longer bound to the material-pleromatic environment—but it is bound to, or identified with, the biological body. The self, as body-ego, is dominated by instinctual urges, impulsiveness, the pleasure principle, involuntary urges and discharges—all the id-like primary processes and drives described so well by Freud and others. For this reason, we also call the body-self the "typhonic self"—the typhon, in mythology, was half human, half serpent (uroboros).

THE INTERMEDIATE REALMS

Eventually, however, true *mental* or conceptual functions begin to emerge out of, and differentiate from, the body-self. As language develops, the child is ushered into the world of symbols and ideas and concepts, and thus is gradually raised above the fluctuations of the simple, instinctual, immediate, and impulsive body-ego. Among other things, language carries the ability to picture things and events which are not *immediately* present to the body senses. "Language," as Robert Hall put it, "is the means of dealing with the nonpresent world."[137]

By the same token, then, language is the means of transcending the simply present world (language, in the higher realms of consciousness, is itself transcended, but one must go from the preverbal to the verbal in order to get to the transverbal; we are here talking about the transcendence of the preverbal by the verbal, which, although only half the story, is an extraordinary achievement). Through language one can anticipate the future, plan for it, and thus gear one's present activities in accordance with tomorrow. That is, one can delay or control one's present bodily desires and activities. This is, as Fenichel explains, "a gradual substituting of actions for mere discharge reactions. This is achieved through the interposing of a time period between stimulus and response."[39] Through language and its symbolic, tensed structures, one can postpone and channel the otherwise immediate and impulsive discharges of simple biological drives. One is no longer totally dominated by instinctual demands but can to a certain degree *transcend* them. And this simply means that the self is starting to differentiate from the body and emerge as a mental or verbal or syntactical being.

Notice again: As the mental-self emerges and *differentiates* from the body (with the help of language), it *transcends* the body and thus can *operate* upon it using its own mental structures as tools (it can delay the body's immediate discharges and postpone its instinctual gratifications using verbal insertions). At the same time, this allows a sublimation of the body's emotional-sexual energies into more subtle, complex, and evolved activities.

Thus, a fairly coherent mental-ego eventually emerges (usually between ages four and seven), differentiates itself from the body (after the Oedipal stage), transcends the simple biological world, and therefore can to a certain degree operate on the biological world (and the earlier physical world), using the tools of representational thinking. This whole trend is consolidated with the emergence (around age seven) of what Piaget calls "concrete operational thinking"—thinking that can *operate* on the concrete world and the body using concepts.

By the time of adolescence, another extraordinary differentiation begins to occur. In essence, the self simply starts to differentiate *from* the concrete thought process. And because the self starts to differentiate itself from the concrete thought process, it can to a certain degree *transcend* that thought process and therefore *operate* upon it. It is thus not surprising that Piaget calls this—his highest stage—"formal operational," because one can operate on one's own thought (i.e., work with linguistic objects as well as physical ones), a detailed operation which, among other things, results in the sixteen binary propositions of formal logic. But the only point I wish to emphasize here is that this can occur because consciousness differentiates itself from concrete thought, thus transcends it, and hence can operate upon it—something it could not do when it *was* it. (Actually, this process is just beginning at this stage—it intensifies at the higher stages—but the overall point seems fairly clear: Consciousness is *starting* to transcend the verbal ego-mind.)

This overall verbal ego-mind is known in Mahayana Buddhism as the *manovijnana* (*mano* means "mind"; same root), in Hinduism as the *manomayakosha,* in Hinayana Buddhism as the fourth and fifth *skandhas* (words and thoughts); it is also the fourth and fifth *chakras,* the latter, the *visuddha-chakra,* being the lower of verbal-rational mind. It is basically Freud's mature ego and secondary process, Arieti's language and conceptual levels, Loevinger's conscientious and individualistic stages, Sullivan's syntaxic mode, Maslow's belongingness and self-esteem needs, and so on. These are all very general but adequate correlations. (For a more precise alignment, see chapter 9.)

Now as consciousness begins to transcend the verbal ego-mind, it can integrate the ego-mind with all the lower levels. That is, because consciousness is no longer identified with any of these elements to the exclusion of any others, all of them can be integrated: the body and mind can be brought into a higher-order holistic integration. This stage has been referred to as the "integration of all lower levels" (Sullivan, Grant, and Grant), "integrated" (Loevinger), "self-actualized" (Maslow), "autonomous" (Fromm, Riesman). My favorite descriptive phrase comes from Loevinger's statement of Broughton's work: his highest stage, stage 6, is one wherein "mind and body are both experiences of an integrated self."[78] This integrated self, wherein mind and body are harmoniously one, we call the "centaur." The centaur: the great mythological being with animal body and human mind existing in a state of at-one-ment.

As I mentioned, both Eastern and Western psychology are in general agreement as to the nature of these lower levels, from pleroma to body to ego-mind to centaur. But the West has contributed a rather exact understanding of a phenomenon that is only vaguely understood in the East: namely, the process of dynamic repression. For what Western psychology discovered is that as higher-order levels of consciousness *emerge* in development, they can *repress* the lower levels, with results that range from mild to catastrophic.

In order to take into account this process of dynamic repression, we simply use the Jungian terms "shadow" and "persona." The shadow is the personal unconscious, a series of "feeling-toned complexes." These complexes are images and concepts which become "contaminated" by the lower levels—in particular, the emotional-sexual (typhonic)—and thus are felt, for various reasons, to be threatening to the higher-order structure of the ego-mind. These complexes are thus split off from consciousness (they become shadow), a process which simultaneously distorts the self-concept (the ego), and thus leaves the individual with a false or inaccurate self-image (the persona). If the persona and shadow can be reunited, then the higher-order integration of the total ego can be established. That, in very general terms, is the major aim of most orthodox Western psychotherapy.

So far, then, we have these major levels of increasing integration and transcendence: the simple and primitive fusion-unity of the pleroma; the next higher-order unity of the biological body-self; then the mental-persona, which, if integrated with the shadow, yields the higher-order unity of the total ego; and finally the centaur, which is a higher-order integration of the total ego with all preceding and lower levels—body, persona, and shadow.

THE HIGHER REALMS

With the exception of transpersonal psychology, the centaur level is about the highest level of consciousness taken seriously by Western psychology. The existence of levels above or higher than the centaur is thus viewed by Western psychology with a somewhat jaundiced eye. Western psychologists and psychiatrists either deny the existence of any sort of higher-order unities, or—should they actually confront what seems to be a higher-order level—simply try to pathologize its existence, to explain it by diagnosis. Thus, for indications as to the nature of any higher levels of consciousness, beyond the ego and centaur, we have to turn to the great mystic-sages and perennial philosophers, East and West. It is some-what surprising, but very significant, that most of these sources agree almost unanimously on the nature of the "farther reaches of human nature" (hence, indeed, the title *"perennial* philosophy"). There are, in fact, these traditions tell us, higher levels of consciousness—as far above the ego-mind as the ego-mind is above the typhon. And they look like this:

Beginning with (to use the terms of yogic *chakra* psychology) the sixth *chakra,* the *ajna chakra,* consciousness *starts* to go transpersonal or gen-uinely transcendental. It begins to enter what is called the "subtle sphere." This process quickens and intensifies as it reaches the highest *chakra*—the *sahasrara*—and then goes supramental as it enters the seven (some say ten) higher stages of consciousness within and beyond the *sahasrara.* The *ajna,* the *sahasrara,* and the seven or so sublevels are, on the whole, referred to as the subtle realm (although the exact wording is a matter of semantic choice).

For convenience's sake, we speak of the "low-subtle" (or "psychic") and the "high-subtle." The low-subtle is epitomized by the *ajna chakra,* the "third eye," which is said to include and dominate psychic events and certain lower forms of mysticlike experiences. Patanjali has an entire chapter of his *Yoga Sutras* devoted to this plane and its structures (called *siddhis*). According to some texts, this level can tend to display actual paranormal events but does not *have* to do so; it is *defined* simply by its intensification of consciousness and the beginning of the opening of the eye of contemplation. We call it "psychic" simply as a reminder that even if paranormal events might more easily occur here, they are said to reach *no higher* than this, the lowest of the transcendental realms.

The high-subtle begins at the *sahasrara* and extends within and be-yond to various subphases of extraordinarily high-order transcendence, differentiation, and integration. I am not going to present an exhaustive breakdown of this realm and its various (seven to ten) subphases. Be-sides, the *surface structures* of this realm are naturally different from culture to culture and tradition to tradition. The *deep structure* of this overall realm, however, is simply that of *archetypal form;* it is marked by transmental *illumination, intuition,* and beginning *gnosis,* which brings a profound insight into the fundamental or Archetypal Forms of being and existence itself. It is not *Formless,* however, or radically transcendent, but rather expresses insight into the subtlest forms of mind, being, deity, and manifestation.

In Theravadin Buddhism, this is the realm of the four "*jhanas* with form," or the four stages of concentrative meditation into archetypal "planes of illumination" or "Brahma realms." In *vipassana* or insight meditation, this is the stage-realm of initial or pseudonirvana, the realm of illumination and rapture and initial transcendental insight. This is the realm of *nada* and *shabd* yoga, of high religious intuition and literal inspiration; of *bija-mantra;* of symbolic visions; of blue, gold, and white light; of audible illuminations and brightness upon brightness; it is the realm of angelic forms, *ishtadevas,* and *dhyani*-buddhas, all of which—as we will soon explain—are simply high archetypal forms of one's own being (although they initially and necessarily appear "other"). It is the realm of *Sar* and *Sat Shabd,* of Brahma the Controller, of platonic Forms and Demiurges. Dante sang of it thus:

> Fixing my gaze upon the Eternal Light
> I saw within its depths,
> > Bound up with love together in one volume,
> > The scattered leaves of all the universe. . . .
> Within the luminous profound subsistence
> > Of that Exalted Light saw I three circles
> > Of three colors yet of one dimension
> And by the second seemed the first reflected
> > As rainbow is by rainbow, and the third
> > Seemed fire that equally from both is breathed.

Keep in mind that this is what Dante *saw,* literally, with his eye of contemplation. He is not simply waxing poetic, but using mandalic poetry to sing of what he saw.

The psychiatrist Dean, pioneer in the new field of metapsychiatry, reports this:

> An intellectual illumination occurs that is quite impossible to describe. In an intuitive flash, one has an awareness of the meaning and drift of the universe, an identification and merging with

creation, infinity and immortality, a depth beyond depth of revealed meaning—in short, a conception of an over-self, so omnipotent . . .[33]

In Hinduism, this general realm is called the *vijnanamayakosha*; in Mahayana Buddhism, this is the *manas*; in Kabbalah, it is Gevurah and Hesed. Aspects of this subtle realm have been called the "over-self" or "over-mind"—as in Aurobindo and Emerson. The point is simply that consciousness, in a rapid ascent, is differentiating itself entirely from the ordinary mind and self, and thus can be called an "over-self" or "over-mind"—almost like calling the ego an "over-body" or "over-instincts," since the mental-ego transcends and reaches over the simple feelings and perceptions of the typhon. The over-mind simply embodies a transcendence of all lower mental forms, and discloses, at its summit, an intuition of That which is above and prior to mind, self, body, and world—something which, as Aquinas would have said, all men and women would call God.

But this is not God as an ontological other, set apart from the cosmos, from humans, and from creation at large. Rather, it is God as an archetypal summit of one's own Consciousness. John Blofeld quotes Edward Conze on the Vajrayana Buddhist viewpoint: " 'It is the emptiness of everything which allows the identification to take place—the emptiness [which means "transcendental openness" or "nonobstruction"] which is in us coming together with the emptiness which is the deity. By visualizing that identification 'we actually do become the deity. The subject is identified with the object of faith. The worship, the worshipper, and the worshipped, those three are not separate.' "[16] At its peak, the soul becomes one, literally one, with the deity-form, with the *dhyani*-buddha, with (choose whatever term one prefers) God. One dissolves into Deity, *as* Deity—that Deity which, from the beginning, has been one's own Self or highest Archetype. In this way only could St. Clement say that he who knows himself knows God. We could now say, he who knows his over-self knows God. They are one and the same.

Now all of this might sound rather "far out," of course, to the skeptical scientist, the empiricist, the rationalist. But I would like you to simply consider the implications of the *possible existence* of the subtle realm. What *if* the mystic-sages are right?

The whole point would be that in the subtle realm—and especially the high-subtle—a very high-order differentiation and transcendence is occurring. Mediated through high-archetypal *cognitive forms*—those that lie immediately beyond formal-operational in the developmental sequence—consciousness is following a path of transformation-upward which leads beyond the gross body-mind and merely rational ego. This transformation-upward, like *all* the others we have studied, involves the *emergence* of a higher-order deep structure, followed by the shifting of *identity* to that higher-order structure, and the differentiation or *dis-identification* with the lower structures (in this case, the ego-mind and centaur). This amounts to a *transcendence* of the lower-order structures, which thus enables consciousness to *operate* on and *integrate* all of the lower-order structures, an integration that, at this high level, simply leads to various forms of *samadhi* or mystical union or identity. Viewed thus, the "super-natural" is simply the next *natural* step in overall or higher development and evolution.

Lex Hixon has described one form of the subtle deep-structure called an *ishtadeva*. The *ishtadeva* is simply a high-archetypal form of cognition evoked in certain meditations on the path of form—a type of inner cognitive vision, directly perceived with the eye of contemplation. I realize that some people would say that the *ishtadeva* is "just a mental image" and doesn't *really* exist—but that is to simultaneously reduce *all* mental productions: might as well say that mathematics is just a mental production and therefore doesn't really exist. No, the *ishtadeva* is real—more than real—in its emergence and perception.

Hixon describes it thus: "The Form or Presence of the *ishtadeva* appears as vibrantly alive, composed from the radiance of Consciousness. We are not projecting the *ishtadeva*. The primal radiance which assumes the form of the *ishtadeva* is actually projecting us and all the phenomena that we call the universe."[61] This high archetypal cognitive form eventually mediates the ascension of consciousness to an *identity* with that Form: "Gradually we realise that the Divine Form or Presence is our own archetype, an image of our own essential nature."[61]

This, however, is not a *loss* of consciousness but an *intensification* of consciousness through a higher-order development, evolution, transcendence, and *identification*: "The *ishtadeva* does not disappear into us; we as individuals disappear into the *ishtadeva*, which now remains alone. Yet there is no loss of our individual being as we blend into the object of our contemplation, for it has been our own archetype from the beginning, the source of this fragmentary reflection we call our individual personality."[61]

The whole point is that the rational ego has not simply swallowed or introjected the high Archetypal Form, but that the prior *nature* of the ego is revealed to *be* that Form, so that consciousness reverts to, or remembers, its own prior and higher identity: "We remain now as a transcendental center of consciousness expressed through the Form or Presence of the *ishtadeva*. We are now experiencing the life of the *ishtadeva* from within. We are consciously meeting and becoming [via higher identification] ourselves in our archetypal and eternal nature."[61]

Now that is, as I said, simply one particular description of development in the subtle realm, and thus its surface structures will naturally be different from other descriptions (and experiences) of the same realm (just as, for example, all mature egos have access to the same basic type of secondary process thinking but don't therefore think the same thoughts). But the realm itself, its actual *deep structures,* appear universally the same. State it in terms of saintly mystical insight or the *jhanas* of Form or *vipassana* pseudonirvana or absorption in the Zen *koan* or *nada-shabd* identity or simple transcendental illumination—the *essential* deep structure of the subtle realm everywhere announces itself: insight into, and absorption as, Archetypal Essence.

THE ULTIMATE REALMS

As the process of transcendence and integration continues, it discloses even higher-order unities, leading, consumately, to Unity itself.

Beyond the high-subtle lies the causal region, known variously as the *alaya-vijnana* (Yogacara Buddhism), the *anandamayakosha* (Hinduism), *pneuma* (Christian mysticism), *karana-sharira* (Vedanta), Binah and Chokhmah (Kabbalah), Dharmakaya (Mahayana), and so on. Again, for convenience, we divide it into the low-causal and the high-causal.

The low-causal, which classically is revealed in a state of consciousness known as *savikalpa samadhi,* represents the pinnacle of God consciousness (or Archetypal-Formal absorption), the final and highest abode of Ishvara, the Creatrix of all realms. This represents the *culmination* of events which began in the high-subtle. In the high-subtle, recall, the self was dissolved or reabsorbed into Archetypal deity, *as* that deity—a deity which from the beginning has always been one's own Self and highest Archetype.

Now at the low-causal, that deity-Archetype itself condenses and dissolves into final-God, which is variously described as an extraordinarily subtle audible illumination or *bija-mantra* or point source from which the individual *ishtadeva, yidam,* or Archetype emerged in the first place.

Final-God (by whatever name and under whatever surface structure appearance) is simply the ground or essence of all the archetypal, pseudo-nirvanic, and lesser-god manifestations which were evoked—and then identified with—in the subtle realms. In the low-causal, all of these Archetypal Forms and illuminations simply reduce to their Source in final-God, and thus, by the very same token and in the very same step, one's own self is here shown to *be* that final-God, and consciousness itself thus transforms upward into a higher-order identity with that Radiance. In Theravadin Buddhism, this is the culmination of the fourth *jhana* (the highest *jhana* of form) and the beginning of the fifth and sixth *jhanas* (the lowest *jhanas* without form); in *vipassana*, this is the great transition insight from the pseudonirvana of subtle-form to the cessation, nirvanic, or formless state of the high-causal; in Zen, this is the seventh of the ten "ox-herding" stages to enlightenment: the transition from formal consciousness to formless consciousness.

Beyond the low-causal, into the high-causal, all manifest forms are so radically transcended that they no longer need even appear or arise in Consciousness. This is total and utter transcendence and release into Formless Consciousness, Boundless Radiance. There is here no self, no God, no final-God, no subjects, and no thingness, apart from or other than Consciousness as Such.

Note the overall progression of the higher-unity structures: In the subtle realm, the self dissolves into archetypal deity (as *ishtadeva, yidam, dhyani*-buddha, audible-illuminations, etc.). In the low-causal, that Deity-Self in turn disappears into final-God, which is its Source and Essence. Here, in the high-causal, the final-God Self is reduced likewise to its own prior Ground: it dissolves into Formlessness, or Infinite and Unobstructed Consciousness. Each step is an increase in consciousness and an intensification of Awareness until all forms return to perfect and radical release in Formlessness.

John Blofeld describes beautifully one form of this general progression from the Vajrayana Buddhist view: "As the rite progresses, this deity [cf. *ishtadeva*] enters the adept's body and sits upon a solar-disc supported by a lunar-disc above a lotus in his heart [these are visualizations used to train concentration]; presently the adept shrinks in size until he and the deity are coextensive [the beginning of the subtle]; then, merging indistinguishably [becoming *one* with deity-form in the high-subtle], they are absorbed by the seed-syllable from which the deity originally sprang [the low-causal]; this syllable contracts to a single point [final-God]; the point vanishes and deity and adept in perfect union remain sunk in the *samadhi* of voidness [the high-causal]."[16]

We already heard Lex Hixon, representing the Hindu view, describe the progression into the subtle realm. But he naturally continues the account into the causal: After the *ishtadeva*-archetype has emerged and one has identified with it (in the high-subtle), then "that Archetype dissolves into its own essence, or ground [the causal]. . . . There is now perfect release into the radiance of formless Consciousness. There is no *ishtadeva*, no meditator, and no meditation, nor is there any awareness of an absence of these. There is only radiance."[61]

Precisely the same sequence is described by Zen texts on *koan* study. After the initial stages of concentrating on the *koan* (this is equivalent to visualizing the *ishtadeva* or *dhyani*-buddha), a point is reached where the individual dissolves into the *koan*—he becomes *one* with the *koan* in a superabundance of consciousness: not a loss of awareness but an extraordinary intensification of it. This is called "the man forgotten"—that is, the separate subject is forgotten in union with the *koan,* which now alone is. This is the subtle state. As this process intensifies, the *koan* itself is forgotten—that is, it dissolves itself into its own prior ground of Formlessness. This is called "the *dharma* (the *koan*) forgotten" or "both man and *dharma* forgotten"—and this is the high-causal of formless *samadhi.* This overall process is so consistently and similarly described by all the traditions which reach this high realm that we can now be quite certain of its general (deep structure) features. They are unmistakable.

Let us note that this state itself—the high-causal of "both man and *dharma* forgotten"—is known as *nirvikalpa samadhi* (Hinduism), *jnana samadhi* (Vedanta); it is the seventh *jhana* (Theravada); the stage of effortless insight and beginning *nirodh/nirvana (vipassana);* and it is the eighth of the ten ox-herding stages in Zen.

Passing through *nirvikalpa samadhi,* Consciousness totally awakens as its Original Condition and Suchness *(tathata),* which is, at the same time, the condition and suchness of all that is, gross, subtle, or causal. That which witnesses, and that which is witnessed, are only one and the same. The entire World Process then arises, moment to moment, as one's own Being, outside of which, and prior to which, nothing exists. That Being is totally beyond and prior to anything that arises, and yet no part of that Being is other to what arises.

And so: as the center of self was shown to be Archetype; and as the center of Archetype was shown to be final-God; and as the center of final-God was shown to be Formlessness—so the center of Formlessness is shown to be not other than the entire world of Form. "Form is not other than Emptiness, Emptiness is not other than Form," says the most famous Buddhist Sutra ("The Heart Sutra"). At that point, the extraordinary and the ordinary, the supernatural and the mundane, are precisely one and the same. This is the tenth Zen ox-herding picture, which reads: "The gate of his cottage is closed and even the wisest cannot find him. He goes his own way, making no attempt to follow the steps of earlier sages. Carrying a gourd, he strolls into the market; leaning on his staff, he returns home."

This is also *sahaja samadhi,* the Turiya state, the Svabhavikakaya—the ultimate Unity, wherein all things and events, while remaining perfectly separate and discrete, are only One. By the same token, this is the radically perfect integration of all prior levels—gross, subtle, and causal, which, now of themselves so, continue to arise moment to moment in an iridescent play of mutual interpenetration. This is the final differentiation of Consciousness from all forms in Consciousness, whereupon Consciousness as Such is released in Perfect Transcendence, which is not a transcendence from the world but a final transcendence as the World. Consciousness henceforth *operates,* not on the world, but only as the entire World Process, integrating and interpenetrating all levels, realms, and planes, high or low, sacred or profane.

And this, finally, is the ultimate Unity toward which all evolution, human and cosmic, drives. And, it might be said, cosmic evolution—that holistic pattern—is completed in and as human evolution, which itself reaches ultimate unity consciousness and so completes that absolute gestalt toward which all manifestation moves.

4

Development, Meditation, and the Unconscious

THE FORM OF DEVELOPMENT

OVERALL, THE PROCESS of psychological development—which is the operation, in humans, of cosmic or universal evolution—proceeds in a most articulate fashion. As we saw in the last chapter, at each stage of development, a higher-order structure—more complex and therefore more unified—emerges through a differentiation of the preceding, lower-order level. This higher-order structure is introduced to consciousness, and eventually the self *identifies* with that emergent structure. For example, when the body emerged from its pleromatic fusion with the material world, consciousness became a body-self: identified with the body. The self was then no longer *bound* to the pleromatic fusion, but it *was* bound to the body. As language emerged in consciousness, the self began to shift from a solely biological body-self to a syntaxic ego—the self eventually identified itself with language and operated *as* a syntaxic self. It was then no longer bound exclusively to the body, but it *was* bound to the mental-ego. Likewise, in advanced evolution, the deity-Archetype emerges, is introduced to consciousness (in the subtle), the self then identifies with and as that Archetype, and operates from that identification. The self is then no longer exclusively bound to the ego, but it *is* bound to its own Archetype, and so on.

The point is that as each higher-order structure emerges, the self even-

243

tually identifies with that structure—which is normal, natural, appropriate. As evolution proceeds, however, each level in turn is differentiated from the self, or "peeled off," so to speak. The self, that is, eventually *disidentifies* with its present structure so as to *identify* with the next higher-order emergent structure. More precisely, we say that the self detaches itself from its *exclusive* identification with that lower structure. It doesn't throw that basic structure away, it simply no longer exclusively identifies with it. The point is that because the self is differentiated from the lower structure, it *transcends* that structure and can thus *operate* on that lower structure, using as tools the newly emergent structure.

Thus, when the body-self was differentiated from the material environment, it could operate on the environment using the tools of the body itself (such as the muscles). As the ego-mind was then differentiated from the body, it could operate on the body and world with *its* tools (concepts, syntax). As the subtle self was differentiated from the ego-mind, it could operate on the mind, body, and world using its structures (*siddhi,* intuition), and so on.

Thus, at each point in psychological growth, we find: (1) a higher-order structure emerges in consciousness; (2) the self identifies its being with that higher structure; (3) the next-higher-order structure eventually emerges; (4) the self dis-identifies with the lower structure and shifts its essential identity to the higher structure; (5) consciousness thereby transcends the lower structure; and (6) becomes capable of operating on that lower structure from the higher-order level; so that (7) all preceding levels can be integrated in consciousness. We noted that each successively higher-order structure is more complex, more organized, and more unified—and evolution continues until there is only Unity, ultimate in all directions, whereupon the force of evolution is exhausted, and there is perfect release in Radiance as the entire World Flux.

A few technical points: Using the terms of linguistics, we say that each level of consciousness consists of a *deep structure* and a *surface structure.* The deep structure is the *defining form* of a level, which embodies all of the potentials and limitations of that level. Surface structure is simply a *particular* manifestation of the deep structure. The surface structure is constrained by the form of the deep structure, but within that form it is free to select various contents. To use a simple example, take a ten-story building: each of the floors is a deep structure, whereas the various rooms and objects on each floor are surface structures. All body-selves are on the second floor; all verbal ego-minds are on the fifth floor; all subtle archetypes are on the eighth floor; the causal is on top and the building itself is Consciousness as Such. The point is that although all verbal egos are quite different, they are all on the fifth floor: they all share the same deep structure.

Now the movement of surface structures we call *translation*; the movement of deep structures we call *transformation*. Thus, if we move furniture around on the fourth floor, that is a translation; but if we move up to the seventh floor, that is a transformation. Thus, each transformation upward marks the emergence in consciousness of a new and higher level, with a new deep structure, within which new translations or surface structures can unfold and operate.

Every time a higher-order deep structure emerges, the lower-order structures are subsumed, enveloped, or comprehended by it. That is, at each point in evolution or development, what is the *whole* of one level becomes merely a *part* of the higher-order whole of the next level. We saw, for example, that the body is, during the earlier stages of growth, the *whole* of the self-sense—that is, the body-ego. As the mind emerges and develops, however, the sense of identity shifts to the mind, and the body becomes merely one aspect, one part of the total self. Similarly, as the subtle level emerges, the mind and body—which together had constituted the whole of the self-system—become merely aspects or parts of the new and more encompassing self.

In precisely the same way, we can say that at each point in evolution or development, a *mode* of self becomes merely a *component* of a higher-order self (e.g., the body was *the* mode of self before the mind emerged, whereupon it became merely a component of self). This can be put in several different ways, each of which tells us something important about development, evolution, and transcendence: (1) what is *identification* becomes *detachment*; (2) what is *context* becomes *content* (that is, the context of cognition and experience of one level becomes simply a content of the cognition and experience of the next); (3) what is *ground* becomes *figure* (which releases higher-order ground); (4) what is *subjective* becomes *objective* (until both terms become meaningless); and (5) what is *condition* becomes *element* (e.g., the mind, which is the *a priori* condition of egoic experience, becomes merely an element of experience in the subtle).

Each of those points is, in effect, a definition of *transcendence*. Yet each is also a definition of a stage of *development*. It follows that the two are essentially identical, and that evolution, as has been said, is actually "self-realization through self-transcendence."

THE TYPES OF THE UNCONSCIOUS

Many accounts of "the unconscious" simply assume that it is there, either as process or as content, from the start, and then proceed to describe its layers, levels, grounds, modes, or contents. But I believe that approach must be supplemented by developmental or evolutionary concerns on the one hand, and dynamic factors on the other.

Let me give a few examples of the problem itself: Transactional Analysis speaks of unconscious (or preconscious) script programming, containing *verbal* commands such as "feel guilty" or "collect anxiety." The job of the script analyst is to discover these commands, make them explicit and conscious, and thus release the client from their compulsive power. For simplicity's sake, let's call this the "verbal-script unconscious."

Let us now note a rather simple point: A preverbal child cannot have a verbal-script unconscious. Rather, language itself will have to *emerge* developmentally, then be loaded with script commands which will then have to sink back below the ordinary threshold of consciousness—at which point, and not before, we may speak of the unconscious script. In the same way, a child in the prephallic stage cannot have a phallic fixation, the preegoic infant doesn't possess unconscious ego-character structure, and so on.

Clearly, what exists in "the" unconscious depends in large measure on developmental concerns—*all* of the unconscious, in all its forms, is not just given at the start. Yet, to continue the story, many writers seem to assume that there is a "transpersonal unconscious" that is present but repressed from the beginning, whereas—if it is like verbal programming, character structure, mental capacity, abstract thinking, and higher structures in general—it is not yet repressed because it has not yet developmentally had the chance to emerge. It is not yet repressed from awareness because it has not yet even tentatively emerged in awareness in the first place.

With this developmental and dynamic, as opposed to static and given, viewpoint in mind, I will now outline five basic types of unconscious processes. These are *types* of unconscious processes, not *levels* of the unconscious (although I will mention those as well). This outline is meant to be neither exhaustive nor definitive, but simply indicative of concerns I feel psychology in general, and contemplative psychology in particular, must address.

1. *The Ground-Unconscious.* By "ground" I intend an essentially neutral meaning; it is not to be confused with "Ground of Being" or "Open Ground" or "Primal Ground." Although in a certain sense it is "all-encompassing," it is basically a developmental concept. The fetus "possesses" the ground-unconscious; in essence, it is *all the deep structures existing as potentials ready to emerge at some future point.* All the deep structures given to a collective humanity—pertaining to every level of consciousness from the body to mind to soul to spirit, gross, subtle, and causal—are enfolded or enwrapped or undifferentiated in the ground-unconscious. All of those structures are unconscious, but they are *not* repressed because they have not yet entered consciousness. Development or evolution consists of a series of hierarchical transformations, unfoldings, or differentiations of the deep structures out of the ground-unconscious, starting with the lowest (matter and body) and ending with the highest (causal and ultimate). When—and if—*all* of the ground-unconscious has emerged, then there is *only* consciousness: all is conscious *as* the All. As Aristotle put it, when all potential has been actualized, the result is God.

Notice that the ground-unconscious is largely devoid of surface structures, for these are basically *learned* during the unfolding of deep structures. This is similar to Jung's idea of the archetypes as "forms devoid of content." As Jung put it, an archetype (deep structure) "is determined as to its content [surface structure] only when it becomes conscious and is therefore filled out with the material of conscious experience."[48] Everyone "inherits" the *same* basic deep structures; but everybody learns *individual* surface structures, which can be quite similar or quite dissimilar from those of other individuals and especially other cultures (but still within the constraints of the deep structures themselves). This is also very similar to Hartmann's conception of an "undifferentiated matrix" or "in-born apparatuses," a concept accepted by virtually all modern schools of psychoanalytic ego psychology. In the words of Blanck and Blanck, "As we presently know it, then, the undifferentiated matrix contains potential ego, id, drive, affect, psyche, soma, and still more to be discovered."[13] I would simply add that that "more to be discovered" includes all the higher levels we have discussed; and that the undifferentiated matrix contains basically only the *deep structures* of all these components and levels, for the surface structures are individually learned and culturally molded, and thus can vary from person to person. This sum of native deep structures, then, we call the ground-unconscious.

Now all of the following types of the unconscious can be defined in relation to the ground-unconscious. This gives us a concept of unconscious processes that is at once structural and dynamic, layered and developmental.

2. *The Archaic-Unconscious.* Freud's initial pioneering efforts in psychoanalysis led him to postulate two basically distinct psychic systems: the system-unconscious, as he called it, and the system-conscious. The unconscious was, he felt, *generated* by repression: certain impulses, because they were dynamically resisted by the system-conscious, were forcefully expelled from awareness. "The unconscious" and "the repressed" were basically the same.

Eventually, however, Freud came to speak, not so much of the system-conscious and the system-unconscious, but rather of the ego and the id, and these two formulations did not overlap very clearly. That is, the ego was *not* the same as the system-conscious, and the id was not the same as the system-unconscious. First of all, parts of the ego (the superego, the defenses, and the character-structure) were *unconscious*; and parts of the id were unconscious *but not repressed*. In his words, "We recognize that the Ucs. does not coincide with the repressed; it is still true that all that is repressed is Ucs., but not all that is Ucs. is repressed."[44]

Not all that is unconscious is repressed because, as Freud came to see, some of the unconscious simply finds itself unconscious from the start—it is not first a personal experience which is then repressed, but something that, as it were, *begins* in the unconscious. Freud had once thought that the symbols in dreams and phantasies could be traced back to real life personal experiences, but he came to see that many of the symbols found in dreams and in phantasies could not possibly have been generated by personal experience. "Whence comes the necessity for these phantasies and the material for them?" we hear him ask. "There can be no doubt about the instinctual sources; but how is it to be explained that the same phantasies are always formed with the same content? I have an answer to this which I know will seem to you very daring. I believe that these *primal phantasies* . . . are a phylogenetic possession. In them the individual . . . stretches out . . . to the experiences of past ages."[47] This phylogenetic or "archaic heritage" included, besides instincts, "abbreviated repetitions of the evolution undergone by the whole human race through long-drawn-out periods and from prehistoric ages." Although Freud differed profoundly from Jung on the nature of this archaic heritage, he nevertheless stated that "I fully agree with Jung in recognizing the existence of this phylogenetic heritage."[48]

For Jung, of course, the "phylogenetic heritage" consisted of the instincts and the mental-forms or images associated with the instincts, which he eventually (and unfortunately) termed the *archetypes*. For Jung, instinct and archetype were intimately related—almost one. As Frey-Rohn explains it, "The connection between instinct and archetypal image appeared to [Jung] so close that he drew the conclusion that the two were coupled. . . . He saw the primordial image [the "archetype"] as the self-portrait of the instinct—in other words, the instinct's perception of itself."[48] As for these archaic-images themselves:

> Man inherits these images from his ancestral past, a past that includes all of his human ancestors as well as his prehuman or animal ancestors. These racial images are not inherited in the sense that a person consciously remembers or has images that his ancestors had. Rather they are predispositions or potentialities for experiencing and responding to the world in the same ways that his ancestors did [they are, that is, archaic deep structures].[58]

Such is the archaic-unconscious, which is simply the most primitive and least developed structures of the ground-unconscious—the pleroma (physical matter), the uroboros (alimentary drives), the typhon (emotional-sexual energies), and various primitive mental-phantasmic forms. They are initially unconscious but unrepressed, and some tend to remain unconscious, never clearly unfolded in awareness. Self-reflexive awareness is out of the question with these structures, so they always retain a heavy mood of unconsciousness, *with* or *without* repression (which is a significant point). The "prevailing quality of the id," said Freud, "is that of being unconscious,"[46] and that is the *nature* of the id, not something *created* by repression.

Incidentally, I do not share Jung's enthusiasm over the archaic images; and I do not equate the archetypes, which are highly advanced structures lying in the high-subtle and low-causal, with the archaic-images, which are, as Jung himself said, instinctual or typhonic counterparts. I agree with most everything Jung says about the archaic images as archaic images, but I do not equate them with the archetypes per se. (See chapter 7.)

At any rate, following both Freud and Jung, we can say in general that the somatic side of the archaic-unconscious is the id (instinctual, limbic, typhonic, pranic); the psychic side is the phylogenetic phantasy heritage. On the whole, the archaic-unconscious is not the product of personal experience; it is initially unconscious but not repressed; it contains the earliest and most primitive structures to unfold from the ground-unconscious, and, even when unfolded, they tend toward subconsciousness. They are largely preverbal and most are subhuman.

3. *The Submergent-Unconscious.* Once a deep structure has emerged from the ground-unconscious and taken on various surface structures, those surface structures, for various reasons, can be returned to a state of unconsciousness. That is, once a structure has emerged, it can be submerged, and the total of such structures we call the submergent-unconscious. The submergent-unconscious is that which was once conscious, in the lifetime of the individual, but is now screened out of awareness.

Now the submergent-unconscious can include, in principle, every structure that has emerged, whether collective, personal, archaic, subtle, and so on. It can contain collective elements that have clearly and unequivocally emerged and then been suppressed, or it can contain personal elements molded and learned in this lifetime and then suppressed, or it can contain a mixture of both. Jung has written extensively on just that subject, and we needn't repeat him here. But we should notice that even Freud was aware of the difference between the archaic-unconscious id and the submergent-unconscious id, even if it is occasionally hard to perfectly differentiate them. "In the course of this slow development certain contents of the id were . . . taken into the ego; others of its contents remained in the id unchanged, as its scarcely accessible nucleus. During this development, however, the young and feeble ego put back into the unconscious state some of the material it had already taken in, dropped it, and behaved in the same way to some fresh impressions it might have taken in, so that these, having been rejected, could leave only a trace in the id. In consideration of its origin, we speak of this latter portion of the id as *the repressed* [in contrast to the first part which was simply unconscious from the start: the archaic-unconscious]."[46] There is the difference, or rather one of them, between the original archaic-unconscious and the repressed or submergent-unconscious. But, as Freud says: "It is of little importance that we are not always able to draw a sharp line between these two categories of contents in the id. They coincide approximately with the distinction between what was innately present originally [the archaic-unconscious] and what was acquired in the course of the ego's development [the submergent-unconscious]."[46] Notice that Freud arrives at these conclusions on the basis of developmental thinking: "in consideration of its *origin*. . . ."

The submergent-unconscious becomes unconscious for various reasons, and these reasons lie along a *continuum of inattention*. This continuum ranges from simple forgetting through selective forgetting to forceful/dynamic forgetting (the latter alone being repression proper). Of the *personal* submergent-unconscious, Jung states:

> The personal unconscious . . . includes all those psychic contents which have been forgotten during the course of the individual's life. Traces of them are still preserved in the unconscious, even if all conscious memory of them has been lost. In addition, it contains all subliminal impressions or perceptions which have too little energy to reach consciousness. To these we must add unconscious combinations of ideas that are still too feeble and too indistinct to cross over the threshold. Finally, the personal unconscious contains all psychic contents that are incompatible with the conscious attitude.[68]

Simple forgetting and lack of threshold response constitute the *subliminal submergent-unconscious*. Dynamic or forceful forgetting, however, is repression proper, Freud's great discovery. The *repressed submergent-unconscious* is that aspect of the ground-unconscious which, upon emerging and picking up surface structures, is then forcefully repressed or returned to unconsciousness due to an incompatibility with conscious structures (for which, see the next section).

The personal aspect of the repressed submergent-unconscious is the *shadow*. Once rendered unconscious, the shadow can be strongly influenced by the archaic-unconscious (following primary process laws and the pleasure principle, which dominate the typhonic realms), although this is definitely a relative affair. I agree with Jung, for instance, that the shadow *can* be verbal and highly structured (similar in structure and content to the ego/persona). Actually, there seems to be a continuum of unconscious structure, ranging from the highly structured verbal components of the unconscious (e.g., scripts) all the way down to the primal chaos of the unstructured or barely structured *materia prima,* the pleromatic fusion base of the archaic-unconscious. Needless to say, one of the major reasons for repressing the shadow is that it becomes a vehicle for the archaic-unconscious: loaded with instinctual impulses which are felt to be incompatible with the ego.

4. *The Embedded-Unconscious.* We come now to that aspect of the unconscious which most puzzled Freud, but which is nonetheless one

of his greatest discoveries. Recall that Freud abandoned the conscious-unconscious model in favor of the ego-id model because "we recognize that the *Ucs.* does not coincide with the repressed; it is still true that all that is repressed is *Ucs.*, but not all that is *Ucs.* is repressed." Besides the archaic-unconscious, which was unconscious but unrepressed, Freud found that "it is certain that much of the ego is itself unconscious." At the same time, he began to locate the *origin* of repression in the ego, because "we can say that the patient's resistance arises from his ego. . . ."[43]

The point was this: Repression *originates* in some part of the ego; it is some aspect of the ego that represses the shadow-id. But Freud then discovered that part of the ego was itself unconscious, *yet it was not repressed.* He simply put two and two together and concluded that the *unrepressed* part of the ego was the *repressing* part. This part he called the superego: it was unconscious, unrepressed, but repressing. "We may say that repression is the work of this superego and that it is carried out either by itself or by the ego in obedience to its orders . . . portions of the both of them, the ego and the superego themselves, are unconscious."[45] But *not* repressed.

Before we try to make sense of this unrepressed but repressing structure, I must briefly recap my general theory of repression, a theory based on the works of Piaget, Freud, Sullivan, Jung, and Loevinger. In essence, we have this: The process of *translation,* by its very nature, tends to screen out all perceptions and experiences which do not conform to the basic limiting principles of the translation itself. This is normal, necessary, and healthy, and forms the basis of "necessary and normal defense mechanisms"—it prevents the self-system from being overwhelmed by its surroundings, internal or external. This is normal "inattention," and—in contrast to a plethora of theories which maintain that such "filtering" is reality corrupting—it is absolutely essential for normal equilibration.

Should, however, binds arise in the translation process of any level, then the individual mistranslates his self and his world (which means that he distorts or deletes, displaces or condenses, aspects of the deep structure that could just as well exist correctly as surface structures). This can occur in any number of ways, and for any number of reasons—and it can be expressed in terms of "energy thresholds" or "informational distortions." The essential point is that the individual is now selectively inattentive or forcefully restrictive of his awareness. He no longer simply translates his self and world (via "normal inattention"), he translates *out,* or edits, any aspects of his self and world which are threatening (via forced and *selective* inattention). This mistranslation results in both a *symptom* and a *symbol,* and the job of the therapist is to help the individual retranslate ("the interpretation") his symbolic symptoms back into their original forms by suggesting *meanings* for the symbol-symptoms. ("Your feelings of anxiety are really feelings of masked rage.") Repression is simply a form of mistranslation, but a mistranslation that is not just a mistake but an *intentional* (even if unconscious) editing, a dynamic repression with vested interests. The individual does not just forget: he doesn't want to remember.

We saw that at each level of development, the self-sense identifies with the newly emergent structures of that level. When the body emerged from the pleroma, the self identified with it; when the verbal-mind emerged, the self identified with it; and so on. Further, it is the nature of an exclusive identification that one does not and cannot realize that identification without *breaking* that identification. In other words, all exclusive identification is unconscious identification—by definition and fact. At the moment the child realizes that he *has* a body, he no longer is *just* the body: he is aware of it; he transcends it; he is looking at it with his mind and therefore cannot be *just* a body any longer. Likewise, at the point the adult realizes he has a mind, he is no longer just a mind—he is actually starting to perceive it from the subtle regions beyond mind. Prior to those points, the self was more or less exclusively identified with those structures and therefore *could not realize it.* The self could not see those structures because the self *was* those structures.

In other words, at each level of development, one cannot totally see the seer. No observing structure can observe itself observing. One uses the structures of that level as something with which to perceive and translate the world—but one cannot perceive and translate those structures *themselves,* not totally. That can occur only from a higher level. The point is that each translation process sees but is not seen; it translates but is not itself translated; *and it can repress but is not itself repressed.*

The Freudian superego, with the defenses and the character-structure, is those aspects of the ego level with which the self is unconsciously *identified,* so much so that they cannot be *objectively* perceived (as can the rest of the ego). They translate without being translated—they are repressing but unrepressed. This fits very well with Freud's own thoughts on the matter, because he himself felt that (1) the superego is created by an *identification* ("identifications replace object-choices"), and (2) one of the aims of therapy is to make the superego conscious—to see it as an object and thus cease using it as something through which to see and (mis)translate the world. This is simply one instance of the overall evolution process we earlier described, where—once one has identified with a newly emergent structure, which is necessary and desirable—one *then* becomes free of that structure by dis-identifying with it, later to integrate it in a higher-order unity. I should quickly mention that, according to Freud, the superego is frequently severe and "masochistic" because contaminated (regressively) by the archaic-unconscious.

Anyway, the superego is simply one instance of what we call the *embedded-unconscious:* because it is embedded *as* the self, the self cannot totally or accurately see it. It is unconscious, but *not* repressed. It is that aspect of the ground-unconscious which, upon emergence, emerges *as* the self-system and so remains essentially unconscious, possessing the power to send other elements to the repressed-submergent-unconscious. Again, it is unrepressed but repressing. This can and does occur at every level of consciousness, although the specifics naturally vary considerably, because the tools of resistance are simply the structures of the given level, and each level has quite different structures (for example, when the body-ego *was* the embedded-unconscious, it used not repression but introjection and projection as the modes of mistranslation, because introjection and projection are part of the primary process structure which dominates the typhonic-body realms). However, this whole process assumes its most violent, pathological, and characteristic forms with the mental-egoic level(s). All stages of development possess their own embedded-unconscious, but those lower than the mental-egoic are not really strong enough to generate fierce repression (the archaic-id is originally unrepressed *and* unrepressing), and those higher than the mental-egoic become so transcendent and integrated that repression—as we ordinarily think of it—tends to fade out. The higher realms do possess their own forms of resistances, generated by their respective embedded-unconscious, but this is a matter for a separate study (see chapter 9).

5. *The Emergent-Unconscious.* Let us now examine someone who has evolved from the pleroma to the body-self to the ego-mind. There still remain in the ground-unconscious the deep structures of the subtle and causal realms. These structures have not yet emerged; they cannot, as a rule, emerge in consciousness until the lower structures have emerged and consolidated. At any rate, it is certainly ridiculous to speak of realizing the transpersonal until the personal has been formed. The transpersonal (the subtle and causal) realms are not yet repressed—they

are *not* screened out of awareness, they are not filtered out—they simply have not yet had the opportunity to emerge. We do not say of a two-year-old child that he or she is resisting the learning of geometry, because the child's mind has not yet developed and unfolded to the degree that he or she could even begin to learn mathematics. Just as we do not accuse the child of repressing mathematics, we do not accuse him of repressing the transpersonal . . . not yet, that is.

At *any* point on the developmental cycle, those deep structures which have not yet emerged from the ground-unconscious are referred to as the *emergent-unconscious*. For someone at the ego (or centaur) level, the low-subtle, the high-subtle, the low-causal, and the high-causal are emergent-unconscious. They are unconscious, *but not repressed*.

Now supposing that development is not arrested at the ego-centaur realm—which is usually the case at this point in history—the subtle will of itself begin to emerge from the ground-unconscious. It is not really possible to set timetables for these higher realms and stages, because a collective humanity has only evolved to the ego level, and thus only levels leading up to that have been determined as to emergence. In general, however, the subtle *can* begin to emerge after adolescence, but rarely before. And for all sorts of reasons, the emergence of the subtle can be resisted and even, in a sense, repressed. For the ego is strong enough to repress not only the lower realms but also the higher realms—it can seal off the superconscious as well as the subconscious.

That part of the ground-unconscious whose emergence is resisted or repressed, we call, appropriately enough, the *emergent-repressed unconscious*. It is that part of the ground-unconscious which—*excluding developmental arrest*—remains unconscious *past* the point at which it could just as well become conscious. We are then justified in looking for reasons for this lack of emergence, and we find them in a whole set of defenses, actual defenses, against transcendence. They include rationalization ("Transcendence is impossible or pathological"); isolation or avoidance of relationship ("My consciousness is supposed to be skin-bounded!"); death terror ("I'm afraid to die to my ego; what would be left?"); desacralizing (Maslow's term for refusing to see transcendent values anywhere); substitution (a lower structure is substituted for the intuited higher structure, with the pretense that the lower *is* the higher); and contraction (into forms of lower knowledge or experience). Any or all of these defenses simply become part of the ego's translation processes, such that the ego merely continues to translate when it should in fact begin tranformation.

Because psychoanalysis and orthodox psychology have never truly understood the nature of the emergent-unconscious in its higher forms, then as soon as the subtle or causal begins to emerge in awareness—perhaps as a peak experience or as subtle lights and bliss—they are all in tithers to explain it as a breakthrough of some archaic material or some past repressed impulses. Since they do not know of the emergent-unconscious, they try to explain it in terms of the *submergent*-unconscious. They think the subtle, for example, is not a higher structure emerging but a lower one reemerging; not the transtemporal coming down but the pretemporal coming back up. And so they trace *samadhi* back to infantile breast-union; they reduce transpersonal unity to prepersonal fusion in the pleroma; God is reduced to a teething nipple and all congratulate themselves on explaining the Mystery. This whole enterprise is starting to fall apart, of its own weight, because of the ridiculous number of things psychoanalysis is forced to attribute to the infant's first four months of life in order to account for *everything* that subsequently emerges.

At any rate, with an understanding of these six types of the unconscious (the ground-unconscious, archaic-unconscious, submergent-unconscious, embedded-unconscious, emergent-unconscious, and emergent-repressed-unconscious), as well as of translation/transformation and the stages of development presented in the last chapter, we can now turn to a quick study of meditation and the unconscious.

MEDITATION AND THE UNCONSCIOUS

Most of the accounts of meditation and the unconscious suffer from a lack of concern with developmental or evolutionary factors. They tend simply to assume that the unconscious is *only* the submergent-unconscious (subliminal, filtered, screened, repressed, or automated), and thus they see meditation as a way to *reverse* a nasty state of affairs created in this lifetime: they see it as a way to force entry into the unconscious. Meditation is pictured as a way to lift the repression, halt the filtering, deautomate the automating or defocalize the focalizing. It is my own opinion that those issues, however significant, are the most secondary aspects of all types of meditation.

Meditation is, if anything, a sustained instrumental path of transcendence. And since—as we saw—transcendence and development are synonymous, it follows that meditation is simply *sustained development* or growth. It is not primarily a way to reverse things but a way to carry them on. It is the natural and orderly unfolding of successively higher-order unities, until there is only Unity, until all potential is actual, until all the ground-unconscious is unfolded as Consciousness.

Meditation thus occurs in the same way all the other growth/emergences did: one translation winds down and fails to exclusively dominate consciousness, and transformation to a higher-order translation occurs (a higher-order deep structure emerges, which then underlies and creates new surface structures). There is differentiation, dis-identification, transcendence, and integration. Meditation *is* evolution; it *is* transformation—there is nothing really special about it. It seems quite mysterious and convoluted to the ego because it is a development beyond the ego. Meditation is to the ego as the ego is to the typhon: developmentally more advanced. But the same process of *growth* and emergence runs through the whole sequence—the way we got *from* the typhon to the ego is the same way we go from the ego to Spirit. We grow, we don't dig back.

My first point is that most accounts of meditation assume that the transpersonal realms—the subtle and causal, by whatever names—are parts of the submergent-unconscious or repressed-submergent-unconscious, and that meditation means lifting the repression. And I am suggesting that the transpersonal realms are really part of the emergent-unconscious and meditation is just speeding up the emergence.

However—and this is what has so confused the picture—when a person (say, a young adult) begins meditation, all sorts of different things begin to happen, many of which are only incidentally and remotely related to the actual growth and transcendence process itself, and this greatly complicates the overall picture of meditation. With that problem in mind, I would first like to discuss the nature of the meditative stance itself, and then its general and complete course.

To begin with, we note that every *transformation* in development necessitates the surrendering of the particular present *translation* (or rather, the exclusiveness of that translation). For the average person, who has already evolved from the pleroma to the typhon to the ego, transformation into the subtle or causal realms demands that egoic-translation wind down and be surrendered. These egoic-translations are usually composed of verbal thoughts and concepts (and emotional reactions to those thoughts). Therefore meditation consists, *in the beginning,* of a way to *break conceptual translating* in order to open the way to subtle-level transformation.

In essence, this means *frustrate* the present translation and encourage the new transformation. As explained in *No Boundary,* this frustration/encouragement—on *any* level, typhon to ego to subtle to causal—is strategically brought about by *special conditions,* and these special conditions—again, on *any* level—simply embody a set of activities or functions characteristic of the next higher or sought-after level.[136] Psychoanalysis, for instance, speaks of the *selective frustrations* needed to help the infant move from a typhonic-impulsive body-self to a delayed and controlled mental-egoic self (the same type of selective frustrations the analyst must use in helping a neurotic *fixated* at infantile levels move to more channeled and mature responses); in this case: *"Put it into words, not impulses!"*

Just so, in moving *from* the ego-mind to the subtle or causal realms, selective frustrations *of* the ego-mind by the special conditions of meditative practice are necessary. In principle, this is no different than asking a child to put into words something he would rather act out typhonically. We are asking the ego to go one step further and put into subtle forms that which it would rather think about conceptually or verbally. Growth occurs by adopting higher translations until one can actually transform to that higher realm itself.

For example, the *yidam* or *ishtadeva:* individuals are shown a symbol of the *yidam*-deity, a symbol which, precisely because it embodies a higher state, corresponds to nothing in this present reality. They construct or translate this symbol into their own consciousness, to the point that the subtle-*yidam* actually emerges from the ground-unconscious into full awareness. Individuals eventually *identify* (as we explained with *all* development) with this higher structure, which breaks their lower translation as ego and raises them to a higher structure.

The Master (guru, roshi, etc.) simply continues to frustrate the old translations, to undermine the old resistances, and to encourage the new transformation by enforcing the special conditions (in this case, visualization of the *yidam*). This is true in *all* forms of meditation—concentrative or receptive, mantric or silent. In concentrative meditation, the special condition has a defined form; in receptive meditation, it is "formless"—both are enforced special conditions, however, and the individual who drops his formless or defocal awareness is chastised just as severely as the one who drops his *koan.*

Since some of the major characteristics of the higher realms include transtemporal timelessness, love, no avoidances or attachments, total acceptance, and subject-object unity, these are most often the *special conditions* of meditation—"Stay in the Now always"; "Recognize your avoidances of relationship"; "Be only Love in all conditions"; "Become one with your meditation and your world"; "Accept everything since everything is Brahman"; and so on. Our parents helped us move from the first floor of consciousness to the fifth floor by imposing the special conditions of language and egoic self-control. Just so, the Master helps us move from the fifth floor to the higher floors by imposing the special conditions of the higher upon us as practice.

It does not, in essence, matter whether the special conditions are a concentrative-absorptive or a receptive-defocal mode of meditation. The former breaks the lower and egoic translation by halting it, the latter by watching it. What they both have in common is what is essential and effective about both: jamming a translation by concentration or watching a translation by defocalizing can only be done from the next highest level. They both accomplish (eventually) the same goal, the breaking of a lower-order translation resulting in a higher-order transformation. Both are also intensely *active* processes. Even "passive receptivity" is, as Benoit said, activity on a higher plane. (This is not to say, however, that the receptive-defocal mode and the concentrative-absorptive mode are identical, or that they produce the same secondary results. This will become obvious when we outline the course of a typical meditation.)

Before discussing what transpires in meditation, however, it is important to realize that not all schools of meditation aim for the same general realm of consciousness. Rather, as we have already suggested in the previous chapters, the transpersonal and superconscious realms really break down into several different levels (low- and high-subtle, low- and high-causal, etc.). Very few religions are aware of all of these distinctions, and thus many have more or less "specialized" in one level or another. Hence, meditative practices themselves break down generally into three major classes (cf. Free John).

The first is the Nirmanakaya class, which deals with bodily or typhonic energies and their transmutation or transformation into the low-subtle region, culminating at the *sahasrara*. This includes *hatha* yoga, *kundalini* yoga, *kriya* yoga, and particularly all forms of tantric yoga. The goal of the Nirmanakaya class, as I mentioned, is the *sahasrara*, the crown *chakra*, and it is exemplified by Patanjali.

The second is the Sambhogakaya class, which deals with the high-subtle regions, and aims for the seven (to ten) subphases of subtle growth and audible illuminations secreted within and beyond the *sahas-*

rara. This includes Nada yoga and Shabd yoga, and is exemplified by Kirpal Singh.

The third is the Dharmakaya class, which deals with the causal regions. It operates through neither tantric energy manipulation (the first five or six *chakras*) nor subtle light and sound absorption (the seventh *chakra* and the higher subphase *chakras* beyond), but rather through inquiry into the causal field of consciousness itself, inquiry into the root of I-ness or the separate self-sense, even in and through the Transcendent Witness of the causal region, until all forms of subject-object dualism are uprooted. This class is exemplified by Sri Ramana Maharshi, Maha-Ati Vajrayana, Zen Buddhism, and Vedanta Hinduism. At the terminal point of each path, one *can* fall into the prior Suchness of all realms, the Svabhavikakaya, although this is both easier and more likely the higher the path one initially adopts.

Let us now assume that a young adult takes up the practice of Zen in either its concentrative-*koan* or receptive-*shikantaza* form. Both of these are Dharmakaya practices, and so we will expect to see, if carried through to completion, not only a higher-causal culmination, but all sorts of lower-level manifestations in the intermediate stages.

To start with, the meditation practice begins to break the present egoic-translation by either halting it (*koan*) or watching it (*shikan*). Washburn has given an excellent account of some of the specifics of this process.[123] (His "reduction of intensity threshold" and "immobilization of psychic operations" are two ways of describing the winding down of a level's translations, which is prerequisite for both lower-level derepression and upward-transformation.) As the present egoic-translation begins to loosen, then the individual is first exposed to the *subliminal-submergent unconscious* (the nonrepressed-submergent-unconscious in general), which includes, among other things, the "innumerable unnoticed aspects of experiences, aspects tuned out due to habit, conditioning, or exigencies of the situation."[123] All sorts of odd memories float up, screen memories, insignificant memories, memories that are not repressed, merely forgotten or preconscious. Months can be spent "at the movies," watching the subliminal-submergent reemerge in awareness and dance before the inward eye.

As meditation progresses, however, the more resistant aspects of the egoic-translation are slowly undermined and dismantled in their exclusiveness. That is, the *embedded-unconscious* is jarred loose from its unconscious identification with the self and thus tends either to emerge as an actual object of awareness or to at least lose its hold on awareness.

Washburn states that psychic immobilization (the halting of egoic-trans-lation) "brings unconscious psychic operations into awareness by inter-fering with their normal functioning," so that "one can begin to look *at* it, rather than, as hitherto had been the case, merely looking *through* it."[123] I think that is an important point, but I would add that it applies basically to the embedded-unconscious (and parts of the repressed-sub-mergent-unconscious); but we don't bring, for example, the emergent-unconscious into awareness by "interfering with it" but rather by allow-ing it to emerge in the first place, just as we don't bring mathematics into awareness by interfering with it but by first learning it.

At any rate, the embedded-unconscious, by being "interfered with," starts to shake loose its habitual hold. Now recall that the embedded-unconscious translations were the unrepressed but repressing aspects of the self-system of a given level. Naturally, then, as the repressor is re-laxed, the repressed tends to emerge. That is to say, the *repressed-sub-mergent-unconscious* now tends to float—or sometimes erupt—into awareness. The individual confronts his shadow (and, on occasion, pri-mal or archaic phantasies from the archaic-unconscious). An individual can spend months or even years wrestling with his shadow, and this is where orthodox therapy can certainly complement meditation. (Inciden-tally, notice that what is released here is the repressed-submergent-unconscious, and not *necessarily* the subtle or causal emergent-unconscious, unless they are part of the emergent-repressed-unconscious screened out by the *same* defenses wielded against the shadow. This is indeed possible and even probable to a certain degree, but on the whole the defenses against the repressed shadow and those against an emergent God are of a different order, and up to this point in meditation, we are basically working with the former.)

Thus, what has happened, up to this stage in meditation, is that the individual—through the loosening of the egoic-translation and its em-bedded-unconscious—has "relived" his life up to that point. He has opened himself to all the traumas, the fixations, the complexes, the im-ages, and the shadows of all the prior levels of consciousness which have so far emerged in his life—the material-pleromatic, the alimentary-uroboric, the typhonic emotional-sexual, the verbal, and the mental-egoic. All of that is up for review, in a sense, and especially up for review are the "sore spots"—the fixations and repressions that occurred on the first five floors of his being. All of that occurring, and notice: *none* of it is yet of the *central* meditative state.

Incidentally, Washburn has suggested that only receptive meditation leads directly and immediately to the unconscious, whereas absorptive meditation "is so immersed in its object that all else, including messages from the unconscious, is unavailable to awareness; and for this reason confrontation with the unconscious can occur only after the object has been discarded, or after the practice has been concluded."[123] Again, I think that is quite true, but it applies to only some aspects of the developmental unconscious, particularly the archaic-, submergent-, and embedded-unconscious. While the concentrative practice is fully active, none of those aspects of the unconscious can "squeeze in." However, it does not apply to, for example, the subtle emergent-unconscious, because in the state of subtle absorption in the *yidam, mantram,* or *nada,* one *is* directly in touch with that previously unconscious state. Even if one doesn't cognize it as an object, which one doesn't, one is still intuitively alive to the subtle as the subtle. The concentrative path *disclosed* this subtle-realm aspect of the emergent-unconscious in a perfectly direct and immediate way, *during* the practice itself.

But while in the subtle, concentratively absorbed (*jhana*), it is true that no *other* objects tend to arise in awareness, and that would include, for example, the shadow. The subtle meditation does help to break the egoic-translation, however, so that when one ceases subtle absorption, one is indeed open to shadow-influx, just as Washburn describes. With receptive meditation, of course, one is open to whatever arises whenever it arises, and so one "sees" the shadow on the spot as it de-represses.

At any rate, as the subtle itself begins to emerge from the ground-unconscious, various high-archetypal illuminations and intuitions occur. I described the subtle realm earlier, and so needn't repeat it here. The point is that subtler and subtler translations emerge, are eventually undermined, and transformation to new and subtler translations occurs. This is nothing more than *development* in the subtle realm.

> It is the strongest impulses that are affected first, and as they dim, the meditator begins to discern more subtle ones—just as the setting of the sun brings the stars into view. But these more subtle impulses themselves wane, which allows even more subtle ones to be discriminated. Interestingly, this is not an absolutely continuous process, for during sitting meditation there occur interludes or virtual silence during which, it seems, one passes through some kind of psychic "membrane" that divides the present level from the next, subtler level. Once this divide has been passed, psychomental activity resumes . . . ; but its character is now much finer and more rarefied.[123]

The "membranes" are simply the translation processes of each level, which screen out the other levels and divide the present level from the rest; the "passing of this divide" is simply transformation to a higher, subtler, and "more rarefied" translation. "The new threshold [the new translation] that is established in this way can itself be reduced [transformed] by continued meditation, and this one too, and so on. In each case a new spectrum of lower-intensity, subtler objects becomes accessible to the meditator's inner sight."[123]

Although these subtle sounds and illuminations are the goal of the Sambhogakayas, they are all viewed as *makyo* (or inferior productions) by the Dharmakayas. Thus, if meditation continues into the causal realm, all prior objects, subtle or gross, are reduced to gestures of Consciousness as Such, until even the transcendent witness or I-ness of the causal realm is broken in the Great Death of Emptiness, and the unparalleled but only Obvious state of *sahaj* is resurrected. This is called *anuttara samyak sambodhi*. It is without recourse. At this final transformation, there are no longer any exclusive translations occurring anywhere; the translator "died." The mirror and its reflections are the same.

And so proceeds meditation, which is simply higher development, which is simply higher evolution—a transformation from unity to unity until there is simple Unity, whereupon Brahman, in an unnoticed shock of recognition and final remembrance, grins silently to itself, closes its eyes, breathes deeply, and throws itself outward for the millionth time, losing itself in its manifestations for the sport and play of it all. Evolution then proceeds again, transformation by transformation, remembering more and more, unifying more and more, until every soul remembers Buddha, as Buddha, in Buddha—whereupon there is then no Buddha and no soul. And that is the final transformation. When Zen Master Fa-ch'ang was dying, a squirrel screeched on the roof. "It's just this," he said, "and nothing more."

5

Physics, Mysticism, and the
New Holographic Paradigm

I N THE PRECEDING CHAPTERS we have seen that there might indeed exist the possibility of a "new and higher" or comprehensive-integral paradigm, one that at least attempts to include monological sciences, dialogical sciences, mandalic sciences, and contemplative sciences. I have not really presented such a paradigm in anything resembling a fully completed version; I have simply suggested and outlined what some of its central features might be. But I hope I have done so with enough persuasion to suggest that such a paradigm is at least a genuine *possibility*, grounded in a spectrum of solid methodologies, and open at every point to consensual review. At the very least, we have seen the disastrous consequences of trying to base such a paradigm on only *one* of the various modes of knowing available to the soul.

In the past few years, however, one such paradigm—generally called the "holographic paradigm"—has received much enthusiastic and international attention. And yet, for all its good intentions, it is based almost solely on empirical physics and empirical brain physiology and, indeed, claims to ground mystical states themselves in empirical data. As Lawrence Beynam eulogized this new theory: "We are currently undergoing a paradigm shift in science—perhaps the greatest shift of its kind to date. It is for the first time that we have stumbled upon a comprehensive model for mystical experiences, which has the additional advantage of deriving from the forefront of contemporary physics."[11]

While we all can certainly appreciate the fact that certain physicists are no longer *denying* the reality of mystical-transcendental states, we must nonetheless look with suspicion on this particular "new paradigm," simply because, in the final analysis, it seems shot through with profound category errors. In this chapter, then, we will look carefully and critically at each point of the holographic paradigm, pointing out exactly the problems involved. In the next chapter, I will present an interview that simplifies and summarizes not only the critique of this chapter, but also the overall topics we have discussed thus far.

THE PERENNIAL PHILOSOPHY

In order to understand how the new holographic paradigm fits into the overall scheme of things, it is necessary to have an overall scheme of things to begin with. The perennial philosophy has always offered such a scheme, and for purposes of convenience, it is one I will use here.

In what follows, I will summarize the *philosophia perennis*—leaving, however, enough details to work with—and then apply this philosophy to an elucidation and critique of both the "holographic paradigm" and the "new physics," touching briefly on each of the key points involved.

The most striking feature of the perennial philosophy/psychology is that it presents being and consciousness as a nested hierarchy of dimensional levels, moving from the lowest, densest, and most fragmentary realms to the highest, subtlest, and most unitary ones. In Hinduism, for example, the lowest level is called the *annamayakosha,* which means the level made of food—that is, the physical body and the material cosmos. The next level is *pranamayakosha*—the sheath made of biological functions, life-breath, emotions, bioenergy, and so on. Both of these levels, in Mahayana Buddhism, are referred to as the five *vijnanas*—the realm of the five senses and their physical objects.

The next highest level, according to Hinduism, is the *manomayakosha,* "the sheath made of mind." In Buddhism, this is called the *manovijnana*—the mind that stays (myopically) close to the five senses. This is approximately the level we in the West would call intellect, mind, mental-ego, secondary process, operational thinking, and so on.

Beyond conventional mind, according to Hinduism, is the *vijnanamayakosha* (what Buddhists call *manas*). This is a very high form of mind, so high, in fact, that it is better to refer to it by a different name—

the most common being "the subtle realm." The subtle is said to include archetypal processes, high-order insights and visions, ecstatic intuition, an extraordinary clarity of awareness, an open ground-consciousness that reaches far beyond the ordinary ego, mind, and body.

Beyond the subtle lies the causal realm (Hinduism: *anandamaya-kosha;* Buddhism: tainted *alayavijnana*). This is a realm of perfect transcendence, so perfect that it is said to reach beyond the conception, experience, and imagination of any ordinary individual. It is a realm of formless Radiance, of radical insight into all of manifestation, blissful release into infinity, the breaking of all boundaries, high or low, and of absolutely panoramic or perfectly mirrorlike wisdom and awareness.

Passing through the causal realm, consciousness reawakens to its absolute abode. This is Consciousness as Such, and not only is it the infinite limit of the spectrum of being, it is the nature, source, and suchness of each level of the spectrum. It is radically all-pervading, one without a second. At this point—but not before—all levels are seen to be perfect and equal manifestations of this ultimate Mystery. There are then no levels, no dimensions, no higher, no lower, no sacred, no profane, so matter-of-factly so that Zen describes it thus:

> As the wind sways the willows
> Velvet beads move in the air.
> As the rain falls on the pear blossoms
> White butterflies lilt in the sky.

The above summary would give us approximately six major dimensions—physical, biological, mental, subtle, causal, and ultimate (listed below). Now many traditions greatly subdivide and extend this model (the subtle, for instance, is said to consist of seven levels). But aside from that it is important to understand that *all* major perennial traditions agree with that general hierarchy, and most of them agree right down to details. Further, this hierarchy is not a nicety of philosophical side issues; for these traditions, it is the fundamental core of the perennial wisdom insofar as it can be stated in words. It is fair to say, then, that any account of the mystic's "world view" that leaves out this type of nested hierarchy is seriously inadequate.

According to the perennial traditions, each of these various levels has an appropriate field of study. The study of level–1 is basically that of physics and chemistry, the study of nonliving things. Level–2 is the realm of biology, the study of life processes. Level–3 is the level of both psychology (when awareness is "turned in") and philosophy (when it is "turned out"). Level–4, the subtle, is the realm of saintly religion; that is, religion which aims for visionary insight, halos of light and bliss, angelic or archetypal intuition, and so on. Level–5, the causal, is the realm of sagely religion, which aims not so much for higher experiences as for the dissolution and transcendence of the experiencer. This sagely path involves the transcendence of all subject-object duality in formless consciousness. Level–6, the ultimate, awaits any who push through the final barriers of levels 4 and 5 so as to radically awaken as ultimate consciousness.

1. Physical—nonliving matter/energy
2. Biological—living, sentient matter/energy
3. Psychological—mind, ego, logic, thinking
4. Subtle—archetypal, transindividual, intuitive
5. Causal—formless radiance, perfect transcendence
6. Ultimate—consciousness as such, the source and nature of all other levels

Notice that these different disciplines, like the levels which they address, are a nested hierarchy. That is, just as each level of the spectrum *transcends* but *includes* its predecessor, so each higher study envelops its junior disciplines—but not vice versa. Thus, for example, the study of biology uses physics, but the study of physics does not use biology.

That is another way of saying that the lower levels do not and cannot embrace the higher levels. The primary dictum of the perennial philosophy is that the higher cannot be explained by the lower or derived from the lower. (In fact, as we will see, the lower is created from the higher, a process called "involution.")

Even though the various dimensional-levels are hierarchic, this does not mean they are radically separate, discrete, and isolated from each other. They are indeed *different* levels, but different levels *of* Consciousness. Therefore, it is said that the various levels mutually interpenetrate one another. Here is an excellent description:

These "worlds" [or dimensional-levels] are not separate regions, spatially divided from one another, so that it would be necessary to move in space in order to pass from one to another. The higher worlds completely interpenetrate the lower worlds, which are fashioned and sustained by their activities.

What divides them is that each world has a more limited and controlled level of consciousness than the world above it. The lower consciousness is unable to experience the life of the higher worlds and is even unaware of their existence, although it is interpenetrated by them.

But if the beings of a lower world can raise their consciousness to a higher level, then that higher world becomes manifest to them, and they can be said to have passed to a higher world, although they have not moved in space.[109]

The various levels, then, are mutually interpenetrating and interconnecting. *But not in an equivalent fashion.* The higher transcends but includes the lower—*not* vice versa. That is, all of the lower is in the higher, but not all the higher is in the lower. As a simple example, there is a sense in which all of the reptile is in man, but not all of the man is in the reptile; all of the mineral world is in a plant but not vice versa, and so on. "The more highly evolved," explains Wachsmuth, "always contains in itself the attributes of the earlier, yet always develops as a new entity, an activity clearly distinguishable from that of the other."[109]

Thus, when the mystic-sage speaks of this type of mutual interpenetration, he or she means a *multidimensional interpenetration with nonequivalence.*

The explanation, by the mystic-sages, of this multidimensional interpenetration forms some of the most profound and beautiful literature in the world.* The essence of this literature, although it seems almost blasphemy to try to reduce it to a few paragraphs, is that "in the beginning" there is only Consciousness as Such, timeless, spaceless, infinite, and eternal. For no reason that can be stated in words, a subtle ripple is generated in this infinite ocean. This ripple could not in itself detract from infinity, for the infinite can embrace any and all entities. But this subtle ripple, awakening to itself, *forgets* the infinite sea of which it is just a gesture. The ripple therefore feels set apart from infinity, isolated, separate.

This ripple, very rarefied, is the causal region (level–5), the very beginning, however slight, of the wave of selfhood. At this point, however, it is still very subtle, still "close" to the infinite, still blissful.

---

* What follows is, approximately, a combination of the *Lankavatara Sutra, The Tibetan Book of the Dead,* and Western existentialism. For a more detailed account, see *The Atman Project.*[137]

But somehow not really satisfied, not profoundly at peace. For in order to find that utter peace, the ripple would have to return to the ocean, dissolve back into radiant infinity, forget itself and remember the absolute. But to do so, the ripple would have to die—it would have to accept the death of its separate self-sense. And it is terrified of this.

Since all it wants is the infinite, but since it is terrified of accepting the necessary death, it goes about seeking infinity in ways that prevent it. Since the ripple *wants* release and is *afraid* of it at the same time, it arranges a *compromise* and a *substitute*. Instead of finding actual God-head, the ripple pretends itself to be god, cosmocentric, heroic, all-sufficient, immortal. This is not only the beginning of narcissism and the battle of life against death, it is a *reduced* or *restricted* version of consciousness, because no longer is the ripple *one* with the ocean, it is trying itself to *be* the ocean.

Driven by this Atman-project—the attempt to get infinity in ways that prevent it and force substitute gratifications—the ripple creates ever tighter and ever more restricted modes of consciousness. Finding the causal less than perfect, it reduces consciousness to create the subtle (level–4). Eventually finding the subtle less than ideal, it reduces consciousness once again to create the mental (3). Failing there, it reduces to the pranic, then material plane, where, finally, exhausting its attempt to be god, it falls into insentient slumber.

Yet behind this Atman-project, the ignorant drama of the separate self, there nonetheless lies Atman. All of the tragic drama of the self's desire and mortality was just the play of the Divine, a cosmic sport, a gesture of Self-forgetting so that the shock of Self-realization would be the more delightful. The ripple *did* forget the Self, to be sure—but it was a ripple *of* the Self, and remained so throughout the play.

Thus, this movement from the higher into the lower—which is involution—is at once an act of pure creation and effulgent radiance (on the part of Atman), and a tragic tale of suffering and epic unhappiness (on the part of the self-ripple attempting the Atman project). The ultimate aim of evolution—the movement from the lower to the higher—is to awaken *as* Atman, and thus retain the glory of the creation without being forced to act in the drama of self suffering.

During the course of our universe's history (and science helps us here), we have evolved from level–1 (which began approximately fifteen billion years ago with the Big Bang) to level–2 (which occurred several billions of years later when matter awakened into some realization of life) to level–3 (which so far has been reached fully by humans only).

Evolution is, as it were, half completed. "Mankind," said Plotinus, "is poised midway between the gods and the beasts."

But in the past course of human history, some men and women, through the evolutionary discipline of higher religion, succeeded in pushing their own development and evolution into level–4: that of saintly religion and the first intuition of a transcendental reality, one in essence, lying above and beyond the ordinary mind, self, body, and world. This "beyond" was poetically called heaven; this oneness was called the one God. This intuition did not fully occur until around 3000 B.C., with the rise of the first great monotheistic religions. (Prior to that time, there were only polytheistic realizations—a god of fire, a god of water, etc. This was really sympathetic magic, stemming from a simple manipulation of level–2, emotional-sexual energies and rites.) By the time of 500 B.C., however, certain evolutionary souls pushed their development into the causal—Christ, Buddha, Krishna, the great axial sages. Their insights were drawn out and extended to produce what the Tibetans called the Svabhavikakaya path—the path of level–6, or already realized Truth, the path of Zen, Vajrayana, Vedanta. What remains is for the world to follow suit, via evolutionary or process meditation, into the higher realms themselves.

According to the perennial philosophy, not only does this whole process of involution and evolution play itself out over centuries, it repeats itself moment to moment, ceaselessly and instantaneously. In this moment and this moment and this, an individual starts out at infinity. But in this moment and this moment and this, he contracts away from infinity and ends up reduced to the level of his present adaptation. He *involves* to the highest point he has yet *evolved*—and all the higher realms are simply forgotten, rendered unconscious. This is why all meditation is called remembrance or recollection (Sanskrit *smriti*, Pali *sati*, as in *satipatthana*, Plato's *anamnesis*, Sufi *zikr*—all are precisely translated as "memory" or "remembrance").

This whole panoply of higher levels generating the lower moment to moment, and of the dazzling interpenetrating of each level with the others, and of the extraordinary dynamics between the levels, all occurring in a field of effulgent radiance—all this is meant when the mystic-sage speaks of multidimensional interpenetration with nonequivalence.

The fact that the mystic-sages speak so often of the difference between levels, and emphasizes those differences, does not mean they neglect the relationships between the elements on a *given* level. In fact, the mystics are precise in their understanding of the community of elements constituting each level. Since all of the elements are "made of" the same density of consciousness—since they are all *of* the same level—they are all perfectly interpenetrating and mutually interdependent, in an *equivalent* fashion. That is, no element of any *given* level is higher, or more real, or more fundamental than the others, simply because they are all made of the "same stuff" (which means, same density of consciousness).

Thus, on the physical plane, no elementary particle is "most fundamental" (they all seem to bootstrap). On the nutritional plane, no vitamin is ultimately more essential (take away any one and you're equally dead). In the moral sphere, no virtue is greater than another—they all seem to involve each other (as Socrates knew and as Maslow discovered for B-values). In the subtle, all archetypes are equivalent reflections of the Godhead, just as all *Sambhogakayas* are equivalent reflections of the *Dharmakaya*.

The point is that all the elements of a given level are roughly equivalent in status and mutually interpenetrating in fact. All in one and one in all—holographically, as it were. But, by virtue of hierarchy, any element from a senior level is higher in ontological status than any element of a junior dimension (e.g., the virtue of compassion is not equivalent with a quark). This mutual interconnectivity of the elements of any *single* level is *one-dimensional interpenetration with equivalence*. It is a type of *heterarchy* existing within each level of *hierarchy*. Heterarchy means that no element is superior to another; it means that there is an *equivalence* of all parties in a unitary pattern. "Holographic" is simply the strong version of heterarchy, where each part is so equivalent that they actually contain each other. For our simpler and general purposes, we will use "holography" and "heterarchy" interchangeably, since the important point is that both are nonhierarchical. Thus, the simplest way to summarize the mystic's world view would be:

1. Heterarchy within each level
2. Hierarchy between each level

With this background information, we come to the new paradigm.

PHYSICS AND MYSTICISM

One of the frequently mentioned doctrines of mysticism is that of "mutual interpenetration," as presented, for instance, in the Kegon school of

Buddhism, Meher Baba's *Discourses,* the Five Ranks of Soto Zen, and so on. By "mutual interpenetration" the mystic means *both* forms of interpenetration discussed above: one-dimensional and multidimensional, heterarchic and hierarchic, horizontal and vertical.

Think of the six levels of consciousness as a six-story building: the mystic means that all the elements on each floor harmoniously interact, *and* most importantly, each of the floors interacts with each other. As for this multileveled interaction, the mystic means that the physical elements interact with the biological elements which interact with the mental which interact with the subtle which interact with the causal which pass into infinity, each level superseding its predecessor but mutually interpenetrating with it. And thus, speaking of *all* these levels the mystic says, to use Meher Baba's words, "They all interpenetrate one another and exist together."

Now it happens that modern-day physicists, working with the lowest realm—that of material or nonsentient and nonliving processes—have discovered the *one-dimensional* interpenetration of the material plane: they have discovered that all hadrons, leptons, and so on are mutually interpenetrating and interdependent. As Capra explains it:

> Quantum theory forces us to see the universe not as a collection of physical objects, but rather as a complicated web of relations between the various parts of a unified whole. . . . All [physical] particles are dynamically composed of one another in a self-consistent way, and in that sense can be said to "contain" one another. In [this theory], the emphasis is on the interaction, or "interpenetration," of all particles.[30]

In short, speaking of these subatomic particles and waves and fields, the physicist says, "They all interpenetrate one another and exist together." Now a less than cautious person, seeing that the mystic and the physicist have used precisely the same words to talk about their realities, would thereby conclude that the realities must also be the same. And they are not.

The physicists, with their one-dimensional interpenetration, tell us that all sorts of atomic events are interwoven one with the other—which is itself a significant discovery. But they tell us, and can tell us, nothing whatsoever about the interaction of nonliving matter with the biological level, and of that level's interaction with the mental field—what relationship does ionic plasma have with, say, egoic goals and drives? And beyond that, what of the interaction of the mental field with the subtle, and of the subtle with the causal, and the reverse interaction and inter-penetration all the way back down through the lower levels? What can the new physics tell us of that?

I suggest that the new physics has simply discovered the one-dimensional interpenetration of its own level (nonsentient mass/energy). While this is an important discovery, it cannot be equated with the extraordinary phenomenon of multidimensional interpenetration described by the mystics. We saw that Hinduism, as only one example, has an incredibly complex and profound theory of how the ultimate realm generates the causal, which in turn generates the subtle, which creates the mind, out of which comes the fleshy world and, at the very bottom, the physical plane. Physics has told us all sorts of significant things about that last level. Of its predecessors, it can say nothing (without turning itself into biology, psychology, or religion). To put it crudely, the study of physics is on the first floor, describing the interactions of its elements; the mystics are on the sixth floor describing the interaction of all six floors.

Thus, as a blanket conclusion, even as an approximation, the statement that "The world views of physics and mysticism are similar" is a wild overgeneralization and is based, as one physicist recently put it, "on the use of accidental similarities of language as if these were somehow evidence of deeply rooted connections."[10]

Further, physics and mysticism are not two different approaches to the same reality. They are different approaches to two quite different levels of reality, the latter of which transcends but includes the former. That is to say, physics and mysticism do not follow Bohr's complementarity principle. It is not generally understood that *complementarity,* as used in physics, means two *mutually exclusive* aspects of, or approaches to, one interaction. Physics and mysticism are not a complementarity because an individual can be, at the same time and in the same act, a physicist *and* a mystic. As we said, the latter transcends but includes the former, not excludes it. Physics and mysticism are no more two mutually exclusive approaches to one reality than are, say, botany and mathematics.

This whole notion of the complementarity of physics and mysticism comes from ignoring levels 2 through 5. It then appears that physics (level–1) and mysticism (level–6) are the only two major approaches to reality. From this truncated view of reality springs the supposed "complementarity" of physics and mysticism. This claim is not made for sociology and mysticism, nutrition and mysticism, or botany and mysticism; no more so physics and mysticism. They can all *complement* each other, it is true, but they are *not* a *complementarity* as defined by physics.

What *is* new about the new physics is not that it has anything to do with higher levels of reality. With a few minor exceptions (which we will soon discuss), it does not even attempt to explain or account for level–2 (let alone 3–6). Rather, in pushing to the extremes of the material dimensions, it has apparently discovered the basic holography of level–1, and that, indeed, is novel. There, at least, physics and mysticism agree.

Yet even here we must be careful. In the rush to marry physics and mysticism, using the shotgun of generalization, we tend to forget that quantum reality has almost no bearing whatsoever in the actual world of macroscopic processes. As physicist Walker puts it, in the ordinary world of "automobiles and basketballs, the quanta are inconsequential." This has long been clearly recognized by physicists. The quantum level is so submicroscopic that its interactions can for all practical purposes be ignored in the macro world. The intense interactions between subatomic mesons, which sound so mystical, are not observed at all between macro-objects, between rocks and people and trees. As Capra carefully explains it, "The basic oneness of the universe . . . becomes apparent *at the atomic level* and manifests itself more and more as one penetrates deeper . . . into the realm of *subatomic particles*" (italics mine).[30]

But it is precisely in the *ordinary* realm of rocks and trees that the mystic *sees* his mutual interpenetration of all matter. His basic oneness of the universe does not "start at the atomic level." When the mystic looks at a bird on wing over a cascading stream and says, "They are perfectly one," he does not mean that if we got a super microscope out and examined the situation we would see bird and stream exchanging mesons in a unitary fashion. His unitary vision is an immediate impact expressing his personal realization that "All this world in truth is Brahman."

That is to say, even the agreement between mystic and physicist on level–1 must be looked upon either as somewhat tenuous or as a fortunate coincidence. Ask almost any physicist if the connections between, say, a macroscopic tree and river are as intense and unitary as those between subatomic particles, and he will say no. The mystic will say yes.

That is a fundamental issue and shows, in fact, that the physicist and mystic aren't even talking about the same world. The physicist says: "The ordinary Newtonian world is, for all practical purposes, separate and discrete, but the subatomic world is a unified pattern." The mystic says, "The ordinary Newtonian world is, as I directly perceive it, one indivisible whole; as for the subatomic realm, I've never seen it."

The issue here is crucial, because, as Jeremy Bernstein, professor of physics at the Stevens Institute, explains, "If I were an Eastern mystic the last thing in the world that I would want would be a reconciliation with modern science."[10] His point is that it is the very *nature* of empiric-scientific discoveries that they ceaselessly change and alter, that last decade's scientific proof is this decade's fallacy, and that no major scientific fact can escape being profoundly altered by time and further experimentation. What *if* we said that Buddha's enlightenment just received corroboration from physics? What then happens when, a decade from now, new scientific facts replace the current ones (as they must)? Does Buddha then lose his enlightenment? We cannot have it both ways. If we hitch mysticism to physics now, mustn't we ditch it then? What does it mean to confuse temporal scientific facts with timeless contemplative realms? "To hitch a religious [transpersonal] philosophy to a contemporary science," says Dr. Bernstein, "is a sure route to its obsolescence."

THE IMPLICATE ORDER

The same types of difficulties surround the popular use of the concept, introduced by David Bohm, of an "implicate order" of matter. The public at large, and many psychologists in particular, look upon the implicate realm as if it transcended physical particles and reached somehow into a higher state of transcendental unity and wholeness. In fact, the implicate realm does not transcend matter—it "subscends" matter and expresses a coherence, unity, and wholeness of the entire physical plane, or level–1. It does indeed go beyond explicate matter, but in a subscending or underlying manner, not a transcending one. As a matter of fact, the concept explicitly *excludes* any higher realms such as mind and consciousness.

This is made very clear by Bohm himself. First of all, Bohm is clearly opposed to trying to introduce mind or consciousness into the formalism of quantum mechanics (QM), as some physicists would like to do. As he and Hiley put it in a recent paper, "We show that the introduction of the conscious mind into physics . . . is motivated by certain quite general considerations that have little to do with quantum mechanics itself. This approach is contrasted with our own investigations using the quantum potential. . . . Our aim is, in fact, to *describe this order without bringing in the observer in any fundamental role*" (italics mine).[18] The conclusion of Bohm's work is that there seem to be certain quantum phenomena that "present us with a new order or a new structure process, that does not fit into the Newtonian scheme."[18]

This new order, in general terms, is the implicate (holographic or holomovement) realm. Bohm's theory is that explicate matter rests upon a sea of implicate physical energy of extraordinary magnitude and potential, and that the equations of quantum mechanics "are describing that [implicate order]."[17] In one sense, then, the implicate realm goes way beyond explicate matter: "Matter is like a small ripple on this tremendous ocean of energy. . . . This implicate order implies a reality immensely beyond what we call matter. Matter itself is merely a ripple in this background."[17]

But in the final analysis, this implicate sea, although "finer" than explicate matter, is still of the realm of *physis* or nonliving mass/energy in general. This is obvious because (1) Bohm has already *excluded* higher realms such as mental consciousness, from quantum mechanics, and (2) the equations of QM are said to "describe the implicate order." The unfolding from the implicate realm is, he says, "a direct idea as to what is meant by the mathematics of [quantum mechanics]. What's called the unitary transformation or the basic mathematical description of movement in quantum mechanics is exactly what we are talking about."[17] Now QM equations do not define biological life, or level–2; they do not describe mental life, or level–3; they do not describe subtle or causal or absolute realms either. They describe something going on in the realm of *physis* and nowhere else. Besides, Bohm clearly states that "the implicate order is still matter."[17]

It is to Bohm's credit that, in his theoretical writings, he makes it very clear that he is not trying to introduce consciousness or mind into the QM formalism, or trying thereby to "prove" higher states of being with equations that are clearly descriptive not even of animal life (level–2) but rather of nonsentient processes. For it is certainly true that if the implicate realm rests on an interpretation of the facts generated by QM, then it just as certainly has no fundamental *identity* with any of the levels of 2 through 6. In short, the implicate order, as I would state it, *is the unitary deep structure (holography) of level–1*, which subscends or underlies the explicate surface structures of elementary particles and waves.

At the same time, Bohm himself is perfectly aware that the notion of a nonlocal implicate order of *physis* is still far from the only possible interpretation of QM, and far, in fact, from being the absolute case anyway: "At present," he says, "it is necessary to resist the temptation to conclude that everything [in the physical realm] is connected to everything else regardless of space and time separations. The evidence to date indicates that the nonlocal effects [what the public has come generally to call "holographic" or "implicate order" events] arise under very special conditions and any correlations that have been established tend to be broken up rather quickly so that our traditional approach of analysing systems into autonomous subsystems is, in general, quite valid."[18]

The important point is that the mystic's insight does not rest on what these physicists finally decide.*

MIND AND QUANTUM MECHANICS

Unlike David Bohm, and unlike the great majority of physicists, there are a handful of avant-garde physicists who not only want to inject "mind" into the equations of QM, but insist on it as well. Wigner, Walker, Muses, and Sarfatti are producing elaborate mathematical explanations that purport to show the crucial role of consciousness in the formulations of QM. It is these types of formulations, above all else, that have brought the physicist wandering into the backyard of the mystic—or at least the parapsychologist.

The impetus for these formulations lies in what is called the "measurement problem," and the measurement problem is shorthand for some very sophisticated and elaborate mathematical equations and certain paradoxes they generate.

The problem itself concerns this type of dilemma: the mathematics of QM can determine, with great precision, the *probability* that a certain quantum event will occur in a certain environment (at a certain place or

---

* I am, in this chapter, leaving out the most radical and pervasive difference between mysticism and any sort of physical or holographic paradigm, because it is also the most obvious. Namely (1) the comprehension of holographic principles is an act of mind, whereas the comprehension of mystical truth is an act of transmental contemplation, and (2) if holographic theories are actually said to describe transcendent truths, or to be the same as actually transcending, a fallacy known as category error occurs. Some have even suggested that a simple learning of the holographic paradigm would be the same as actual transcendence, in which case these hypothetical theories are not just wrong, they are detrimental.

at a certain time), but it can never predict *the* precise environment itself. It can say, for instance, that the chance of finding a quantum particle in area *A* is 50 percent, in area *B,* 30 percent, and in area *C,* 20 percent. But it cannot, under any circumstances, say that a particular event *will* occur in area *A* (given the above probability distribution). Thus, the particular event is not looked upon as a single entity or occurrence, but rather as a "tendency to exist," which, in this example, would be *defined* by an equation (or probability amplitude) that says, in effect: 50 percent *A*/30 percent *B*/20 percent *C.*

Now the odd thing is that the event, when it occurs, *does* occur in just *one* area. It is almost (not quite) as if a statistician were trying to predict which of three doors you are likely to walk through, and, for various reasons, he winds up with the results: 50 percent chance of door *A,* 30 percent door *B,* 20 percent door *C.* He cannot predict exactly which door it will be, just the percentages. But when you finally walk through the door, you go through only *one*—50 percent of you doesn't go through door *A,* 30 percent through *B* and 20 percent through *C.*

But beyond that, the analogy breaks down. The statistician has reasons to believe that you exist before you walk through any of the doors—he can go look at you, for one. But the physicist has no such assurances about his quantum particles, because there is *no way* he can go look at the particle (for our less than accurate purposes, let's just say it's too small to see perfectly). The *only* way he can look at the particle is by using certain instruments—that is, by *measuring* it in some sense. But to measure the particle he has, as it were, to get it through the doors of his instruments. And there is the problem: to find out what's behind the door, the physicist has to use a door. In all cases, his phenomena can be detected only as they walk through various doors, and the equations describing these "walks" are purely probabilistic: say, 50/30/20.

The physicist therefore faces a conceptual problem: prior to measurement, *all* he can say about a quantum event is that it *is* (not has) a certain tendency to exist (e.g., 50/30/20). The event itself, if left alone (not measured) will "propagate through space-time" according to the Schroedinger wave function, which, if squared, gives the probability of finding the event in a certain environment (50/30/20). But prior to the actual measurement, there is *no way whatsoever* to know precisely in which region the particle will occur. Yet, when it is finally detected, it does occur in *one* region only (say *B*) and does not spread out through the three doors. This is called the collapse of the state vector or wavepacket, because when measurement determines that the particle is in *B,* the probability of its being in *A* or *C* collapses to zero. The collapse of the state vector means that the event *jumped* from being a "tendency to exist" ($50A/30B/20C$) to a "real occurrence (*B*)."

Hence the problems. Does measurement itself "cause" the collapse of the wavepacket? Does the actual particle even exist at all prior to measurement? If we say it does exist (which seems common sense), how can we know for sure, since there is *no* way to tell, and since our mathematical equations, which otherwise describe perfectly this realm, tell us only 50/30/20? If we deny the equations, how can we deny the fact that they otherwise work so well?

Aside from a large number of philosophers who maintain (not without certain justifications) that what collapses the wavepacket is not mind or matter but bad metaphysics, there are several different schools of thought on this "measurement problem," offered by the physicists themselves:

1. *The Copenhagen Interpretation.* The vast number of physicists follow this school, which maintains that the collapse of the wavepacket is at bottom purely random. There is no need for an explanation. Since there is no way to get behind the door, there is no behind the door.* QM is a complete explanation as it stands, and there is no need or possibility to "look behind the scenes" and try to figure out whether the event is there or not prior to measurement. In all fairness, it should be said that there are many good, if not absolute, reasons for adopting this view. It should also be said, as is often pointed out, that Einstein himself violently rejected this view (with the exclamation "God does not play dice with the universe!"), even though every objection he forwarded to this interpretation was brilliantly parried by Bohr and others, using Einstein's own theories. At the same time, I repeat that this (and the following) are species of extremely popularized explanations. But within that disclaimer, the Copenhagen Interpretation says that the probability 50/30/20 is all we can know and all there is to know; which door the particle goes through is purely random.

2. *The Hidden Variable Theories.* These theories maintain that there are indeed specifiable factors lying "behind the scenes" of the collapse of the wavepacket. These subquantal processes are described by presently hidden variables, but it is possible that they will eventually become technically accessible. In the crudest of terms, this theory says that quantum events are not purely random, and that the particle goes through a par-

---

*This is crudely stated, but it is also the basis of the charge of bad metaphysics.

ticular door for a "hidden" reason, a reason that the particle "knows" and that we should be able to find out. Bohm and his colleagues, working with the quantum potential (and implicate order), belong to this school. Bell's theorem, which has received much popular attention, is often used by some advocates of this school to point to the apparent nonlocal (not confined to a local region of space causality) "transfer" of information between widely isolated regions of space. Bell's theorem is generally taken to mean that, if QM is otherwise correct, and if there are some sort of hidden variables, then those hidden variables are nonlocal—a type of "instant" causality not separated by time or space. Bohm and his colleagues take this as an example of a possible implicate order; Sarfatti takes it as an example of faster-than-light "communication"; others (such as Einstein) take it as nonsense.

3. *The Many Worlds Hypothesis.* This is proposed by Everett, Wheeler, and Graham (EWG). According to the Copenhagen Interpretation (theory #1), when the 50A/30B/20C particle is measured and is found to occur in region B, then the other two possibilities (A and C) collapse—they simply do not occur (just as, for instance, if you toss a coin and it comes up heads, the possibility of it being tails collapses to zero). Now according to EWG, *all* of the mutually exclusive possibilities contained in the wave function *do* occur, but in different branches of the universe. At the moment the particle hits B in this universe, two other universes branch off, one of which contains the particle hitting A, and one of which contains the particle hitting C. Or, as soon as I catch "heads" in this universe, I *also* catch "tails" but in an entirely different universe. Neither "I" knows the other. This has been developed in a very sophisticated mathematical fashion.

It's easy, upon hearing that type of theory, to sympathize with François Mauriac: "What this professor says is far more incredible than what we poor Christians believe." But the real point is that it is already obvious that what is called the "new physics" is far from a consensus as to the nature of subatomic reality, a fact that will eventually lead us to certain suggestive conclusions. In the meantime, we move on to the fourth major theory generated by the "measurement problem."

4. *The Matter/Mind Connection.* This theory has many different forms, but in keeping with our popularized presentation, we can say that the theory in general suggests the following: If measurement itself collapses the wavepacket, then isn't measurement in some way *essential* to the manifestation of this material event? And *who* is doing the mea-

surement? Obviously, a sentient being. Is not *mind,* then, an influence on—or even creator of—matter?

This general view, in one form or another, is held by Wigner, Sarfatti, Walker, and Muses. "In my opinion," says Sarfatti, "the quantum principle involes *mind* in an essential way . . . mind creates matter."[104] Walker equates the hidden variables, assuming they are there, with consciousness; Muses plugs consciousness into the quantum vacuum potential. But Beynam sums it all up as: "It is consciousness itself that collapses the state vector." It is this theory we want now to examine, because this is said to be *the* connection between physics and parapsychology/mysticism.

To begin with, is there anything in the perennial philosophy which would accord with the general statement, "Mind creates matter"? The first-approximation answer is definitely affirmative. Matter is held, by all traditional philosophies, to be a precipitate in the mental field. But they express it more precisely. It is not directly mind (level–3) which creates matter (level–1), but prana (level–2) which does so. Mind creates prana; prana creates matter.

Thus, the physicists would be more precise, according to tradition, if they said not "mind" but "prana," "bioenergy," or "biological sentience" was directly senior to matter. Von Weizsacker has already done so explicitly (using the word "prana"), and so have several others. This would not be a problem for these physicists, because the characteristics they already ascribe to "mind" as being necessary for the wavepacket collapse are actually characteristics of prana. That is, these physicists usually don't say "concepts," "ideas," or "logic" collapses the state vector. Rather, they use such terms as "biological systems" (Sarfatti), "sentient being" (Walker), "sensation" (Wigner), and these are distally characteristic of mind but proximally characteristic of prana (or any living system). Mind could also collapse the vector, but via prana. This would also fit Sarfatti's suggestions, because all biological systems would contribute to random quantal Brownian movement, but a disciplined mind (not present in animals) might *control* it.*

All of which sounds as if this version of QM is right in accord with

---

* It should be said that, while I will end up disagreeing with this school of QM as to the nature of the *generation* of matter from mind, I do not rule out that they may have some important things to say about the *influence* of mind on matter, *after the fact* of matter's generation from mind. This is a very dilute agreement, but an agreement nonetheless, and certain very select areas of parapsychology (not mysticism at large) might find resonance with these theorists.

the mystic view, at least as far as levels 1 and 2 are concerned (i.e., level–2 creates level–1). Yet again we must be very precise here, because premature conclusions are much too easy to draw.

First of all, when the mystic says that matter is created by prana, he does not mean that prana itself must be present in a manifest fashion (and from this point on, for ease of recognition, I will use "mind" instead of "prana," remembering the important qualifications given above). That is, mind does *not* create matter by perceiving it, or sensing it, or "measuring" it—which is, as we saw, the form of the theory held by the QM physicists under discussion. Rather, matter simply precipitates out of mind whether mind is paying attention or not. In fact, during involution, mind generates matter and then "disappears" from the scene altogether. It doesn't stay around to watch matter and thereby generate it.

In this fashion, the traditional philosophy avoids entirely the otherwise ridiculous dilemma: if mind creates matter by perception or actual contact (as participator-observer), then what occurred, say, 10 billion years ago when there was only matter and no minds? Science is rather certain that biological life appeared only billions of years *after* matter. Prior to that time, there was no life, no mind. If mind has to measure or observe matter in order for the latter to exist (or have its wavepacket collapsed), we arrive at absurdity.

This view—that mind generates matter by the effect of the "participator-observer"—is like saying the chicken (mind) *sees* the egg (matter) and thereby creates it. No chicken to see the egg, no egg. The traditional view says that the chicken (mind) lays or gives birth to the egg (matter) and thereby creates it; what the chicken does after that is its own business—the egg continues to exist, perceived or not. In fact, during involution, the chicken is, well, buried. What it leaves behind is a reduced version of chicken-ness, a reduced version of mind called matter (the egg). But the egg-matter has enfolded in it the potential to actualize ("hatch") a new chicken, or mind itself, which is just what happens in evolution. But in no case does the chicken create the egg by watching it.

It is for similar reasons that most physicists themselves reject this version of the QM interpretation. As David Bohm himself explains: "The introduction of the conscious mind into physics by Wigner is motivated by certain quite general considerations that have little to do with quantum mechanics itself." And speaking of this tendency to hastily conclude that observation by mind is needed to produce matter (measurement), Bohm answers succinctly: "Indeed this is often carried to such an extreme that it appears as if nothing ever happens without the observer.

However, we know of many physical processes, even at the level of quantum phenomena, that do occur without any direct intervention of the observer. Take for example the processes that go on in a distant star. These appear to follow the known laws of physics and the processes occur, and have occurred, without any significant intervention on our part."[18]

In short, the perennial philosophy would agree that matter is created out of mind (prana), but through an act of precipitation and crystallization, not perception and measurement. But QM can account, *if* at all, for *only* the latter theory, and therefore the agreement of QM and mysticism on this point is purely coincidental. Should, therefore, this particular interpretation of QM prove incorrect (and I agree with Bohm and others that it will), it would not affect one way or the other the world view of the mystic-sage.

But my point does not concern whether any of the above four QM interpretations is right or wrong. And there are even others we haven't really discussed at all—superluminal connections, simple statistical interpretations, quantum logic interpretations. These issues are extremely complex and difficult, and it will take decades to work out their implications. However, what we can do now is reach certain immediate conclusions:

1. The "new physics" is far from a grand consensus as to the nature of even subatomic reality. To hook transpersonal psychology/mysticism to the consensus of the new quantum physics is not possible, because there is no consensus. Those connections that have been drawn between physics and mysticism are of the pick and choose variety. The actual details of the various QM interpretations are, as we have seen, largely mutually exclusive. Simply to take a detail from one interpretation, then another, a little bootstrap here, a little implicate order there, is, in the words of physicist Bernstein, "a travesty and a disservice" to the theories involved.

2. Even if we could draw several tight parallels, to hook transpersonal psychology to physics is still "the surest route to oblivion." To paraphrase Eckhart, if your god is the god of today's physics, then when that physics goes (tomorrow), that god goes with it.

3. The most important point is that no matter which version of QM theory is finally accepted, this will not profoundly affect the mystic's vision or world view. First of all, in no case could it *invalidate* the mystic world view. When Newton's "fractured world view" was "truth," this

did not invalidate the mystic vision. If the Copenhagen Interpretation is the "truth," this will not invalidate the mystic vision. If *any* of the QM interpretations are true, this will not invalidate the mystic vision. And therefore, as any epistemologist will tell us, in no case could an interpretation *validate* the mystic world view. If there is no conceivable physical test that would disprove the mystic view, and there isn't, then there is no conceivable one which could corroborate it either.

4. It is sometimes said that the new physics at least *accords* with the mystic world view. I think we can easily agree that certain aspects of some interpretations of mathematical quantum formalisms, when placed into everyday English, sound similar to aspects of the mystic's view, not of the world (levels 1–6), but of level–1. The mystic's insight, however, does not find its validation nor explanation in that possible accord. But if this accord helps "legitimize" mysticism in the public's eye; if it at least does not cause its proponents to radically deny mystical states as hallucinatory; if it opens the way to a fuller acceptance of mystical experience—then, by all accounts, we will indeed have the new physics to thank.

Beyond that point, however, take Bernstein's warning with you: thank the new physics for agreeing with you, but resist the temptation to build your transpersonal models upon the shifting sands of changing level–1 theories.

THE HOLOGRAPHIC BRAIN

While the holographic/implicate theories of physics deal unequivocally with level–1, the theories of holographic brain processes deal, apparently, with level–3, or mind and memory. In tandem, then, these theories would cover, more or less, levels 1–3.

But beyond that, it is suggested by some that *if* the mind were holographic, then this could also account for higher, transpersonal experiences via the mind melting down into the holographic blur beyond explicit distinctions. This holographic blur is called a "frequency realm," where, supposedly, objects in space and time "do not exist." The holographic blur or frequency realm is described as: "No space, no time—just events (or frequencies)."

Let us pass by the difficulties of having *events* existing without *any sort* of space or time; let us also ignore the fact that physical objects (space-time *things*) are needed to produce holograms in the first place.

Aside from that, how might this holographic-mind fit with the perennial philosophy?

To start with, it is fundamentally the storage of memory-information that is said to occur on the principles of optical holography. The mechanisms of holography are explained by mathematical transforms, one of whose intriguing properties is that—in mathematical terms anyway—space and time seem at one stage to be left out, and the desired temporal results are retrieved through a readout function of frequency information. This has led to the notion of a frequency realm—the notion that space/time objects come out of "no space, no time frequencies."

I have no doubt that that is basically true—that memory is holographically stored, just as is said. I also think that the research demonstrating this is brilliant. But beyond that, how this relates in any fashion to transcendent states is far from clear. To be sure, there are similarities of language—the holographic blur ("no space, no time") sounds like a mystical state. It also sounds like passing out. There is a world of difference between pretemporal consciousness, which has no space and no time, and transtemporal consciousness, which moves beyond space and time while still embracing it. "Eternity," after all, "is in love with the productions of time." This in no way proves that the holographic blur is not a transcendent state; it demonstrates that one cannot judge so on the basis of language correlations.

Nonetheless, it is said that a shift to a "perception of the holographic blur" would produce transcendent states. Since it is memory which is holographically stored,* what would it actually mean to shift to a perception of the storage bin of personal memory? Would this be nirvana, a direct consciousness which transcended but included all manifestation?

By the accounts of the theory itself, I do not see that it would or could result in anything but an experience of one's own memory storage bin, properly blurred and without benefit of linear read-out. How one could jump from a blur of one's own memory to a crystal consciousness that transcends mind, body, self, and world is not made clear at all. It is a wild theoretical leap to move from "personal memory is holographically stored" to "therefore all minds are part of a transpersonal hologram."

I think instead that we are allowing certain superficial similarities of language to rule the day. The above is example enough, perhaps, but beyond that there exists the whole notion of a "transcendent frequency

---

* The "perception" of the physical frequency realm is discussed later in conjunction with William Tiller's critique of the holographic paradigm.

realm beyond space and time"—which is said to be the implicate holographic blur. This notion, it seems to me, gains credence only from the oddities of the mathematics involved, which translate "things" into "frequencies" and thus allow a slip of language to pass for transcendent truths. The "frequency realm" transforms are assumed to refer to experiential realities in a way that is not only unbelievable, but frankly self-contradictory.

The transform of "things" into "frequencies" is not a transform of space/time into "no space, no time," but a transform of space/time objects into space/time frequencies. Frequency does not mean "no space, no time"; it means cycles/second or space per time. To read the mathematics otherwise is more than a quantum leap; it is a leap of faith.

This "theory has gained increasing support and has not been seriously challenged. An impressive body of research in many laboratories has demonstrated that the brain structures see, hear, taste, smell and touch by sophisticated mathematical analysis of temporal and/or spatial frequencies [hence the primacy of frequency realm]."[98] I do not challenge the theory; I repeat, and mean, that I am straightforwardly impressed. I am not impressed, however, by speculations that call "*temporal* and/or *spatial* frequencies" by the name "no space, no time." And it is in just that semantic slip that this theory *sounds* transcendentally alive.

Needless to say, this semantic sleight-of-hand, which replaces personal blur with transpersonal unity, helps neither the brilliant work of these brain researchers—Pribram for example—nor the difficult task of transpersonalists attempting to explain transcendence.

Aside from the above, we have still another strand of argument which has been proposed. For this strand, let us assume anyway that the mind *in general* is holographic in its operations. Would this fit with the perennial philosophy, and beyond that, would it possibly account for higher levels of consciousness?

I am afraid that, even given this generous lead, we fare no better. First of all, the fact that the deep structure of the mental field is holographic would not in itself account for transpersonal levels, or levels 4–6. The reasons, according to the perennial traditions, are that (1) *every* level is a holography, not just mind, and (2) the experience of any level's holography does not take one *beyond* that level, but merely opens up deeper insights *into* that level. Just as the holography of level–1 does not imply nor demand level 2, 3, 4, 5, or 6, so the holography of level–3 doesn't automatically account for any of the levels above it (levels 4, 5, or 6).

Likewise, the actual experience of the holography of level–3 would not necessarily—nor even likely—involve levels 4, 5, or 6. The ordinary surface mind (level–3) experiences itself as separate and somewhat isolated from other minds. To experience the holography of level–3 would be, at most, to experience a strong resonance with, and even overlapping of, other minds. It would produce a direct experience of actual interpersonal empathy.

But interpersonal empathy is not transpersonal identity. In states of transpersonal awareness (beyond certain introductory practices), whether mind is present or not, explicit or implicit, standing out or holographically blurred—all of this is irrelevant. The higher realms transcend but can easily include mind, and whether mind itself arises doesn't matter. The *existence* of higher states cannot be explained in terms of something that may or may not happen to a lower state, whether that state is unfolded and projected or enfolded and blurred. You might as well say you can explain level–2 by sufficiently blurring level–1. This disguised reductionism led Willis Harman to comment, "These holographic theories still would interpret the primary datum, consciousness, in terms of something else ultimately quantifiable [i.e., in terms of lower physical level measurements]. These theories are not yet of the new science, but rather of the old, in which the attempt is made to explain away consciousness rather than to understand it."[98]

Finally, we might heed William Tiller's suggestions: "The holographic [theory of brain perception] has focused largely on the sensor apprehension of this representation at the physical level of consciousness [level–1]. [We might do better] to opt for a multidimensional [hierarchical] representation of consciousness and possible structures of the universe for its manifestation. Without such an extension beyond the purely physical perception frame, the scope of any 'new paradigm' will be severely limited."[98]

Tiller hints at two points. First, the "frequency realm" said to be so transcendent is really prescendent: it's just the chaotic "blooming buzz" of physical level–1 frequencies before the brain can sort them into higher-order organization. An actual experience of that "primary reality" would be, in fact, pure regression, not transcendence. Second, holography cannot account for hierarchy, and thus the whole theory, as a paradigm, falls flat in the most important area of explanation.*

---

* I am not questioning the fact that perception and memory occur as suggested in this hypothesis. I am questioning whether, beyond that, this hypothesis could have anything to do with transcendent realities. My conclusion is that it only *appears* to

Conclusions and Assessments

There are several beneficial repercussions coming from the "new physics" and the "holographic paradigm," even if we conclude, as I think we must, that the latter constitutes nothing close to a comprehensive or even adequate paradigm. But among the benefits are:

1. The interest of influential physicists in metaphysics. This has taken two different forms. First, the willingness to postulate unmeasurable and undetectable orders of *physis* lying behind or subscending explicate energy/mass. This is Bohm's quantum potential/implicate order. Second, the willingness of physicists to acknowledge the necessity of ultimately including references to levels higher than *physis* in their accounts of *physis*. As Wheeler put it, "No theory of physics that deals only with physics will ever explain physics."[104] And Sarfatti: "Therefore, *meta* physical statements are absolutely vital for the evolution of physics,"[104] whereupon Sarfatti introduces the notion of "mind creating matter." But even if that were true in the fashion proposed by Sarfatti, the perennial philosophy would remind him to add: "And you then need meta-mental to explain mind, which brings you to the subtle; and you then need meta-subtle to explain that, and so on in such fashion until, like an asymptotic curve that approaches an axis but never reaches it until infinity, you arrive at Consciousness as Such."

2. The reductionistic fury of mechanistic science seems to be finally winding down, and physics is opening itself—and by impact of authority, many other fields as well—to open systems of unending novelty and creativity. This is especially evident in the work of I. Prigogine, whose theory of dissipative structures is as beautiful as it is profound. Dissipative structures are simply a mathematical way to *allow* for the evolution of higher, more organized states from less complex structures. Dissipative structures are not actually explanations of life or mind, as is some-

---

have something to do with actual transcendence because of the oddities of the math involved and because of a less than precise manipulation of language. Particularly questionable is the jump from "each personal memory is equally distributed in every cell of the individual brain" to "therefore each individual mind is part of a transpersonal hologram." The holographic paradigm is described as "one in all and all in one"—where "one" means "individual memory/cell" and "all" means "all individual brain cells." From that accurate statement a quick substitution is made: "One" comes to mean "one individual" or "one person" and "all" comes to mean, not all other personal brain cells, but all other persons, period.

times said, but rather descriptions of what has to happen to matter in order for higher realms to unfold. To actually identify the essence of a higher level as simply being a dissipative structure is like saying the *Mona Lisa* is simply a concentration of paint.

3. The whole movement of new physics and new paradigm at least demonstrates that there is profound, serious, and rapidly growing interest in perennial concerns and transcendent realities, even among specialists and fields that a decade ago could not have cared less. No matter that some of what is said is premature, *that* it is said is extraordinary.

4. Books such as *The Tao of Physics* and *The Dancing Wu-Li Masters* and publications such as Marilyn Ferguson's *Brain/Mind Bulletin* are introducing vast numbers of people not only to the intrigue of Western science and physics, but also to aspects of Eastern wisdom and thought, and in ways that simply would not have been possible before.

My point, therefore, in criticizing certain aspects of the new paradigm is definitely *not* to forestall interest in further attempts. It is rather a call for precision and clarity in presenting issues that are, after all, extraordinarily complex and that resist quick generalization. And I say this with a certain sense of urgency, because in our understandable zeal to promulgate a new paradigm, which somehow touches bases with physics at one end and mysticism at the other, we are liable to alienate both parties—and everybody in between.

From one end of the spectrum: already certain mystically or transpersonally oriented researchers—Tiller, Harman, W. I. Thompson, Eisenbud—have expressed disappointment in or total rejection of the new paradigm.

From the other end: already many physicists are furious with the "mystical" use to which particle physics is being subjected. Particle physicist Jeremy Bernstein recently unleashed a broadside on such attempts, calling them "superficial and profoundly misleading."[10] And no less an authority than John Wheeler—whose name is always mentioned in the "new paradigm" and in a way he finds infuriating—recently released two scathing letters wherein, among several other things, he brands the physics/mysticism attempts as "moonshine," "pathological science," and "charlatanism." "Moreover," he states, "in the quantum theory of observation, my own present field of endeavor, I find honest work almost overwhelmed by the buzz of absolutely crazy ideas being put forth with the aim of establishing a link between quantum mechanics and parapsychology"[51]—and transpersonal psychology, for that matter. He has asked, and Admiral Hyman G. Rickover has joined him, to have all sanctions of the American Association for the Advancement of Science removed from any endeavor tending toward transpersonalism, a sanction that Margaret Mead, years ago, fought so hard to obtain.

The work of these scientists—Bohm, Pribram, Wheeler, and all—is too important to be weighed down with wild speculations on mysticism. And mysticism itself is too profound to be hitched to phases of empirical scientific theorizing. Let them appreciate each other, and let their dialogue and mutual exchange of ideas never cease. But unwarranted and premature marriages usually end in divorce, and all too often a divorce that terribly damages both parties.

6

Reflections on the New Age Paradigm

AN INTERVIEW

ReVision Journal: Of various authorities in the transpersonal field, you seem to be one of a very few who have expressed strong reservations about the so-called holographic theories. I wonder if you could tell us why.

Wilber: Well, it's very difficult in a short discussion to explain the various lines of critique. The holographic paradigm is immensely exciting at first glance, I think, but the more you go into it, the more it begins to lose its appeal. You simply have to take all sorts of strands—epistemological, methodological, ontological—and follow them up.

RV: Then you agree with certain theorists, such as Peter Swartz of The Stanford Research Institute, that the holographic paradigm is a nice metaphor but a bad model of reality?

Wilber: It is a bad model, but I'm not sure it's even a good metaphor. The holographic paradigm is a good metaphor for pantheism, but not for the reality described by the perennial philosophy.

RV: How do you mean that?

Wilber: Well, the perennial philosophy—the term was made famous by Huxley but coined by Leibniz—the transcendental essence of the great religions—has as its core the notion of *advaita* or *advaya*—

"nonduality," which means that reality is neither one nor many, neither permanent nor dynamic, neither separate nor unified, neither pluralistic nor holistic. It is entirely and radically above and prior to *any* form of conceptual elaboration. It is strictly unqualifiable. If it is to be discussed at all, then, as Stace so carefully pointed out, it must involve paradoxical statements. So, it is true that reality is one, but equally true that it is many; it is transcendent, but also immanent; it is prior to this world, but it is not other to this world—and so on. Sri Ramana Maharshi had a perfect summary of the paradox of the ultimate: "The world is illusory; Brahman alone is real; Brahman is the world."

RV: So if you leave out any of those paradoxical aspects, you end up advocating one side of a subtle dualism?

Wilber: Yes. The transcendentalists, and also the monists, agree that "the world is illusory and Brahman alone is real," but they overlook the equally true but paradoxical fact "Brahman is the world." On the other hand, pantheism is the reverse, and perhaps worse—it agrees that "Brahman is the world," or the sum total of the universe, but it overlooks the equally important fact that Brahman is radically prior to the universe.

RV: Why is that "worse"?

Wilber: Because pantheism is a way to think about spirit without having to actually transform yourself. If God is merely the sum total of the empirical universe, you don't need to fundamentally enlighten yourself to see that god, because *that* god is already clunking around in your visual field. Pantheism is the favorite god of the empiricists—the "nothing morists," as Plato would say—those who believe in "nothing more" than can be grasped with the hands.

RV: And the perennial philosophy maintains that the absolute is immanent in the world but also is completely transcendent to it?

Wilber: Yes. Plato's cave is still an excellent analogy, as long as we remember its paradoxical nature. There are the manifest shadows in the cave; there is an absolute Light of reality beyond the cave; and ultimately they are not-two . . .

RV: The shadows and the Light . . .

Wilber: Yes. But none of those three points can be overlooked, as Ramana said. Now the problem with pantheism is that it mistakes the totality of the universe with that which is radically prior to or beyond the universe. That is, pantheism confuses the sum total of all the shadows *in* the cave with the Light beyond the cave. And the danger of that philosophy is that, if one thinks Godhead is merely the sum of things and events in the universe, the sum of shadows in the cave, then one ceases to try to get *out* of the cave. One merely contemplates one's own level of adaptation, and tries to add up the parts.

RV: What's the danger with its opposite world view, that of extreme transcendentalism?

Wilber: A hatred of the shadows. It shows up in violent asceticism, in antimaterialism, and especially in antisexual ethic and life repression. The idea is that the world itself is somehow evil, whereas all that is evil is the world perceived apart from, or other to, God. When God is seen to be in the world, as the world, the world is radically divine. Grace, as St. Thomas said, is supposed to perfect nature, not obliterate it.

RV: So you were saying the hologram is a good metaphor for pantheism.

Wilber: Yes, in my opinion, because it basically deals only with the totality of parts, the holographic blur, and its relation to individual parts. In the hologram, the sum total of the parts is contained in each part, and that sum-of-the-parts-being-in-each-part is supposed to reflect the transcendental oneness underlying the manifold separateness. But the only way you can say that the hologram is a metaphor for Brahman or Tao is by reducing Brahman to that sum of the parts, which is then present in each part. But that by itself is exactly pantheism.

RV: You mean the whole is not the same as Brahman, or the absolute?

Wilber: No, of course not. Brahman is *in* the world *as* the *whole world*, it is true, but the whole world in and by itself is not exclusively Brahman, because you could theoretically destroy the whole world but that wouldn't destroy Brahman or Buddha Nature or Tao. Anyway, pantheism makes the mistake of confusing the whole world with Brahman, and the hologram is a good metaphor for the whole/part relation.

RV: And you're not saying that is totally wrong, just partial.

Wilber: Yes, it covers the immanent but not the transcendent aspects of the absolute.

RV: What about the notion that the holographic paradigm posits a frequency realm or implicate order under the explicate order of events. Isn't that analogous to the unmanifest, or the Light beyond the cave?

Wilber: Well, again, I think that is initially the obvious thing to say, and a lot of people have agreed with it. I'm not sure it holds up, however. To begin with, Bohm's implicate order is directly related to something like a vast sea of quantum potential energy, out of which there crystallize, so to speak, concrete matter events. These events are related not by field forces, Einsteinian or Newtonian, but by their degree of implication, or how far out of the matter-energy sea they have emerged.

RV: That implicate sea has been compared by many to the unmanifest and infinite source of the mystics.

Wilber: Yes, I know, but the problem is that the quantum potential is merely tremendously huge in size or dimensions; it is not radically dimensionless, or infinite in the metaphysical sense. And you simply cannot equate huge in size, potential or actual, with that which is without size, or prior to any dimensions, high or low, subtle or gross, implicate or explicate.

RV: So the implicate sea, potential or actual, is really quite different from the infinite ground of mysticism.

Wilber: In my opinion, that's exactly right. They merely sound similar if described in superficial language, but the actual difference is profound. But see, David Bohm is perfectly aware of that. That's why he speaks of the "source" as being beyond both the explicate and implicate spheres. Somehow, people seem to ignore that part of what he says.

RV: OK, and Pribram's holographic brain?

Wilber: If you take a tape recorder and record various sounds, the tape will store those sounds or "memorize" them. So will storage systems based on optical holography. The noises come in all dynamic and flowing—or temporal—but they get translated into a "frozen" or "timeless" state in the tape. But just because the information is stored in a "timeless" fashion doesn't mean that the tape recorder is in a transcendental or eternal state. The human brain also stores information, perhaps holographically; in the process it naturally translates it from a dynamic or moving state into a "timeless" or stored condition, and when you call up that information you read it out from this frozen state. But this "timeless" or frozen condition has little to do with a metaphysical or mystical eternity. For one thing, break the tape recorder—destroy it—and there goes your eternity. An eternity dependent for its existence on a temporal structure, tape or brain, is a strange eternity.

RV: But what about the frequency realm?

Wilber: Yes, the brain is said to read out information by analyzing frequencies, or by plugging into a realm where "there is no space, no time, only events (or frequencies)." Now I am not questioning that theory; I'm sure the brain does analyze spatial and/or temporal frequencies. I just don't see that that has anything to do with a transcendental ground which is eternal and infinite. First of all, frequency means cycles per second or space per time. The same is true of "event densities." The fact is, the so-called frequency realm is simply a realm with space-time structures different from those of the linear or historical mind, and the mind has to impose its structures upon the less structured frequency realm. But in any event, or in any way you wish to interpret it, the frequency realm still has *some sort of structure,* whether that structure be blurred, vibratory, frozen, or whatever. And structure cannot be confused with that which is radically without structure, or perfectly dimensionless, transcendent, and infinite. If you do mistake that frequency realm for some sort of eternal ground, instead of seeing that it is simply less structured noise, then it appears that you're dealing with some sort of mystical theory, whereas you're actually dealing with the simple mechanics of sensorimotor perception.

RV: But that theory is frequently coupled with Bohm's ideas.

Wilber: Yes, that is initially the obvious thing to do. If you equate the frequency realm with the implicate order, and then equate the unfolded or read-out information with the explicate realm, it naturally appears that you have a paradigm which covers the emergence of manifest thought and things from an unmanifest and timeless ground.

RV: But since both the implicate order and the frequency realm have some sort of form . . .

Wilber: Yes, it's not a good metaphor for the perennial philosophy. At best, it's a decent metaphor for pantheism.

RV: In your original critique of the holographic theories [see chapter 5], you used the concept of nested hierarchy quite often. Do you still feel it is important?

Wilber: Yes, absolutely. If we return to Plato's analogy, there are the objects in the cave and there is the Light beyond—but the point is that some objects are closer to the opening of the cave. That is, there is a gradation in ontology—as Huston Smith summarized the essence of the world's great mystical traditions, "Existence is graded, and with it, cognition." That is, there are levels of being and levels of knowing, leading, as it were, from the very back of the cave up to and through the opening.

RV: And the absolute is the highest level of this gradation?

Wilber: Not exactly, because that would be dualistic. It is paradoxical, again. The absolute is both the highest level of reality *and* the condition or real nature of every level of reality. It is the highest rung on the ladder, *and* it is the wood out of which the ladder is made. The rungs in that ladder are both the stages of evolution at large and the stages of human growth and development. That was Hegel's and Aurobindo's and Teilhard de Chardin's message; evolution is moving through the waves in the Great Nest of Being—starting with the lowest, or matter, and moving to biological structures, then to mind, then to subtle and causal realms, and finally to supermind or spirit. It's not that the absolute or supermind only comes into existence at that last stage—it existed all along, but could only be *realized* when consciousness itself evolved to its highest estate. Once we get out of the cave we see there is and always has been *only* Light. Prior to that final and highest stage, there seems to be nothing but shadows, but we don't realize they are shadows, having no point of comparison. So, anyway, the absolute is both the highest stage or goal of evolution and the ever-present ground of evolution; your real and present condition and your future potential or realization. Anything less than that paradox is dualistic.

RV: Where does hierarchy fit in?

Wilber: Well, the stage-levels of evolution and ontology *are* the hierarchy. But hierarchy only covers one half of the paradox—it covers the fact that certain levels are closer to the Light than others. The other half of the paradox is, of course, that all things are already and fully Buddha, just as they are. All things are already One, or always already One, and all things are trying to evolve toward the One, or omega point.

RV: That's why you are Buddha but still have to practice.

Wilber: Yes, if Buddha were not omnipresent, it would not be Buddha, but if it were only omnipresent, you would be enlightened right now. Dogen Zenji has made all that very clear. But if you leave out any side of that you get into theoretical trouble. You could paraphrase Orwell: "All things are God, but some things are more God than others." The first part of that is God's omnipresence; the second part is God's hierarchy. The stage-levels of evolution show increasing structural organization, increasing complexity and integration and unity, increasing awareness and consciousness. There is even a sense in saying, as Smith and Schuon and the traditionalists do, that each higher level is more real, or has more reality, because it is more saturated with Being. In any event, evolution is hierarchical—rocks are at one end of that scale, God the Omega is at the other, and plants, reptiles, mammals, humans, and *bodhisattvas* fill up the middle, in that order. *And,* God is the very stuff, the actual essence, of *each* stage-level—God is not the highest level, nor a different level itself, but the reality of all levels.

RV: I think you are right that most or all of that has been overlooked by the holographic theories, but is all of that really necessary for a basic paradigm? Aren't you being picky?

Wilber: I know what you mean—why not take the paradigm and run? Don't spoil a good thing; physicists are talking mysticism! [Laughing] I can see the headlines now: "Scientists at M.I.T. today announced they discovered God. That's right, God. Asked whether God was compassionate, merciful, all-pervading, radiant, all-powerful and divine, a senior researcher was heard to say, 'Gee, we're not sure; we think it's a photon.' "

Look, it was some of the proponents of the holographic theories that claimed they had a paradigm that could explain the fundamentals of mystical religion. So we go to the authorities on mystical religion, or the perennial philosophy in general, and see what they say. According to Huston Smith, for example, four levels of being are the absolute minimum you can use to explain the world's great mystical religions. Those are physical-body, symbol-mind, subtle-soul, and causal-spirit. No major religion recognizes less than that. Many, however, give a more detailed cartography, frequently involving seven levels—the seven *chakras,* for instance, of kundalini yoga, which is probably the most archetypal paradigm of existence ever devised. The seven generally are: (1) physical or material, (2) emotional-sexual (*prana* or bioenergy), (3) mental, (4) higher mental or psychic, (5) subtle or archetypal, (6) causal or unmanifest, and (7) ultimate or unqualified.

Finally, you can, if you are very careful, group these levels into three broad categories, for convenience, say. Since most people have evolved to the mental level(s), it's useful to speak of those levels below the mind—the material and biosensory realms—as premental or submental, and those above it—soul and spirit—as transmental. That gives us three general realms, known variously as matter, mind, and spirit; or subconscious, self-conscious, and superconscious; or instinct, reason, and intuition, and so on. Those three realms, for instance, have been explicitly mentioned by Hegel, Berdyaev, and Aurobindo.

RV: All of which has been overlooked . . .

Wilber: All of which has been overlooked. The problem with the popular holographic theories, as well as the general "new physics and Eastern mysticism" stuff, is that they collapse the hierarchy. They go from saying "All shadows are ultimately illusory" to saying "All shadows are equally illusory." That is, they latch on to such phrases as "All things are One" or "Separate entities don't exist" or "Isolated things are merely shadows" and then overlook the distinctions between the shadows themselves. They collapse the shadows; they collapse the hierarchy.

RV: Now you said "popular" theories. Do the more academic versions escape this problem?

Wilber: The theories don't, but I think many of the theorists do. Most of the people who either introduced the physics/mysticism thing or at least used it for effect have increasingly refined and sophisticated their views. David Bohm has clearly moved toward a more articulated and hierarchical view, even if he objects to the word hierarchy. And Fritjof Capra never said that physics and mysticism were the same, although he did try to draw so many parallels that the public thinks he did. Anyway, he has moved quite beyond his introductory statements in *Tao of Physics.* I'm just afraid the public never will. They have latched onto physics equals mysticism with such passion that Capra's new and more sophisticated—and necessarily complicated—ideas will never reverse the tide. Anyway, it's not so much those scholars, or ones like Renée Weber who are trying to interpret their findings for us, that I have in mind when I criticize the pop mysticism and the new physics or holographic craze. But definitely the holographic paradigm, in and by itself, falls into that pop mysticism, and I simply think that is a real problem.

RV: Now that hierarchy collapse which occurs in the holographic paradigm—that's related to the error of pantheism, correct?

Wilber: Yes. Almost identical. It mistakes the sum of illusions for reality. You take the phenomena, the shadows, claim they are "all one," and then confuse that sum total of shadows with the Light beyond. As Schuon put it in a blistering attack, pantheism denies distinctions on precisely the plane that they are real. It confuses an essential with a substantial identity. That's also exactly what the holographic paradigm does.

RV: The implications of that collapse would be what? Or, well, what does a theory lose when it loses those various dimensions?

Wilber: It loses all the differences in methodologies, epistemologies, and cognitive interests. All of those crumble.

RV: Could you back up?

Wilber: First off, each higher level cannot be fully explained in terms of a lower level. Each higher level has capacities and characteristics not found in lower levels. This fact appears in evolution as the phenomena of creative emergence. It's also behind synergy. But failing to recognize that elemental fact—that the higher cannot be derived from the lower—results in the fallacy of reductionism. Biology cannot be explained only in terms of physics, psychology cannot be explained only in terms of biology, and so on. Each senior stage includes its junior stages as components but also transcends them by adding its own defining attributes.

RV: Which generates hierarchy . . .

Wilber: Yes. All of the lower is in the higher but not all the higher is in the lower. A three-dimensional cube contains two-dimensional squares, but not vice versa. And it is that "not vice versa" that creates hierarchy. Plants include minerals but not vice versa; the human neocortex has a reptile stem but not vice versa, and so on. Every stage of evolution transcends but includes its predecessor—as Hegel said, to supersede is at once to negate and to preserve.

RV: But that doesn't apply to Godhead or the absolute, does it?

Wilber: It applies to the paradoxical aspect of God that is the highest of all levels of being. God contains all things but all things do not exclusively contain God—that would be pantheism.

RV: The other side of the paradox is that what every person or thing is, whether enlightened or not, is still only God.

Wilber: Yes. Anyway, each stage-level of the hierarchy is, as Huston Smith pointed out, a more or less unified totality that can stand on its own, so to speak. Likewise, all of the elements of each level are said to be mutually interdependent and interrelated. Each level of hierarchy, in other words, is a type of holography.

RV: So the elements of *a given level* are mutually interacting. But what about elements from *different* levels? How do they interact, or do they?

Wilber: They interact, but *not* in a mutual or absolutely equivalent fashion, and for the simple reason that they aren't equivalent. If the higher levels contain attributes not found on the lower levels, you simply can't have bilateral equivalence between them. My dog and I can interact on the level of sensorimotor perception, but not on the level of symbolic mind—I mean, we don't discuss Shakespeare.

RV: But don't the Eastern traditions say that all things are perfectly, mutually interpenetrating?

Wilber: No, that's pure pop mysticism. The actual traditions are much more sophisticated than that. But I suppose you are referring to Hua Yen Buddhism, or Kegon—the school associated with the *Avatamsaka Sutra.*

RV: That seems to be the most often quoted or referred to.

Wilber: According to Hua Yen, there are four fundamental principles of existence, none of which can be dismissed. One is *shih*, which means "separate thing or event." Two is called *li*, which means "transcending principle or pattern." Three is called *shih li wu ai*, which means "between principle and thing there is no obstruction," or perhaps "between noumenon and phenomena there is no boundary." And four is called *shih shih wu ai,* which means "between phenomenon and phenomenon there is no obstruction." Now the last item has been seized, isolated from its context, and made the basis of pop holistic philosophy. It's very misleading.

Anyway, the point is that the world is indeed an interrelated and interpenetrating series of thing-events, but not in the merely one-dimensional fashion of pop mysticism. All things interact through karmic association and karmic inheritance, but those of greater structural organization do not act absolutely equivalently with their junior dimensions, nor can junior dimensions embrace senior ones.

RV: OK, but now we come to the crux of the matter. What about the absolute? Isn't it equally at every point?

Wilber: It is, as I said, paradoxical. All of the absolute is equally at every point, *and* some points are closer to the absolute than others. The hierarchy deals with the manifest universe, where there are levels of increasing reality (or decreasing illusion) leading up to the absolutely real. And those levels are not one-dimensionally and equivalently interacting. I don't know of a single authority on the perennial philosophy—Smith, Schuon, Guénon, Coomaraswamy, Pallis—who would make that type of statement, or who would deny relative hierarchy.

RV: But couldn't physics have discovered the other side of the paradox—the absolute oneness or infinite whole underlying the manifest world?

Wilber: Follow it through. We already saw that what physics has found is actually a unified interaction of material shadows; it discovered that various physical particulars are interrelated processes—but interrelated shadows aren't the Light. As for the implicate order, we saw it was actually a huge energy dimension; it wasn't radically dimensionless or metaphysically infinite. And if you mean that physics could actually have evidence, concrete evidence, for the absolute . . . Well, the absolute itself, being all-pervading and all-inclusive, is not other to any phenomenon and therefore could not be detected by any sort of instrument or show up in any sort of equation. That which can be functionally useful in an equation must be a variable *different* from other variables, but the absolute is different from, or set apart from, absolutely nothing.

RV: I see; so there is no way it could even enter an equation or make any difference in terms of theoretical information?

Wilber: None whatsoever, or else it would be itself merely more information, which would make it perfectly relative, or nonabsolute.

RV: Then what is it that the new physics *has* discovered? I mean, if it's not the Tao, what is it?

Wilber: In my opinion, it is simply the holography of level–1, or the fact of material or physical energy interrelation. The biologists discovered the holography of their level—level–2—about thirty years ago; it's called ecology. Every living thing influences, however indirectly, every other living thing. The sociopsychologists discovered the holography of the mental level—the fact that the mind is actually an intersubjective process of communicative exchange, and no such thing as a separate or radically isolated mind exists. Modern physics—well, it's what, almost a century old now?—simply discovered the analogous holography on its own level, that of physical-energetic processes. I don't see any other way to read the actual data.

RV: OK, but now why couldn't that physical holography actually be the *same* oneness underlying the biological and psychological and other levels? Why couldn't all of these approaches—physics, biology, psychology, and so on—simply be approaching the same underlying holistic reality from different angles?

Wilber: Start by explaining what you mean by "different angles," and you will find you are necessarily reintroducing the very differences you wished to overcome by saying "one reality." That is, you have merely moved the problem back one step. *If* there are these fundamentally different approaches to one reality, then tell me first *why* the approaches *are* different. Tell me why the study of physics is different from the study of literature, for instance. As you pursue that question very carefully, you will find that those differences are not merely arbitrary. They are not simply interchangeable or equivalent approaches, because they take as their subject matter various classes of events that *are* different because they display different dimensions of structural organization and evolutionary advance and developmental logic. The approach to studying hydrogen is fundamentally different from the approach to studying, say, the meaning of *Hamlet,* if for no other reason than that the one is submental and the other is mental. Now those are *not* two different approaches to the same reality, they involve two different levels of reality. Further, that reality—the absolute as absolute—is disclosed in its entirety or essence only on the highest or ultimate level of being. And then only to the soul that has itself evolved perfectly to that estate.

RV: I understand. So there's only one more possibility—can't you say that since all things are ultimately made of subatomic particles, physics *has* shown us an ultimate oneness?

Wilber: All things are not ultimately made of subatomic particles; all things, including subatomic particles, are ultimately made of God. But you mention the most popular position, which is really an extreme form of reductionism. It's popular, I guess, because it fits the hierarchy collapse.

RV: Reduce all things to material particles, then discover the particles are holographic, then claim that that holography is the Tao.

Wilber: Yes, that's right. There's a strange appeal in the simplicity of the reductionism. Part of the problem is simply that the physicists are so used to working with the material world, they tend to call it "*the* world" or "*the* universe," and so they say things like "Physics has proven all things in the world are one," when of course it has done no such thing. It has not explained or even touched bio-ecological unity, let alone sociopsychological community, and so on. Physics deals with four major forces—strong and weak nuclear, electromagnetic and gravitational. But it can't tell you anything about the force of emotional-sexuality, which comes into existence on level–2. It can't tell you about what constitutes good literature, or how economics works, or why children have Oedipal complexes, or the meaning of a dream, or why people commit suicide, and so on. All of those are mental symbolic events that begin on level–3. Physics doesn't deal with "*the*" world, you see? As I say, the whole thing has been very misleading.

RV: But there are important parallels, is that right?

Wilber: You mean parallels between the various levels, laws of the various levels?

RV: Yes. I mean, can't the laws of physics tell us something, anything, about the higher levels?

Wilber: Yes, I think they can, but we have to be very careful here. The lower will display its version of an analog law first—the lower emerges first in any developmental sequence, and so it is extremely tempting to say that the lower stands in a causal relation to the higher analog law. That's why I went to such pains in *Up from Eden* to point out that the higher comes *through* the lower, then *rests on* the lower, but doesn't come *from* the lower.

RV: It comes from, or gains its reality from, its senior dimension, not its junior dimension, correct?

Wilber: Yes, via the process of involution.

RV: Maybe we can come back to that point. For now, what is an "analog law"?

Wilber: The idea is simply that every event and principle on a lower level is merely a reduced version or a reflection downward or a lesser degree of those events and principles found on higher levels.

RV: Could you give some examples?

Wilber: This is not a novel idea; it's extremely well developed in the traditional philosophies. According to Hinduism, for example, the absolute bliss of Brahman goes through a series of stepped-down versions, or dilutions, until it appears as the sexual thrill of orgasm. In Christian mysticism, you find such ideas as that natural law is simply a partial version of mental rationality, which itself is merely a reduced reflection of the Divine Logos. The Buddhist *vijnana* psychology holds that there are four classes of consciousness, each being a stepped-down version of Universal Mind. This is correlated with the idea of the four bodies of Buddha; which is almost identical to the Vedanta notion of four bodies and four major states of awareness—gross, subtle, causal, and ultimate or *turiya*. The point, with reference to bodies, is that the body or substance of a physical entity, such as a simple rock, is actually a reflection downward of the freedom and vitality of the subtle body associated with mind, and the subtle body itself is merely a trickle of the causal body— and *that* is just a contraction in the face of eternity or *turiya*.

RV: The idea also exists in the West?

Wilber: Oh yes; I assure you you can give just as many examples, from the neo-Platonists to the Victorine mystics. Interestingly, it forms the crux of one of the most influential of modern Western philosophers—Whitehead.

RV: Was he influenced by the traditionalists?

Wilber: He must have been aware of them, but I think he came to the notion more or less on his own. You know, the truth will out and all. I'd like to think the obviousness of the truth simply couldn't escape one such as Whitehead. Anyway, he took the notion of junior dimensions being essentially reduced versions of senior ones, and completely turned the typical approach to reality on its head. He said that if you want to know the general principles of existence, you must start at the top and use the highest occasions to illumine the lowest, not the other way around, which of course is the common reductionist reflex. So he said you could learn more about the world from biology than you could from physics; and so he introduced the organismic viewpoint which has revolutionized philosophy. And he said you could learn more from social psychology than from biology, and then introduced the notion of things being a society of occasions—the notion of compound individuality. Naturally, he held that the apex of exemplary pattern was God, and it was in God, the ultimate compound individual, that you would ground any laws or patterns found reflected in reduced versions in the lower dimensions of psychology, then biology, then physics. The idea, which was brilliant in its statement, was that you first look to the higher levels for the general principles of existence, and then, *by subtraction,* you see how far down the hierarchy they extend. You don't start at the bottom and try to move up by addition of the lower parts, because some of the higher parts simply don't show up very well, or at all, on the lower rungs. Perhaps his favorite examples were creativity and love—God, for Whitehead, was especially love and creativity. But in the lower dimensions, the creativity gets reduced, appearing in humans as a modicum of free will but being almost entirely lost by the time you get to atomic particles. Maybe we could say that the Heisenberg uncertainty principle represents all that is left of God's radical freedom on the physical plane. But the point is that if you try to understand the cosmos in the reverse direction, from atoms up, you are stuck trying to account for free will, for creativity, for choice, for anything other than a largely deterministic cosmos. The fact is, even with its little bit of Heisenberg indeterminacy, the physical universe is much more deterministic than even level–2, biological beings. Any good physicist can tell you where Jupiter will be located a decade from now, barring disaster, but no biologist can tell you where a dog will move two minutes from now. So Whitehead, by looking to illuminate the lower by the higher, and not vice versa, could make creativity the general principle, and then understand determinism as a partial restriction or reduction of primary creativity. If, on the other hand, you start at the bottom, then you have to figure out a way to get free will and creativity out of rocks, and it just won't work. That it is reductionistic is the nicest thing you can say about such approaches.

RV: That's extraordinary, because I've seen so many attempts by new age thinkers to derive human free will from electron indeterminacy, or to say that human volition is free *because of* the indeterminate wave nature of its subcellular components, or some such.

Wilber: Yes, it appears the thing to do. It's a reflex thing to do—finally, after decades of saying the physical universe is deterministic and therefore human choice is an illusion, you find a little indeterminacy in the physical realm and you go nuts. It's only natural you then try to explain human freedom and even God's freedom as a blowup of the lowest level. You get so excited you forget you have just pulled the reductionist feat of the century; God is that big electron in the sky. The intentions are so good, but the philosophy is so detrimental. And imagine this: there are plenty of physicists who feel that the physical realm really is purely deterministic—Einstein, for one—and that future research may disclose subatomic variables that *are* purely causal. I'm not saying that will or will not happen, but theoretically, what if it does? Does poor God then lose Its creative power? The day the determinate variables are found, does human will evaporate? You see the problem?

RV: Yet so many new age thinkers are using physics and neurophysiology to establish their claims of higher transcendence or mysticism or just human free will.

Wilber: Yes, and in a way that even orthodox philosophers find horrifyingly reductionistic. Let me read you a quote from a recent president of the American Philosophical Association: "The body can be free, no matter what may be true according to quantum laws; and moreover, it could not be free by virtue of the latter alone. For if its freedom is merely that of electrons, then, as has been well said, it is freedom of the electrons but not of the body. This objection to some recent attempts to treat human freedom as simply derivative from quantum mechanics and nerve structure is, I believe, quite valid." The point, of course, applies even more so to the Tao, and yet new agers seem to be applying it even less.

RV: I think all that is very clear. But now on a popular level, a general level, is there anything wrong with such books as *The Dancing Wu Li Masters* or *The Tao of Physics* or any of the other new age, new paradigm books?

Wilber: I'm simply saying that you have to be very careful about the statements you make if you want to extend them from popular hyperbole into a real and enduring paradigm. Statements like "The universe is a harmonious, interrelated whole" or "All things are One" or "The universe is dynamic and patterned, not static and fixed" are superb introductory material; we've all used them to get our points across in a general way. But beyond that, they are very misleading.

RV: How, specifically?

Wilber: Well, if you take two columns and in column *A* you write words like fixed, static, isolated, manyness, discrete, and in column *B* you write fluid, dynamic, pattern, holistic, oneness; then I would guess the vast majority of new age thinkers imagine that the mystical view is column *B*. But in fact mysticism is concerned with transcending *both* column *A* and *B*. Column *B* is just as dualistic as column *A*, for the simple reason that the two columns are opposites or mirror images and thus both are partial. Reality is *not* holistic; it is not dynamic, not interrelated, not one and not unified—*all* of those are mere concepts about reality. As Chuang Tzu said in "Three in the Morning," to say all things are one is just as dualistic as to say all things are many. That's why Zen says reality is "Not-two! Not-one!" That is not some sort of very subtle or terribly sophisticated mystical doctrine. It is the simplest and most fundamental of all mystical doctrines. Murti's classic, *The Central Philosophy of Buddhism,* has made that very clear, certainly for Mahayana, as have writers from Schuon to Guénon to Coomaraswamy for the other traditions. That is simple, bottom-line mysticism.

RV: The absolute cannot be qualified in any sense?

Wilber: Correct, including the sense you just gave it. The absolute—and here we have to speak somewhat poetically—cannot be characterized or qualified because it is not set apart or different from any thing and therefore could not be described as one thing or event among others. It is *nirguna,* without attributes, or *shunya,* void of characterization. Since there is no place outside the absolute, there is no place you could take up a stance so as to describe it. If you could get outside it, it would cease to be the absolute.

RV: And so . . .

Wilber: Well, here's a crude analogy. Say the entire universe consists of only three objects—a square one, a round one, and a triangular one. God is not the sum of those objects, whether they are considered things or events. . . .

RV: As pantheism maintains. . . .

Wilber: Yes; God is not the sum of those objects because you could destroy those objects and God would still exist. Therefore neither can you describe God as being any of the attributes of each thing—God is not a circular square triangle. And most important, God is not another object in addition to the three objects. God is not One Thing set apart from the many. God is not a dynamic thing, a holistic thing, or a patterned thing.

RV: Staying with your analogy, can you say anything about what God would be?

Wilber: As long as you remember it is a metaphoric and not descriptive statement. God is not one thing among many things, or the sum of many things, or the dynamic interaction of many things—God is the condition, the nature, the suchness, or the reality of each thing or event or process. It is not set apart *from* any of them, yet neither is it in any way confined *to* them. It is identical *with* the world, but not identical *to* it.

RV: Is that why you earlier said the absolute is prior to the world but not other to the world?

Wilber: Yes. That is the doctrine of *tathata,* or suchness—Eckhart called it the *isness* of each thing-event; the Taoists call it *tzu jan,* the so-ness of every object; it is also very close to the meaning of both *dharma,* for Buddhism, and *sahaj,* for Vedanta. Anyway, the doctrine of suchness, combined with the doctrines of *advaita* or nonduality and *shunyata* or unqualifiability, form the most fundamental and elemental starting point for all mystical traditions, although the terminology is, of course, different.

RV: And it's those basics that seem to get left out of so many new age accounts of science and mysticism?

Wilber: I think so, yes. Apparently the author wants to say that modern science has discovered that certain objects are actually processes and not static things, or triangles and not circles, and so the Tao is triangular, just as good ole physics says. But, in fact, the Tao contains things and it contains events, but it can be characterized by neither. It is not different from them, but neither is it defined by them.

RV: And you could also say that because the frequency realm is actually a different realm from the read-out realm, these are merely two *different* realms, and so the one could not be the mystical suchness of the other?

Wilber: Yes, that would be another important point. The frequency realm is simply one realm among others, not one without a second. I hadn't thought of it that way before, but that's true. Please let me say again that I think the frequency realm does exist, but that I honestly think it just doesn't have anything to do with mystical events or with a truly transcendent-immanent ground, and you've simply given another and very fundamental reason why.

RV: I wonder if we could now move on to the notion of epistemology, because you said earlier that the evolutionary hierarchy is also a hierarchy of knowledge. Could you elaborate?

Wilber: Each level of the Great Chain is a level of prehension, as Whitehead might say. Each level prehends, or somehow touches or cognizes, its environment. As we said earlier, each level is a stepped-down version of absolute consciousness. Anyway, if we use our simple three-level hierarchy of body, mind, and spirit, then the three corresponding modes of knowing are sensory, symbolic, and intuitive. The Christian mystics refer to them as the eye of flesh, the eye of reason, and the eye of contemplation. Even Aristotle was perfectly aware of these realms—he referred to them as *techne, praxis* (or *phronesis*), and *theoria*.

RV: And they are hierarchic?

Wilber: Yes. Just as the eye of reason transcends but includes the eye of flesh, the eye of contemplation transcends but includes the eye of reason.

RV: Can science as we know it be extended to cover all three realms? Can we have a higher science of being?

Wilber: Yes, I think we can speak of these higher realms and their knowledge as being scientific, but we have to be extremely careful by what we mean. Look at it this way; we have at least these three modes of knowing—sensory, symbolic, and contemplative. These modes correspond to the physical body, the mind, and the spirit. That is simple enough, but it becomes a little more complicated when you realize that the mind, for instance, can look not only at its own realm but at the other two realms as well, and in each case you could get a fundamentally different type of knowledge. Here, I could draw it like this:

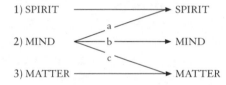

RV: So we have three basic modes and realms of knowledge: the physical-sensory, the mental, and the spiritual. (These are numbered 1, 2, and 3.) And then, within the mental mode itself, we have, what, three subsets?

Wilber: Subsets is fine. . . . (These are lettered a, b, and c.)

RV: Depending upon which of the three realms the mental mode takes as its object?

Wilber: Yes. Following my favorite orthodox philosopher, Jürgen Habermas, we can characterize the three mental subsets like this. When the mind confines itself to sensory knowledge, the mode is called empirical-analytic, and its interest is technical. When the mind works with other minds, the mode is hermeneutic, phenomenological, rational, or historic, and its interest is practical or moral. We now add the mystic view, which Habermas doesn't directly cover, and we say that when the mind attempts to cognize the spiritual realm, its mode is paradoxical or radically dialectical, and its interest is soteriological. Here, I'll put it on the diagram.

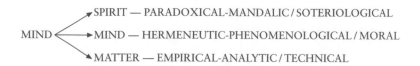

SPIRIT — PARADOXICAL-MANDALIC / SOTERIOLOGICAL

MIND — MIND — HERMENEUTIC-PHENOMENOLOGICAL / MORAL

MATTER — EMPIRICAL-ANALYTIC / TECHNICAL

RV: What exactly is hermeneutics?

Wilber: The study of interpretation and symbolic meaning. In the hands of such sophisticated philosophers as Gadamer or Ricoeur, it really comes to mean mentality in general, or symbolic intentionality and meaning and value. See, the reason that empirical-analytic studies are so limited—limited, in fact, to the sensory realm—is that they can't even disclose the nature or meaning of mental productions. There is no empirical test, for instance, which will disclose the meaning of *Macbeth,* or the meaning of value, the meaning of your life, and so on. Meaning is a mental production and can be determined only by interpretation, or what Heidegger called the hermeneutic circle.

RV: Most people understand what you mean by empirical-analytic. Could you comment on the third subset, the paradoxical?

Wilber: The idea is simply that when the mind attempts to reason about the absolute, it will necessarily generate paradoxes, for exactly the reasons we have been discussing. When reason operates in this mode, we call it paradoxical. I have also heard the word "mandalic reason" used, and I like that. Either one is fine.

RV: Now you are saying that mandalic reason is not contemplation, but it does have its uses, correct?

Wilber: Yes, exactly. Both of those points should be emphasized. The first is that paradoxical or mandalic reason—which is what results when you try to think or write about the Tao or Spirit or Buddha Nature—is not itself spirit, nor does it disclose spirit per se. Here, let me just number all five modes like this:

SPIRIT ——— 1 ———▶ SPIRIT (TRANSCENDELIA)

MIND ——— 3 ———▶ MIND (INTELLIGIBILIA)

MATTER——— 5 ———▶ MATTER (SENSIBILIA)

Number 5 is simple sensory-material or sensorimotor perception. Number 4 is empirical-analytic mental knowledge, or mind's ideas about the sensorimotor world. Number 3 is hermeneutic and introspective and phenomenological knowledge, or mind's knowledge about mind. Number 2 is paradoxical or mandalic reason, or mind's attempt to think about spirit. Number 1 is spirit's direct knowledge *of* spirit, which is nonmediated or nonsymbolic knowledge, intuitive and contemplative.

RV: And your first point is that #2 should not be confused with #1.

Wilber: Yes, and that is an extremely elemental point. There is no way to directly understand spirit except by radical spiritual transformation, or the direct opening of the eye of contemplation in your own case. You can read, think, and write about the Tao all day, and none of that is the Tao. No mental theory is even close to Brahman.

RV: And since, if you do reason about Tao, you will only generate paradoxes, there is no way to state one position over another. I mean, you can't say the Tao is dynamic flux, because that's half of a dualism in the paradox.

Wilber: That's true. You can't say it without contradicting yourself, as both Nagarjuna and Kant clearly pointed out.

RV: I'm not sure I follow that point.

Wilber: Well, suppose you say the Tao is constantly changing, that nothing is permanent, everything changes. That's a self-contradiction, because you are claiming everything changes except, apparently, the fact that everything changes, which must therefore be a *permanent* fact. It won't work. Same thing happens if you claim reality is relative, dynamic, one, and so on.

RV: So the Tao is permanent and impermanent?

Wilber: Or neither, or even neither-neither, as Nagarjuna would have it. But you see the point—reason generates paradoxical statements when it tries to grasp the absolute.

RV: But your second point was that that type of reason has certain uses?

Wilber: Definitely so, as long as we don't confuse mandalic reason (#2) with actual intuition-contemplation (#1). One of its uses is to try to hint to other minds what God might be like. Hegel used such dialectical reason with great force, although he always came too close to confusing it with spiritual intuition. Another purpose, which was used with extraordinary skill by Nagarjuna, is to use the dialectic to demolish reason itself and thus pave the way for actual contemplation, or prajna.

RV: How, exactly?

Wilber: Nagarjuna would be faced by an opponent who wished to characterize the absolute—the Brahmins claimed God was absolute being, certain nihilist Buddhists claimed it was extinction, others claimed it was pattern, others said it was monistic or unitary, and so on.

RV: All of which are partial and dualistic?

Wilber: Yes, and Nagarjuna would demonstrate that point by turning the opponent's logic back on itself, at which point it would contradict itself. See, if you try to make a statement about reality as a whole, then your statement is part of that reality, at which point it becomes like a hand trying to grasp itself or a tongue trying to taste itself. You end up either in an infinite regress or in a blatant contradiction. Nagarjuna would use this inherent limitation in reason to exhaust reason's attempts to grasp spirit, at which point, if the thing is done carefully, you become more open to actual contemplative insight—the mind just shuts up, and in the gap between those thoughts, prajna is born, or at least can be. But as far as reality goes, it is neither being nor nonbeing, nor both nor neither—those were Nagarjuna's four categories, and they were based on the Buddha's original "inexpressibles." Whatever reality is, it can only, only be "seen" upon satori, or via actual contemplative insight (mode #1).

RV: And if you try to state what is "seen" you will only generate paradox. . . .

Wilber: Yes, but those paradoxes, used skillfully, as *upaya*, constitute mandalic reason (mode #2)—and that is one of its uses.

RV: We were talking about science, about a higher science.

Wilber: Well, as I said, we have to be very careful here. If by science you mean consensual and experimental knowledge, then all realms, including the higher, can be scientific. [See chapter 2.] But they cannot be merely sensory-empirical; nor are all of them directly involved in forming *theories.*

RV: Because a theory is a mental production?

Wilber: Yes. The sensory mode—#5—does not itself form theories because it is presymbolic. And the spiritual mode—#1—does not itself form theories because it is transsymbolic; its actual operation is immediate and nonconceptual insight.

RV: So that limits theoretic activity to the three mental subsets.

Wilber: The activity itself, yes. It is only the mental modes that form theories, although the theories themselves can try to take account of the other realms, realms which themselves do not directly form theories. Of course, classical science was theory directed toward the biomaterial realm. That is, it was empirical-analytic theory or mode #4. The mind creates a theory-map of the objective biomaterial world, looks carefully at that world, usually by altering that world in controlled ways, and then fits the map to it. A good map becomes a model, and a model that is never disproven becomes a law.

RV: What about theory in mode #3?

Wilber: That is phenomenological philosophy, introspective psychology, intersubjective communication, interpretation, value systems, and so on. This mode does form theories or maps of what the subjective and intersubjective world is like.

RV: But those theories are not checked by empirical-analytic means, because they aren't sensory referents?

Wilber: That's right; they are checked by hermeneutical procedures, by interpretation, by communities of like-minded interpreters, by direct phenomenological apprehension, and so on.

RV: Could you give an example?

Wilber: What you and I are doing right now. We are exchanging meaning, symbolic meaning, and arriving at interpretive understanding. "What do you *mean* by that?"—meaning, you know. That is not an empirically reducible event, and it cannot be explained by physics, chemistry, or biology. *Hamlet* is not made of electrons; it is constructed of symbolic units of meaning which, if reduced to the paper on which they are written, are simply destroyed. But I suppose a classic example is Freud. Despite his rampant attempts at sociobiological reductionism— and it was absolutely rampant—his methodology was almost entirely hermeneutic and phenomenological, which is why I think he still has much to tell us, and why so many structuralists are returning to him for insight. Lacan is now said to be the foremost psychological thinker in Europe, and Lacan is two things: a structuralist in the line of Lévi-Strauss and a brilliant Freudian. Anyway, Freud's methodology was basically to watch the client's production of words and symbols and then try to figure out what those symbols might really mean. His assumption was that a dream, for instance, must occur on two levels, because the client is actually the author of the dream—it's her or his dream—but the client either professes not to understand its meaning or suffers the dream as a passive witness. The dream, in other words, is composed of two texts, a manifest text and a latent or hidden text. And it's the hidden text that is causing the problems. So part of the analyst's job is to find this hidden text, decipher it, and interpret it to the client. It's like finding an Egyptian hieroglyphic, and no merely sensory evidence will help here, because what you are dealing with is how trains of subjective symbols slide over each other to create a world of meaning, intention, value, desire, and so on. It's exactly like a Rorschach blot—the empirical blot is fixed and given; it's composed of so much ink arranged in just one way. But the symbolic meanings that can ride on that blot are numerous, and they can't be determined by empiricism at all. So Freud's technique was to use linguistic dialogue in order to disclose hidden texts, then translate or interpret those texts so as to make the meaning of hidden symptoms more transparent to the client. It was that transparency, where before there had been opaqueness, that helped effect the cure. The interpretation, in other words, leads to insight or understanding. Through repeated observations and interpretations, Freud was able to create various maps or theories of the psychological sphere, theories that could not be tested empirically, like mere behaviorism, but which *could* be tested by those who were willing to take up the discipline of introspective interpretation. That Freud's reductionism crippled many of his maps and theories is sad, but that is not the fault of his methodology. It was a pure case of in garbage, out garbage.

RV: So mode #3 can be theoretic in that it also forms and uses maps and models of its own level.

Wilber: Yes, but its verification test is hermeneutic, not empiric. Or rational-phenomenological, not sensory. Or linguistic, not physical. If you wish, call it phenomenological science [dialogic science; see chapter 2].

RV: And mode #2. That's paradoxical—can that be theoretic?

Wilber: I think so, but theory in a looser sense. As I said, paradoxical reason has its uses, as long as we are careful. Theory in this sense would involve creating maps or cartographies of the higher and transcendental spheres, for the aid of those who have not yet seen them, and also for general knowledge purposes. Mandalic maps, as it were, and mandalic science [chapter 2].

RV: Could you check those maps?

Wilber: Yes, but only by actually transforming to the spiritual realm, or by awakening mode #1. You absolutely could not verify them using empiric or hermeneutic procedures.

RV: But would those maps also be paradoxical?

Wilber: Yes, definitely. It sometimes doesn't appear that way because each system, merely for consistency, usually works with only one side of the paradox. Thus the Buddhists will call the highest level Void, Hindus will call it Being, the Taoists will claim it is ever-changing, and the Christians will say it is everlasting. All are right—or wrong; it makes no difference. It's paradoxical. You see, paradox is simply the way nonduality looks to the mental level. Spirit itself is not paradoxical; it is not characterizable at all. But when the mind tries to think about it, then nonduality shows up as two contradictory opposites, both of which can be shown to be equally plausible because neither is complete by itself. The best you can do therefore is affirm *both* sides of the duality, or deny them both. The former gives you paradox; the latter, double negative. I use mandalic reason to cover both, although it applies better to paradox. But my point is that neither of them should be confused with mode #1 or actual contemplation—true contemplative or transmental and transtheoretical science: the science of Spirit *as* Spirit, not merely as symbolized by mind. So all these various modes can be called "scientific," as long as we are careful in each case to explain exactly what we mean. My only worry has been that advocates of a "new and higher" science all too often have in mind one of these modes, usually the empiric, and they want to expand that mode over all the others. That results in reductionism, which leads to hierarchy collapse, which involves the fallacy of equivalent shadows, which gives pantheism. . . . So use "science" any way you wish, but first please say what you mean by the term, give its methodology, distinguish it from other modes and disciplines, and then we'll see what you've got.

R V: On the notion of the applicability—or inapplicability—of empirical science to higher realms, such as the mental-subjective or the transcendental-spiritual; doesn't research in brain physiology—which is empirical—tell us something about mind and its operations?

Wilber: Yes, of course. Brain research is extremely exciting and important, but I think it is also extremely limited.

R V: In what sense?

Wilber: Well, take Freud's thoughts on the matter. In his last book he stated pretty clearly that even *if* we could figure out every connection between the brain and consciousness, then—and these are his own words—"it would at most afford an exact localization of the processes of consciousness and would give us no help toward understanding them." As I said—and as almost everybody has recently discovered—Freud was primarily interested in hermeneutics—in interpretation and meaning and symbolic discourse.

R V: His first major book was *The Interpretation of Dreams.*

Wilber: Yes. Even if we can localize the dream—say, in the right hemisphere—and even if we can describe its chemical components, we still don't know its *meaning.* That meaning is discoverable only in the hermeneutic circle, only in my life's history and its intentions.

RV: Mode #3 and not #4.

Wilber: Yes. And this insight is now producing an entire renaissance in nonempirical, nonreductionistic, nonbiological psychology. You have the interpersonal or object-relations theorists—Sullivan, Guntrip, Fairbairn, Jacobson, Erik Erikson. You have the linguists and structuralists—Lacan, Piaget, Kohlberg, Roy Schafer, Ricoeur. The information theorists—Bateson being the most famous. All of these are related to symbolic transfer or hermeneutics, and it's revolutionizing psychology.

RV: Can you give a short example, say in terms of pathology?

Wilber: Sure. Originally symptoms were conceived in energetic or biophysical terms: The id pushes here, the ego pushes back, the compromise is a substitute gratification in the form of a symptom. The shadow, or personal unconscious, was a product of forces. Very thermodynamic. Now without denying that bioenergetics are also involved, the new understanding simply points out that the self is not so much a present biophysical event as it is a story or a history. The self, the mental self anyway, is a linguistic structure, a creation of history and a creator of history. It lives via communication or dialogue, it is constructed of units of meaning or symbols, and it lives out a course in time or history. It is a story; it is a *text*. And the only way you understand *War and Peace*, for instance, is by good interpretation. What does it really *mean*, see? What does my life mean? Where is it going? Why am I doing this? What value does this have for me? And that's hermeneutics.

RV: And pathology?

Wilber: Pathology is related to bad interpretation or maybe misinterpretation. And the shadow is no longer the seat of unconscious forces, it's the seat of misinterpretation. In a sense, the shadow is a hidden text or subtext, and so it produces scripts whose *meanings* baffle you—bad hermeneutics, or poor hermeneutics, as when the person says, "I don't know why I did that, wonder what it means?" The shadow is a text you secretly write, a text whose authorship you refuse to admit.

RV: And so therapy?

Wilber: Is a process of assuming or reassuming the authorship or responsibility for your own life text, your own self.

RV: And none of that can be easily explained in empirical or physiological terms?

Wilber: The hermeneutics? No. But I would like to add that the system I'm working with utilizes both the bioenergetics of the body's prana, or emotional-sexual distributions, and the mental units of meaning that transcend but include the simpler bioenergetic feelings. Both are important, but the hermeneutics more so. In the seven-level scheme I gave earlier, diet and exercise deal basically with level–1; bioenergetics and emotional-sexual cathexis deals with level–2; and hermeneutics and symbolic interpretation deals with level–3 and part of level–4. None of those can be tossed out. The problem with pure hermeneutics is that it tries to say the id is just language, which is silly. A dog has sexual impulses and no language. Humans have both. Trying to reduce one to the other is just not useful. They both slot in the nested hierarchy.

RV: And so, is empirical physiology without any fundamental use for the understanding of mental hermeneutics?

Wilber: No, no, that's reverse reductionism, I didn't say that. Hermeneutics transcends but includes the effects of physiology, as I have said for each level of the hierarchy. So the effects of physiology can be best understood in terms of degeneracy theory, I think.

RV: Which is?

Wilber: If you look at every stage in evolution, what you find is that—this has been pointed out often—each higher stage is synergistic to its junior components; it includes them but is more than them.

RV: That's "transcends but includes."

Wilber: Yes, same idea; synergy is the same idea. Bring lifeless matter together in certain complex ways, and you generate something that is more than the sum of its parts. You generate life or prana. Life is synergistic in reference to matter and cannot be reduced to, or fully explained by, matter. Likewise, bring prana together in certain complex ways, and symbols begin to emerge. But symbols—or psychology—cannot be explained by life—or biology—just as biology cannot be explained by rocks. Each is synergistic in reference to its predecessors. Now the opposite of synergy is degeneracy. If A is degenerate to B, then two or more states of B can be sustained on top of a single state of A. For example, if you make a telephone call, then a certain amount of electrical energy is passing along the lines. But information is also passing along the lines, and you cannot tell how much information, what type of information, or the quality of information that is being transmitted on the mere basis of the amount of energy supporting it. For example, with the same amount of energy—say, 100 kilowatts or whatever—you could say "Hello, how are you" or "zizzy lollop thud." The former carries information; the latter, mere noise. Several *different* states of information transfer can be sustained on the *same* state of energy exchange. In this case, energy is degenerate with regard to information.

RV: And that occurs at all stages of evolution?

Wilber: Yes, at every level of the nested hierarchy. Really, it's a simple notion; it's just the opposite of synergy.

RV: And you see that relationship in the brain and mind?

Wilber: I think that is certainly a possible explanation. The brain is basically the biophysical substrate for the mental processes. We would also expect spiritual processes to leave their footprints in the biophysical substrate, either directly or via the mind. But in no case could mind or spirit be reduced to brain or explained entirely or merely by brain physiology. The Rorschach blot is still a good analogy: There is one physical substrate, the actual ink blot, but it supports several different mental interpretations, and you can't say the interpretations are just ink. I think it's the same with brain and mind.

RV: The brain is degenerate with regard to mind?

Wilber: Yes. That would mean that the changes in brain physiology would not be correspondingly as significant as the changes in mind values. For instance, I can be in the beta brain-wave state, and have two successive thoughts of wildly different truth-values, say, "2 + 2 = 4" and "2 + 2 = 5." The difference in EEG between those thoughts is extremely small, but the difference in truth-value is tremendous. So there *are* physiological correlates, but they are degenerate with regard to mind. The differences in physiology are not as significant as the differences in the truth-values of the propositions. Incidentally, notice that you cannot establish the truth or falsity of the propositions by any amount of physiological studies. You have to go outside the brain's physiology, into the intersubjective circle of logic and communication, in order to verify mental truths, because, as we've said, mind transcends but includes physiology, and the truths of the former cannot be entirely contained in the truths of the latter. No amount of EEG sophistication could help you prove or disprove Keynes's theory of macroeconomics, for instance.

RV: But that would still give brain physiology an important effect on mind but not a causal effect, correct?

Wilber: Yes. This theory still gives us a definite brain-mind connection and interaction, but it doesn't postulate wild dualism on the one hand or simple monism or identity on the other. Further, it suggests that the brain is as complex as it is because nothing less complicated could serve as the biophysical substrate for logical and symbolic processes, but it avoids the reductionism of saying, for example, that literature is fancy electrons.

RV: So theoretically, if we understood brain physiology in depth, we could produce general states and moods and improve the substrate, like memory capacity and so on, but we could not produce specific thoughts or ideas in the mind.

Wilber: Yes. Changing physiological states would be like changing Rorschach blots. You would get a whole new series of moods and responses, but you couldn't control all the specific mental interpretations or actual contents. So brain would still have a significant effect on mind but not a determinant or causal effect on mind. This also fits very well, I think, with such researchers as Elmer and Alyce Green, who maintain that "all of brain is in the mind but not all of the mind is in the brain."

RV: That's hierarchy and degeneracy.

Wilber: Absolutely. But this still leaves us with the important tasks of mapping out the degenerate relationships between mind and brain, and also between spirit and brain. Correlations of brain waves with dreaming, for example.

RV: And because of degeneracy, you can tell from physiological changes *that* a person is dreaming but not exactly what he or she is dreaming?

Wilber: Yes, that's exactly degeneracy.

RV: This is slightly off the topic, but what *would* determine the dream content?

Wilber: Well, a quick answer would be that the past history of the text-self is now getting a reading, especially its hidden subtexts. The shadow is on stage. And the content of the shadow is not determined by present physiology as much as it is by past history, the actual past events that constitute the story and the history that this person recognizes as a self. That's why Habermas calls this mode the hermeneutic-*historic.* And finally, that's why Freud was drawn to the idea of trying to trace the *historical* genesis of symptoms. He wanted to use a historical reconstruction method to help the person see when he or she began to write hidden or secret or guilty texts and stories, to see how the person repressed the shadow by creating a secret author. The secret author shows up in dreams and symptoms, and the job of the therapist is to help the person *interpret* the meaning of the symptoms—you know, "your anxiety is really masked or hidden rage"—until the person can re-own them, re-authorize them, re-author them. So even if physiology can't tell us what the shadow says or means, it can tell us when it is on stage—and that's tremendously important. I think the same thing will hold true of any psychospiritual correlates we can find in the biophysical substrate. So these correlations, even though they are degenerate, are very important.

RV: And this theory allows us to look for correlations of the higher in the lower without having to reduce the higher to the lower?

Wilber: That's my opinion, yes.

RV: In a related vein, what do you think of Prigogine's work? Doesn't it offer an empirical basis of higher transformations?

Wilber: In my opinion it doesn't, because I agree literally with Marilyn Ferguson that Prigogine's work—I'll read this—"bridges the critical gap between living systems and the apparently lifeless universe in which they arose."

RV: In other words, it applies basically to the gap between level–1 and level–2 in the seven-level hierarchy?

Wilber: I think so. It describes the complexities of material perturbations that allow life or prana to emerge through—but not from—matter. They are really exciting equations, but they don't easily or clearly cover the higher levels, levels 3 through 7.

RV: Why not? Surely it has some general applicability?

Wilber: Well, it is definitely true that there are analog laws on all levels of the hierarchy, as we earlier said. The question is not whether transformation occurs on all levels, because it does; the question is which level of structural organization do these equations actually describe? I think it is fairly well agreed that these equations deal primarily with thermodynamic energies and entropy, not with symbolic information and not with transphysical and transmental insight. Dissipative thermodynamic structures seem best representative of biomaterial transforms, or levels 1 and 2. They are *examples* of general transformations, therefore, but not paradigmatic among them. They are a subset of evolutionary transformations, and not the sole or exemplary type. As we earlier put it, they are downward reflections, or reduced versions, of the transformations that occur on the higher levels, and so naturally they all have certain similarities, just as the electron and human will are "indeterminant." But trying to use the lower-level manifestation of the general principle to explain the higher-level prototype of that very principle is what we want to try to avoid. So I think Prigogine's work is very important, not because I can then say he has proven the laws of psychological or spiritual transformation, but because he has demonstrated that the transformation process itself extends all the way down the hierarchy to the lowest levels. It shows up in an extremely reduced form, as we would expect, but there it is.

RV: So thermodynamic dissipative structures would be degenerate with regard to higher transformations?

Wilber: Yes. With respect to the brain-mind interface, if dissipative structures apply to levels 1 and 2, it follows they would apply to the brain or biophysical substrate of the mind, and thus assume the importance, limited but definite, that we discussed earlier.

RV: But are there ways to explore and verify any of the higher modes themselves, since they aren't empiric?

Wilber: Yes, of course. There is phenomenological investigation and its verification in a community of intersubjective interpreters—just as you and I are doing now. There is contemplative practice and its verification by a community of transsubjective meditators—as happens, say, between Zen Master and student [see chapter 2].

RV: But using phenomenology and hermeneutics as an example, wouldn't mere interpretation make truth a wildly subjective affair?

Wilber: It depends upon the caliber of the community of interpreters. Real philosophy, psychology, and phenomenology—not behaviorism and not positivism, those are empiric and not rational affairs—depend in large measure upon the quality of the community of interpreters. Good interpreters, good thinkers, ground good phenomenology. They discover those truths that apply to the subjective realm, and in that sense the truths are subjective truths. But that doesn't mean mere individual whim. First of all, a bad interpretation will simply not mesh with general subjective consensus. It is rebuffed by a reality that is subjective but very real and very lawful, just as a bad empiric fact is rebuffed by other facts. Second, a phenomenological truth, in order to be recognized as truth, must be *tested* in a community of like-minded interpreters, just as an empiric fact, to be so, must be tested against the community of other facts. It's no mere wishful thinking and subjective license. The hermeneutic test is just as stringent and demanding as the empiric test, but of course the empiric test is easier because it is performed by a subject on an object, whereas phenomenology is performed by a subject on or with other subjects. Much more difficult.

RV: Isn't that what has helped reductionism so much? Everybody wants the methodological elegance of physics?

Wilber: I think so. We are lured into thinking physics has *the* method, instead of seeing that physics is working with the simplest level of structural organization and thus produces relatively simple and easily reproducible truths.

RV: But aren't you pulling a type of reverse reductionism yourself? I mean, when we look into the subatomic world it's every bit as complex as the biological world or the human symbolic world.

Wilber: Well, it's complex, but not as complex as higher levels, for the simple reason that a human being contains electrons but electrons don't contain human beings. Thus all the complexities of the electron are contained in humans, but humans also contain other complexities found only in humans—guilt, anxiety, despair, desire.

RV: Yes, I see. So we should give equal or greater emphasis to rational-phenomenology and hermeneutics and so on?

Wilber: Yes, certainly, but hermeneutics alone is not the ultimate answer. See, just as empiricism wants to reduce symbol to sensation, hermeneutics wants to reduce spirit to symbol. It wants to claim God is a mere idea, or only an idea, in the community of intersubjective interpreters. It refuses to include in its methodology the practice of contemplation—mode #1—and thus it fails to see that God can be verified as a transcendental reality by a community of transsubjective meditators.

RV: Even though, on the mental plane, various communities of meditators would interpret spirit differently. Mind is degenerate to Spirit.

Wilber: Exactly. When the mind speaks of spirit, it generates paradox or contradictory interpretations. That's as it should be. But what is verified in meditation itself is not a particular interpretation of spirit, but a direct and immediate identity with and as spirit, and that occasion is not subject to interpretation because it is not a symbolic or mediated event. On the mental level, however, there are only interpretations of the event, most paradoxical, and that is inescapable. "They call Him many who is really one."

RV: Aren't there a lot of paradoxes in modern physics—what have been called "quantum koans"—and couldn't that suggest that physics is somehow involved in fundamental reality, in mandalic logic?

Wilber: Yes, that point has been raised a lot. But first off, just because the absolute always generates paradox doesn't mean that paradox always indicates the absolute, OK? But beyond that, I personally think there are very few genuine paradoxes in any branch of science. A real paradox, remember, means that two mutually contradictory occasions are known to occur simultaneously and equally. For instance, if at this very moment it is raining and not raining on my house, that would be a real paradox.

RV: What about wavicles—a particle acting as a wave in one situation, and a particle in another?

Wilber: Well, that's the point; it is a wave in one situation and a particle in another. In any given experiment, it never acts equally and absolutely as a perfect wave and a perfect particle simultaneously. It oscillates, or alternates, its mutually exclusive truths, and that is a complementarity, not a real paradox.

RV: Are there no genuine paradoxes in science or philosophy?

Wilber: I wouldn't put it that strongly, but I think it is safe to say that most apparent paradoxes turn out to be ordinary contradictions, which simply means you have made a confused step somewhere. In empiric research, contradictions usually indicate that a series of experiments have been run incorrectly. It is usually cleared up by more refined research. In rational-conceptual inquiry, what seems to be a paradox usually results, as Russell and Whitehead demonstrated in *Principia Mathematica,* from violating the theory of logical types. Even though Spencer Brown has suggested ways to reformulate the types theory, it is still extremely useful. Bateson almost made an entire career out of it.

RV: To put it bluntly, what is it?

Wilber: It simply states that a class cannot be a member of itself. It came up in trying to define number as the class of all classes similar to a given class. But the idea is very simple: The class of all chairs is not itself a chair, the class of all apples is not itself an apple, the alphabet is not itself a letter, and so on. Anyway, if you violate the logical typing of your symbols, then you generate a pseudoparadox. It's not a real paradox because it's just based on bad semantics. For instance, if you take one word-symbol, say, "chair," and then give it two meanings, each of a different logical type, then create a sentence using that word, you can generate a pseudoparadox. You might say, "That chair is not a chair." It is a particular chair but is not a universal chair, not the class of all chairs. When semanticists say—Korzybski's famous utterance— "Whatever you say a thing is, it isn't!"—that's not a real paradox. What they mean is that "whatever you say a thing is"—that is, the name you give it, the symbol you use to describe it—is not to be confused with the particular thing itself. The former is the class; the latter, the member, and the class is not a member of itself—that is a direct application of logical typing, and it is behind much of modern semantics and the map/territory theories. And it says that wherever you generate what looks like paradox, you've confused your logical types.

RV: I remember that theory now. Isn't it the way Russell solved the famous paradox about the Cretan who said, "Everything a Cretan says is a lie"? Since a Cretan said it, was he telling the truth or lying?

Wilber: Yes, the idea was that the Cretan was making a statement about statements, and that is of a logical type different from statements in general, and so he wasn't contradicting himself. You judge the statement and the meta-statement on their own terms, decide in each case whether it is true or false, and there goes the paradox. See, the theory of logical types is really just a way to group classes and sets into a hierarchy of increasing comprehensiveness. Each level in the Great Chain, for example, is of a higher logical type, even though not all of the levels themselves are actually made of logic. And in that larger sense, the theory of logical types—which says don't confuse types—says "don't collapse the hierarchy."

RV: Didn't the types theory also lead to the double-bind theory of schizophrenia?

Wilber: It really was the heart of most of Bateson's work. What happens in schizophrenia, according to Bateson, is that two messages of different logical types contradict each other, and the person, who takes both to be equally true, oscillates between them, until he shakes himself to pieces, so to speak. Because he cannot easily differentiate logical types, he takes both messages, which are merely contradictory, as being equally true or paradoxical. Then he can neither reach a compromise with them nor throw one of them out, because they are now equal but opposite.

RV: He's in a double bind.

Wilber: He's in a double bind. He violated logical typing, which generated a pseudoparadox which shakes him apart. It happens in any sort of information feedback system. If you take a machine that is supposed to turn itself "on" at a given lower limit and "off" at a given upper limit, and then you start moving those limits together, the machine will turn off and on in increasingly shorter intervals. If you then collapse the difference between the limits, the machine will tell itself to turn off at the same time it tells itself to turn on. It's caught in a "paradox" and right there in front of your eyes it will shake wildly until it breaks down. Anyway, I am saying that just as in such schizophrenic thinking, and unless you are explicitly using mandalic reason, then paradox usually means there is actually just a contradiction somewhere—it indicates sloppy thinking, not transcendental reason. In empirical-analytic theory and research as well as in phenomenological-rational theory and research, what appears to be a paradox is usually an indication of pathology in your system—something went wrong somewhere. Instead of saying I'm working with the Tao, I'd go back and retrace my tracks.

RV: You earlier mentioned Whitehead and how, in your opinion, he didn't exactly agree with the holographic theories. I think what you said then was clear enough, but the more I think about it the more confusing it is.

Wilber: How so?

RV: It is generally thought that Whitehead's philosophy fits the holographic theories in at least two ways. One, he said everything in the cosmos interacts with everything else. And two, doesn't his philosophy fit with the notion, made famous by the Heisenberg uncertainty principle, that the subject affects the object when it perceives it? Or do you disagree with Whitehead there?

Wilber: Well, no, I generally agree with Whitehead, but Whitehead disagreed with both those ideas.

RV: Didn't Whitehead say that everything prehends everything else in the cosmos?

Wilber: What he said was that a thing prehends everything in its actual universe, and its actual universe consists only of its ancestors, not its contemporaries and not its descendents.

RV: I don't follow.

Wilber: Whitehead maintained that the universe consists of a series of occasions which come into existence for a few seconds or so and which then fade into cosmic memory, so to speak—very like the Hinayana Buddhist notion of momentary *dharma*-events. Anyway, each entity or occasion, as it comes into existence, is regarded as a subject, and this subject prehends, or is somehow aware of, its immediate predecessors or those occasions that helped to form it. So those predecessors, or ancestors, are objects to the present event, the subject. As that subject passes, it becomes object for its descendents, and so on. So each subject prehends all of its ancestors, to some degree, however minimal—but notice that no event can prehend its descendents, and no event can prehend its contemporaries.

RV: Why not?

Wilber: Because events just coming into existence don't have time, so to speak, to get to know each other. Two truly simultaneous events are without mutual influence at the precise time of their simultaneity. They haven't had the chance to enter the causal or karmic stream. The influence they do have will be on the occasion that immediately succeeds it—that influence is causality in Whitehead's system. If two subjects are in the same vicinity, the odds are high that they both may become object for the same eventual subject. But otherwise, no interaction. And an entity cannot prehend its descendents any more than Christopher Columbus could be aware of you or me.

RV: So an entity prehends all its ancestors, but not its contemporaries and not its descendents?

Wilber: That is Whitehead's view, yes.

RV: And you agree with that?

Wilber: Yes.

RV: But what about precognition. Isn't that an example of a present occasion prehending a future one, or a descendent?

Wilber: Look, if precognition is absolutely real and absolutely possible, then all events are already absolutely determined for all time. There is then no such thing as free will, no such thing as actual creativity or true free emergence, there isn't even such a thing as Heisenberg's uncertainty principle. The universe is, through all times and on all levels, absolutely a deterministic machine. I don't buy it, myself.

RV: OK, what about the second point, the idea that physics has supposedly proven that the subject in many ways creates its object.

Wilber: Are you asking whether I agree or whether Whitehead does?

RV: Start with Whitehead.

Wilber: He disagrees absolutely. And remember Whitehead was perfectly aware of modern quantum mechanics.

RV: He denied quantum mechanics?

Wilber: No, he denied, or at least refused to embrace, some of the terribly unsophisticated philosophical interpretations of QM, such as that the object is created or even altered when prehended by a subject.

RV: What was his idea?

Wilber: As each occasion comes to be, as it becomes subject, it prehends its ancestors or causal objects and is thus changed by the objects, or formed by its immediate past. But the object is not changed, and indeed could not be changed, by its subject or by being prehended, because the object now only exists in or as the past, and you can't alter the past by merely thinking about it or prehending it. Again, it's like saying that what Columbus did could affect you, but what you do now does not affect Columbus. Whitehead's point was that, since all events are coming to be and ceasing to be in a stream of flux, change, or time, then essentially the same thing applies during the milliseconds involved.

RV: You agree?

Wilber: Yes, definitely. That is simply another way of saying that the subject contains the object but the object doesn't contain the subject, and *that* is simply another way to say that there are indeed nonmutual or nonequivalent relationships. Hierarchy is, of course, the strong version of that fact.

RV: So you don't agree with the new age theories that say the human brain as subject creates the objective world it perceives?

Wilber: It might indeed create order in its world of perception, or in the material world of noises, but it doesn't create that world itself.

RV: If it did there would be an infinite regress?

Wilber: Yes. But the point can be established more easily—the human brain didn't evolve until 6 million years ago, but the cosmos is 13 billion years old. There were lots of things around before brains existed. As for the so-called participant-observer in physics, or the necessity for the object to be perceived by mind in order to collapse its state vector, the vast majority of physicists—including David Bohm's classic 1975 paper that perfectly shredded Jack Sarfatti's wild claims on the subject—find the idea either unnecessary or downright ridiculous. But many new age theorists think they must believe in the idea because they confuse the events occurring on the merely physical level with the entire Tao; they think that because Buddha Nature or God is one with all things in the act of perceiving-creating them, that the human mind itself must try to do the same thing for electrons.

RV: What about such related topics as the Whorf-Sapir hypothesis, the idea that language, or the mind, creates the world, and that different languages in fact create different worlds. There seems to be a lot of support for that notion.

Wilber: There is a partial truth there, but it is very confused, because again we have failed to say what we mean by the phrase, "the world." Do we mean the physical world, the biological world, the sociological world, what? Because, you see, I believe that the Whorf-Sapir hypothesis is perfectly wrong in reference to the physical, biological, and submental spheres in general. I do not believe that the linguistic mind creates rocks and trees, although obviously it creates the words with which we represent those entities. A diamond will cut a piece of glass no matter what words we use for "diamond," "cut," and "glass."

RV: So if there were no human minds, there would still be physical and biological entities in existence.

Wilber: Yes. Again I remind you of the obvious fact that those levels antedated the human brain or mind by billions of years.

RV: So where is the Whorf-Sapir hypothesis correct?

Wilber: Symbols do not create the material or biological spheres—levels 1 and 2—but they do create, literally, the mental spheres—level-3 and parts of level-4. But it's not just that there are these higher mental levels and that symbols reflect them. The higher mental levels *are* symbols. They are *made* of symbols the way a tree is made of wood. So notice we have these two general realms under discussion—the mental and the submental—and that symbols play a different role with regard to each. They basically *reflect* the submental world but they help to *create* the mental world. In the first case they basically *represent;* in the second, they also *present.* For example, the symbol "rock" represents an independently existing rock. Take away the symbol, and the rock, or whatever it is, is still there. Language does not create that world. But entities such as envy, pride, poetry, justice, compassion, goals, values, virtues exist only in and as a stream of symbols. Take away the symbols and those entities are gone. Alter the symbols, and you shift the sense of those entities. Different languages do exactly that, and that is where the Whorfian concepts find some applicability.

RV: Now isn't the difference between the symbols that *represent* the submental realms and the symbols that *create* the mental realms the same as the difference between empirical-analytic modes and hermeneutic-historic modes?

Wilber: Definitely—same thing. And that's why the methodologies, the interests, the structures, and the verification processes are so different in the two modes. See, if you are working with the empirical-analytic mode, then you are basically working with the "mirror" model of truth—the model made famous by the positivists, such as Wittgenstein's early work. Propositions are true if they reflect the facts correctly—that type of thing. An empiric proposition is true if it more or less accurately mirrors or pictures or represents the sensory world. That is all as it should be. That model is fine for empirical truth [see chapter 2 for details]. But when it comes to the purely mental or phenomenological world, the simple mirror or only reflective model no longer works. In a sense you are still doing reflective work—you know, you are still proposing theoretic maps and models, as we earlier discussed; but you are no longer using symbols to represent nonsymbolic occasions. You are using symbols to look at other symbols, a process which *creates* new worlds with new possibilities and new truths, and those truths are not empirical or merely sensory, and so a simple mirror model no longer works. Or we could put the analogy like this: With empiric propositions you are trying to mirror the lower realms in symbols so as to better comprehend them. But in the mental world, where symbols look at symbols, it's like using one mirror to reflect another mirror which reflects the reflection, and so on in a circle of meaning that you and I co-create whenever we talk. That is the hermeneutic circle. The self is aware of itself only by taking the role of other—but the same is equally true of the other. So here we are, two mirrors in discourse, co-creating each other in communicative exchange. And the way you find your way around in that world, that hermeneutic circle, is radically different from dropping rocks and seeing if they fall at the same speed in a vacuum, right? In empiricism, the symbols you use to represent the world simply represent the world, more or less. But in the mental and linguistic world, the symbols you use to represent that world are also involved in creating that world, and there is the great difference.

RV: What happens if you ignore that difference?

Wilber: The phenomenologists try to make all empirical truths into mere subjective co-creations. You know, the human mind helps co-create dirt, and so on. Similar to the overextended version of the Whorf-Sapir hypothesis. The empiricists, on the other hand, try to reduce the hermeneutic circle to mere sensory transactions. Since they can't find any sensory referents, however, they proclaim mind to be a black box. They refuse to try to map out the hermeneutic circle and instead content themselves with monitoring muscle twitches, as Tolman put it. Philosophy degenerates into only positivism, and psychology degenerates into only behaviorism.

RV: So an overall paradigm . . .

Wilber: An overall paradigm, in my opinion, would have to include all of the modes of knowing we have discussed, and all the correlative methodologies. It would include sensory investigations and empirical-analytic hypotheses and tests. It would include hermeneutic-historic investigations and interpretations, conceptual analyses and syntheses. It would include mandalic cartographies of the higher realms, however paradoxical at spots, and it would include an actual summons to contemplative practice. Further, the overall paradigm, its simple existence, would demand a social evolutionary stance, a social policy geared to help human beings evolve through the stage-levels of existence. This would involve both attempts to help vertical transformation to higher levels and also attempts to clear up the distortions and oppressions that have occurred horizontally on the levels already in existence. The vertical is connected with soteriological interests; the horizontal is the normative or emancipatory interests, as Habermas uses the term.

RV: Couldn't that lead to "we-know-best-for-you" social engineering?

Wilber: No, because in this paradigm transcendence cannot be forced. There are only *participants* in emancipation. You can only force slavery; you can't force a person to be free.

RV: It seems to me that your major concern over the holographic or new age paradigms in general is that most of these issues in methodology and epistemology are overlooked or ignored. The hierarchy, as you say, has collapsed.

Wilber: What happens is that when the hierarchy is collapsed, you lose all these relative distinctions. The different methodologies—sensory, empirical-analytic, mental, and so on—collapse. And the different interests of human inquirers—technological, moral, emancipatory, soteriological—all collapse. And all sorts of other problems start up. That was the problem with the original holographic paradigm. Since they had only two levels, then the frequency realm had to be the same as the implicate realm, and the read-out information had to be the explicate realm. And dissipative structures had to be the link between the frequency realm and the fold-out information—and so on. But then Bohm stated that the implicate level wasn't ultimate; there was a realm "beyond both." That gives three realms. Recently, he has spoken of several levels of the implicate realm. That gives us maybe six levels in all. Now that's much closer to the perennial philosophy. My own feeling is that as soon as he starts describing these realms in a little more detail, he's going to end up describing the traditional Great Chain. He's already speaking of "relatively independent subtotalities"—pretty much Huston Smith's definition of realm or level for the perennial philosophy.

RV: In the last interview in *ReVision,* he tended to include matter and thought as one realm.

Wilber: Well, I think that is part of the problem he might have inherited from Krishnamurti. Because Krishnamurti is so interested in the Light, he almost refuses to even discuss the shadows. Hence, he tends to commit hierarchy collapse and lump things like matter and symbol together.

RV: Because all shadows are ultimately illusory he thinks they are equally illusory.

Wilber: Yes, that's hierarchy collapse. I think Bohm stepped into this rather loose philosophy, and so he tended to include matter, prana, and mind as more or less equivalent parts of the explicate sphere. He then had to look at the implicate sphere as something that existed more or less equally alongside or under material things and mental thoughts. He thus veered off from the traditional view, which would say that what is implicate to matter is simply élan vital, prana, the life force.

RV: So prana is the implicate order in which matter is embedded?

Wilber: I think that would be correct, traditionally. But that doesn't preclude the possibility that matter rises from a physical energy sea. This seems to me the original meaning of Bohm's physical implicateness or, at least, quantum potential. My point is that both matter and the physical energy sea crystallize out of prana. In that sense, prana is implicate to matter.

RV: And prana is what? Or mind relates to prana how?

Wilber: Prana is implicate to matter but explicate to mind; mind is implicate to prana but explicate to soul; soul is implicate to mind but explicate to spirit; and spirit is the source and suchness of the entire sequence. (You have to be very careful with terminology here—you can almost reverse the sequence of wording, depending upon your definition of "implicate." If by implicate you mean enfolded as in "enveloped," then prana envelops or implicates matter, or contains it. This might seem trivial but I have seen many writers use Bohm's concept in what are really diametrically opposed senses. I am using implicate to mean the larger ground out of which the explicate emerges.) Anyway, in my opinion, because Bohm originally didn't distinguish systematically between matter, prana, and mind, he started looking horizontally for hidden dimensions of implicateness, failing to see that those three realms are already vertical dimensions of implicateness with regard to each other. But I think he's looking carefully at his scheme, but we'll have to wait and see.

RV: One last question. Anybody who knows you knows that you'd much rather work on your own writing than critique the works of others. What jarred you away from your own work?

Wilber: Well, the notion was rapidly spreading that all you have to do to be a mystic is learn a new mental worldview. If you actually think you can include the absolute Tao in a new paradigm—and get anything other than a mass of contradictions and paradoxes—then you foster the idea that by merely learning the new paradigm, whatever it may be, you are actually transcending—really transcending. I have actually heard that claim made. That is a disaster. So naturally you're moved to put your two cents in. But the fact that spiritual transformation takes years of meditative or contemplative practice, that it takes moral and physical purification, that it takes, or is helped by, direct contact with a living adept in divine realization, that it takes a direct opening of the eye of contemplation and has nothing to do with merely learning another mental paradigm—all of that was being left out. You know, we went through all this with Alan Watts. God knows nobody did more for mystical studies, especially Zen, than Alan, and I don't know a single person of my generation interested in transcendence who wasn't touched deeply by the man. Nobody could write like Watts, nobody. But it was just that—words. It was only at the end of his life that he rather surreptitiously began to admit that the core of Zen is, in fact, zazen. But by then, most of the people who began with Alan were now with Suzuki Roshi or Sazaki or Soen or Katagiri—that is, they were actually practicing, actually working on spiritual transformation. That is not Square Zen, as Alan finally admitted. Thus, the only good function of a book on Zen should be to persuade the reader to engage in zazen and to encourage those already practicing to continue and deepen their efforts. In the same way, the only major purpose of a book on mysticism should be to persuade the reader to engage in mystical practice. It is precisely like a cookbook: You give recipes and invite the reader to go out and perform the recipe, actually do it, and then taste the results. You are not supposed merely to learn the recipes, memorize the recipes, and then claim you're a cook. But that is exactly what many—not all—of the proponents of the new paradigm have in mind. As Watts himself would say, it's like eating the menu instead of the meal. The new paradigm is just a new menu, but nobody's talking about the meal anymore, and that is unfortunate, don't you think?

7

The Pre/Trans Fallacy

W E HAVE SEEN that one of the greatest obstacles to the emergence of a truly comprehensive or integral paradigm is the attempt to base it on only one of the several modes of knowing available to the soul—an attempt known as category error. For it now seems certain that until the full spectrum of knowing is acknowledged, the full spectrum of being—the comprehensive worldview—will likewise remain hidden, obscured, elusive.

But there is another obstacle to the emergence of a comprehensive worldview, and by all accounts this obstacle is the most fascinating of all. In its various forms, this obstacle, this fallacy, has infected psychologists from Freud to Jung, philosophers from Bergson to Nietzsche, sociologists from Lévy-Bruhl to Auguste Comte; it lurks as equally behind the mythological and romantic worldviews as behind the rational and scientific; it exists to this day in both the attempts to champion mysticism and the attempts to deny it. Until this obstacle is overcome, until this major fallacy is exposed, a truly comprehensive worldview will, I believe, most definitely continue to evade us. This obstacle we call the "pre/trans fallacy"; this chapter is an attempt to unravel it.

The essence of the pre/trans fallacy is easy enough to state. We begin by simply *assuming* that human beings do in fact have access to three general realms of being and knowing—the sensory, the mental, and the spiritual. Those three realms can be stated in any number of different ways: subconscious, self-conscious, and super-conscious; or prerational, rational, and transrational; or prepersonal, personal, and transpersonal.

The point is simply that, for example, since *pre*rational and *trans*rational are both, in their own ways, *non*rational, then they appear quite similar or even identical to the untutored eye. Once this confusion occurs—the confusion of "pre" and "trans"—then one of two things inevitably happens: the transrational realms are *reduced* to prepersonal status, or the prerational realms are *elevated* to transrational glory. Either way a complete and overall world view is broken in half and folded in the middle, with one half of the real world (the "pre" or the "trans") being thus profoundly mistreated and misunderstood. And it is *that* misunderstanding which will concern us in this chapter.

THE GENERAL NATURE OF THE PRE/TRANS FALLACY

The concept of the pre/trans fallacy—and let us call it "ptf" for short—stems from both developmental philosophy, which is represented most effectively by Hegel in the West and Aurobindo in the East, and developmental psychology, which is epitomized by Baldwin and Piaget in the West and kundalini yoga in the East. This general developmental-evolutionary view holds that *in the world of maya* all things exist in time; since the world of time is the world of flux, all things in this world are in constant change; change implies some sort of difference from state to state, that is, some sort of *development;* thus all things in this world can only be conceived as ones that have developed. In essence, *all phenomena develop,* and thus true phenomenology is always evolutionary, dynamic, or developmental—this was, for example, the burden of Hegel's *Phenomenology of Spirit.*

According to this viewpoint, then, any given phenomenon exists in and as a stream of development, and one of the best ways to grasp the phenomenon's nature is to attempt to reconstruct its development—trace its history, map out its evolution, discover its *context* not just in space but also in time. That point is crucial in itself, and we shall return to it again and again. But for the moment, let us go straight to the next point: if one attempts to look at the world-at-large in such developmental terms, the world itself appears to be evolving in a definite direction, namely, toward higher levels of structural organization, toward greater holism, integration, awareness, consciousness, and so on. Indeed, a brief glance at the evolutionary record to date—matter to plant to lower animal to mammal to human—shows a pronounced growth toward increasing complexity and awareness.

Many philosophers and psychologists, looking at this evolutionary course, have concluded that not only can phenomena be best understood as ones that have developed, but that development itself is heading toward noumenon. We are all familiar with Teilhard de Chardin's evolutionary conception of the omega point and with Aurobindo's evolutionary drive toward the supermind, but the same concept was held in the West by such philosophers as Aristotle and Hegel. Hegel, for example, maintained that "The Absolute is Spirit [in] the process of its own becoming, the circle which presupposes its end as its purpose and has its end as its beginning. It becomes concrete or actual only by its development. . . ."[31] The "end" of which Hegel speaks is similar to supermind and omega—it is a state of "absolute knowledge" where "Spirit knows itself in the form of Spirit."

Thus history (evolution) was, for Hegel as for the perennial philosophy in general, the process of the self-actualization of Spirit. Significantly, Hegel maintained that this developmental process occurs in three major stages. It begins with nature, the lowest realm—the realm of matter and of simple bodily sensations and perceptions. This realm we shall be calling the *prepersonal* or the *subconscient*. Hegel often speaks of subconscient nature (i.e., the prepersonal realm) as a "fall" (*Abfall*)—but it is not that nature is set against Spirit or divorced from Spirit. Rather nature is simply "slumbering Spirit," or "God in His otherness." More specifically, nature is "self-alienated Spirit," or the *lowest* form *of* Spirit in its return *to* Spirit.

In the second phase of the return of Spirit to Spirit, or of the overcoming of self-alienation, development moves from (prepersonal) nature to what Hegel calls the self-conscious stage. This is the stage of typical egoic or mental awareness—the realm we shall be calling personal, mental, and self-conscious.

Finally, according to Hegel, development culminates in the Absolute, or Spirit's discovery of Spirit as Spirit, a stage/level we shall be calling transpersonal or superconscious.

Note, then, the overall sequence of development: from nature to humanity to divinity, from subconscious to self-conscious to super-conscious, from prepersonal to personal to transpersonal. This is represented in figure 1. Precisely the same three major stages can be found in Berdyaev and Aurobindo, and Baldwin comes very close to it

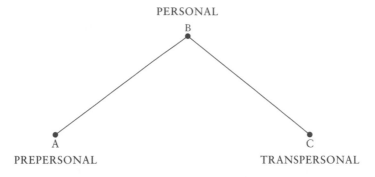

FIGURE 1

with his notion of prelogical, logical, and hyperlogical. In any case, the conception has an extremely broad grounding.

We need only one last theoretical tool. If the movement from the lower to the higher is evolution, then the reverse, the movement from the higher to the lower, is *involution*. (See fig. 2.) Nature became a "fall" or "slumbering God" or "self-alienated Spirit" through the prior process of involution, or the descent and "loss" of the higher in the lower. Call it the Big Bang, when matter—the lowest realm—was flung into existence out of the Void (*shunyata*). Evolution is the subsequent reversal of the Abfall, the return of Spirit to Spirit via development. Aurobindo has written extensively on this subject, and I shall do no more than recommend his works. It should be said, however, that one may take involution symbolically and metaphorically, or one may take it literally and metaphysically, but in no case should involution be confused with any movement or sequence of movements in *evolution*. That would be like confusing growing up with being conceived. In any event, even if we totally reject Hegel's or Aurobindo's cosmological notions of involution, we can nevertheless certainly speak of involution in the general sense of moving from higher to lower—in this sense, it is simply the

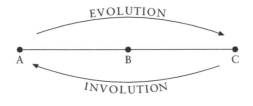

FIGURE 2

phenomenon of regression. Either of these interpretations will suffice for this chapter.

But now we return to the overall process of *evolution,* or growth and development in general, and here is where the ptf comes in (I'll give its simplified form first, and we can refine it as we go along):

Since development moves from prepersonal to personal to transpersonal, and since both prepersonal and transpersonal are, in their own ways, nonpersonal, then prepersonal and transpersonal tend to appear similar, even identical, to the untutored eye. In other words, people tend to confuse prepersonal and transpersonal dimensions—and there is the heart of the ptf.

This fallacy has two major forms: the reduction of the transpersonal to the prepersonal, which we call ptf-1, and the elevation of the prepersonal to the transpersonal, or ptf-2. With reference to figure 1, the point is that if the subtle but drastic differences between *A* and *C* are not understood, then the two ends of one's developmental map are collapsed into each other. In ptf-1, *C* is collapsed or *reduced* to *A* (and thus ceases to exist *as C*)—figure 3. In ptf-2, *A* is *elevated* to *C* (and thus ceases to exist *as A*)—figure 4. Instead of two legs of development, we get a single axis.

This collapse instantly creates two opposed world views. Since the real world still contains *A, B,* and *C,* then ptf-1 and ptf-2 will still run into the whole spectrum of existence, but both will necessarily interpret the world in light of their respective deficiencies. Thus, correlative with the two forms of ptf, there are generated two major worldviews—*reductionism* and *elevationism*—precisely as shown in figures 3 and 4.

Now both of these world views recognize the personal realm, and,

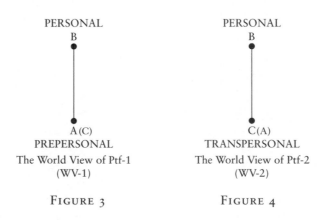

PERSONAL
B

A (C)
PREPERSONAL
The World View of Ptf-1
(WV-1)

FIGURE 3

PERSONAL
B

C (A)
TRANSPERSONAL
The World View of Ptf-2
(WV-2)

FIGURE 4

moreover, in both views development is thought to have *culminated* in the personal realm (this is because the personal realm is the pivot point B, the only point the two views have in common). Beyond that, the two world views diverge dramatically, but their characteristics can be read with frightening accuracy from figures 3 and 4, respectively.

Worldview one (WV-1) sees development moving from a prepersonal source in nature, through a series of intermediate advances, to a culmination in the "high point" of evolution, that of human rationality. It recognizes no higher source or goal of development, and it vehemently denies the necessity of even mentioning such supposedly "higher" levels. Man is a rational being, and rationality is all that is necessary to comprehend and order the cosmos. It looks very much like orthodox science.

WV-2, on the other hand, sees development moving *from* a spiritual source ("in heaven") to a culmination in a "low point" of alienation, that of a sinful humanity or of the individual and personal ego. History is thus the history of a falling down, not a moving up, and mankind (or personal ego) is at the *end* of the fall, just as depicted in figure 4. It looks a lot like orthodox religion.

Now the difficult and intricate part is that while the pre/trans fallacy itself is simply an error, the two worldviews generated by the two ptfs are half true and half fallacious—and *that* is what has made it so hard to decide on their relative merits. They are true when dealing with the half of development that they have not exalted or reduced, and fallacious when dealing with the half they have so mistreated. To be more specific:

We can look basically at overall development in terms of both (1) its nature, or its components—which involve prepersonal, personal, and transpersonal aspects, and (2) its directionality—which entails some sort of understanding (implicit or explicit) of evolution and involution. We would then expect each of these two major but partial worldviews to say something true and false about both the nature and directionality of development. That is, each of these worldviews contains *two* important truths and *two* major errors. Specifically, and with regard in each case to nature and direction: WV-1 is correct in maintaining that (1) we possess a prepersonal, irrational, and subconscious component, which did indeed precede the rational and personal in evolution, and (2) the direction of actual or historical evolution is indeed from the lower to the higher. It is wrong when it (1) denies the existence of a transpersonal component and thus (2) denies that there can be a real moving down or descent from Spirit, an involutionary Abfall from union with and as Godhead.

WV-2 is correct in maintaining that (1) there is a transpersonal component to the cosmos, and (2) there is some sense in which we are all "in sin," or living alienated and separated from a supreme identity with Spirit. It is wrong, however, in maintaining that (1) the individual ego, or rational thinking personhood, is the height of alienation from Spirit, and wrong in thus maintaining that (2) a true Eden *preceded* the ego in *evolution.*

The last two points perhaps require clarification. WV-2 maintains, as one block view, that the rational ego is the high point of alienation from Spirit and that, therefore, *evolution* prior to the ego was a Garden of Eden free from original sin. Correlatively, then, the rise of ego (Adam) is, of practical purpose, synonymous with the rise of original sin.

But that is simply the world view of ptf-2. In fact, as both Hegel and Aurobindo demonstrated, *original alienation,* or the high point of alienation, starts with material nature. Nature, or the prepersonal world, is *already* self-alienated Spirit, without any help whatsoever from the ego; and further, nature is the *greatest* point of alienation from Spirit. WV-2 misses the crucial point because it sees clearly only the movement from C to B, and thus misviews the existence of the leg B to A, which constitutes the actual extreme of spiritual separation. The ego (B) is merely the first structure developed enough to self-consciously *recognize* that the world is *already* fallen from Spirit. What happened in the historical Garden of Eden (some hundreds of thousands of years ago) was not the instigation of original sin (or original separation from Spirit) but the original apprehension of an already original separation. The fact that the ego can now *choose* to act toward Spirit, or choose to deny it, merely adds to the illusion that the ego's existence alone is the instigator of all alienation in the cosmos.

In other words, WV-2 confuses the real Fall that occurs in involution with a supposed fall that occurred in evolution. And it is forced to do so simply because it only recognizes clearly the axis between B and C, and therefore fails to take accurate account of the *prior* fall to low-point A. It then appears that with the evolutionary rise of ego, Spirit reaches its zenith of alienation, whereas in fact, with the rise of ego, Spirit is halfway back home: It has gone from the prepersonal subconsciousness of nature to the personal self-consciousness of Spirit. The fact that the ego, as a halfway house back to Spirit, is the first structure intelligent enough *to be aware of* the already fallen state of existence, makes it appear incorrectly that the ego caused the disease itself, when in fact it is half-way through the cure.

To be sure, the ego is certainly *part* of the fallen or alienated world, and as the first recognizer of this alienation, it suffers doubly. This new suffering makes the ego think that since it did not suffer yesteryear, yesteryear must have been a transpersonal bliss, whereas it was merely a prepersonal ignorance. Nature is asleep in sin, and God is awake without sin—but human beings are caught in the middle: awake *with* sin. Or: Nature is unconscious imperfection, God is conscious perfection, but poor humanity is conscious imperfection. Now human beings can indeed act "sinfully," by choosing against Spirit, or they can act "morally," by choosing Spirit, but that choice, however crucial, still rests upon a sea of already prior alienation. It is not that by choosing wrongly men and women introduce alienation; it is that by choosing correctly they are helping to overcome it.

But failing to grasp that point not only devalues the place of ego, it elevates and romanticizes nature. Nature, instead of being seen as unconscious imperfection, is viewed as unconscious perfection, as if there could be perfection outside of Self-realization. But it then appears that the previous stages of evolution—the prepersonal, subhuman, subconscious stages—constituted some sort of transpersonal heaven, whereas they really added up to nothing but physical forces and animal impulse.

Thus arose the universal Eden myths, which unfortunately were not taken as an allegory of a prior Abfall constituting involution but as a literal story of what happened in earth's recent *evolution*. Naturally the scientists, who did happen to be correct on the *A*-to-*B* leg of the evolutionary record, proceeded with glee to point out that what preceded human beings was not angels but apes, whereupon most orthodox religions began a long series of undignified retreats and ridiculous apologetics, trying to make as a matter of absolute faith the acceptance of the *wrong* half of their otherwise acceptable world view.

Now that is a simple and general introduction to the ptf and its two basic forms of worldviews. What we will do in the rest of this chapter is examine these two forms of ptf as they have appeared, and are still appearing, in psychological, anthropological, and sociological theories. But I must make very clear what the following discussion attempts to do and what it does not attempt to do. Because this is an introductory presentation, I shall usually only give one (occasionally two) *general* examples of each ptf we shall discuss, avoiding technical details where possible. This does not mean these are the only examples, or necessarily even the most significant ones, but only that they more readily lend themselves to our discussion. The fact that a particular theorist is explicitly mentioned as following a ptf in one instance does not necessarily mean she or he commits the fallacy in all other instances. Also, I do not mean to imply that various theories always fall cleanly into one or the other of these two ptf world views (although that happens quite often)—there are several minor variations on this fallacy, with some occasional combinations and mixtures between its two forms. Finally, many important theorists completely, or at least largely, avoid ptf collapse. Besides Aurobindo, Baldwin, Hegel, and Berdyaev, whom we have already mentioned, I would like to include Maslow and Assagioli among the many transpersonalists who, in my opinion, do not commit significant pre/trans fallacies. My overall goal is simply to use several different examples to suggest how the pre/trans fallacy might be lurking behind various theories, personal and transpersonal, and how we might begin to redress the respective imbalances.

EXAMPLES OF PTF IN PSYCHOLOGICAL THEORIES

In the *The Atman Project*, I took a dozen or so variables and described how human psychological development moves through the three general realms with regard to each variable. These variables included time, space, abstract logic, ego, self-control, socialization, conventional morality, subject/object differentiation, the notion of union or wholeness, verbal mentality, perceptual clarity, angst-guilt, and death-terror. The point, in general, was that development tends to move from, for example, prelogical to logical to translogical modes (cf. Baldwin); from preconventional to conventional to post-conventional morality (cf. Kohlberg); from presubject/object differentiation to subject/object differentiation to transsubject/object differentiation; from prepersonal id to personal ego to transpersonal spirit; and so on with each of the variables.

The conclusion was that unless it is clearly understood how pretemporality differs from transtemporality, how preegoic impulsiveness differs from transegoic spontaneity, how prepersonal ignorance differs from transpersonal emptiness, how preverbal impulse differs from transverbal insight, how prepersonal fusion differs from transpersonal union, and so on through almost every conceivable variable, then the ptf swings into action in either of its two notorious forms.

With regard to human psychological development, the two major examples of ptf-1 and ptf-2 are, respectively, Freud and Jung (although, as we will see, they do not exhaust the field). Freud correctly recognized the prepersonal id (A) and the personal ego (B), but he reduced all spiritual and transpersonal experiences (C) to the prepersonal level; transtemporal insights are explained as pretemporal id-impulses; trans-subject/object *samadhi* is claimed to be a throwback to presubject/object narcissism; transpersonal union is interpreted as prepersonal fusion. In every respect, Freud follows WV-1 (fig. 3). WV-1, of course, is not confined to Freud. It is standard, orthodox, unquestioned Western orthodoxy—Piaget to Sullivan to Adler to Arieti.

In my opinion, Jung errs consistently to the opposite side. He correctly and very explicitly recognizes the transpersonal or numinous dimension, but he often fuses or confuses it with prepersonal structures. For Jung there are only two major realms: the personal and the collective—and as Assagioli himself pointed out, Jung thus tends to obscure the vast and profound differences between the *lower* collective unconscious and the *higher* collective unconscious; that is, the prepersonal collective and the transpersonal collective realms. Thus, not only does Jung occasionally end up glorifying certain infantile mythic forms of thought, he also frequently gives a regressive treatment of Spirit. In any event, he and his followers thus tend to recognize only two major realms—ego and Self—and human development is therefore viewed as occurring along an ego-Self axis, which is actually drawn precisely as in figure 4, with Self at bottom and ego at top. This is pure WV-2, and, as we shall see, it is generally accepted by many transpersonal psychologists, even those who disavow Jung.

Incidentally, the Jungians do recognize that development occurs in two major phases: the development and then the transcendence of the ego. So far, so good. However, since they are working more or less with only one *actual* leg of development (B-C), they are forced into making that single axis do double duty. Instead of seeing development as going from A to B to C, they see it as going from C to B and then *back* to C. Not unconscious prepersonal to personal to transpersonal, but unconscious transpersonal to personal to transpersonal. Not preego to ego to transego Self, but Self to ego back to Self. Instead of Fig. 1, they have in mind fig. 5, which, for convenience, they depict precisely as in fig. 4. (The fact that fig. 5 has two legs should not conceal its ptf-2 essence.)

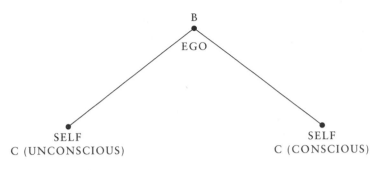

FIGURE 5

In these types of theories, the prepersonal realm *qua* prepersonal realm seems to get left out. However, what actually happens, behind the theoretical scenes, is simply that the prepersonal realm gets elevated to quasi-transpersonal status. Among numerous other results (which we will investigate below), it might subsequently appear as a type of infantile psychological Garden of Eden. And while we can agree that infancy is free of certain conceptual anxieties, that "freedom" is not due, in my opinion, to transpersonal protection but prepersonal ignorance, a point on which Maslow was equally insistent.

Such theories, in effect, posit a type of U-turn right in the middle of development—a simple and predictable result of ptf-2 collapse. But this U-turn also seems bolstered by a related misunderstanding. Instead of seeing that involution goes from C to B to A, and evolution goes from A to B to C, it views A-to-B as involution (or the movement of "greatest" alienation—called "alienation from Self" in Jungian theory) and B-to-C as the "sole" movement of evolution. It consequently overlooks or denies that A-to-B is the *first* part of evolution, and that, as far as involution or alienation goes, it is A, not B, that stands farthest from Self (or Spirit). Thus the ego-mind, in true WV-2 form, mistakenly appears as the high point of alienation, instead of the high point of self-conscious recognition of already alienation and the halfway point of *return* to Self, or the overcoming of already alienation.

In my opinion, besides Jung and his followers, this ptf-2 and its worldview is found, although in different outer forms and to different degrees, in a large (but certainly not total) number of transpersonal psychologists, in the immensely influential works of Norman O. Brown, in Matte Blanco's *The Unconscious as Infinite Sets*, in my own early works, *Spectrum of Consciousness* and (to a lesser degree) *No Boundary*, in Welwood, Alan Watts, aspects of Bergson, Wordsworth, and virtually all romantic psychologists and philosophers. Since it is understood that Spirit is beyond ego, but since the nonegoic realms are not clearly differentiated into preegoic and transegoic, the result is a pervasive devaluation of ego and/or elevation of preego. It might be necessary, then, to remind ourselves, as Meher Baba put it:

> Human consciousness would be no more than a repository of the accumulated imprints of varied experiences did it not also contain the principle of *ego-centered integration*. The process [that is ego] implies capacity to hold different experiences together as parts of a unity and the capacity to evaluate them by mutual relation. The integration of the opposites of experience is a condition of emancipating consciousness from the thraldom of [prepersonal] compulsions and repulsions which tend to dominate consciousness: and the *early attempts in securing such integration are through the formation of the ego.*
>
> The part played by the ego in human life may be compared with the function of the ballast in a ship. The ballast keeps the ship from too much oscillation; without it, the ship is likely to be too light and unsteady and in danger of being overturned. The psychic energy would be caught up in the mazes of dual experience and would be frittered away were there no provisional nucleus to bind together the active tendencies born of the relatively independent instincts inherited from [prepersonal] animal-consciousness. The formation of the ego serves the purpose of giving a certain amount of stability to conscious processes, and secures a working equilibrium which makes for organized life.[69]

Thus, concludes Baba, "it would be a mistake to imagine that, as the ego arises only to vanish, it fulfills no need in the long journey of the soul. Though the ego is not meant to be permanent since it can be transcended and outgrown through spiritual endeavor [leg *B* to *C*], the phase of ego-formation [*A* to *B*] must nevertheless be looked upon as necessary for the time being."[69]

The ptf-2 misunderstanding, which devalues ego and elevates preego, takes on ominous proportions when it comes to some (but certainly not all) forms of "avant-garde" or "human potential" or "humanistic/transpersonal" psychotherapies. Put simply, the problem is that many, perhaps most, people who seek or need therapy are suffering in large part from *prepersonal* fixations, dissociations, and obsessions, and haven't the ego-strength to transcend those subhuman angers, impulses, and drives which therefore threaten to overwhelm their very existence. Introduced to a purely WV-2 therapist, they are invited to "let-go" of the very structure—that of egoic conceptualization and integration— that they are in such desperate need to create and strengthen. Such WV-2 therapists overlook the elemental fact that, in devaluing ego and elevating preego realms—realms such as body, feeling, impulse, sensation, experiential immediacy, *chakras* 1–3—they are actually championing realms which are *more* self-centric and narcissistic than the ego, and realms which therefore (if not transcended) actually constitute much of the very problem that they seek to overcome.

There is a marvelous passage in Salinger's *Franny and Zooey* that keys this whole issue. Franny, becoming deeply drawn to contemplative (transpersonal and mystical) practices, decides that all misery in the world is, in essence, the fault of ego, and that the ego consequently must go. As someone sarcastically but accurately explains her views, "Everything's ego, ego, ego, and the only intelligent thing for a girl to do is lie around . . . and beg God for a little mystical experience that'll make her nice and happy." Finally Zooey reacts: "You keep talking about *ego*. My God, it would take Christ himself to decide what's ego and what isn't. . . . But don't go screaming about egos in general. In my opinion, if you really want to know, half the nastiness in the world is stirred up by people who aren't using their true egos. Take your Professor Tupper. From what you say about him, anyway, I'd lay almost any odds that this thing he's using, the thing you think is his ego, isn't his ego at all but some other, much dirtier, much less *basic* faculty."

Baldwin, who skillfully avoided ptf, elegantly pointed out that in the highest stage of growth (*B* to *C*), "Consciousness achieves a freeing *from* logic as before [*A* to *B*] she worked to secure the freeing *of* logic." The point, of course, is that one can indeed be freed *from* ego-logic, but if and only if one frees, liberates, and establishes ego-logic *in the first place*. The majority, the vast majority, of common pathological problems derive from a miscarriage of development that prevents the conscious movement *from* self-centric, infantile, and prepersonal modes *to* rational, integrative, and conscientious ego-structures. Most neurotics suffer not because of lack of ego-transcendence, but from the prior lack of ego-esteem, and therapy must be, first and foremost, the *facilitator of strong ego-esteem* and then—but only then—the facilitator of ego-transcendence.

In my opinion, Jungian psychology manages to avoid such therapeutic, if not theoretic, WV-2 problems, simply because it so highly emphasizes that one must first strengthen ego, *then* transcend it. And yet that is the crucial insight missing from so many human-potential therapies, those which, caught in the notion that the ego is the height of alienation-pathology, end up strengthening the very modes that are actually the source of the problem, while denigrating the only structure capable of solving it.

PTF IN SOCIOLOGY AND ANTHROPOLOGY

In *Up from Eden,* I extended and clarified the discussion of ptf (in ways we shall soon examine) and also tried to point out some of the ways both its forms seem to have infected anthropological and sociological theories.

We have already mentioned briefly the two forms as displayed in anthropological theories. WV-1 forms the basis of general Darwinian evolutionary theory, which correctly sees evolution as moving from lower to higher, and reminds us, as Darwin said, that "man still bears in his bodily frame the indelible stamp of his lowly origin." But the strict theory of natural selection, a true WV-1, suffers from not acknowledging the role played by Spirit in evolution. It consequently attempts to derive the higher *from* the lower instead of from Spirit, and further refuses to see any *higher* stages of evolution. WV-1 is, of course, standard, orthodox Western anthropology.

It has as its opposite or mirror image the Eden corpus—Eden interpreted as literal evolution instead of as prior involution. From this WV-2 angle, Eden is seen, not as a state of prepersonal ignorance and immersion in self-alienated nature, but as some sort of actual, transpersonal heaven on earth. The necessary rise of self-conscious ego is then misinterpreted as a fall from a heavenly and spiritual estate, whereas it is simply an anxious halfway point on the way back from the lowest reach of self-alienation and subconsciousness to a real superconscious heaven in actualized Spirit. This WV-2 theory is not confined to a religious myth; there is a whole and vastly influential school of anthropology that takes it as just so. They consequently imbue what are often primitive and barbaric rites of preegoic stages with all sorts of transegoic symbolism, and read deeply mystical insights into crude rites of ritual butchery. They damn the rise of modern intelligence and slander the use of logic, and make it all appear believable by elevating every inarticulate slobber of the savage to a transcendental status, so that the poor mental-ego, by comparison, appears the devil incarnate. From its more dilute and secular forms, such as the romantic anthropology of Rousseau (the idea of the "noble savage"), to its more religious forms, which see the sacrifice mythology of the Bronze Age as the Golden Age of Transcendence, to its outright decadence theories, such as those of Klagess, that see the rise of reason as a fundamental error in the cosmos, this whole WV-2 anthropology—which places the present mental-ego at the end of a long slide downhill, a slide whose results outweigh any corresponding advances—has been immensely influential in its various guises.

Incidentally, Max Schlerer, as Berdyaev notes, "has established four types of anthropological theory: (1) The Jewish-Christian—the creation of human beings by God and the Fall; (2) the ancient Greek conception of men and women as the bearers of reason; (3) the natural science view of men and women as the products of evolution . . . ; (4) the decadence theory which regards the birth of consciousness and reason as biological retrogression, a weakening of life [and creation of angst]."[9] The overall theory we are presenting here attempts, by taking out what are suggested to be ptf elements in *each* view, to make possible a general synthesis of *all* of them. We have already examined what, in my opinion, constitute both the true and false halves of the first three theories. I simply add here that we even make room for the decadence theory, *if* it is understood that humanity's early evolution (*A* to *B*) does indeed involve an increase in guilt, anxiety, and angst-sickness, *not* because human beings are becoming fundamentally weaker in nature but because they are becoming more complex, with increasing responsibilities in consciousness (as was carefully explained in *Up from Eden*). With those ptf corrections in mind, not only do I agree with each of those theories, I absolutely endorse them.

We come now to sociological theories, specifically those addressing the "new age." On the one hand, there are those who, like Christopher Lasch and Peter Marin, clearly show that much of the so-called new age is actually infected with, if not based on, narcissistic regression and self-centric fixation. I personally happen to agree with the great bulk of their analyses, and consequently I think that we transpersonalists are going to have to get very straight, very fast, and evidence the most rigorous of intellectual discrimination and conceptual clarity, if we are to avoid theoretical oblivion.

Unfortunately, like most subscribers to WV-1, Lasch and others throw out the baby with the bathwater. After tracing the prepersonal rampage of the new age narcissism, they are forced (explicitly or implicitly) to include in the pathological heap all transpersonal experiences as well, simply because they have no way to tell the difference between prepersonal regression and transpersonal progression. They thus assume that every time there arises a consciousness not exclusively bound to history, ego, time, or logic, the person involved must be regressing into presocial and preegoic worlds, overlooking the fact that the person might, just might, be contacting transtemporal and transegoic truths. These critics would be forced, by their very reasoning, to the conclusion that Christ must have been hallucinating, Lao Tzu was psychotic, Buddha was schizophrenic, and so with Plato and Hegel, Aurobindo and all.

The new age enthusiasts, such as Roszak—or any of those who have suggested that we are or will soon be experiencing the greening of America, the new cultural revolution, a great transpersonal wave—often seem to err in the opposite direction (ptf-2). In their understandable haste to move beyond ego, they frequently fail to specify clearly in which direction that movement is or should be occurring. Two things then tend to happen: They either elevate preegoic license to the status of transegoic freedom (as the "*dharma* bums" did), or they simply denigrate the role of mind, ego, secondary process and logic, and in its place they argue for a mode that is called simply "nonegoic," "nonrole bound," "nonlogical," and so on. In such cases, this "nonegoism" usually conceals a mixture and confusion of preegoic fantasy with transegoic vision, of preconceptual feelings with transconceptual insight, of prepersonal desires with transpersonal growth, of preegoic whoopee with transegoic liberation. Jack Crittenden, in a long and thoughtful review of this whole stance, concluded, "It seems that Roszak, along with many other chroniclers of the Aquarian Age, misconstrues ego license for ego transcendence."[32]

Perhaps the problem is that such chroniclers correctly see that future evolution involves a conscious resurrection of Spirit, but they muddle that realization with the thought that almost any mode that isn't mental-egoic must be transcendent. And so, as they look around at the present social and world situation and see the widespread disintegration of logic, they tend to conclude that imminent spiritual transformation is at hand, overlooking the extraordinarily ominous indicators that what is at hand might be prepersonal holocaust, not transpersonal enlightenment. Their writings then tend to see every social disintegration as "creative" and every pathology as cause for jubilation. We repeat that the true half, the true aspects, of their writings are extremely important; but, taken at face value, they fail to discriminate ego transcendence from ego annihilation. Thus, aside from misreading present-day sociological trends, they often end up recommending a course of action that is actually a mixture of up and down: They inadvertently advocate now progression, now regression, now New Age, now Dark Age, now breakthrough, now breakdown.

Whenever a Lasch-type gets together with a Roszak-type, sparks fly. The new agers deny that their movement is narcissistically tinged just as vehemently as Lasch and others deny that they have an antispiritual bias. Each tends to claim simply that the other is fundamentally prejudiced in his or her world view, or that the other is a victim of old paradigms. I am trying to suggest that both may be partially right (and partially wrong), and that both need to be untangled from any ptfs they conceal and then integrated in a sane fashion. This is all the more urgent, given the present-day social turmoils. Granted that standard mental-egoic translations are beginning to fail, and that society at large is undergoing some kinds of significant transformations. But in which directions? Transegoic or preegoic or some exotic mixture of both? Unless we spot the nature of the disease, we had better be very careful about the cures we advertise.

TRANSCENDENCE, REPRESSION, AND REGRESSION

The course of development is defined at every stage by increasing differentiation, integration, and transcendence. It is not that transcendence per se occurs only in the highest realms—although it certainly occurs there royally—but that each stage of growth, no matter how lowly, *transcends its predecessor* to some degree by definition and by fact. Thus, for example, the mind transcends and animates the body just as Spirit transcends and inspires mind.

But this places a burden on each successive stage of development, for not only must it cleanly transcend or differentiate from its lower predecessor, it must *integrate* and *include* that lower level in its own higher wholeness and greater structural organization. As Hegel said, "To supersede is at once to negate and to preserve"—that is, to transcend and to include; to transcend and thus negate the partiality and lopsidedness of the lower level but to include and thus preserve its essential structures and functions. For example, to transcend mind in Spirit is not to lose mind or destroy mind but merely to include mind in the higher-order wholeness of the superconscient. What is negated is the exclusivity of mind; what is preserved is the capacity of the mind.

One of the main themes of *The Atman Project* is that if development miscarries at any point, then instead of differentiation there is dissociation, instead of transcendence, repression. The higher stage does not transcend and include the lower, it dissociates and represses it (or aspects of it). The dissociated component—now cut off from the conscious sweep of ongoing development and structuralization—sends up its disturbing derivatives in the form of pathological symptoms and symbols. In these instances, as Freud demonstrated, therapy involves, in some sense, a reintegration of the dissociated aspects, a re-membering of components previously dismembered.

This becomes especially obvious if we look at the general transition(s) from the prepersonal to the personal realm, which was Freud's specialty. Freud's essential message was that the personal realm—mind, ego, logic—can and too often does repress the prepersonal realm—id, emotion, sex, nature. The famous Oedipus complex—a rebellion against father (law and culture) and incestuous return to mother (sexuality and nature)—simply represents a failure to transform from prepersonal to personal, with consequent fixation, dissociation, and pathology.

As this general understanding began to reach the public at large, it actually seemed to bolster antirationality and romantic regression, due to a simple misunderstanding. Individuals at large mistakenly thought that abstinence from (or discipline of) emotional-sexuality was the same as the repression of emotional-sexuality. Thus common wisdom began to recommend as "healthy" the general indulgence and overindulgence of emotional-sexual release. In the span of a few decades, large blocks of Western culture traded repression of sex for fixation to and obsession with sex. The *same* dissociation of mind and body was at work, but individuals were now exploiting the body side of the split, where previously they had at least the virtue, however misplaced, of hanging to the mental side. *Repressive* culture was replaced by *regressive* culture, and the cult of Narcissus was everywhere upon us.

In the hands of such intellectuals as Wilhelm Reich, the regression from mind to body was given alibi. Reich started with the extremely important idea that mental-egoic character structure was responsible for large-scale libido-body (or orgone) repression. The fundamental problem, said Reich, was to heal the split between mind and body, thus resurrecting a total psychophysical organism. So far, so good. The problem, however, was that Reich increasingly began to "heal" the body-mind split by championing *only* the body and its orgone energies. He went from saying that body unrepressed by mind is higher than body repressed by mind, to saying that body is higher than mind, period. This is really a modern psychological version of the Eden myths: blame the repression of the lower, not on something the higher may or may not do, but on the *very existence* of the higher—then throw out the higher; that is, cure the repression by regression.

But Reich, and especially his modern followers, in effect covered their tracks by renaming the body level. They called it the "body-mind." Now in my opinion there is indeed a bodymind level, because there is a developmental progression from the body to the mind with a further and consequent possibility of integrating mind and body into a higher-order wholeness of bodymind union (the centaur). That is, the developmental progression is body to mind to bodymind. However, the neo-Reichians (among numerous others) frequently collapse the body and the body-mind levels and refer ambiguously to "*the* bodymind." Instead of body and mind and bodymind, they have only mind and bodymind. The body *qua* body seems to get left out, *except* that, in neo-Reichian style, what they mean by "bodymind" usually turns out to be the preverbal body all by itself, and therefore what is really getting left out is the actual union of verbal-mind and feeling-body—the true bodymind (centauric) union. Further, since what they call "bodymind" is said to be a "higher reality" than the mind, all they have done is put the mind back on the lowest rung of the ladder by elevating the preverbal body to exalted status, and by giving that body a newspeak name that makes the whole affair sound holistic.

This miniature pre/trans fallacy (and the reason that it is a ptf will be explained shortly) can be found even in the works of such sensitive psychologists as Carl Rogers. According to Rogers, there are two major realms of awareness, the conceptual self and the experiential self. The experiential realm is variously called organismic sensing, organismic experiencing, or ongoing psychophysiological flow. The implication is that the psychophysical realm is in fact a bodymind (centauric) integration. But Rogers frequently uses the term to mean what we would recognize only as the body, or feeling-experience and emotional-valuing. Thus, he states that traditionally his theory of the psychophysiological flow was indeed "stressing primarily the emotional-experiential component of being." His theory was thus widely viewed as similar to sensory awareness, felt meaning, experiential therapy, body-based awareness, and so on. But of late he has begun to emphasize that the experiential flow or organismic feeling is really "more than heightened sensory awareness of internal bodily states and of limbic system activities. It is the integration of this [body] awareness with awareness of those functions represented by the neocortex [mind]."[101]

My point is that one cannot have it both ways. One cannot use a psychophysical or bodymind-union concept to refer to "the inherent wisdom of the body," and then claim it is also and really a total integration of logic-mind and body-feeling. And if by the concept one really means just integrating capacity in general, then there is every reason to assign that function more to the mind than to the subhuman body, as Meher Baba said.

Rogers is very careful to try to avoid such ambiguities, and more often than not he succeeds. But in the hands of less capable psychologists, his theory tends frequently to support and encourage the elevation of the body past the mind to bodymind status. Instead of body-sensing, mental-insight, and bodymind integration, there is only "bodymind experiencing" versus mental-logic—and there is the mini-ptf that has tended to denigrate linguistic communication and devalue the very structures that allow men and women to transcend body-bound and narcissistic impulse.

(It should be said that I am a staunch supporter of body-oriented therapies and recommend them, along with diet and exercise, as the first step of any overall therapy [especially Yoga, Rolfing, focusing, Alexander]. We all seem generally out of touch with the body and must begin by rebuilding the base. It is one thing, however, to recontact the body so as to reintegrate it, quite another to recontact the body and stay there. Unless the released body-feelings are taken up and made a part of the higher stream of *communicative exchange* and *intersubjective sharing,* they merely reinforce an isolated I-ness. For it is *only* the mind, via symbol-exchange in communicative discourse, that reaches intersubjective and interpersonal bonding. The body as body is merely self-referential; it cannot take the role of other and thus cannot enter community. It merely senses and emotes over its own separate self-existence. The body is merely subjective; the mind is intersubjective; spirit is transsubjective—and the lower you go on that ladder, the more narcissistic and self-centric you become. In therapy, it is necessary to reverse this trend, and so we start at the bottom with body-therapies. But we certainly don't stay there, and we don't elevate muscle twitches above mental insight.)

But my point in bringing all this up is merely to suggest what historically happened when a genuine *transpersonal* orientation was introduced to this prevailing humanistic notion that distinguished and recognized basically only a "bodymind" and a mind, with mind on the lowest or at least lower rung. Since mind was pictured as the lowest or most alienated level, and since "bodymind" (read body) was thought to be higher, then supermind or big mind was imagined to lie in and through the direction of the "bodymind." Here was the scheme:

mind
"bodymind"
supermind

My suggestion is that the scheme should have been:

body
mind
bodymind
supermind

And, in fact, since by "bodymind" most writers actually (if unwittingly) meant body, their scheme amounted actually (if unwittingly) to confusing supermind or Spirit with the very *end limit of a sequence of regression* from the mind to the body (an end limit we will soon describe as the primary matrix). The point is that the neo-Reichian legacy often played straight into ptf-2 and its world view: the personal, logical, conceptual mind is a devalued structure, and almost any other mode, from bodily feelings to emotional sensing, is theoretically viewed or actively pursued as part of the higher consciousness. And although this did not solely cause, it certainly did not stem, the subsequent theoretical disaster.

The Primary Matrix

Beginning with Freud's initial speculations and culminating with such research-theorists as Hartmann, Klein, Jacobson, Spitz, and Mahler, it was becoming increasingly obvious that the earliest stages of infant development were ones of narcissistic fusion: the infant does not clearly differentiate self from other, subject from object, inside from outside but, rather, lives in a primary matrix where such distinctions are as yet largely absent (the pleroma).

The metapsychological problem arises: How to interpret the primary matrix? What meaning could it have? What role might it play in subsequent development?

In a sense, the Jungians gave the first real metatheory: The primary matrix represents the original, primal, all-encompassing unity of ego and Self. In fact, they suggested, the primary matrix *is* the primary Self (or, technically, an unconscious identity with Self), the total-unified wholeness at the start, prior to separate ego development. Now we said that Freud's own speculations were leading toward this type of original primary-matrix self, and so it is not surprising that modern Jungian thought has already joined in part with many neo-Freudian schools, especially the British Kleinians and the American object-relationists and certain ego-psychologists. In essence, their central point of agreement is stated popularly by Brown as follows: "Freud says not only that the human ego-feeling once embraced the whole world [the primary-matrix self], but also that Eros drives the ego to recover that feeling. In primal narcissism [original matrix] the self is *at one with a world of love and pleasure;* hence the ultimate aim of the human ego is to reinstate what Freud calls 'limitless narcissism' and find itself once more at one with the whole world in love and pleasure."[26]

Already we are handed a problem, because the phrase "at one with the *whole world*" gives the primary matrix a connotation of almost universal wholeness. But surely the infant could not be one with the *whole* world. The infant is not one with the mental world, the social world, the personal world, the subtle world, the symbolic world, the linguistic world, the communicative world—because, in fact, none of those yet exist or have yet emerged. Infants are not one with those levels, they are perfectly ignorant of them. One might as well claim a dog is one with the United Nations because it does not display conflict toward it. Rather, what infants are basically one with, or fused with, is just the material environment and the biological mother—they cannot distinguish their physical body from the physical environment—no levels higher than that enter this primitive (pleromatic) fusion state. It is prepersonal, not personal *or* transpersonal.

Thus, it is a grand ambiguity to refer to this early fusion state as a "oneness with the whole world," if by "whole world" we mean anything other than primitive bio-material fusion. And further, that primitive fusion-matrix simply cannot be equated, in my opinion, with the Self or with Self-identity. But there exactly was the problem with the Jungian (and neo-Jungian) view, which maintained that this early state was an identification with Self, an *identification that is subsequently lost in development and then regained in enlightenment* (precisely as depicted in figure 5, and here our argument joins up with our preliminary discussion of this WV-2 theory). For the Self is the totality of psychological structures, not the lowest psychological structure; the totality has not yet manifested itself in the infant, and it is impossible to be actually one with only a potential, just as you cannot actually eat a potential apple. *Or,* if you do take that view metaphorically and say that the Self is always present even if unrealized (or unconscious), then you must also admit that *all* levels, prior to enlightenment, are one with Self in an unconscious fashion, but then it makes no sense whatsoever to say that that state is *lost* in subsequent development. Either way, the view is fallacious.

Now what *is* lost in subsequent development is the relatively blissful ignorance of the subconscious, prepersonal, bio-material fusion. That is, the infant does break an identity, not with Self, but with the prepersonal matrix (the pleroma). And further, it is precisely the personal ego that has the consciousness, strength, and power to break and transcend that primitive fusion, and thus move, not away from Self, but halfway back to Self.

What role, then, if any, does the Self play in development? We can begin by agreeing with Vedanta that *all* levels and stages are one with Self, but prior to enlightenment, this oneness is unconscious (or unrealized). The prepersonal state—as with Aurobindo's subconscient and Hegel's nature—is also in essence one with Self, but since it is the state of "God in His otherness," then ignorance (*avidya*) or unconsciousness is at its extreme limit, and thus awareness is poorly developed or absent altogether (this is the primary matrix). With the next major stage, the personal ego rises above the prepersonal sphere and shakes off some measure of unconsciousness, and thus awakens as a self-conscious, self-reflexive entity. The ego is also essentially one with Self in a still unrealized fashion, but it at least begins to consciously awaken to the Self in a half-measure (contrasted with the prepersonal stage, which consciously realized no measure).

The ego, then, is no longer protected by ignorance but not yet saved by Self, and *therefore* it, alone of all the stages, experiences guilt, angst, and despair. But that angst, as it appears in evolution, is not, to repeat, a sign of alienation from or deintegration of Self, but the symptom that a cure for the disease of Self-alienation is half in progress. In evolution, the loss of the prepersonal ignorance does indeed introduce angst, but that angst is not a symptom of a just-broken ego-Self unity but of a just-transcended ego-animal slumber. Most WV-2 theorists, since they conflate preego and transego, tend to take the rise of ego and angst as indicators of a fall down from Self, whereas in evolution it actually signals a rise up from subconsciousness. It's not *real* decadence, it just feels like it. And while I attach much significance to, and make abundant theoretical room for, the developmentally emergent feelings of angst and decadence and regret and guilt, I do not interpret them along the lines of ptf-2.

At any rate, in the final major stage, individual consciousness returns itself to its Self, now in a fully conscious and realized form, so that Spirit knows itself as Spirit in Spirit, with a subsequent and final overcoming of angst and alienation.

Since the Self was both the *ground* of every stage of development and the *goal* of every stage of development, it is perfectly acceptable to say that the Self was present all along, "guiding," "pulling," and "directing" development, so that *every* stage of development is drawn closer and closer to Self-realization (as when Jantsch characterized evolution as "self-realization through self-transcendence"). What seems objectionable is confusing the transpersonal with the prepersonal leg, and then assigning to the prepersonal matrix an exalted status of Self-identity *which is simultaneously denied* to the higher structure of the mental-ego, and *then* covering the obfuscation by saying the first Self-identity is unconscious anyway, and *then* denying even *that* status to the mental-ego. This is nothing but a vicious and denigrating attack on the ego, fueled by ptf-2.

But our theoretical problems with the primary matrix are not over, because we still have to examine ptf-1. To begin with, right where the Jungians place the unconscious Self, the orthodox Freudians place the unconscious id. In that regard anyway, the Freudians seem correct (development goes id to ego to Self), but then we already expect the Freudians to have the more accurate view of the prepersonal to personal leg. In my opinion, there *is* a transpersonal Self (Jung), but the primary matrix is prepersonal (Freud). The problem comes when Freudians are faced with a truly transpersonal and actually mystical event, for then they are forced to explain it as regression to the primary matrix, or regression/fixation to primary narcissism and omnipotent valuation (cf.

Ferenczi). Now I believe there is most definitely such a regression, in both is useful forms—called regression in service of ego, wherein the ego can occasionally relax its upward growth by slipping back to lower levels, gathering strength and moving forward again—and in its pathological forms—mild regression/fixations in neurotic symptoms and full-scale regression/fixation in psychotic reactions. But the transpersonal Self—and true mystic union—lies in *precisely* the opposite direction. As *The Atman Project* tried to suggest, mysticism is not regression in service of ego, but evolution in transcendence of ego.

But—and without letting the Freudians off the hook—the immediate problem was that, to make it all worse, many transpersonalists, spearheaded by various Jungians, countered this wrong half of the Freudian WV-1 with nothing but the wrong half of their WV-2. Instead of working to the other and high end of the spectrum, they began fighting with the Freudians for control of the same low territory—the primary matrix. The problem was (and still is) that many transpersonalists see the primary matrix and want to use it as a base of operations for the *unio mystica,* or transcendent oneness (overlooking the fact that the primary matrix is presubject/object, not transsubject/object, and prepersonal fusion, not transpersonal union). They have therefore been perfectly willing and even eager to use the *Freudian* notion of regression in service of ego in order to explain and even validate mystical experience. Prince and Savage did precisely that, and Deikman's classic paper on mysticism explains it as a deautomatization—"a shift to a structure *lower in the hierarchy,*"[84] a move downward "towards dedifferentiation," a shift "in the direction of primitive thought"—that is, regression. And he rests the whole argument on a confusion of transpersonal union with prepersonal fusion. But notice that his explanation is not meant to denigrate mysticism; it is an attempt to validate it, to ground it, to explain it in "real" terms—and it is now widely accepted by transpersonalists as *the* explanation of mystical union.

We can see the same "primary matrix" difficulties running through various anthropological and sociological theories, because modern anthropological research (from Lévy-Bruhl to Gebser to Cassirer) has established as highly likely the fact that primal men and women lived in a type of *participation mystique,* a vague indissociation of self and group, self and nature, self and animals (hence totemism, the clan-self, kinship ritual, etc.). Participation mystique can, of course, sound very transcendent, holistic, holographic, or whatnot, until you carefully examine the evidence. It soon becomes obvious that paleohumans did not transcend subject and object, they simply couldn't differentiate them in the first place. Participation mystique is not a capacity; it is an incapacity. Participation mystique, in fact, is an almost exact phylogenetic parallel of the ontogenetic primary matrix—it is a prepersonal and prerational fusion state, out of which subsequent men and women, in the form of mental-ego, eventually managed to evolve.

But already you can guess what theoretical uses have been made of this concept. On the one side, WV-1 theorists—who are correct in picturing participation mystique as a predifferentiated state—take any state of *actual* transcendence and claim it is a throwback to the primitive fusion of paleohumans. These "critiques" can be put with terrifying assurances of what will happen to someone in "transpersonal states," simply because what *did* occur in the *prepersonal* realms of participation mystique was quite often horrifying—human sacrifice, blood feasts, cannibalistic orgy, and mass suicide/regicide.

Jonestown, for instance, is probably a perfect example of group regression to participation mystique, or egoic dissolution and self-clan fusion, with subsequent, will-less obedience to totem "master," with emotional-sexual obsessions, sadistic rituals, and mass human sacrifice. WV-1 anthropologists and sociologists are quite right in pointing that out. Problem is, they are forced to apply similar analyses to transpersonal communities headed by actual spiritual masters. Since they cannot theoretically tell the difference between a transpersonal community or *sangha* and a prepersonal clan or cult, such theorists are convinced that all contemplative master-student communities are always on the edge of Jonestown.

Just to make sure, they consult a psychiatrist—who, as a likely subscriber to WV-1, cannot distinguish prepersonal helplessness and dependence on a father figure from transpersonal surrender and submission to a spiritual master—and the psychiatrist assures the sociologist that all such devotees are indeed mass hysterics with borderline personalities and dangerously low self-esteem. In their understandable and perhaps justifiable attempts to save us from Jim Jones and the Reverend Sun Myung Moon, such theorists come very close to saving us from Socrates, Christ, and Buddha.

To return to the other side of the anthropological fallacy: WV-2 theorists agree that there is (or was) a participation mystique among paleohumans, but they use it to bolster their Eden view of yesteryear. We needn't go into the specifics, since we have already discussed WV-2 anthropology. Suffice it to say that these anthropologists elevate participation mystique to a quasi-transcendental status, and embue the horrifying rituals often accompanying it with mystical significance—ritually murdering a sacrificial victim is "really" a form of "transcending self" ("that takes care of *that* ego"). In pure WV-2 form, participation mystique, like the primary matrix, is elevated from prepersonal fusion to transpersonal union (or unconscious transpersonal union, in the more sophisticated versions of fig. 5).

Translate this whole discussion into the realm of pathology, and it is no surprise that where the WV-2 psychologists see the supreme Self, the WV-1 psychologists see the supreme pathology. The former therefore tend to see all psychotics as half-saints, while the latter see all saints as half-psychotic. (Examples, respectively: Norman O. Brown, *Love's Body,* and Group for the Advancement of Psychiatry, *Mysticism: Spiritual Quest or Psychic Disorder?*) It seems that until both sides cease fighting each other with the incorrect half of their ptf world views, both real saints and real psychotics will continue to be misrepresented and therefore victimized.

One final note: not only is there a difference between "pre" and "trans," there is a difference between "pre" and "de"; that is, depersonal is not to be confused with prepersonal or transpersonal. For example, in saying that the actual psychotic is regressing to a prepersonal stage, which I agree is in part what happens, it does not follow that the prepersonal stage is a schizophrenic disease. As Bleuler pointed out long ago, the schizophrenic in some ways regresses to child-level, say age three, but the three-year-old child is not a little schizophrenic. Age three is not a disease. The lower levels are prepersonal, but the schizophrenic is *de*personal—and there the vast difference. On top of the regressive movement itself, the depersonal crash carries with it the cascading fragments of higher structures that have ruinously disintegrated. In every way it is a nightmare of destructuring and devolving. And if depersonal cannot be confused with prepersonal, even less can it be called on to explain transpersonal. But when ptf occurs, just that confusion is made, in either of the two basic directions: depersonal psychotics are called saints, and transpersonal saints are called psychotic.

Summary: Our more refined developmental map can be presented as in figure 6, and we can then summarize our discussion very quickly. In my opinion, Freud is more or less correct in his articulation of 1, 2, and 3, but he denies the existence of 4 and collapses 5 into 1—and that gives perfectly the WV-1 of figure 3.

On the other side: Jung clearly believes in, and often eloquently eluci-

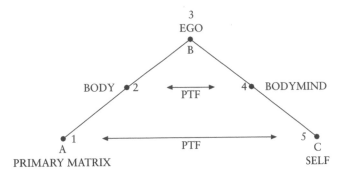

FIGURE 6

dates, 5, but he frequently elevates or confuses 1 with it, thus generating the WV-2 of figure 4. And this WV-2 was strengthened by the humanistic mini-ptf: they articulate well the existential, integrated, bodymind union, 4, but, under the neo-Reichian conflation, they often elevate or confuse 2 with it. On this side, the neo-Reichian conflation has joined with the Jungian primary matrix conflation to present an almost invincible WV-2 theory, while on the other, the early Freudian research has today culminated in, and joined with, the extremely influential and widespread school of orthodox ego psychology, to generate a perfect and perfectly entrenched WV-1.

FREUD, EROS, AND THANATOS

Just as numerous theorists—both pro and con—have eagerly used the Freudian notion of regression in service of ego to explain (or explain away) the *nature* of mysticism, so several theorists—again both pro and con—have been drawn to Freud's concept of thanatos (or something similar to it) as a possible explanation for the *dynamic* of mysticism. The starting point is that, as is well known, mystical experience involves "ego-transcendence" or "ego-death"—that is, apparently some sort of thanatos-like elements. From this point, the theorists line up on opposing sides of the same concept: if you are for transcendence, then you interpret thanatos as a drive to surrender ego and find unity in Spirit; if you are against transcendence, then you interpret thanatos as a drive to abdicate ego and regress to morbid id. Norman O. Brown, Charles Garfield, Ronald Laing, and perhaps the majority of transpersonal psychologists would line up on the first side; Freud, Ferenczi, Ernest Becker, and orthodoxy, on the second.

By now you might expect that I shall claim both sides are half-right and half-wrong, and that is true enough. But in this case the discussion becomes extremely intricate, for not only do we have to tease out possible ptf elements from these concepts, we have to wade through a swamp of semantic confusion, primarily about the word "death," but also and consequently about the word "life," for both of these terms have been used to mean something very, very good and something very, very bad. At the very least, then, we are faced with distinguishing between (1) death in the bad sense (premature and useless destruction, or simple degeneration) and (2) death in the good sense (connected with "ego-death" in transcendence); and consequently the difference between (3) life in the good sense (promoting unity and vitality) and (4) life in the bad sense (refusing to give up the "life" of the old so as to make room for the new). As we shall see, all four of these meanings have been used indiscriminately by modern theorists, with resultant and almost total confusion.

Perhaps we can best begin to sort things out by describing some of the actual dynamic factors of structural development without specifying their possible life-death connotations. Once that is done, we can then assign various shades of life-death meaning to them—in both what we are calling "good" and "bad" senses—and use this assignment to analyze the various death-transcendence theories.

To begin with, we have already seen that there are two major "directions" of consciousness movement: The first is ascending, progressive, evolutionary; the second is descending, regressive, involutionary. The evolutionary movement is marked by a series of structures that display ever-increasing holism, transcendence, integration, and unity. The involutionary movement is simply a shift in the opposite direction—it is a move *down* the nested hierarchy and thus is marked by increasing alienation, fragmentation, lack of unity, and disintegration. Where the aim of evolution is the resurrection of the ultimate Unity in only Spirit, the aim of involution is the return to the lowest unity of all—simple matter, physical insentience, dust.

Now, not only are individuals moved vertically to *change* levels (i.e., evolve or involve), they are moved horizontally *within* levels. The former we call *transformation*, the latter, *translation*. Although it is acceptable to view translation or horizontal movements as tangential derivatives of transformative factors (i.e., as compromises of evolutionary and involutionary drives), it would be helpful if we could also specify the translative forces in their own terms; that is, what, in general, drives horizontal translation?

Without excluding other and more complex elements, we can for simplicity's sake mention two major dialectical forces of translation. For, with regard to any given structure, an individual basically has two drive-choices: to *preserve* the structure or to *alter* it. The first, the preservation factor, seeks to consolidate, close, and fortify the elements of the present structure or level of consciousness. This is similar to Piaget's notion of assimilation and the psychoanalytic concept of alloplastic regulation—the structure remains essentially unchanged and the environment is fitted to it.

Against this preservation factor there looms the possibility of the altering, rearranging, or changing of the present structure itself. This is similar to Piaget's accommodation and the psychoanalytic autoplastic regulation—the structure must change in order to fit the environment. We may, in the most general sense, refer to it as the release factor, since some present configuration is being released and subsequently altered, or even abandoned altogether. The overall point is that *within* a given level, the individual's actions are a dialectic of preserving, acting, and holding that structure on the one hand, and an altering, rearranging, or releasing that structure on the other. We can display our two translative (horizontal) forces and the two transformative (vertical) forces as follows:

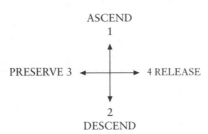

With that display as background, we can now reexamine the various theories of life-death-transcendence, starting with Freud. In *An Outline of Psychoanalysis*,[46] Freud gives a classic (and final) statement of his drive theory. "After long hesitancies and vacillations," he begins, "we have decided to assume the existence of only two basic instincts, *Eros* and *the destructive instinct*. . . . The aim of the first of these basic instincts is to establish ever greater unities . . . —in short, to bind together." We shall qualify this in a moment, but so far that instinct is what we have called the ascent factor—the evolution to ever higher unities and totalities, drive #1.

Freud continues: "The aim of the second is, on the contrary, to undo connections and so to destroy things. In the case of the destructive instinct we may suppose that its final aim is to lead what is living into an inorganic state. For this reason we also call it the *death instinct*." Freud, of course, was severely criticized by everybody, including his own followers, for proposing the death instinct (thanatos), but clearly it is exactly what we have in mind with the descent factor (#2), or the involutionary drive. It is simply the impulse to move to a lower level in the hierarchy, and its final aim, as we said earlier, is therefore insentient matter. In that sense, it is a death instinct, a death drive, a primal masochism. Not a fear of death, but a drive toward it.

Now I do not agree with everything Freud said about this instinct (or its counterpart), nor do his statements exhaust the theoretical dynamics of death, but so far, and within only the definitions I have given, I agree completely with Freud's assessments of both eros and the death instinct.

It should be said, however, that I reject entirely the notion that eros is generated only in the soma and consequently displaced to mind. In my opinion, *each* level is defined by its own unitive tendencies in the arc of evolution, and, as a matter of fact, the higher levels (such as mind) possess more holism and holistic drive—more eros—than the lower ones (such as libido). For example, biological or body-sex eros can only form a union with two bodies at a time, whereas mental eros can unite whole peoples in a community of discourse, and spiritual eros can unite the entire manifest universe in radical oneness. I share none of Freud's biological, sexual, libidinous reductionism. Not only can spirit-transcendence not be reduced to id, neither can ego-mind.

Notice, too, that because Freud is working within WV-1, he correctly sees that the aim of involution is the return to the lowest level of all (inanimate matter), but he refuses to see that the aim of evolution is the resurrection of ultimate unity in Spirit. "If we assume," he says, "that living things came later than inanimate ones and arose from them, then the death instinct fits in with the formula we have proposed to the effect that instincts tend towards a return to an earlier state. In the case of Eros (or the love instinct) we cannot apply this formula. To do so would presuppose that living substance was once a unity which had later been torn apart and was now striving towards re-union."[46] Of course, for the perennial philosophy, that is *exactly* what happened—all things were "torn apart" from Spirit-unity during prior *involution,* and evolution, driven by love (#1), is now reuniting and re-membering all elements in a climb *back* to unity-Spirit. That, for example, was precisely Plato's view ("This becoming one instead of two [is] the very expression of humanity's need. And the reason is that human nature was originally One and we were a whole, and the desire and pursuit of the whole is called love"). Incidentally, Plato's *Symposium* was exactly what Freud was trying to deny with this passage. Needless to say, I side with Plato.

At any rate, this overall discussion gives us the meaning of death in the bad sense—a driving toward less unity via contraction and fragmentation—and life in the good sense—ascending to higher unities via love and expansion. These are factors #1 and #2 in our display.

What we need now is the sense in which death may be good and life bad. For we have seen, first off, that what has sparked so much interest in Freud's thanatos or death instinct is that transcendence seems to involve some sort of ego-death, and this death must be "good" in some sense. What sort of death is good?

To begin with, the ego-death as actual transcendence has absolutely nothing to do with Freud's thanatos. Rather, actual transcendence demands the death of the present structure in the sense that the structure must be *released* or let-go of in order to make room for the higher-order unity of the next structure. The *release factor* in this case is indeed a type of *death;* it is a real dying to an exclusive identity with a lower structure in order to awaken, via love-expansion or transcendence, to a higher-order life and unity. In this sense, such death-and-transcendence occurs at every stage of growth, matter to body to mind to bodymind to spirit. One accepts the death and release (#4) of the lower stage in order to find the life and unity of the next higher stage, and so on until either growth arrests and preservation (#3) alone sets in, or actual Spirit is resurrected in the Great Death of final transcendence and ultimate unity.

That is death in the "good" sense—the release factor (#4) allowing subsequent ascent. The reverse of that is simply the refusal to release and transcend, and that is the preservation factor (#3) gone rigid, sterile, and overbearing. One quits all transformation and seeks merely to preserve one's present structure of consciousness. And while preservation has its important functions, in this case it serves merely stagnation and life gone rigid—and there, finally, is our last factor, life in the "bad" sense. This is the factor the Buddhists have in mind when they speak of attachment, clinging, permanence, fixation, and unyieldingness.

Since we have established two major but different meanings of both life and death, let us distinguish them with uppercase initial letters, thus:

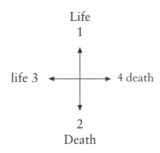

Now we are in a position to easily untangle the various life-death-transcendence theories. To begin with, the "good" factors, those promoting growth, unity, and transcendence, are Life and death. The "bad" factors, those preventing growth and transcendence and even urging the reverse, are life and Death. Already you can see the semantic problems, for these various meanings simply are not differentiated in most modern theories, and the semantic confusions have insinuated themselves deeply into present-day theories to produce several contradictions. I shall give only two major examples.

1. We already mentioned that Buddhism maintains that grasping, clinging, and a desire for permanence (*trishna/svabha*) are the root problems of suffering, simply because those factors prevent growth, and it is only growth leading to Spirit (*dharmakaya*) that can remove suffering (*dukhka*). It therefore recommends life denial and an embrace of self-death (*anatta*). This has led to all sorts of charges that Buddhism is, on the one hand, antilife, antilove, antipurpose, and, on the other, death-obsessed, nihilistic, and necromaniacal.

But, of course, when Buddhists say that the cause of suffering is life-desire, they are repudiating not Life but life. They disavow not love, openness, growth, and transcendence, but status-quo clinging, attachment, fixation, and fear of change (*anicca*). Conversely, the self-death recommended is not Death but death, not regression but release, not involution but accommodation.

Perhaps this confusion started with Schopenhauer, who nobly tried to interpret the Upanishads and *Prajnaparamita Sutras* for the West, but who, in trying to argue for death, always sounded like Death, and in denying life always sounded as if he hated Life. In any case, it is a confusion as deep-seated as it is unfair.

2. We come now to the modern death and transcendence theories, notably those of such theorists as Brown, Laing, Garfield. For, amidst

the extremely significant conceptualizations that these researchers are putting forward, there seems to lie a ptf in the form of a persistent ambiguity about the nature of ego-death itself. Put simply, *they do not always or clearly distinguish between ego-death leading to transcendence and ego-death leading to regression*. The ego *dies* in each case, but how different the deaths! And these theorists rarely distinguish them—they confuse or conflate death and Death, factors #4 and #2.

Garfield, for example, suggests that if "the drive to intentionally alter consciousness possesses a thanatomimetic element, as suggested by Robert Kastenbaum and Ruth Aisenberg, then it may well be that this hypothesized drive to thanatomimesis (and its experiential core, ego-loss or ego-death experience) is also innate."[52] Because this does not distinguish between ego-death leading to transcendence and ego-death leading to regressive dissolution (i.e., #4 and #2), Garfield then falls straight into the course of adopting Freud's thanatos (#2)—the drive to material Death—in an attempt to explain the drive to transcendent Life: "In fact," he says, "Freud's description of the operation of Thanatos, the death instinct, approximates, if not duplicates, phenomenological accounts of the Eastern notion of the highest state of consciousness, i.e., satori, nirvana, etc."[52] That is incorrect on both Freud's side and the Eastern side.

Yet this fallacy—or at least theoretical ambiguity—has gained widespread acceptance among transpersonalists, largely, I suppose, because it fits so well with that other widely adopted WV-2 belief, namely, that the primary matrix—that primitive and prepersonal fusion state—is some sort of transpersonal union. Since Freud's thanatos does indeed have as its aim the primary matrix of prepersonal de-struction, and since this matrix is mistaken to be Self, then it appears that Freud's thanatos has as its aim ego-death in transcendence, whereas in fact its aim is ego-dissolution in regression.

In my opinion, what these transpersonal theorists mean to say is that the mystic union demands not the Death of the ego, but the death of the ego—the death and transcendence, the death and release (#4), of the ego-mind in order to discover the higher Life and Unity of Spirit. That death is truly experienced *as* a death, *is* in fact a death, and so naturally looks like a death. It just isn't Death. As they stand now, however, lacking this elemental distinction, the present-day theories represent a truly bizarre marriage:

The *wrong* half of WV-1 (its reductionism: "mysticism is really just thanatomimetic regression in service of the ego") has joined up the *cor-*

rect half of WV-2 (there *is* a transcendent Self), with the even more bizarre but reverse corollary that the *correct* half of WV-1 (in total regression the ego dissolves back into prepersonal fusion) is being used to explain the *incorrect* half of WV-2 (the oceanic matrix is Self). In short, as the false half of Freudianism was joined to the true half of transpersonalism, the true half of the former was used to explain the false half of the latter.

As an ironic twist on this whole ptf confusion, take one last example: Freud—precisely as described above in the Buddhist example—happened to completely misunderstand nirvana as Life-extinction, instead of life-extinction. Nirvana, for Freud, was complete dissolution, the return to dust. Therefore, Freud explicitly referred to thanatos—which does aim for dust, so to speak—as the *nirvana principle.* Now Garfield (and numerous others), coming from the perfectly opposite angle and trying correctly to explicate nirvana as a truly transcendent state, runs into Freud's concepts. The result is ironic. For, in my opinion, Garfield is right about the existence of a transcendent-nirvana, but wrong about Freud's thanatos; Freud is right about thanatos, but wrong about nirvana. Consequently, however, because of this almost seamless overlap of the two wrongs, they both can use the *same* sentence ("Thanatos gives nirvana") to describe their fundamentally different worldviews.

As for death-drive, Jung criticized thanatos, saying that humans actually possess phobos, a fear of death, not a drive to death. In my opinion, both are true. Phobos is related to death [#4]—it is the *fear of release,* or the fear of dying to a particular structure, and this phobos remains as long as the life [#3] of the structure is not surrendered in its exclusivity. Both phobos and thanatos are present in the psyche, but phobos definitely plays the more decisive role. But now the crowning confusion—most of the neo-Freudians trying to use Freud's concept of thanatos actually use it to mean phobos. Thus, if you want to use the otherwise important insights of these theorists, you end up using the word thanatos to mean phobos—as occasionally I did in *The Atman Project.* But so goes the promised semantic nightmare. Perhaps, however, if you simply remember the four actual dynamic factors, regardless of their arbitrary names, you will be able to figure out what the various theorists actually mean.

I must end by emphasizing the significance of the true half of the new transpersonal theories, such as those of Brown, Garfield, and Laing. For their collective import is that higher growth is bought only by ego-death, a notion that, almost for the first time in history, gives us a genuine sense of the importance and place of death in the overall scheme of Life. My only point is that we must distinguish between ego-death (#4) leading to transcendence and ego-death (#2) leading to regression. Then we can champion death and release, not Death and regress, and we can urge surrender of life and attachment, not Life and love.

A REFINEMENT

I wish in this last section on the theoretical nature of ptf to outline very briefly the refinements given to it in *Up from Eden*. The essential point is that, although we speak of the ptf as a confusion of "pre" and "trans" around a central pivot, this does not mean that there are *only* three structures involved. To speak of development as moving from preego to ego to transego, for instance, does not mean that there are really and only three stages of growth. In fact, there are a dozen (or more) major structure/stages, and the pre/trans fallacy can be committed with regard to *any* of them. The point is merely that, with reference to any structure X, it is easy to confuse a preX structure with a transX one (or vice versa). We have already examined the neo-Reichian confusion of the body stage (which precedes mind) with the bodymind stage (which succeeds mind). This is every bit as much ptf as is the confusion of id and God; less conspicuous perhaps, but ptf nonetheless.

In *Up from Eden* I therefore examined eight or so major structures of consciousness in order to discover how they may have been subjected (in the context of both historical development and present-day theories) to either ptf-1 or ptf-2. The structure/stages examined, in order of phylogenetic and ontogenetic development, were:

1. Matter—or material fusion, the lowest stage of structural organization, recapitulated in humans via the primary matrix or pleroma.
2. Body—simple sensorimotor intelligence and emotional-sexual drives.
3. Magic—the first symbolic cognitive mode, the primary process, which confuses inside and outside, whole and part, subject and predicate, image and reality.
4. Mythic—higher representational thought, but still incapable of formal-operational insight; still anthropomorphic; mixture of logic with previous magic.

5. Mental-rational—egoic rationality and formal-operational logic.
6. Bodymind—integration of formal and verbal mind with emotional body; the centaur.
7. Psychic—actual psychic capacity, or the *beginning* of transpersonal modes.
8. Subtle or archetypal—home of archetypes, or exemplary and transindividual patterns of manifestation.
9. Causal—ultimate unity in only Spirit.

My conclusions were that, almost without exception, some lower structure, such as magic, has been and still is confused with some similar-appearing higher structure, such as psychic, and then either the former is elevated to the latter, or the latter reduced to the former. In other words, the pre/trans fallacy. These ptf confusions are summarized in figure 7. We have already seen examples of primary matrix-Spirit ptf and of body/bodymind ptf. As for the others, a few brief comments:

Magic, or unrestrained and unrefined belief in action at a distance, ontogenetically characterizes the thinking of two- to four-year-olds, principally because they cannot yet distinguish image from reality or symbol from thing, hence believe that to manipulate the one is to manipulate the other. This mode can sound very holistic and holographic and all that, until you really dig into the actual case details. Then you realize that magic does not unite subject and object, it fuses and confuses them; and it does not holographically integrate whole and part, it simply can't tell them apart in the first place. I am confident that the simplest study of any good developmental psychologist, Werner to Arieti to Piaget, will disabuse anybody of the notion that childhood magic is some sort of heavenly holographic display.

Nonetheless, magic is almost always confused with psychic, or the

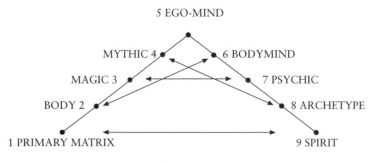

FIGURE 7

actual display of some sort of transcendental vision based *not* on the fusion of subject and object but on the beginning transcendence of subject and object. This ptf, of course, goes both ways: Freudians claim all psychic is really magic, and parapsychologists occasionally rig up elaborate laboratory experiments in an attempt to prove that magic is really psychic.

A similar confusion seems to exist with regard to myth and archetype, and here Jung apparently stands most to blame. It's rather hard to pin Jung down here, because he ended up using the word "archetype" in several different ways. But his classic definition of an archetype is a mythic-archaic image or form collectively inherited. Unfortunately, however, the archaic-mythic level lies on the prepersonal or at least pre-rational side of the developmental divide. Apparently, the fact that certain archaic-mythic images are *collectively inherited* was confused by Jung to mean that they are *transpersonally located,* whereas they are merely part of the lower, prepersonal, collective unconscious. We all collectively inherit ten toes, but that doesn't mean that if I directly experience my toes I am having a transpersonal experience. Besides, when Jung explicitly locates the "archetypes" as the exact counterpart of the biological body instincts, his position is obvious. Notice, in this regard, that Freud stated explicitly that he agreed with Jung's notion of a phylogenetic heritage, but that it was in every respect a prerational (*not* transrational) legacy. There, anyway, Freud seems to be in the correct half of his WV-1.

In my opinion, Jung was correctly trying to say that beyond the rational ego there lie important realms of consciousness; unfortunately, as we earlier explained, he failed to clearly distinguish the preegoic realms—which contain infantile magic and childish myth—from transegoic realms—which contain actual psychic and real archetypes. Having thus fallen into WV-2, I believe that Jung spent much of his life trying to elevate primitive mythic images to subtle archetypes.

Archetypes, as used by Plato, St. Augustine, and the Buddhist-Hindu systems, refer to the *first* forms of manifestation that emerge from causal Spirit in the course of the creation of the universe. That is, in the course of *involution,* or the emergence of the lower from the higher, the archetypes are the *first created forms,* upon which *all subsequent creation is patterned* (from the Greek *archetypon,* meaning "that which was created as a pattern, mold, or model"). Thus, the archetypes lie, or have their formal location, in the subtle region (level #8 in fig. 7).

Consequently, archetype has two related but slightly different meanings. One, the archetypes are exemplary and transindividual patterns of existence lying in the upper limits of the spectrum. But two, every structure on every lower level (1 through 7) that can be said to be present collectively, can be said to be archetypal or archetypally determined. The lower structures themselves are not *the* archetypes, but they *are* archetypally or collectively given. Thus, the deep structure of the human body *is* archetypal, as is the deep structure of matter, magic, myth, mind, psyche. But to experience *the* archetypes means to experience level #8, and not, as we said, to experience archetypal toe, and even less to experience some sort of archaic-mythic imagery. I am not denying that, on occasion, some spiritual insight might be expressed in mythic images; I am denying that they are its source. Thus, mythic images are not *the* archetypes; as for being archetypal, so are *all* other deep structures, so there is nothing especially or preeminently archetypal about mythic images—on both counts, Jung's use of the term archetype is incorrect, in my opinion. We can easily agree with him when he more accurately states that the ego and all other major psychological forms are *archetypal,* for indeed they are, but then always in the next breath he's back to claiming that by archetypal he means mythic, and off we go again.

Once Jung confused mythic image with transpersonal archetypes, he could then claim that "the archetypes" were inherited from *actual* past evolution—they live on in us as a reflection of the actual form of yesterday's cognitions. And while it is true that we have inherited the past structures of development, those structures lie on the ape side, not angel side, of the divide. But, for Jung, the archetypes thus came to mean the collective inheritance of the *early* stages of *evolution,* whereas *the* archetypes actually refer to structures at the opposite end of the spectrum. In short, Jung placed the archetypes toward the beginning of evolution, whereas they actually exist at the beginning of involution. Had he avoided that confusion, he could have seen that the *ascent* of consciousness was drawn *toward* the archetypes *by* the archetypes themselves. This would have removed them from the wrong end of the spectrum, where they were forced (unsuccessfully) to do battle with Freud's archaic heritage. It would also have placed Jung firmly in league with Plato, Plotinus, and others. Finally, it would have relieved Jung and his followers from the extremely uncomfortable predicament of having to view the archetypes as both very primitive and very divine. Jungian therapists are forced to alternately worship archetypes and tremble in their presence, simply because their "archetypes"—being in fact a ptf mixture of real archetype and very primitive myth-forms—wobble between transrational glory and prerational chaos. Here, I believe, Jung's theories are in dire need of revision.

Finally, I need hardly mention the reverse fallacy: orthodox analysts and psychologists usually take any truly archetypal material and hold it up as perfect examples of infantile or regressive mythic (or magic) cognition.

CAUTIONS

I would like to end this chapter by pointing out some of the typical mistakes that are often made when one begins to apply ptf to an understanding of various theories. Since the general form of unwinding a ptf is to go from a *bipole* such as

to a tripole such as

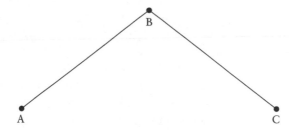

it is important to remember that not every bipole conceals a ptf in need of teasing apart. Certain fundamental bipoles, such as yin/yang, heaven/earth, light/dark, left/right, active/passive, rest/motion, one/many, good/evil—whatever else they may be, they are not examples of ptf-bipoles. They are dualities inherent in maya; they are transcended not by teasing one of the poles apart, but by uniting, integrating, and transcending both, equally, in the Tao. Thus, ego/nonego is a ptf-bipole, yin/yang is not; rational/mystical is a ptf-bipole, active/passive is not.

The problem, however, is that some theorists use real or structural bipoles in order to support and carry their own versions of a ptf-bipole. For example, in the brain the left/right hemisphere is a structural bipole. We don't handle it as a ptf-bipole and then try to introduce *three* "hemispheres." The *L* and *R* hemispheres are real enough. Unfortunately, many researchers such as Ornstein use a ptf-bipole, such as personal/transpersonal or rational/mystical or egoic/nonegoic, then try to cram this false bipole into the structural hemispheric bimodes. The result, of course, is that the *L-H* gets logic, ego, time, and language, and the *R-H* gets everything nonlogical, nonegoic, mystical, and so on. This leads Ornstein and others into that disaster of championing nonlogical modes without specifying whether they are prelogical or translogical. Worse, it makes it appear that there is no difference between prelogical, preegoic, prepersonal and translogical, transegoic, transpersonal, because there are only two hemispheres and one of them is already taken. Since one hemisphere is definitely logical, the other must just be nonlogical—there's no room for pre and trans. This results precisely because a ptf-bipole is forced into a real bimodal structure.

But what, then, could the *L* and *R* hemispheres represent, if not two different modes of knowing termed rational and mystical? We might begin by noting that, in the course of human cognitive development, the individual progresses through, and then has access to, at least a half-dozen major, different, perfectly discrete modes or levels of knowing. For argument's sake, we'll simply use Piaget's four major stages—sensorimotor, concrete representational, concrete operational, formal operational—then add two higher stages—say, the psychic and subtle levels—to include transcendent modes. Since we have at least these six major modes of knowing, but only two hemispheres, doesn't it seem obvious that the two hemispheres don't represent two modes of knowing—for in fact there are at least six—but rather represent two different aspects of every mode of knowing, that is, two components present at each of the six structures of knowledge?

I suggest that the *L-H* simply specializes in the sequential-digital-logical component of any mode of knowing, and the *R-H* specializes in the pattern-analogic-spatial component. But *every* mode of knowing (with the possible exception of the very lowest and highest, which we will discuss below) contains these two necessary components. As Foulkes's landmark study, *A Grammar of Dreams,* demonstrated, even dreams have a logic, or a sequential unfolding, frame by some sort of frame. There is a dream time (L) just as much as a dream space (R). Conversely, even mathematical logic (L) utilizes images and pattern recognition (R). This also fits perfectly with Piaget's studies, which demonstrated that both the logic (L) and fantasy (R) of cognition follow the *same basic deep structures* of the given level of cognition. Thus both L and R are simply two aspects of each level, not two different levels themselves.

Finally, if you will look at any diagram of the yoga *chakras,* you will see exactly what I am suggesting: There are six major structures (*chakras*) of knowledge-consciousness, *each* of which has a left and right component, or *ida* and *pingala*. These two components exist *equally* at each mode of knowing, from the bodily modes to the mental modes of the psychic and subtle ones. Then, at the forehead and into the crown, they merge into each other and *both* disappear in highest transcendence. It is not that L is egoic-rational and R is nonegoic-mystical. It is that L and R are present at all six stages of knowing, and that the lowest two stages are preegoic, the middle two, egoic, and the upper two, transegoic. L and R have, precisely, nothing to do with it.

My final cautionary note is that when we say that, for example, ego/nonego is a ptf-bipole and that there are really two different forms of nonego (pre and trans), we mean that statement only as a semantic convenience. That A and C *appear* similar is never, in my opinion, because they actually and structurally *are* similar, *in anything other than an empty sense*. A has more in common with B than with C, and C has more in common with B than with A.

If I may finish with a personal note, I would say that, if I have occasionally appeared harsh in my criticism of those theories that seem to me fallacious, it is in almost every instance due to the fact that I once embraced those fallacies with enthusiasm, especially in their WV-2 form. And, as Husserl observed at the turn of the century, one is most vehement against those errors that one recently held oneself. In my subsequent attempts to take the true half from each major ptf world view, I realize that I run the risk of being disowned by both sides, going down eventually with Shaw's epigram ("He has no enemies but is intensely disliked by all his friends"). Nonetheless, if the true marriage of science and religion—WV-1 and WV-2—is ever to be effected in other than a spurious or empty sense, if we are ever to have a truly comprehensive paradigm, my best judgment is that absolutely no other course is available. We shall take the true from both and discard the false from both, or we shall continue to try to integrate the muddled half truths of each.

8

Legitimacy, Authenticity, and Authority in the New Religions

A DEVELOPMENTAL-STRUCTURAL APPROACH

ON THE WHOLE, the new religious movements in America are singularly problematic. Perhaps no other phenomenon has caused as much public comment, commotion, or confusion. The Moonies, "brainwashing," Jonestown, cults, Scientology, deprogramming, Jesus Freaks, the Children of God, Hare Krishnas, Synanon—the list itself seems a concatenation of all that might be sinister.

On the one hand, it is certainly true that a great number of the "new religious movements" are—at least in hindsight—disastrous, and Jonestown is paradigmatic. Yet, on the other, some of them seem—at least in theory—genuinely beneficial, even enlightening. The best of Vajrayana, Zen, Taoism, and Vedanta, for example, have graced magnificent civilizations and apparently epitomized the summit of the human idealistic spirit, and there is no reason to suppose that an infusion of such spirit could not resonate with and enrich our own highest wisdoms. Heidegger, for instance, stated that "if I understand Zen scholar Suzuki, this is what I have been trying to say in all my writings,"[6] and we have already seen that the very search for a new and more comprehensive paradigm was generated in large measure by the knowledge claims of transcendental mysticism, predominantly Eastern in form.

It appears that not *all* the "new religions" are merely sophomoric platitudes or mind-numbing cultisms. The great problem, of course, is how to tell the difference. That is, how to devise any sort of *believable* scale or criteria for differentiating the more valid "religious movements" from the less valid or even harmful. This is all the more urgent for those who are striving to present a "new and higher" or comprehensive paradigm, simply because a considerable portion of the transcendental claims of the new paradigm is prompted by or even based on some of the new and specifically mystical religions, and we had better be able to offer believable criteria for differentiating the select "some" (e.g., Zen) from all the rest (e.g., Charles Manson). To Zen scholars, this might seem an outrageously unfair equation, but the simple fact is that the public at large—and many influential scholars—have already simply lumped together, under the single title of "those new religions," all endeavors that are nonorthodox in their religious claims. The burden of "de-lumping" or differentiating these in fact quite different endeavors accordingly falls now, unfairly, on the genuinely transcendental scholars.

In such a terribly complex and problematic field, even a very general and somewhat imprecise scale would be better than none, as long as the scale itself could be externally verified in its general outlines according to the germane criteria of modern psychological and sociological sciences. Acknowledging these broad limitations, I believe several such general scales exist. In fact, throughout this book we have been working with one such (tentative) overview model—a developmental and structural view of the overall "spectrum of consciousness." The lower and intermediate portions of this model are based on the works of Piaget, Werner, Arieti, Kohlberg, Loevinger, Erikson, Freud, and so on; the higher portions are based on the *philosophia perennis*. But the important point is that the existence of each of the stage-levels of this model is open to injunctive inquiry and verification (or rejection). And it is this external verifiability—should it indeed prove sound—that confers upon this type of overview model its *potentially believable* status, and thus allows it, within broad limits, to act as a scale for the *adjudication* of any particular psychosocial engagement, including "religious involvement."

Now by "adjudication" I mean precisely this: We have no difficulty in saying, for instance, that a person at stage-5 moral development (à la Kohlberg) is at a *higher* stage than someone at stage-2. Nor do we have any difficulty in saying that a person at formal-operational (à la Piaget) is at a *higher* stage than someone at preoperational. Nor in saying that conscientious-ego structure is *higher* than conformist-ego structure

(Loevinger). Nor so on through a dozen stages openly described by developmentalists as constituting successively *higher* occasions. Just so, with a *general* overview model of psychosocial development on the whole—one that included not only the lower and intermediate stages of Kohlberg, Piaget, Loevinger, and others, but also the upper levels and stages of subtle and causal occasions—we would be better able to judge—adjudicate—the relative *degree of maturity* or *authenticity* of any psychosocial production, moral, cognitive, egoic, or—in this case—religious (and "new religious").

We introduced this general overview model in chapters 3 and 4; we will be looking at it again in the next chapter. For the purposes of this chapter, we will simply work with seven of its major levels. They are:

1. *Archaic.* This includes material body, sensations, perceptions, and emotions. This is roughly equivalent, for instance, to Piaget's sensorimotor intelligence, Maslow's physiological needs, Loevinger's autistic and symbiotic stages, the first and second *chakras*, the *annamayakosha* (physical food) and *pranamayakosha* (élan vital).

2. *Magic.* This includes simple images, symbols, and the first rudimentary concepts, or the first and lower mental productions, which are "magical" in the sense that they display condensation, displacement, "omnipotence of thought," and so on. This is Freud's primary process, Arieti's paleologic, Piaget's preoperational thinking; the third *chakra*. It is *correlated* (as explained in the next chapter) with Kohlberg's preconventional morality, Loevinger's impulsive and self-protective stages, Maslow's safety needs, and so on.

3. *Mythic.* This stage is more advanced than magic, but not yet capable of clear rationality or hypothetico-deductive reasoning, a stage Gebser explicitly termed "mythic." This is essentially Piaget's concrete operational thinking; the fourth *chakra;* the beginning of *manomayakosha* (Vedanta) and *manovijnana* (Mahayana). It is *correlated* with Loevinger's conformist and conscientious-conformist stages, Maslow's belongingness needs, Kohlberg's conventional stages, and so on.

4. *Rational.* This is Piaget's formal operational thinking, propositional or hypothetico-deductive reasoning; the fifth *chakra;* the culmination of *manomayakosha* and *manovijnana*. It is correlated with Loevinger's conscientious and individualistic stages, Kohlberg's postconventional morality, Maslow's self-esteem needs, and so on.

5. *Psychic.* Here I am including the centaur and the low-subtle as one general level. "Psychic" does not necessarily mean "paranormal," although some texts suggest that certain paranormal events may more

likely occur here. Rather, it refers to "psyche" as a higher level of development than the rational mind per se (e.g., Aurobindo, Free John). Its cognitive structure has been called "vision logic," or integrative logic; the sixth *chakra*; the beginning of *manas* (Mahayana) and *vijnanamayakosha* (Vedanta). It is correlated with Loevinger's integrated and autonomous stages, Maslow's self-actualization needs, Broughton's integrated stage, and so on.

6. *Subtle.* This is, basically, the archetypal level, the level of the "illumined mind" (Aurobindo); the culmination of *manas* and *vijnanamayakosha*; a truly transrational (not prerational and not antirational) structure; intuition in its highest and most sober sense; not emotionalism or merely bodily felt meaning; home of Platonic forms; *bija-mantra, vasanas*; beginning of seventh *chakra* (and sub-*chakras*); start of Maslow's self-transcendence needs, and so on.

7. *Causal.* Or the unmanifest ground and suchness of all levels; the limit of growth and development; "Spirit" in the highest sense, not as a Big Person but as the "Ground of Being" (Tillich), "Eternal Substance" (Spinoza), "Geist" (Hegel); at and beyond the seventh *chakra*; the *anandamayakosha* (Vedanta), *alayavijnana* (Mahayana), Keter (Kabbalah), and so on.

As we have seen, those seven general structure-stages of development can be further reduced to *three general realms:* the prerational (subconscious), the rational (self-conscious), and the transrational (superconscious) (see diagram).

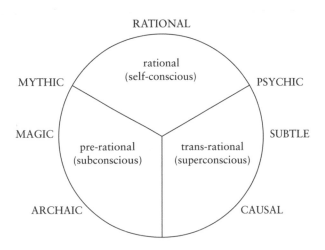

THE PRE/TRANS FALLACY

In the previous chapter, we saw that one of the great problems with discovering an overall model of development is that, although the rational or self-conscious realms are almost universally agreed upon, the other two realms are almost as universally confused. That is, because the prerational and the transrational realms are, in their own ways, nonrational, they appear similar or even identical to the untutored eye. This confusion generally leads to one of two opposite mistakes: either the transrational is *reduced* to the prerational (e.g., Freud), or the prerational is *elevated* to the transrational (e.g., Jung).

We called any of those confusions the "pre/trans fallacy," and it is the pre/trans fallacy that, in my opinion, rests precisely at the center of the controversy over "the new religions"—*because,* I will suggest, about half of the new religions *are* prerational, and about half are *transrational,* and *that* is the strange mixture of trick and treat that has made this whole issue so extraordinarily difficult to unravel.

But whatever we decide on that particular point—we will pursue it below—I would like to remind the reader that this general model—which we have simplified as prerational, rational, and transrational, or prepersonal, personal, and transpersonal, or subconscious, self-conscious, and superconscious—is based on *developmental* and *structural* criteria that are potentially open to external and experimental verification (as are, e.g., Piaget's or Kohlberg's works). This model is offered hypothetically and experimentally, not dogmatically and conclusively. But *if* it proves sound, then we will be able to draw certain significant conclusions on the nature of the "new religions," not to mention the "old."

LEGITIMACY VERSUS AUTHENTICITY

Recall that the basic defining form of each level is its *deep structure,* whereas a particular element or component of each level is a *surface structure.* A change in deep structure we call *transformation;* a change in surface structure, *translation.* We now introduce a simple notion: Any psychosocial institution that validates or facilitates translation we call *legitimate;* any that validates or facilitates transformation we call *authentic.*

Legitimacy, so defined, is a *horizontal* scale. It is a measure of the degree of integration, organization, meaning, coherence, and stability of or within a given level of structural adaptation or development. One of the greatest needs of individuals—an overarching need—is to find legitimacy at their present level of development, whatever that level may be. For example, persons at the magic-protective level seek legitimacy, or sanctified existence, via the safety or self-protective (preconventional) needs of their animistic and narcissistic world view. Persons at the mythic-membership (conventional) level seek legitimacy through conformist belongingness, trying to be sanctified by the group. Persons at the rational (postconventional) level seek legitimacy via conscientious or self-esteem needs: they can legitimate their existence only by following their own conscience and by interacting with similarly structured social institutions. One of the great tasks of any society is to provide its members with a legitimate and legitimizing world view, one that is capable of validating existence on the average expectable level of structural development reached by its members. (In our society, the average expectable level is approximately mythic-rational.)

Authenticity is a *vertical* scale. It is a measure of the degree of transformation offered by any particular psychosocial institution. Every society has to act as a *pacer* of transformation up to its average expectable level of structural adaptation, and thus it must provide authentic modes of transformation up to and including that level (generally, this task falls to family, educational, and occasionally religious systems). In our society, for example, we attempt to move or develop individuals up to the rational level, or at least the mythic-rational. Those at the archaic level often have to be institutionalized, and those at the magic level are labeled psychotic and subsequently isolated. But somewhere around the mythic-rational stage, our society's force as a pacer of authentic transformation (or vertical growth) drops out, and any higher growth or authenticity has to occur either on one's own or in microcommunities of the higher- and like-minded. In any event, this power and degree of transformation we call authenticity.

Any given religion, like any other psychosocial production, can be judged on the basis of both its legitimacy and its authenticity. That is, does it seek merely to confirm, validate, and sanctify a person at his or her present stage of adaptation, or does it seek to transform a person to genuinely higher levels of growth and development? Not merely help a person *translate* better, but *transform* significantly? Now *both of these scales are important.* Even authentic religions (i.e., ones that explicitly engage transrational, transpersonal, superconscient realms) have to be legitimate on their own levels, and even a legitimate but not very authentic religion (e.g., exoteric Protestantism, civil religion, lay Shintoism) can serve as a stabilizing and organizing force on its own level. It's just that, like prerational and transrational, legitimacy and authenticity are often, even usually, confused (especially by the sociologists of religion). Among other things, this makes it appear that a seeker of higher authenticity is no different than a seeker of sturdier legitimacy. It completely confuses two independent scales, and that—along with the pre/trans fallacy—makes it appear that all the "new religions" are essentially identical in motive. In the recent Graduate Theological Union seminar series (which we will discuss below), Dick Anthony, an influential sociologist of religion, responded to these distinctions, making the following very succinct and important summary:

> This is a theme that has come up over and over again. We need to distinguish between transpersonal criteria, in other words, groups that are authentically spiritual in some transpersonal sense, versus groups which aren't, and then another dimension, which is groups which are in some sense or other legitimate, such as civil religious sects, or conventional religious groups, or whatever; and groups can deviate in a negative way along either one of those dimensions. And the dimensions interact, so you get a kind of four-cell table. And when we try to make everything fit along some unidimensional criterion of value, then everything falls apart.[55]

The last two sections might be summarized in one sentence: It is these two confusions—pre and trans, and legitimate and authentic—that have so helped to muddle the study of the new religions (as well as the emergence of a new paradigm). I will now attempt to study the new religions without these confusions.

THE CRITERIA

Our methodology is simple: we take the particular socio-religious movement, examine its statements, actions, and belief systems, and subject these to (1) a *developmental-structural analysis* in order to determine its degree of authenticity or vertical maturity; and (2) a *surface-functional analysis* in order to determine its type and degree of legitimacy or horizontal integration and stability.

First, its authenticity. Is it *archaic,* with moments of self-other indissociation, primary narcissism, primitive fusion, oral needs, perhaps even cannibalistic or murderous (homicidal or suicidal) impulses? Or is it *magical,* with "omnipotence-of-thought" rituals (e.g., voodoo, witchcraft), emotional-sexual impulses, magic beliefs, self-clan confusion (totemism)? Or is it *mythical,* with intense conformity needs, a Cosmic Parent world view, authoritarian figure "representative" of the Parent, mythic ritual, emphasis upon in-group (saved) versus out-group (damned), and lack of rational justification? Or does it seem to contain truly transcendental aspirations—aspirations that are defined not by their prerational dogmatism but by their transrational injunctions? Is it psychic, subtle, or even causal—these are characterized by genuine study and discipline aimed at effecting authentic transformation, and in ways that can be impartially determined by strict developmental-structural analysis?

In short, with regard to authenticity, is the group in question prerational (archaic, magic, mythic) or transrational (psychic, subtle, causal)?

Second, we analyze the psychosocial productions of the movement in order to determine their type and degree of legitimacy. That is, we are looking for the degree of integration, meaningful engagement, purpose, and stability offered at the particular level characteristic of the group's degree of authenticity. How and why, within its general level of belief structure, does the group earn its legitimacy? How does it validate its existence? What sanctions are used? How coherent and organized are they? Most importantly, is legitimacy conferred by a whole society or by a tradition or by a single person? That is, within the given level of structural adaptation, who or what has the final power to tell you that you're OK?

Overall, then, once we determine the group's level of authenticity, or its vertical degree of maturity and development, we then try to determine its type and degree of legitimacy, or its horizontal scale of integrative meaning and stability. And it is especially these two scales that can help us tease apart the various strands of the "new religions." But there is one other scale or factor that is also important: the type and degree of *authority* evidenced by the group leader(s).

Authority

I am going to shorten and simplify this discussion drastically by approaching authority from an angle almost opposite to that usually taken: I am going to discuss not what constitutes "bad" authority—fascist dynamics, authoritarian personalities, group subservience to superego projections, and transference hypnosis—but what constitutes "good" authority; that is, under what circumstances would most people agree that an authority is necessary? What is a benign, useful, nonproblematic authority?

One type of benign authority is the "functional authority," the person who by special training is authorized to perform certain tasks and functions, for example, plumbers, doctors, lawyers. That type of authority is nonproblematic because subjection to it is voluntary. But there are even certain types of *involuntary* subjection to authority that are also generally thought to be nonproblematic—law enforcement, for example. But the best example is probably compulsory education, because its existence is based upon a developmental argument and upon society's need to act as a pacer of development up to at least a certain average-expectable level of adaptation.

The benign authority in this situation is, of course, the teacher. And the teacher has a peculiar form of authority. If, for example, a student says, with regard to a particular task, "But why do I have to do it that way?" the teacher's final authority is, "Because I say so. Once you have learned to do it that way—once you have graduated—you can do it any way you wish. But experience has shown us that that is the best way to learn that task, and that is how you are going to do it in my class if you want to pass."

Now, even though that is a compulsory authority, it is viewed as benign, nonproblematic, and necessary, because (1) it is effecting development, and (2) it is *phase-temporary* or *phase-specific*. That is, the teacher's authority over the pupil is temporary; it effectively evaporates once the pupil's degree of understanding approaches that of the teacher (supposedly symbolized by graduation). At that point, the pupil can become a teacher—and can even disagree with his or her previous teachers.

Phase-specific authority seems inescapable in any process of education (development). Even in higher or noncompulsory education, the gap between the teacher and pupil's understanding of a topic confers on the teacher a phase-specific authority that is only annulled when and if that gap is sufficiently closed. At that point, teacher and pupil become more or less equals; prior to that point, phase-specific authoritarianism seems inescapable.

Now we cannot conclude from those examples that *all* functional and phase-specific authority is benign and nonproblematic. But we can conclude that authority which is *not* functional or phase-specific might very likely be problematic, because then the only major reasons left for its existence are those that tend to fall in the category of "bad" authority—authority that does not serve a necessary (objective) function or a phase-specific (subjective) growth, but rather rests on certain psychological dynamics of "master-slave" (Hegel), "power-over" (Fromm), "superego projection" (Freud), "transference hypnosis" (Ferenczi), "herd mentality" (Hegel/Berdyaev), "emotional plague" (Reich), and so on.

For this presentation I have chosen the shortcut of not attempting to explain the nature of all those various conceptions of "bad" authority; rather, I have simply suggested two major characteristics of "good" authority (functional and/or phase-specific), and then added: if the authority in question displays neither of those "good" characteristics, odds are that that authority is or will be problematic. (And the reader can fill in the nature of the "problem" using whatever theory he or she wishes.)

If we take each of the dimensions or variables we have discussed—authenticity, legitimacy, and authority—and look at their "bad" manifestations, we arrive at a tentative list of *problematic factors,* the more of which any group contains, the more problematic the group probably is (or will become): (1) engagement of a prerational realm, (2) engagement of a "permanent" authority figure, and (3) engagement of a fractured, isolated, and/or single-source legitimacy.

Some Concrete Examples

In a recent Graduate Theological Union seminar series, which capped a year-long research project, some dozen or so "new religious movements" were carefully examined (including in-depth interviews with their proponents). Of those dozen, approximately three out of four were deemed—by orthodox and transpersonal scholars alike—to be problematic, or at least to have degenerated into problematic status. These included such movements as Jonestown, Synanon, an unfortunate twist on Psychosynthesis, and the Unification Church (Moonies).

What emerges from those transcripts is a *general pattern of problematic groups,* and that pattern unmistakably correlates with the three "bad" criteria suggested above. The paradigm for this, of course, was Jonestown. It was (1) prerational (eventually sinking past mythic-belongingness needs to magical-sexual ritual to archaic sacrifice); (2) it was headed by a permanent and not phase-specific authority (the "father" Jim Jones, who was even so addressed); and (3) its legitimacy—the very OKness of every member—rested upon a sole person (isolated legitimacy).

But a similar pattern could be observed in most other problematic groups, even those existing in entirely different circumstances (although few degenerated to the final degree of Jonestown). An unfortunate example is the atypical situation that arose in one particular school of Psychosynthesis. I say "atypical" because Psychosynthesis itself is by and large a rather sophisticated and authentic teaching, and what happened to one of its schools is simply not indicative of its theoretical potential.

This particular group began as a concerned community of individuals—virtually all of whom seemed at or near a rational level of structural adaptation—apparently interested in pursuing an authentic transrational growth and development. Through a series of events that can only be conveyed by the original (and quite terrifying) transcripts, the upward transformation began to go sour. What followed was classic group regression into prerational realms, a regression that almost ended in a Jonestown.

We can follow this regression using virtually any of the developmental schemes we have discussed—Piaget, Kohlberg, Loevinger, Maslow, our own overview model. The individuals apparently started out at the self-esteem (conscientious) stages, interested in the higher realms of self-actualization and self-transcendence. As that upward development began to go sour, individuals not only failed their own self-esteem needs, they apparently began to regress to conformist-belongingness modes. Individuality was shunned; the "group ego" began to demand allegiance. In place of rational individuality and logical inquiry there arose mythic-membership and the "wall of terror" that demanded and compelled group allegiance. *Conformity* to the particular world view was now the arbiter of *legitimacy:* to leave the group was "to die." (This is all the more extraordinary because the people so caught up were extremely well-educated—doctors, lawyers, and other professionals.) The move toward and into prerational realms was well under way; nobody was encouraged, or even allowed, to rationally question the teachings. Criterion #1—prerationality—was already in evidence.

Worse, the sole arbiter of "the teaching" soon focused on *one* individual, a situation that represented the abandonment of phase-temporary authority in favor of a for-all-practical-purposes *permanent* authority (criterion #2). This person—call him Smith—was looked upon as the sole and permanent leader of the organization. Eventually Smith began to be perceived (by himself and all others) as the sole and individual bearer of *legitimacy:* Smith, and Smith alone, had the final power to tell you if your actions were or were not OK (criterion #3). So blatant was this power that Smith would spend hours—literally hours— "processing" individuals, either directly or by phone, telling them exactly what to think, feel, and do in order to be OK, to be legitimate, to be validated. And, given the group regression to intense conformity needs, virtually no one objected.

The situation worsened, on the part of both master and slave. Mythic-belongingness and group conformity soon regressed to the magical stage of primary process cognition and delusional reference systems. Invisible forces—graphically described—were "out to get them"; both master and slave became, literally and clinically, paranoid (as was, e.g., Jim Jones). Had not extraneous circumstances interrupted this pattern, it might indeed have ended in archaic, masochistic, and literal sacrifice: since the world doesn't understand us, in fact, since they are all out to get us, let us get ourselves first, as a heroic statement.

Although not all problematic groups follow exactly that overall pattern, or at least do not follow it to such extremes, I believe the pattern itself is general enough to be considered essentially paradigmatic. I usually refer to this general pattern as the "cult-clan and totem master." "Cult-clan" refers to the general absence of self-esteem, conscientious, or postconventional needs, with consequent herd mentality. "Totem master" refers to the permanent authority figure that usually rides herd. "Totem" emphasizes the magical-mythical connotations given to this father figure, and "master" emphasizes the extraordinary power of legitimation rested in this individual (for psychodynamic reasons). Thus, Jim Jones was the totem master or temporal father of his entire community. He was not representative of the "eternal self" of each individual, as is an authentic guru. Rather, he was viewed as the *temporal* and even biological father of the group—a belief apparently supported by bizarre sexual-fertility (magical) rituals. Not "our Father who art in Heaven," but "our father who art next door." But regardless of actual sexual practices (they seem rather rare), the totem master is viewed as somehow being the temporal father of the entire group, literally or figuratively. He is *totemically* "in" the group and the group is "in" him, magically or mythically so. It is no accident that Jones, Moon, and Manson were often referred to as "father" (*not* meaning priest), and that more than one totem master has found *Führer* and *Vater* synonymous.

Such seems to be the general pattern of especially problematic groups: engaged in prerational realms, headed by a permanent and not phase-specific authority, and based on isolated, separative, or clannish legitimacy: the cult-clan and totem master. However much the specifics vary—and they vary immensely—I believe that is the single, simplest generalization that can adequately summarize the especially problematic "new religious" sects.

A Corroborative Scheme

In this section I would like to mention very briefly the work of Dick Anthony and Tom Robbins, because they have categorized the new religions according to three (nondevelopmental) dimensions, and these dimensions tangentially support my own criteria. Those dimensions are (1) charismatic/technical, (2) one-level/two-level, and (3) monistic/dualistic.[55]

The monistic/dualistic dimension refers to whether a group believes that all individuals are ultimately one with Godhead (regardless of particular belief), or whether only a select "in-group" can achieve exalted status. One-level religion tends to look at the manifest or *presently* available level (usually material) as the arena of salvation, whereas two-level religion tends to see liberation as occurring in a transtemporal realm. Charismatic religion tends to center on the personality of the group leader, whereas technical religion tends to center on certain impersonal techniques and practices (or traditions).

Those three dimensions are not judgmental—they simply categorize, in terms perfectly acceptable to the various groups, the *types* of cognitive maps or belief systems embraced by each group itself. It is a simple classificatory scheme (see fig. 8). Beyond that scheme, however, Robbins and Anthony have attempted to pinpoint those cells that seem to be problematic. This is what they found on the average (there are exceptions):

Negative or problematic groups tend to be one-level, while positive groups tend to be two-level. Charismatic groups tend to be more problematic than technical groups. And dualistic groups tend to be more problematic than monistic groups.

MONISTIC

	TECHNICAL	CHARISMATIC
One-Level	est Scientology Circle of Gold	Charles Manson Family Messiah's World Crusade Om Cult
Two-Level	Vedanta Hinduism Integral Yoga Zen Buddhism	Meher Baba Muktananda Bubba (Da) Free John

DUALISTIC

	TECHNICAL	CHARISMATIC
One-Level	Positive Thinking Robert Schuller Church of Hakeem	Unification Church (Moonies) People's Church (Jonestown) Synanon
Two-Level	Catholic Charismatic Renewal Groups Neo-Pentacostal Groups	Jesus Movement Christ Commune Christian Liberation Front

(Adapted by permission from D. Anthony)

FIGURE 8

Now what I am suggesting is that the developmental-structural criteria we have outlined form the substructure of the conclusions reached by Anthony and Robbins. Thus, dualistic groups tend to be more problematic than monistic groups because they foster the pseudostructural notion that only *some* people are qualified for (or can evolve to) the highest estate. This leads to an extreme emphasis on the in-group versus the out-group, which itself invites prerational regression to exclusively or overblown conformist or cultic involvement with separate and separative legitimation. Monistic religions, on the other hand, acknowledge temporary differences in development but emphasize potential equality or unity in only God.

One-level religions tend to be more problematic than two-level religions simply because they disregard vertical growth and development, and thus are always open to reinterpreting their own (however mediocre) level of structural adaptation as *the* highest level (as long as one merely adopts fully its present *legitimacy* criteria—a technique perfected by est). Genuine authenticity is ditched in favor of sturdy legitimacy, and the present level of development, however intermediate, is made the arena of final salvation. Two-level religion, on the other hand, *is* two-level because it refuses to equate the present level with the ultimate level (except in a paradoxical sense), and thereby holds open the possibility, indeed the necessity, of higher growth and development.

Charismatic religion is more problematic than technical (or traditional) religion because it necessarily relies on the authority of a sole person. Should the person prove to be less than genuine, then charismatic religions can degenerate into sole authority and isolated legitimacy—with all the problems therein. Technical religion, on the other hand, takes as ballast either an impersonal technique or a historical tradition, thereby counterbalancing the possibly idiosyncratic whims of any potentially totem master.

If we take the more problematic pole of each of these three dimensions and put them together, we arrive at the worst possible combination for a "new religion": one-level/charismatic/dualistic; second worst is one-level/charismatic/monistic. One-level, we saw, tends toward cultic separatism, and charismatic can tend toward permanent and sole authority. In short, the worst possible combinations follow exactly the general pattern of the "cult-clan and totem master." And if you look at those two cells in figure 8, you will indeed find *the* disastrous cults, Manson to Jonestown to Synanon to Moonies.

Conversely, at the other extreme, completely opposite in all three dimensions, are the monistic/two-level/technical religions—integral yoga (Aurobindo), Buddhist meditation, Vedanta, and so on—precisely the "new religions" that are at the forefront of the new and transcendental paradigm.

THE NONPROBLEMATIC GROUP

According to Anthony and Robbins, the nonproblematic group will likely be monistic, two-level, and technical. Or, more realistically, we could recommend two out of that three: if the movement is charismatic, hope it is monistic and two-level; if dualistic, hope it is technical and two-level, and so forth.

In terms of developmental-structural criteria, we can suggest the following. A positive, authentic group will likely:

1. *Be transrational, not prerational.* Specifically, it will utilize teachings and disciplines that engage higher, subtle, and/or causal levels of structural adaptation, *not* prerational or irrational engagements. These disciplines generally involve sustained practice, concentration, and will; they explicitly rest on a moral foundation, which usually includes appropriate dietary and sexual relations; and they are at least as difficult to master and complete as is, say, a doctorate.

Most orthodox sociologists, unfortunately, seem intent upon seeing *all* "new religions" as nothing but a search for a new legitimacy prompted by the breakdown of traditional, orthodox, or civil religions, and fail to even consider that some of the new religions—the expressly transrational ones—are also in search of a higher *authenticity,* an authenticity *never* offered by the old religions. Say what you will, exoteric Protestantism never offered widespread, authentic, mystical, transcendental, superconscient experience. It offered, at best, a sturdy legitimacy at the *mythic* level. Some of the new religions are explicitly and structurally in search of that authentic, not merely legitimate, dimension (e.g., Zen, Vedanta, Raja Yoga, Vajrayana, etc.).

On the other hand, these authentic disciplines ought not be confused with the plethora of "pop mystical" and "quasi-therapeutic" movements. The laid-back, blissed-out, Marin County high is exactly what these authentic disciplines are not; Beat Zen, dharma bum, go with the here/now—that, too, is exactly what these disciplines are not. In fact, virtually all of such Beat Zen approaches are based on the pre/trans fallacy. As *Serial* so whimsically put it, "Everybody knew, in these days of heightened consciousness, that the rational mind was a screw-up; the really authentic thing to do was to act on your impulses." That, of course, is exactly the prerational mood that has so distorted mystical and Eastern teachings, and, alas, that prerational approach is behind perhaps 50 percent of humanistic, transpersonal, and "human potential" movements—not to mention the "new religions" so dubiously allied with them. Even worse, this pop mysticism, all-is-one, Beat Zen, has been used by more than one religious cult to rationalize their monstrosities. ("Since all is one," said Charles Manson, "nothing is wrong.")

2. *Anchor legitimacy in a tradition.* Legitimacy offered by a tradition—say, Christianity, Sufism, Buddhism—tends to be less problematic

than legitimacy offered by a single person (leader), simply because it is less open to permanent, isolated, single-authority-figure domination and distortion. If, for example, you are a Buddhist meditation master, it is infinitely more difficult to proclaim yourself permanent authority and sole arbiter of legitimacy, because there lies behind you, as ballast, 2,500 years of corrective teaching. *Lineage,* in other words, is one of the greatest safeguards against fraudulent legitimacy.

3. *Have a phase-specific authority.* It is common knowledge that virtually all authentic Eastern or mystical traditions maintain that the guru is representative of one's own highest nature, and once that nature is realized, the guru's formal authority and function is ended. The guru is guide, teacher, or physician, not king, president, or totem master.

Buyer beware, then, of any religious movement headed by a permanent authority. Or—it comes to the same thing—any authority that cannot, at least in principle, be replaced. Even Dalai Lamas and Popes can be replaced by their successors; but there was, and could be, no replacement for Jim Jones or Charles Manson; when they die, their movements generally end or fizzle. Either religious teachers are there to bring you up to their level of understanding—in which case their authority is phase-temporary—or they exist to keep you in your place, which by definition is somewhere below or under them. The list of disastrous cult leaders is a list of permanent, not replacement and not phase-specific, "authorities."

As for the relation between the "good" gurus' authority and their disciples, I have been a participant-observer in almost a dozen nonproblematic new religious movements, Buddhist, Hindu, Taoist. In none of those groups was I ever subjected to any harsh degree of authoritarian pressure (discipline, yes, pressure, no). In fact, the authoritarian pressure in these groups never even equaled that which I experienced in graduate school in biochemistry. The masters in these groups were looked upon as great teachers, not big daddies, and their authority was always that of a concerned physician, not totem boss.

There is another way to state what a nonproblematic authority looks like. That is, a positive group:

4. *Is NOT headed by a Perfect Master.* Perfection exists only in transcendental essence, not in manifest existence, and yet many devotees consider their master "perfect" in all ways, the ultimate guru. This is almost always a problematic sign, because the devotee, in confusing essence with existence, is invited to *project* his or her own archaic, narcissistic, omnipotent fantasies onto the "perfect" guru. All sorts of archaic and magical primary process cognitions are thus reactivated; the guru

can do anything; how great the guru is; in fact, how great I must be to be among the chosen. It is an extremely narcissistic position.

But, of course, the guru eventually displays his or her human side (thank God), but the devotee is devastated, disillusioned, crushed. The devotee then either leaves, because the guru can no longer support the devotee's narcissistic glamour, or tries to rationalize the guru's actions. "Drunk? The master got drunk? Well, you know, like he was just emphasizing the evils of intoxicants by example." The notorious case involving Trungpa—he had a student stripped and verbally abused—was given all sorts of high explanations by his followers, none of whom got the correct one: Trungpa made an outrageous, inexcusable, and completely stupid mistake, period.

Good masters might indeed be divine, but they are also human. Even Christ was said to be one person (Jesus) with two natures (human and divine). Further, the fact that a guru has been thoroughly educated in soul and spirit does not mean he or she has been thoroughly educated in body and mind. I have yet to see a guru run a four-minute mile with his "perfect body" or explain Einstein's special theory of relativity with his "perfect mind." The Perfect Master cannot appear until the humanity in which he or she is grounded—until, indeed, all manifestation—has evolved to its own highest and perfect estate. Until that time, Perfection lies only in transcendence, not in manifestation, so beware the "perfect master."

There is a corollary to this; a positive group:

5. *Is NOT out to save the world.* It has often been pointed out that a very high percentage of those in problematic groups initially entered with apparently very altruistic and idealistic impulses, a desire to help people and better the world. But that "idealism" actually has a structure very similar to that of the "perfect master"—archaic and narcissistic. The underlying impulse is "me and the group are going to change the world," emphasis on me. Further, its narcissistic core is evidenced in the arrogance of the stance itself: we have the only (or the best) way, and we will change the world, that is, we will impose our ideas on the poor ignorant folks out there. Now they may not *state* it that way (I put it rather harshly); but they must in fact feel that way, more or less—how can you possibly presume to help someone, especially without being asked, unless you assume they are in need of help (i.e., inferior) and you are capable of providing it?

This narcissistic "altruism" usually shows up in a missionary zeal and proselytizing fury that no amount of high-sounding "idealism" can disguise. Such obsessive drivenness is always open to problematic occasions, not the least of which is the fact that if you have *the* way, then that end will justify virtually any means, up to and including holy war. And holy war, of course, isn't a sin, it isn't murder, because the people you are killing in order to save aren't really people—they're infidels.

On a smaller scale, in problematic new religious groups, the psychological dynamic is the same, if toned down. But any group "out to save the world" is potentially problematic, because it rests on an archaically narcissistic base that *looks* "altruistic" or "idealistic" but in fact is very egocentric, very primitive, and very capable of coming to primitive ends by primitive means.

9

Structure, Stage, and Self

PART OF THE SEARCH for a comprehensive or integral paradigm has included the attempt to compare and contrast different maps or models of consciousness, Eastern and Western, orthodox and transpersonal, humanistic and mystical. But what virtually all of these models and assessments have tended to overlook—and what, up to this point, our own mandalic maps (e.g., chapter 3) have not explicitly mentioned—is that there is a profound difference between levels or structures of consciousness and stages or phases of consciousness. The former are essentially permanent, enduring, basic components of consciousness; the latter are essentially temporary, transition, or replacement phases of consciousness. Just what that means, and why that distinction seems so important, is the topic of this chapter.

INTRODUCTION

One of the simplest facts of human ontogeny seems to be this: as various structures, processes, and functions emerge in the course of development, some of them *remain* in existence, some of them *pass*. For example, the need for food—the oral/anal alimentary structure—develops in the very earliest stages of development; so does the oral stage of psychosexual development. The need for food remains; the oral stage passes (barring fixation/repression). One never outgrows the need for food; one ideally outgrows the oral stage.

That is by no means an isolated example; in fact, as a crude approximation, it appears that about half of development remains in existence (even if modified), and about half is lost, or passes. In cognitive development, for instance, once a capacity emerges and matures—whether an image, a symbol, a concept, or a rule—it is by and large retained; the higher cognitive structures generally subsume and incorporate the lower ones. In moral development, however, the higher stages do not so much include the lower as *replace* the lower. The lower structures seem essentially to be dissolved or negated. The former might be called *basic structures;* the latter, *transition* or *replacement structures.*

As a simple analogy of how both basic and transition structures might operate in development, take the growth of the United States by annexation of new territories. Hawaii, for example, used to be a sovereign and autonomous nation itself. It possessed its own sense of "selfhood"—or nationality—and its own basic geographical structures (land, rivers, mountains, etc.). When the U.S. annexed Hawaii and eventually made it into a state, two fundamental things happened: the basic geography of Hawaii remained unchanged, and was simply incorporated as part of the U.S. The nationality of Hawaii, however—its existence as an *exclusive* nation—was simply and completely dissolved. It was *replaced* by U.S. nationality. From that point on, Hawaii could no longer declare war on other countries, make treaties, engage in international relations, and so on.

In that analogy there are three fundamental phenomena: the basic geographical *structures,* the *function* of nationality, and the replacement *stages* of actual national identities. I am suggesting that similar phenomena occur in human growth and development. The *basic structures* of human ontogeny are like the basic geographical features—even as growth includes more and more territories, the old ones are not abandoned but included. The *self-system* in human ontogeny is like nationality—it seems to include such basic functions as defense mechanisms ("war"), sense of identity, interpersonal relations, and so on. And the actual *stages of self-development* are like the stages in the growth of nationality—as a new one emerges, it negates, dissolves, and replaces the old one (barring fixation/repression).

These distinctions seem to be significant for several reasons, which I will suggest throughout this presentation. For example, I will argue that the yoga chakras are basic structures but that Maslow's hierarchical needs are replacement structures, and trying to equate them leads to theoretical difficulties. Likewise, the psychological dynamics of basic and replacement structures seem to be fundamentally different, a factor of apparently decisive importance in psychopathology. This theory also seems to suggest a rather clean way to fit Eastern concepts of levels of consciousness with Western concepts of stages of development. Finally, this overall approach has specific implications for developmental psychology in general and meditative-transpersonal psychology in particular.

Developmental psychologists are faced with two fundamental tasks. The first is to determine, as accurately as possible, the data of the human life cycle (ontogenetic development)—in particular, the *chronological sequence* of the emergence of the various psychological structures, systems, and processes. The second is to suggest (and then test) *hypothetical connections* that might account for this temporal ordering. One theoretical approach to these problems that I have found useful is to differentiate between at least two broad categories of developmental psychological phenomena, each possessing two subsets (compare Piaget,[93] and especially Flavell):[41]

Transition structures (where *A* and *B* appear to be different developmental phenomena)—*A* precedes *B* but "disappears" after *B*'s emergence.

Preliminary—*A* is a preliminary version of *B*. In this case, *A* constitutes merely the early "learning" steps in the perfection of *B*, and *A* disappears as *B* is perfected (or *A* gives way to *B*).

Replacement—*A* is not merely a preliminary version of *B*; *B* is of a significantly different order of response which substitutes for or fundamentally replaces *A*. *A* is for all practical purposes lost, and *B* takes its place.

Basic Structures—*A* precedes *B* but remains in existence after *B* appears.

Incorporation—*A* is incorporated in *B*. Once *A* is more or less developed, it serves as an ingredient, subpart, or element of *B* (when *B* emerges). *A* remains largely intact even as it is incorporated in *B*.

Mediation—*A* mediates *B*. The relation of *A* to *B* is that of means to end. *A* is not necessarily a preliminary version of *B*, nor is it necessarily incorporated by *B*, nor is it simply replaced by *B*. It mediates the emergence and development of *B* without itself necessarily becoming involved beyond that point. *A* remains in existence.

This list is not exhaustive. Further, it must be emphasized that "exact definitions of and distinctions among [the four types of relation listed above] remain vague and uncertain and so, consequently, does the assignment of instances to each" (Flavell).[41]

At the very least, it seems that there are clear differences between basic structures and transition structures. This distinction may seem elemental enough, but as Flavell[41] points out, "There has been surprisingly little attention given in the literature to this aspect of the problem." This is all the more surprising, since interest in "stages of growth," "needs" hierarchies, "passages," and stages of self-development, etc., seems to be increasing rapidly, especially in humanistic and transpersonal psychology. However, Flavell's point, which I share, is that conceptions of human development that do not at least implicitly allow for these elemental differences may be seriously limited.

In this presentation I intend to focus on the fundamental differences between basic structures and transition structures, and show that they underscore two fundamentally different types or sequences of human growth and development. In particular, I will suggest that such psychological phenomena as sensation, perception, emotion, cognition, archetype, etc., are basic structures of consciousness, whereas moral sense, modes of self, Maslow's needs hierarchy, etc., are merely transition-replacement structures in consciousness. Attempting to equate these two different patterns of growth leads to severe conceptual difficulties, but I will suggest that the two are nonetheless intimately related, since the former serves as a developmental substrate for the latter.

As an introductory example of these differences, we may point to the work of Piaget and Kohlberg. Piaget[93] has demonstrated that cognitive development proceeds through four major stage/structures: sensorimotor, preoperational thinking ("preop"), concrete operational thinking ("conop"), and formal operational thinking ("formop"). Significantly, each of these cognitive structures is necessary for, and actively contributes to, its successor's operations. Thus, sensorimotor cognition provides the raw data for preop and conop thinking, which in turn provides the material for formop logic. The point is that, even though sensorimotor intelligence emerges and is tentatively well developed by age 2, it does not then cease to be active or important but rather continues to exist and function. Besides its own appropriate activities, it also contributes to and is incorporated in higher structures of consciousness. This is a good example of what all basic structures have in common: once they emerge, they "remain."

Kohlberg's studies, on the other hand, are largely examples of stage-specific replacement structures. Kohlberg[74] has demonstrated that an individual's sense of morality develops through (at least) six major stages. Most importantly, once a person has reached a particular stage—say 5—he or she *virtually ceases all responses characteristic of the lower stages*—in this case, stages 1 through 4 (only 25% stage 4 responses, virtually 0% stage 1, 2, or 3 responses). While each junior stage is necessary for the development of its senior, the junior stages are not incorporated by the senior stages but rather are almost totally replaced by them (a point clearly suggested by Flavell).[41] That is a good example of transition-replacement structures: the lower is a precursor of the higher but is not an ingredient of the higher—it emerges only to be replaced, not incorporated.

In a sense, then, the basic structures are stages of development that are never outgrown; the transition structures are stages that *are* outgrown; the former are stages that *remain as structures,* the latter, structures that serve *basically as stages. Both* of them display structure *and* stage attributes, but with different emphasis. For this reason I will usually refer to the former as basic *structures* (although they also emerge in stages) and the latter as transition *stages* (although they are also temporary structures).

Accordingly, this presentation is divided into three sections. The first deals with the basic structures of consciousness and their development—body, mind, subtle, causal, and so on. The third deals with the major replacement stages of consciousness—moral stages, self-sense stages, Maslow's needs hierarchy, and so on. The second section, "The Self System," discusses what I propose as the theoretical link between them.

THE BASIC STRUCTURES OF CONSCIOUSNESS

Figure 9 is a schematic presentation of some of the basic structures of consciousness. This schema, up to and including vision-logic, is based explicitly on the works of Piaget, Werner, Arieti, and Baldwin, among others. The higher levels—which I have here condensed from five or six levels into two general realms, the subtle and the causal—are based largely on Hindu and Buddhist psychological systems and especially their modern interpreters, for example, Aurobindo, Guénon, Smith, Free John (see Wilber[137]).

This schema suggests that there are vertical developments *between* levels as well as horizontal developments *within* each level (the former we have called transformation; the latter, translation). Further, each level or basic structure seems to have a fairly circumscribed date of emergence, or chronological *starting* point, but no necessarily circumscribed *end* point of development. Thus, for example, formop thinking (the reflexive-formal mind) generally emerges around age twelve, but it can be further developed and exercised throughout one's entire life. The important point is not so much when it can be said to be "perfected," but rather that it rarely appears in any form prior to early adolescence. It is the emergent point, not the end point, that most helps us to locate a process on the hierarchy of structural organization (although that is by no means the only criterion; see Wilber[140]). In the schema of fig. 9, I have therefore listed, at their branch or differentiation points, some generally accepted dates of the first emergence of the various structures.

(The dates of the three most senior levels are set in parentheses because they do not yet seem to be collectively determined. Piaget had

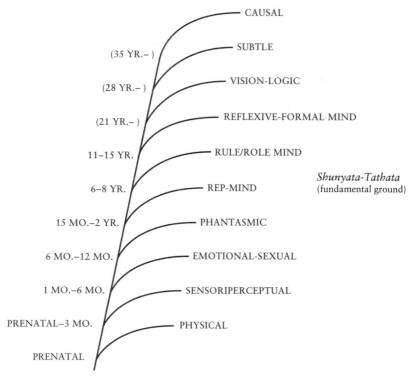

FIGURE 9. The Nested Hierarchy of Basic Structures of Consciousness

demonstrated that, barring abnormality, most individuals will reach a capacity for formop consciousness. But individuals today do not automatically develop beyond that point into the transpersonal regions of subtle, causal, or ultimate transcendence. My tentative hypothesis to account for this is that humanity on the whole has, up to this point in history, *collectively* evolved to the level of formop thinking, and therefore each individual born today is more or less assured of developing to that level. Beyond that level, however, "you're on your own." Conceivably, as more individuals strive for and reach the higher levels, as our ancestors fought for the capacity to reason, then these higher levels will be collectively bequeathed to subsequent progeny. In the meantime, my rather arbitrary earliest-point emergent dates are suggested in parentheses.)

One of the advantages of this type of branching-tree schema (first suggested by Werner) is that it clearly allows for the chronological development *of* and hierarchical ordering *between* the basic structures, without in any way denying ongoing and often parallel development *within* them. For example, the reflexive mind is of a higher order of structural organization than, say, the phantasmic or simple image mind, *and* the reflexive mind always emerges *after* the phantasmic mind—*but* the phantasmic level itself can still display significant development even as and while the reflexive mind is emerging and maturing. This occurs because once a basic structure emerges, then, as was suggested earlier, it *remains* in existence *simultaneously* with the subsequent higher structures; since it does remain it can be continuously and simultaneously developed and exercised. Significantly, this is *not* the case with transition or replacement stages. Persons at level-5 moral development do not simultaneously develop their capacity to be level-1 scoundrels. These stages, being replacements, are mutually exclusive.

It remains to give a brief description of the basic structures themselves, especially in the intermediate levels, which we heretofore have either lumped together (as "mind") or failed to define precisely.

1. *Physical.* The simple physical substratum of the organism (e.g., the first Buddhist *skandha*).

2. *Sensoriperceptual.* Here I am treating sensation, the second *skandha,* and perception, the third, as one general realm; typical sensorimotor cognition.

3. *Emotional-sexual.* The sheath of bioenergy, libido, élan vital, or *prana* (*pranamayakosha* in Vedanta, the fourth *skandha* in Buddhism, etc.).

4. *Phantasmic.* Arieti's term for the lower or image mind; the simplest form of mental "picturing" using only images.

5. *Rep-mind.* It is short for "representational mind," which is similar to Piaget's preoperational thinking. The rep or preop mind can form symbols and concepts, and thus *represent* not only things but classes, but it cannot yet *operate* on or coordinate those representations. Thus, to give a simple example, the rep-mind can count objects, but it cannot easily multiply or divide them—it lacks such *rule* coordination. Another striking feature of representational or preoperational thinking is that it *cannot easily take the role of other.* In other words, it is still very egocentric or narcissistic. In a classic series of experiments, Piaget precisely exposed the heart of preop consciousness: in a typical experiment (I am greatly simplifying), Piaget would place an object, colored green on one side and red on the other, between the experimenter and the child. The child is allowed to examine the object, and then, with the red side facing the experimenter and the green side facing the child, the child is asked what color the experimenter (the other) is now looking at. The child answers "green." The object is turned so that green is now facing the experimenter and red is facing the child, and the question is again asked: what color is the experimenter now looking at? Answer: "red." In other words, in every instance the child imagines that others are seeing exactly what the child is seeing; the child has no real capacity to take the view of other, to cognitively change roles, to assume different perspectives. Because the rep-mind is still "close to the body," it is still bound to naive sensory data. What it *sees* is largely what it *thinks;* hence the incapacity for perspective; hence the egocentrism.

6. *Rule/role mind.* This is similar to Piaget's concrete operational thinking. Conop thinking, unlike its rep-mind predecessor, can begin to take the *role* of others, and can also clearly perform *rule* operations, such as multiplication, division, and class inclusion. It is called "concrete operational" because it is still heavily bound to the immediate, gross, physical-sensory world. It can operate on the concrete world, but cannot yet operate on thought itself. One of the results of this is that conop, like its predecessors, is not a very imaginative or truly creative structure; still bound largely to the concrete and obvious world, it cannot imagine *possible* or *hypothetical* relationships. Again, in a series of extremely telling experiments, Piaget demonstrated that this structure lacks an understanding of "what if" and "as if" statements. That is, conop thinking simply cannot grasp statements such as "*If* this is the case, *then* this is the case"—it cannot grasp higher and nonobvious relationships.

7. *Formal-reflexive mind.* This is similar to Piaget's formal operational consciousness. It is the first structure that can not only think about the world but think about thinking; hence, it is the first structure that is clearly self-reflexive and introspective (although this begins in rudimentary form with the rule/role mind). As such, formop can *operate* not just on concrete things but on subjective thoughts, and thus it is the first structure capable of imagining nonobvious *possibilities.* Among other things, this means it is capable of hypothetico-deductive or propositional reasoning ("if *a,* then *b*"), which allows it to apprehend higher or noetic *relationships.* Thus, far from being an "aridly abstract" structure, with little or no creativity, it is in fact the first truly creative or imaginative structure of cognition, as Piaget's studies clearly demonstrated. In fact—and Piaget is very explicit about this—this is the first stage that a person can become, in the true and best sense of the word, a "dreamer"—one capable of imagining possibilities not given to mere sensory evidence or sensory-concrete operations. And this leads directly to the next structure:

8. *Vision-logic.* Where the formal-mind establishes higher and creative relationships, vision-logic establishes *networks* of those relationships. The point is to place each proposition alongside numerous others, so as to be able to see, or "to vision," how the truth or falsity of any one proposition would affect the truth or falsity of the others. Such panoramic or vision-logic apprehends a mass network of ideas, how they influence each other, what their relationships are. It is thus the beginning of truly higher-order synthesizing capacity, of making connections, relating truths, coordinating ideas, integrating concepts. It culminates in what Aurobindo called "the higher mind," which "can freely express itself in single ideas, but its most characteristic movement is a mass ideation, a system or totality of truth-seeing at a single view; the relations of idea with idea, of truth with truth . . . self-seen in the integral whole."[2] This, obviously, is a highly *integrative* structure; indeed, in my opinion it is the highest integrative structure in the *personal* realm; beyond it lie more transpersonal developments.

9. *Subtle.* The general region of archetypal patterns or transindividual forms. We have already given a detailed breakdown of this realm in chapter 3; the reader is referred to that chapter for specifics.

10. *Causal.* The unmanifest source or transcendental ground of all the lesser structures. Again, a detailed breakdown is given in chapter 3.

11. *Ultimate.* Passing fully through the state of cessation or unmanifest absorption, consciousness is said finally to reawaken to its abso-

lutely prior and eternal abode as spirit, radiant and all-pervading, one and many, only and all. This is Aurobindo's supermind, transcendental and unqualifiable consciousness as such. I am using the paper on which figure 9 is drawn to represent this fundamental ground of empty suchness (shunyata-tathata).

Those are some of the basic structures of consciousness. In the course of development, once they fundamentally emerge they remain in existence, not only fulfilling their own functions and carrying out their own tasks but also contributing to or even acting as ingredients of their senior structures. Although they can continue to grow, they are never outgrown.

SOME TRANSITIONAL ASPECTS ASSOCIATED WITH THE BASIC STRUCTURES

We said that the basic structures of consciousness, although defined as being essentially enduring structures, nevertheless emerge in *stages,* and therefore we would expect each basic structure to have certain temporary or phase-specific phenomena associated with it. And this indeed seems to be the case.

Since the basic structures are essentially *cognitive* structures, the temporary or phase-limited aspects of the basic structures simply concern the shifts in *cognitive maps* or *worldviews* that occur as successively new and higher structures emerge. I'll give several examples, which I'm sure will start to sound familiar:

The worldview of the lowest levels—matter, sensation, and perception (treated together)—we have called "archaic," "pleromatic," "uroboric," and so on. This worldview (so primitive as to hardly merit the name) is largely undifferentiated, global, fused, and confused—it's the way the world looks when you *only* have physical and sensoriperceptual structures. When the higher structures emerge, the archaic worldview is lost or abandoned, but the capacity for sensation and perception is not. The latter are basic and enduring structures, the former is merely the transitional or phase-temporary cognitive map associated with them.

The worldview of the emotional-sexual level we called "typhonic." It is more differentiated than the archaic and more body-stable, but it is still a largely premental world view, bound and confined to the felt present, capable of seeking only immediate release and discharge. When higher structures emerge, the *exclusively* felt-world will disappear; feelings will not.

The worldview of the phantasmic and beginning preop we called "magic." Magic is simply the way the world looks when you *only* have images and symbols, not concepts, not rules, not formal operations, not vision. As in the world of the dream, the phantasmic images display magical condensation and displacement, wish-fulfillment, and release. As higher structures emerge, the magical worldview per se is abandoned, but images and symbols themselves remain as important basic structures.

The worldview of late preop and beginning conop we called "mythic." Myth is the way the world looks when you have concepts and rules, but no formal-operations or rational capacity. When the higher levels emerge, the mythic worldview per se will die down and be replaced, but conop and rule/role will remain as important basic structures. Likewise, as development proceeds into the transrational realms, the exclusively rational worldview—the way the world looks when you only have formop—is replaced with psychic and subtle worldviews, but the capacity to reason remains, and so on.

Thus, the archaic-typhonic worldview (the way the world looks when you only have sensorimotor) is replaced by magic (the way the world looks when you only have preop), which in turn is replaced by mythic (the way the world looks when you only have conop), which itself is replaced by rational (the way the world looks to formop), and so on. The exclusive worldviews—archaic, typhonic, magic, mythic, and so on—are successively abandoned and replaced, but the basic structures themselves—preop, conop, formop, and so on—remain in existence, in awareness, functional and necessary. This is not to say that the old worldviews cannot in some cases be reactivated. All previous worldviews are available in various circumstances but are essentially contextualized by the higher structures.

THE SELF-SYSTEM

Perhaps the most striking feature of the basic structures of consciousness, at least as I have presented them, is that every one of them is *devoid of self*. That is, to no branch of the structural tree in figure 9 can you point and say, *there* is the ego, or there is the self-sense, there is the feeling of personal "me-ness." The reason, I am suggesting, is that each of those basic structures is inherently without self-sense, *but,* in the course of development, a self-system emerges and takes as its successive substrates the basic structures of consciousness. In a sense, the basic structures form rungs in a ladder upon which the self-system then climbs, matter to body to mind to subtle to causal to spirit (generating certain self-transition stages in the process, as we will see).

But our point for now is that no single rung of the ladder, nor any combination of them, can be said to constitute an inherent self. This is very similar to the Buddhist notion of the five *skandhas*—roughly, the physical body, sensation-perception, emotion-impulse, lower cognition, and higher cognition. Each of these is said to be *anatta*, or without self, yet each (temporarily and unavoidably) serves as a substrate of the self-sense. When the self-sense passes through and beyond the *skandha*-structures, and thus ceases to exist in itself, the result is nirvana or selfless radiance, in which the *skandhas* can still continue to function but without the distortions of personalization. Essentially the same idea is found in the psychology of the yoga *chakras,* the Vedanta *sheaths,* and the Mahayana *vijnanas*—each system maintains that there are several basic structures, *sheaths,* or *chakras,* that are fundamentally without separate self-sense, evidenced by the fact that, for example, the enlightened sage has *access* to *all* the basic structures—for example, physical, emotional, mental, subtle—but she or he is not exclusively identified with or bound to them—there are structures *of* consciousness but no separate self *in* consciousness.

But this suggests that the self-system, although *ultimately* illusory, nonetheless serves an absolutely necessary if *intermediate* function. Namely, it is the vehicle of development, growth, and transcendence—or, to return to our simplistic metaphor, the self is the climber of the rungs in the ladder of structural organization, a climb destined to release the self from itself, "lest the last judgement come and find me unannihilate," said Blake, "and I be seiz'd and giv'n into the hands of my own selfhood."

The self-system, then, even if ultimately illusory, is intermediately necessary, appropriate, and functional, and this brings us to the whole topic known generally as self psychology (a phrase first widely used by Maslow to describe his endeavors). It is actually only in the past few decades that self psychology—the study of what the self is, what its functions and constituents are, what developments it undergoes—has begun to receive serious attention. ("Only in the last twenty years has there been a shift in psychology back to the subject's consciousness of self.")[20]

Spearheaded by such theorists as Hartmann, Sullivan, G. H. Mead, Erikson, Rogers, Fairbairn, Kohut, Loevinger, Maslow, and Branden, the study of the nature and function of the self-system has recently become of paramount importance. Indeed, the significance of self psychology might be indicated by the fact that the claim has already been made that "Kohut and Chicago are modern equivalents of Freud and Vienna"[20]— Kohut being the author of the landmark book, *The Restoration of the Self*.

All I wish to do in this section is suggest, on the basis of the above-mentioned theorists, what seem to be some of the major characteristics of the self-system. We might begin by noting that even such antiself psychologist-philosophers as Hume and James felt that the self-sense was connected to memory, or the capacity to connect and organize *this* moment around the *preceding* moment; that is, to *appropriate* the preceding moment by the succeeding one. For James, the innermost self— "the Self of selves"—consisted of "successive acts of appropriation, sustained for as long as one can sustain them."[66]

This definition—the self as locus of appropriation—can of course be used in a perverse fashion—to explain the self by explaining it away (as both Hume and James ended up doing). The idea is that, since the self is "merely" the act of this moment's appropriation of the preceding moment, there *is* no self, only a "stream of consciousness," evidenced by the fact that the self never sees itself as subject but always and only as a stream of objects.

The problem with this theory, however, is that the act of appropriation itself does not entirely enter the stream—and thus neither does the self. Put simply, the fact that the self cannot see itself doesn't necessarily mean there is no self, just as the fact that the eye does not see itself doesn't mean there is no eye. The self as intermediate seer of the stream is not necessarily part of the stream, at least not as entirely as Hume supposed. As appropriator of the stream, the self is constituted by functions *other than* the stream, and those functions are a legitimate field of study and research. Thus, as Brandt points out, it was only after this gap (or dead end) in the Hume-James approach became evident that the study of self psychology could proceed in earnest.[20]

One of the characteristics of the self, then, might be the capacity to appropriate and organize the stream of psychological events in meaningful and coherent ways. This is not very different from the modern psychoanalytic viewpoint which defines the self as "the process of organizing." Beginning with Freud's *The Ego and the Id,* and passing on to Heinz Hartmann, Edith Jacobson, Fairbairn, Spitz, Mahler, Kohut, Blanck and Blanck, the idea of the self as an *active organizer of psychological reality* was increasingly given credence. As Brandt summarizes this general view: "The self [is not merely] a synthesis of the underlying psychic parts or substructures [i.e., not merely a sum of the streams] but an *independent organizing* principle, a 'frame of reference' against which to measure the activities or states of these substructures."[20] Thus, in line with all the above, our first characteristic might be that the self is the executor of psychological organization, integration, and coordination.

In the same way and for the same reasons, the self might be viewed as the *locus of identification*. This is perhaps the most cogent definition or characteristic of the self-system, for the self, in appropriating and organizing the stream of structural events, creates for itself a *selective identity* in the midst of those occasions. This seems perfectly normal and necessary—we need only think of the disastrous results of the incapacity to form a stable self-identity (e.g., Erikson's "identity crisis") or the breakdown of self-identity in the borderline psychoses and neuroses (cf. Kernberg). As a simple generalization, then, I will speak of the self as the locus of identification as well as the center of the sense of identity— the intuitive apprehension of proximate "I-ness" which correlates with the act of appropriation.

Finally, the self might be thought of as the navigator of development, for at any point on the ladder of basic structures (except the two end limits), the self is faced with several different "directional pulls." On the one hand, it can (without limits) choose to remain on its present level of structural organization, or it can choose to release its present level in favor of another. If it releases its present level, it can move up the hierarchy, or it can move down. *On* a given level, then, the self is faced with preservation versus negation, holding on versus letting go, living that level versus dying to that level, identifying with it versus dis-identifying from it. *Between* levels the self is faced with ascent versus descent, moving up the hierarchy to levels of increasing structural organization and integration or moving down to less organized and integrative structures. We have already discussed these factors in chapter 7. For convenience, I'll simply reproduce the figure (see page 407).

The self is located, so to speak, at the crossroads of the display. It must balance the two dilemmas—preserve/release and ascend/descend— and navigate its developmental course of those four compass points. The self does not merely float down the stream of consciousness—for better

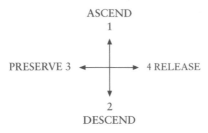

or worse, it pushes and pulls, holds on and lets go, ascends and descends, preserves and releases. How the self as "navigator" handles the resultant tensions and functional dilemmas appears to be a large part of the story of self-development and self-pathology.

Now, *if* the self is indeed the locus of organization, identification, and navigation, then we might expect the course of self-development to include the following: As each of the basic structures begins chronologically to emerge and develop, the self would *appropriate* those structures or *identify* with them (the self as the locus of identification). Once identified with a structure, the self, or the self's preservation drive (#3), would seek to consolidate and integrate the resultant overall self-complex (self plus appropriated basic structure; incidentally, note that the self's world view would be that of the appropriated basic structure—archaic or magic or mythic, etc.). This initial identification, consolidation, and preservation is normal, necessary, appropriate.

If, however, the self *as* self is to *ascend* the hierarchy of structural organization—to grow—then eventually it must *release* or negate its *exclusive* identification with the lower level (or levels) in order to allow a higher identification with more senior levels of structural organization. It must accept the "death," negation, or release (#4) of the lower level—*it must dis-identify with or detach from* an exclusive involvement with that level—in order to ascend (#1) to the greater life, unity, and integration of the next higher level (or levels) of structural organization. Once on the *new* level, the self then seeks to consolidate, fortify, and preserve the self-complex of *that* level (via factor #3), until it is once again strong enough to accept the death of that level, release or negate it, and so ascend to the next developmental level.

Thus, both preservation and negation, or life and death, apparently have important *phase-specific* tasks to accomplish. It is by the preservation-drive that a given level is appropriated, developed, consolidated, and integrated—only by making a level "its own" can the self intimately

organize it. Once that task is accomplished, however, it is only by negation that the self can die to its exclusive identification with that level and
thus ascend to the next higher integration. Pathology seems to develop
if either (or both) of these phase-specific tasks is misnavigated. For example, *fixation* might be thought of as *morbid preservation*—a failure
to release, negate, or die to a given level; the individual thus remains
obsessed with gratifications he or she ought otherwise to have "outgrown." On the other hand, *repression* might be viewed as a type of
morbid negation—a premature death; it is dis-identifying with a component before it is properly integrated, appropriated, and consolidated; the
component is thus merely split off from the personality. The necessary
dis-identification process becomes merely perverse dissociation.

In normal development, the phase-specific task of dis-identification
from a given level seems to serve an extremely important function—
namely, to denude that level of self (since self is the locus of identification). This phase-specific dis-identification does not destroy the level or
the basic structure itself, but merely releases it from being the intermediately necessary substrate of the separate self-sense and returns it to its
prior state of *anatta,* or selfless function and service. To return to our
ladder metaphor: at each stage of growth, as the self steps from lower
rung to a higher, the rungs of the ladder are not destroyed, deformed, or
discarded. What *is* destroyed is the self's exclusive attachment to that
rung.

We are now in a position to examine those self structures that are
negated or released—they are, we have said, examples of transition-replacement structures. In particular, what we will be examining are the
various *self-stages* constructed by a series of *exclusive identifications*
with the hierarchic levels of structural organization or basic structures.
As we will see, these "exclusivity structures" last as long as the self-
attachment to the particular basic structure lasts. Once that identification is released, that exclusivity structure is destroyed.

The Self-Stages of Consciousness

The overall suggestion of this section is that if one takes the nested hierarchy of basic structures (as presented in fig. 9) and then subjects each
level to the influence of a self-system (whose characteristics I summarized above), one will generate the basic features of the stages of development presented and described by researchers such as Maslow,

Loevinger, and Kohlberg. It is almost a process of simple mathematical mapping—for example, if the self is the seat of identification, what would the self look like if it identified with the emotional-sexual level? with the rule/role mind? with the formal mind? with the subtle? As I will try to demonstrate, by asking that question of each of the basic structures, we can generate—in precisely the same order and with quite similar descriptions—the stages of Kohlberg's moral development, Loevinger's ego development, and Maslow's needs hierarchy (to cite only the three examples I have chosen for this presentation).

I am suggesting (1) that the hierarchical stages presented by Loevinger, Kohlberg, and Maslow (also Erikson, Peck, Bull, Selman, Broughton, etc.) are referring to various aspects of *essentially similar* replacement-transition structures, and (2) that these particular types of replacement-transition structures are generated primarily by the enzyme of self-system acting on the substrate of basic structure. Since they are generated when the self's locus of identification centers more or less exclusively on successive basic structures, they can also be called "exclusivity structures."

Claim #1 is put in its strong form by Loevinger: "There is but one major source for all the conceptions of moral and ego [self] development, one thread of reality to which all of the conceptions give varying access."[78] But, to my mind, there is much room for latitude here, and I would (at this stage of our knowledge) prefer to make my own point with the weaker claim of similarity. Kohlberg, for example, feels that self-development is somewhat prior to moral development, and Selman feels that self-interpersonal development is a deep structure against which moralization occurs as surface structure (views I am inclined to agree with).

In addition to those (minor) differences, there are also variations in the comprehensiveness of the various theories of self-stages we are correlating. Thus, for each one of Maslow's stages Loevinger has two (as does Kohlberg, up to a point). It might be that Loevinger is presenting substages; it might be that Maslow was inadvertently lumping different stages together—but that is not our concern for the moment. In all of these cases—the relation of self and moral sense, the number and types of stages and substages, and so on—future research alone will decide the issues. We need only the already acknowledged fundamental similarities between these theories to make our general point; as these systems are refined, we can likewise refine our scheme.

The correlations between the basic structures of consciousness and the hierarchic stages of Maslow, Loevinger, and Kohlberg are presented in figure 10. The correlations between Maslow, Loevinger, and Kohlberg are basically those given by Loevinger herself; further, the correlations between the Piagetian basic (cognitive) structures and the stages of Kohlberg and Loevinger are those suggested by Breger and by Habermas—in any case, these correlations are not merely my own readings of the data. Until research techniques are refined, however, these authorities generally acknowledge that such correlations are open to errors of ± one stage (e.g., some theorists place moral stage 2 under conop, and stage 4 under formop, etc.; these are very important distinctions, but again, quite incidental to our overall conclusions).

Because both the lower and the upper levels are more controversial (more difficult to research and interpret), I will start my discussion of the correlations in the middle—with the representational mind.

The rep-mind, which emerges around age two and predominates consciousness until around age seven, is capable of being *aware* of others but incapable of taking the *role* of others. A self identified with the rep-mind would thus be able to react *to* others but not act in conscious conformity *with* others; to that extent, it would be a rather self-centered or narcissistic structure, aware of its own tenuous and vulnerable existence but unable to fully comprehend the others who may threaten it, with a consequent concern, above all, for its own self-protection. This is, in my opinion, Maslow's safety needs and Loevinger's self-protective stage.

Further, since the rep-mind is also still "close to the body" (Piaget's summary of preop thinking)—or still partially identified and involved with emotional-sexual impulses—this general structure, especially in its beginning development, would display Loevinger's stage of "impulsiveness." The impulsive and self-protective stages correspond to Kohlberg's first two stages of moral development—punishment and obedience (stage 1) and naive hedonism (stage 2). The point is that, since the rep-mind is still close to the body, the self identified with that mind is likewise close to the body and thus largely motivated *by* the body—by concerns over bodily pain and punishment (stage 1) or bodily hedonistic pleasure (stage 2). With little or no actual comprehension of *others,* this overall stage is indeed rightly referred to as self-protective (Loevinger), narcissistic (Freud), egocentric (Piaget), preconventional (Kohlberg), and safety-bound (Maslow).

With the emergence of the rule/role mind, the capacity to take the role or perspective of others emerges. The self identified with the role-

Basic Structures	Maslow (Needs)	Loevinger (Self-Sense)	Kohlberg (Moral Sense)	
Physical Sensoriperceptual		Autistic Symbiotic		
	(Physiological)	Beginning impulsive		
Emotive Phantasmic				
Rep-mind	Safety	Impulsive	I. Preconventional	1. Punishment/ obedience 2. Naive hedonism
Rule/role mind	Belongingness	Self-protective Conformist	II. Conventional	3. Approval of others 4. Law and order
		Conscientious-conformist		
Reflexive mind	Self-esteem	Conscientious Individualistic	III. Postconventional	5. Individual rights 6. Individual principles of conscience
Vision-logic	Self-actualization	Autonomous Integrated		
Subtle	Self-transcendence			
Causal	"			
Ultimate	"			

FIGURE 10. Correlations between Basic Structures and Various Aspects of Self-Stages (Maslow, Loevinger, and Kohlberg)

mind would thus be keenly attuned to the opinions and roles of others and to its own role in the midst of others. Further, since the role-mind is not yet capable of formal operational thinking, the self would have no inner capacity to easily judge the true roles from the false (or fraudulent) ones—it would thus tend merely to *conform* to the role assigned it, especially by authority figures. This, in my opinion, is Maslow's belongingness needs, Loevinger's conformist (and conscientious-conformist) stages, and Kohlberg's overall stage of *conventional* (conformist) morality.

The self identified with the role-mind escapes to some degree its narcissistic imprisonment in its own being and begins to enter the community of other viewpoints. Initially, however, it is "captured" by those viewpoints—hence, conformity. And the self would indeed actively *seek* this conformity because that is now its locus of identification, preservation, and life—to lose conformity is to "die." To lose face, to be an outsider, to not belong—there is the terror of the self identified with the role-mind.

By the time of adolescence, the formal-reflexive mind begins to emerge. This level is, as we saw, the first structure clearly capable of sustained self-reflection and introspection. The self identified with the reflexive mind would thus be involved in conscientious and self-inquiring modes of awareness and behavior. It would have the capacity to question conventional mores (something the role-mind could not easily do) and would thus be involved in postconventional moral decisions. No longer bound to conformity needs, the self would have to rely more on its own conscience, or its inner capacity to formally reflect and establish rationally what might be the good, the true, and the beautiful. Above all, it would have to see itself succeeding in—or at least attempting—this task, since it is now *identified* with the processes of self-reflection. Its "life" is now a process of self-reflection in the midst of other self-reflecting persons, and how it succeeds in this venture of self-reflection largely determines its own inner feelings of worth.

In my opinion, this is exactly Maslow's stage of self-esteem, Loevinger's conscientious and individualistic stages(s), and Kohlberg's postconventional morality. According to Kohlberg, the postconventional level consists of the stage of "morality by individual rights" (stage 5) and morality of "individual principles of conscience" (stage 6), which are almost exactly Loevinger's conscientious and individualistic stages, respectively.

We turn now to some of the highest levels of development, and here of course our data begin rapidly to thin out, but enough remain to conclude our general points. If the development of basic structures continues beyond the formal-reflexive mind, then—I have hypothesized—the next major basic structure is that of vision-logic, which was postulated as being the *highest personal-integrative level of consciousness*. The self identified with this level would thus be expected to attempt to fulfill the highest personal potentials it may possess, as well as to firmly integrate those it has already developed (we called the self-sense at this stage "centauric"). In my opinion, this is Maslow's stage of self-actualization, and Loevinger's integrated/autonomous stages(s). (For reasons that Kohlberg's studies "run out" at this point, see Loevinger,[78] Breger;[21] it's not that moral sensibility runs out at this stage, but that careful research into moralization has not yet been carried out beyond this stage, a situation I believe will soon be remedied.)

Beyond vision-logic lie the various levels of transpersonal structural organization—which, taken as a whole, obviously refers to Maslow's self-transcendence (a region usually ignored or denied by orthodox psychologists). The problem with even Maslow's presentation at this point, however, is that it fades out much too quickly. Although of pioneering importance in its day, Maslow's single category ("self-transcendence") slurs over the increasingly obvious fact that there are probably as many discrete stages of development beyond self-esteem as there are stages leading up to it. The transpersonal realm is far from being a single structure—it houses, in my opinion, at least five levels, perhaps as many as twelve or more (see Brown, Goleman). I simply include Maslow's highest need (self-transcendence) to finish our correlations. As research is expanded and refined, I think the existence of these higher dozen or so transpersonal levels—their characteristics, their development, and their moral correlates (such as the *bodhisattva* vow)—will become more obvious.

As for the very lowest levels, I do not think it necessary—or yet possible—to put the case as forcefully as I have for the middle realms. The reason is obvious: the lowest levels (up to and including the phantasmic) are preverbal; thus research is extremely difficult to conduct and even more difficult to interpret, and I in no way wish to hang my case on wild speculations about the first one or two years of infancy. I will simply say that, in my opinion, the studies of Piaget, Mahler, Spitz, Jacobson, and Fairbairn are definitely amenable to the theory I am here presenting. As for Loevinger's lowest levels (autistic, symbiotic, and beginning impulsive), I have simply listed them next to what I believe are the crucial correlations with the basic structures of consciousness. (Kohlberg has no correlations here because he was working solely and deliberately with verbal reports, and these early stages are entirely preverbal.) In any event, the lowest stages, as with the highest, are especially awaiting further research.

DISCUSSION

Perhaps we can now better appreciate why the self-moral stages can also be called "exclusivity stages," and how and why they differ fundamentally from the basic structures on which they rest. Take as an example the conformity stage(s)—my suggestion is that the actual *need to conform* (e.g., Maslow/Loevinger) is generated in large part by the *attachment to* the rule/role mind. Once that attachment is broken (via phase-specific negation or dis-identification), so is the conformity drive. But the rule/role mind—as a basic structure—is *not* broken; it can and does continue to function, at least as Arieti describes it, both in gathering its own information/rule-processing data and in serving as an ingredient-operand of the formal mind. And notice: A person at the rule/role mind has (barring pathology) *perfect access to and use of all the preceding and lower basic structures*—simultaneous access to the physical body, sensations, perceptions, feelings, images, and representational symbols (words). *However,* a person at the correlative level of self stage—in this example, a person at the conformity stage(s)—does *not* have access to, or does not use and simultaneously exercise, the lower self-stages (because, basically, they no longer exist). A person striving to be a conformist does not simultaneously and equally strive to be an impulsive maverick. As both Loevinger and Kohlberg demonstrated, a person at a given stage of self-moral development rarely gives responses of the lower stages (and the lower or more removed the stage, the less likely the response).

To suggest, however, that the basic structures are root supports of various self transition-stages does not imply that the latter aren't subjected to intermediate operations. This certainly seems the view of Habermas, Selman, and Kohlberg, all of whom tend to see cognitive base structures separated from moralization by interpersonal-self operations. Habermas, for instance, suggests that a single cognitive base structure, when subjected to different degrees of "interactive competence," supports two subclasses of self-moral response (Habermas's correlations of

Piaget's base cognitive structures with Kohlberg's moral responses are exactly as given in figure 10). Further, this degree of "interactive competence" is related directly to "the core of identity formation" (our self-system identification-locus). I myself have already argued (above) that between the basic structures, on the one hand, and the self-moral stages, on the other, lies the self-system and its transcribing operations. Whether this transcription process takes place in one or two stages—indeed, three or four—is an extremely important point, but one that is incidental to our general thesis. At this time, I regard Habermas's discussion, and his correlations, as the most cogent, and therefore they are the ones I have here followed.

Finally, a note on Maslow's needs hierarchy. In my opinion, Maslow's hierarchy is almost entirely one of self-stages, *not* basic structures, of consciousness. I say this because (1) it fits almost perfectly the other schemes of self-stage development, as we have already seen (and as Loevinger emphasized); and (2) it fits very poorly with the traditional maps of basic structures (or levels of consciousness).

Take, for example, the Vedanta *koshas* or sheaths of consciousness—in order of ascending structuralization, they are: the *annamayakosha,* or physical (food) level; the *pranamayakosha,* or emotional-sexual level; the *manomayakosha,* or level of mind; the *vijnanamayakosha,* or level of intuition; and the *anandamayakosha,* or level of transcendental *enstasis* (beyond which lies the selfless being of ultimate spirit, or *sahaj* Brahman). *None* of those levels directly represents a self-sense—they are first and foremost levels of consciousness, not modes of self or self-needs. The Vedanta *koshas* are, in my opinion, perfect examples of *basic structures* (not self-stages). They correlate precisely, although in condensed fashion, with the scheme presented in figure 8, *not* figure 10. The same seems to be true, I would like to emphasize, of the yogic *chakras* (Hindu and Buddhist), the Mahayana *vijnanas,* Aurobindo's levels, the Christian mystic hierarchies, and others.

The perennial traditions are certainly aware of various stage, transition, or phase-temporary phenomena, including both transitional world views *and* self-stages. Meditation, especially, is generally viewed as the unfolding of higher levels or basic structures of consciousness, but an unfolding that is accompanied by all sorts of phase-temporary events and stages (including also the fact that higher stages often include spiraling returns to and recapitulations of lower levels, in all sorts of complex patterns and combinations—see, for example, Brown and Engler's excellent account,[24] and also our own chapter 4). My point is rather that, in attempting to integrate and synthesize Eastern and Western approaches (as well as various Western approaches themselves), the differences between basic structures and transitional-stages ought to be kept in mind, lest we end up comparing apples and oranges. I have, for instance, seen probably a half-dozen attempts to equate Maslow's hierarchy with the yoga *chakras,* and they simply aren't the same phenomena, no matter how closely correlated they certainly are.

I have suggested that Maslow's hierarchy is basically one of transitional self-stages. The one exception is Maslow's physiological needs, his lowest level, which I have put in parentheses in figure 10. One never outgrows the physiological need for food, air, and so on. In other words, the physiological needs are not self-stages or transition-stages per se; nor are they prepotent (giving way to subtler needs: the need for air is never replaced, for example, by the need for belongingness). Thus, in my opinion, Maslow's physiological needs are the only basic structures in his hierarchy; they therefore ought to be replaced (à la Loevinger) with something like the symbiotic or impulsive needs (with the physiological needs moved back to the hierarchy of basic structures). Maslow's list would then be consistently a hierarchy of self-stages—self-impulsive, self-safety, self-belongingness, self-esteem, self-actualization, self-transcendence—and not physical, emotional, mental, subtle, and causal structures.

One last reason that it is important to distinguish basic structures from self-stages is that the two do not necessarily—not even usually—follow the same developmental timetable. They emerge in the same order, but not necessarily at the same time. To return one last time to our ladder analogy, the emergence of the basic structures can run far ahead of the self's willingness to "climb up" them. This, of course, raises many intriguing questions, but they are questions already faced by orthodox developmental psychologists, for it has long been acknowledged that cognitive structures are necessary but not sufficient for moral and self-development. For example, an individual can be at the basic structure of the conop mind but display a moral self-sense anywhere at or below it (but never above it). For just that reason, the actual times of emergence of the basic structures (up to and including formop) are largely *age-dependent* and relatively fixed (as evidenced, for example, by Piaget's cognitive structures and as indicated on figure 9), but the emergence of the self-stages are relatively *age-independent* (as Loevinger and Kohlberg have explained for their stage-structures). The hypothesis that the basic structures serve as substrates for the self-stages is compatible with that data.

In short, these distinctions have important implications for orthodox developmental psychology, because, even though rather elemental, they have been largely overlooked, as Flavell lamented. But they are also important for the scientists, philosophers, and psychologists who are in search of a new and higher transcendental paradigm, lest mere stages be confused with ontological structures (or vice versa). The dynamic, the timetable, the characteristics—these are all different in the development of the basic structures and the development of the self-sense through those structures. And while the former is the substrate for the latter, the two otherwise constitute different development strands.*

---

* [See *Integral Psychology* for the most recent elaborations of this model.]

10

The Ultimate State of Consciousness

Throughout this volume we have pointed out that the Absolute is both the highest state of being and the ground of all being; it is both the goal of evolution and the ground of evolution; the highest stage of development and the reality or suchness of *all* stages of development; the highest of all conditions and the Condition of all conditions; the highest rung in the ladder *and* the wood out of which the entire ladder is made. Anything less than that *paradox* generates either pantheistic reductionism, on the one hand, or wild and radical transcendentalism, on the other. Failure to grasp this paradox of instruction has led more than one modern theorist—in search of the new paradigm—to collapse and equate Spirit with any merely "holistic" findings in physics, biology, or psychology—a confusion of the sum total of the shadows in the cave with the Light beyond the cave. Accordingly, as a counterbalance to this modern and widespread pantheistic reductionism, I have throughout this book largely emphasized the developmental, transcendental, "highest rung" aspect of Spirit.

But, indeed, the other side of the paradox ought not be overlooked in the process. If Spirit is completely transcendent, it is also completely immanent. I am firmly convinced that if a new and comprehensive paradigm is ever to emerge, that paradox will be its heart. Since I have heretofore been emphasizing the transcendental or "highest rung" aspect, I can think of no better way to conclude this volume than with a sustained emphasis on the immanent or omnipresent aspect.

ONE WITHOUT A SECOND

In the *Chandogya Upanishad,* Brahman—the absolute reality, the ultimate state of consciousness—is described in glaringly simple and straightforward terms: the Absolute is "One without a second."[62] That inspired Upanishadic text does not describe the ultimate as the creator, controller, ruler, or lord of a second; neither does it speak of One opposed to a second, nor One outside a second, nor over, above, or beyond a second—but One without a second. The Absolute, in other words, is that which has nothing outside It, nothing apart from It, nothing other to It, a fact expressed in Isaiah as "I am the Lord, and there is none else." All of which means that there is really nothing outside Brahman, nothing outside the Absolute. In the words of an old Zen Master:

> All the Buddhas and all sentient beings are nothing but the One Mind, beside which nothing exists. Above, below, and around you, all is spontaneously existing, for there is nowhere which is outside the Buddha-Mind.[15]

Of course, if there were anything outside the Absolute, that would immediately impose a limitation on It, for the Absolute would then be one outside a second instead of One without a second. And so it is in this sense that Brahman, the Buddha-Mind, the Godhead is called absolutely all-encompassing, all-inclusive, and all-pervading. When the Upanishads say "All the world is Brahman," and "This, too, is Brahman"; when the *Lankavatara Sutra* proclaims that "The world is nothing but Mind," and "All is Mind"; when the *Awakening of Faith* states that "All things are only of the One Mind"; when the Taoist texts insist that "There is nothing outside the Tao; you cannot deviate from It"— well, they mean just that. To quote the apocryphal Acts of Peter:

> Thou are perceived of the spirit only, thou art unto me father, thou my mother, thou my brother, thou my friend, thou my bondsman, thou my steward: thou art All and All is in thee: and thou ART, and there is nought else that IS save thee only.[65]

This being true because, as Christ said in the Gospel of St. Thomas:

> I am the Light that is above them all, I am the All, the All came forth from Me and the All attained to Me. Cleave a piece of wood, I am there; Lift up the stone and you will find Me there.[57]

Now the statement that all the world is really Brahman usually fires up in overly imaginative minds such fancies as uniform, all-pervading, featureless but divine goo; the instantaneous and total evaporation of all diversity and multiplicity, leaving behind an immaculate but amorphous All-knowing, All-merciful, celestial Vacuum. We flounder in such mental frenzies only because we expect the statement "All is Brahman" to be a logical proposition, containing some type of mental information about the universe, and taken thus, we can only picture its meaning to be the reduction of all multiplicity to uniform, homogeneous, and unchanging mush.

But "All is Brahman" should not be mistaken as a philosophical conclusion, a logical theory, or a merely verbal explanation of reality. For the sages of every time and place have unanimously maintained that the Absolute is actually ineffable, unspeakable, utterly beyond words, symbols, and logic. And not because it is too mysterious or too sublime or too complex for words, but rather because it is too simple, too obvious, too close to be caught in the net of symbols and signs. Because there is nothing outside It, there is no way to define or classify It. As Johannes Scotus (Erigena) remarked, "God does not know Himself, what He is, because He is not a *what*; in a certain respect He is incomprehensible to Himself and to every intellect." Or, as Shankara, the Master of Vedanta Hinduism, explains:

> Now there is no class to which Brahman belongs, no common genus. It cannot therefore be denoted by words which signify a category of things. Nor can it be denoted by quality, for it is without qualities; nor yet by activity because it is without activity—"at rest, without parts or activity," according to the Scriptures. Neither can it be denoted by relationship, for it is "without a second" and is not the object of anything but its own self. Therefore it cannot be defined by word or idea; as the Scripture says, it is the One "before whom words recoil."[120]

This, indeed, is also the point of Wittgenstein's philosophy; namely, we cannot make any valid statements about Reality as a whole because there is no place outside it where we can take up a stance so as to describe it. In other words, "we could only say things about the world as a whole if we could get outside the world, if, that is to say, it ceased to be for us the whole world. . . . (But) for us, it cannot have a boundary, since it has nothing outside it."[142] And having no boundary, no limits—being one without a second—it cannot be defined or classified. You can define and classify, for example, a "fish" because there are things that are not fish, such as rocks, trees, and alligators; and drawing a mental line between what is fish and what is not fish, you are able to define and classify it. But you cannot define or say "what" Brahman is, for there is nothing It is not—being one without a second, there is nothing outside It and so nowhere to draw the classifying line.

Hence, the Absolute, the real world as it is, is also called pure Emptiness, since all definitions and propositions and statements about reality are void and meaningless. Even such statements as "Reality is the Limitless" won't quite do, for the "limitless" excludes that which is "limited." Rather, the Absolute is finally Void of all conceptual elaborations, and so even the word "void," if taken to be a logical idea, is to be denied validity. In the words of Nagarjuna:

> It cannot be called void or not void,
> Or both or neither;
> But in order to point it out,
> It is called "the Void."[124]

Since all propositions about reality are void and invalid, the same of course holds true for the statement "All is Brahman," if this statement is taken as a logical proposition. If, for instance, Brahman were taken as a concrete and categorical fact *among other facts,* then "All is Brahman" would be sheerest nonsense: as any logician will tell us, to predicate something of everything is to predicate it of nothing. But Brahman is not so much a fact among other facts, but the Fact of all facts. "All is Brahman" is not a merely logical proposition; it is more of an experiential or contemplative revelation, and while the logic of the statement is admittedly quite flawed, the experience itself is not. And the experience All-is-Brahman makes it quite clear that there is not one thing outside the Absolute, even though when translated into words, we are left with nonsense. But, as Wittgenstein would say, although It cannot be *said,* It can be *shown.*

Now the insight that there is nothing outside of Brahman implies also that there is nothing *opposed* to It; that is to say, the Absolute is that which has no opposite. Thus It is also called the Nondual, the Not-two, the No-opposite. To quote the third Patriarch of Zen:

All forms of dualism
Are ignorantly contrived by the mind itself.
They are like visions and flowers in the air:
Why bother to take hold of them?
When dualism does no more obtain,
Even Oneness itself remains not as such.
The True Mind is not divided—
When a direct identification is asked for,
We can only say, "Not-Two!"[116]

But, as Seng-ts'an points out, "Not-two" does not mean just One. For pure Oneness is most dualistic, excluding as it does its opposite of Manyness. The single One opposes the plural Many, while the Nondual embraces them both. "One without a second" means "One without an opposite," not One opposed to Many. Thus, as we have already hinted, we mustn't picture the Absolute as excluding diversity, as being an un-differentiated monistic mush, for Brahman embraces both unity and multiplicity.

Now the import of what has been said thus far is that since there is really nothing outside the Nondual, there is no point in either space or time where the Absolute is not. And it isn't that a *part* of the Absolute is present in every thing—as in pantheism—for that is to introduce a boundary within the infinite, assigning to each thing a different piece of the infinite pie. Rather, the *entire* Absolute is completely and wholly present at every point of space and time, for the simple reason that you can't have a different infinite at each point. The Absolute, as St. Bona-venture put it, is "A sphere, whose center is everywhere and whose cir-cumference nowhere," so that, in the words of Plotinus, "while it is nowhere, nowhere is it not."

Yet notice that the Absolute can be entirely present at every point of space only if It is itself spaceless. Just as, to use Eckhart's example, your eyes can see things which are colored red only because your eyes them-selves are without red color or "red-less," so also the Absolute can em-brace all space because It is itself without space or "space-less."

Thus, the infinite is not a point, or a space—even a very Big Space—or a dimension among other points, spaces, and dimensions; but is rather point-less, spaceless, dimensionless—not one among many but one with-out a second. In just this fashion, the *whole* of the infinite can be present at all points of space, for being itself spaceless, it does not contend with space and so is free to utterly embrace it, just as water, being shape-less and form-less, can fill containers of all shapes and forms. And since the infinite is present in its entirety at every point of space, *all* of the infinite is fully present right HERE. In fact, to the eye of the infinite, no such place as *there* exists (since, put crudely, if you go to some other place over *there,* you will still only find the very same infinite as *here,* for there isn't a different one at each place).

And so also with time. The Absolute can be present in its entirety at every point of time only if It is itself timeless. And that which is timeless is eternal, for, as Wittgenstein rightly pointed out, Eternity is "not infinite temporal duration but timelessness." That is to say, Eternity is not everlasting time but a moment without time. Hence, being timeless, *all* of Eternity is wholly and completely present at every point of time—and thus, all of Eternity is already present right NOW. To the eye of Eternity, there is no *then,* either past or future.

Point without dimension or extension, Moment without date or duration—such is the Absolute. And while It is nowhere, nowhere is It not. That, simply, is the meaning of omnipresence—the Absolute is simultaneously present everywhere and everywhen in its entirety. "Who sees not God everywhere sees him truly nowhere."

With all of the foregoing, it won't be hard to understand that all metaphysical traditions have universally claimed that the Absolute is literally Unattainable. For if it were possible for a person to *attain* the Absolute, this would imply moving from a point where the Absolute is not to a point where It is—yet there is no point where It is not. In other words, it's impossible to attain It because it's impossible to escape It in the first place. And so it is important to realize that since the Absolute is already one with everything everywhere, we can in no way manufacture or attain to our union with It. No matter what we do or don't do, try to do or try not to do, we can never attain It. In the words of Shankara:

> As Brahman constitutes a person's Self, it is not something to be attained by that person. And even if Brahman were altogether different from a person's Self, still it would not be something to be attained; for as it is omnipresent it is part of its nature that it is ever present to everyone.[120]

Or read carefully the following from the great Zen Master Huang Po:

> That there is nothing which can be attained is not idle talk; it is the truth. You have always been one with the Buddha, so do not pretend you can attain to this oneness by various practices. If, at this very moment, you could convince yourselves of its unat-

tainability, being certain indeed that nothing at all can ever be attained, you would already be Bodhi-minded. Hard is the meaning of this saying! It is to teach you to refrain from seeking Buddhahood, since any search is doomed to failure.[15]

Or, just to push the point home, consider the words of Sri Ramana Maharshi:

There is no reaching the Self. If Self were to be reached, it would mean that the Self is not here and now but that it has yet to be obtained. What is got afresh will also be lost. So it will be impermanent. What is not permanent is not worth striving for. So I say the Self is not reached. You *are* the Self; you are already That.[95]

Thus the Absolute, the Buddha-Mind, the real Self cannot be attained. For to attain union with the Absolute implies bringing together two things, and yet in all reality there is only One without a second. The attempt to bring the soul and God together merely perpetuates the illusion that the two are separate. As the above quotes make clear, the Self is already present, and we're already It.

Now it is sometimes said that whereas we are indeed already one with the Absolute, most of us nevertheless do not realize that this is so; that whereas union with God cannot be attained, *knowledge of that union can be attained;* that whereas we cannot manufacture the Supreme Identity, we can realize it. And that realization, that attainment of the knowledge of our Supreme Identity, is everywhere said to be the very Ultimate State of Consciousness, enlightenment, satori, *moksha, wu,* release, liberation.

Now there is certainly some degree of truth in the statement that we are all Buddhas but don't know it, and that we must therefore attain this knowledge for complete liberation. But on closer inspection this is not entirely satisfactory. For by the truth of nonduality, to know God is to be God: the two are not at all separate. So there is not one thing called God and another thing called knowledge of God. Rather, it is that knowledge is but one of the names of God. And if we cannot attain God, neither can we attain knowledge of God—since the two are actually one and the same. Put it another way: since the Ultimate State of Consciousness *is* Brahman, and since Brahman cannot be attained, neither can the Ultimate State of Consciousness.

If this conclusion seems odd, then go ahead and suppose, on the contrary, that the Ultimate State of Consciousness could be attained, or reached, or entered. What would that imply? Only that that state of consciousness which you *entered* would necessarily have a beginning in time; that that state of consciousness is therefore not timeless and eternal; and that, in short, that state of consciousness is precisely not the Ultimate State of Consciousness. The Ultimate State of Consciousness cannot be entered because it is timeless, without beginning or end, and conversely, any state of consciousness you can enter is not the Ultimate State of Consciousness.

Hsuan-tse heard of a meditation master named Chih-huang, and when he went to visit him, Chih-huang was meditating.

"What are you doing there?" inquired Hsuan-tse.

"I am entering into a *samadhi,* a highest state of consciousness."

"You speak of *entering,* but how do you enter into a *samadhi*—with a thoughtful mind or with a thoughtless mind? If you say with a thoughtless mind, all nonsentient beings such as plants or bricks could attain *samadhi.* If you say with a thoughtful mind, all sentient beings could attain it."

"Well," replied Chih-huang, "I am not conscious of either being thoughtful or being thoughtless."

Hsuan-tse's verdict was swift-coming. "If you are conscious of neither, you are actually in *samadhi* all the time; why do you even talk at all of entering into or coming out of it? If, however, there is any *entering* or *coming out,* it is not the Great *Samadhi.*"[116]

So what does it mean that you can't enter the Ultimate State of Consciousness? What does it mean that never, under any circumstances, at any time, through any effort, can you enter the Ultimate State of Consciousness? Only that the Ultimate State of Consciousness is already fully and completely present. And that means the Ultimate State of Consciousness is in no way different from your ordinary state of consciousness or from any other state of consciousness you might have at this or any moment. "Your ordinary mind, just that is the Tao," says Nansen. Whatever state you have now, regardless of what you think of it and regardless of its nature, is absolutely It. You therefore cannot enter It because you have always been in It from the very beginning.

Of course, this should have been obvious all along. Since the Ultimate State of Consciousness is Brahman, and since Brahman is absolutely all-inclusive, the Ultimate State of Consciousness is equally all-inclusive. That is to say, the Ultimate State of Consciousness is not a state among other states but a state inclusive of all states. This means most emphatically that the Ultimate State of Consciousness is not an altered state of consciousness, for—being one without a second—there is no alternative to It. The Ultimate State of Consciousness is perfectly compatible with every state of consciousness and altered state of consciousness, and there is no state of consciousness apart from or outside of It. As René Guénon explains it, "The state of *Yogi* is not then analogous with any particular state whatsoever, but embraces all possible states as the principle embraces all its consequences."[56]

All of this points inescapably to the fact that you not only are already one with the Absolute, you already know you are. As Huang Po said, "The Buddha-Nature and your perception of it are one." And since, as we have seen, the Buddha Nature is always present, then so is your perception of It. If you maintain that you are Buddha but don't know it, you necessarily introduce a very subtle dualism between the Buddha Nature and your perception of It, imagining that the one is while the other is yet to come, and such is not possible. Truly, as we cannot manufacture the Absolute, we cannot manufacture knowledge of the Absolute. Both are already present.

> Rekison Roshi was asked by a monk, "What is this 'apprehending of a sound and being delivered'?" Rekison took up some fire-tongs, struck the firewood, and asked, "You hear it?" "I hear it," replied the monk. "Who is not delivered?" asked Rekison.[116]

That the Ultimate State of Consciousness is not a state apart or in any way different from the Present State of Consciousness is the point so many people seem to miss. Hence, they misguidedly seek to engineer for themselves a "higher" state of consciousness, radically different from their present state of awareness, wherein it is imagined that the Supreme Identity can be realized. Some imagine that this particular and exclusive "higher" state of consciousness is connected with specific brain-wave patterns, such as predominant amounts of high amplitude alpha waves. Others maintain that an individual's neurological system must undergo several changes, evolving as it were to a point where this "higher" state of consciousness can finally emerge. Some even believe that physiological stress has to be removed through meditative techniques and *then* the "higher" state of consciousness will result. But all this chatter totally overlooks the inescapable fact that *any* state of consciousness that can be entered, or that emerges after various practices, must have a beginning in time, and thus is not and could never be the timeless and eternal Ultimate State of Consciousness.

Moreover, to imagine that certain steps can be taken in order to realize the Ultimate State of Consciousness and attain liberation is actually to make the Ultimate State an *effect*. That is to say, to believe certain stages or various steps or particular practices can lead to liberation is inescapably to make liberation the *result* of these steps, the *consequence* of these stages, the *effect* of these causes. Yet long ago Shankara saw the utter absurdity of such a notion:

> If Brahman were represented as supplementary to certain actions, and release were assumed to be the effect of those actions, it would be temporal, and would have to be considered merely as something holding a preeminent position among the described temporal fruits of actions with their various degrees.
>
> But as Release is shown to be of the nature of the eternally free Self, it cannot be charged with the imperfection of temporality. Those, on the other hand, who consider Release to be the effect of something maintain that it depends on the action of mind, speech, or body. So, likewise, those who consider it to be a mere modification. Noneternality of Release is the certain consequence of these two opinions; for we observe in common life that things which are modifications, such as sour milk and the like, and things which are effects, such as jars, etc., are noneternal.[120]

And what of the opinion that we all have Buddha Nature but as yet just don't know it? And that through some sort of action, such as meditation, we can attain to this knowledge? Shankara is decisive:

> It might be said that Release might be a quality of the Self which is merely hidden and becomes manifest on the Self being purified by some action; just as the quality of clearness becomes manifest in a mirror when the mirror is cleaned by means of the action of rubbing. This objection is invalid, we reply, because the Self cannot be the abode of any action. For an action cannot exist without modifying that in which it abides. But if the Self were modified by an action its noneternality would result therefrom; an altogether unacceptable result.[120]

In short, since the Ultimate State of Consciousness is your Present State of Consciousness, there is obviously no way to cause, produce, effect, or manufacture that which is already the case—and even if you could, the result would be noneternal. But when we imagine that the Ultimate State of Consciousness is different from the state of consciousness we have now, we then foolheartedly seek ways to usher in this supposedly different and miraculous state of "higher" consciousness, totally ignorant of the fact that even if we get this "higher" state of consciousness it is not the Ultimate State because it is the result of certain steps and therefore has a beginning in time. And yet, think we, some knowledge of the Absolute awaits us in this particular higher state of consciousness. But as Eckhart so forcefully explained, if we imagine God can be found in a *particular* state of consciousness, then when that state slips from us, that god slips with it.

"Contrary to widespread belief," writes Alan Watts, "the knowledge and contemplation of the infinite is not a state of trance, for because of the truth that there is no opposition between the infinite and the finite, knowledge of the infinite may be compatible with all possible states of mind, feeling, and sensation. [This] knowledge is an inclusive, not an exclusive, state of consciousness."[125]

In fact, it's only because we keep insisting that the Ultimate State of Consciousness be different from the Present State of Consciousness that makes it so hard to admit to ourselves that we already know our Buddha Nature. We imagine, for instance, that nirvana is different from samsara, that enlightenment is different from ignorance, that Brahman is different from maya (illusion). Yet Nagarjuna clearly states: "There is no difference whatsoever between nirvana and samsara; there is no difference whatsoever between samsara and nirvana. There is not the slightest bit of difference between these two." And Hsuan-chueh begins his celebrated *Song of Realizing the Tao:*

See you not that easygoing Man of Tao, who has abandoned learning
    and does not strive?
He neither avoids false thoughts nor seeks the true,
For ignorance is in reality the Buddha nature,
And this illusory, changeful body is the body of Truth.[116]

And pure Vedanta has never understood maya or illusion to be different from Brahman, but rather as something Brahman is doing. And yet we seek to escape samsara as if it weren't nirvana; we try to overcome ignorance as if it weren't enlightenment; we strive to wipe out maya as if it weren't Brahman. Fénelon, Archbishop of Cambrai, has the only acceptable comment on this state of affairs: "There is no more dangerous illusion than the fancies by which people try to avoid illusion."

Hence, all seeking, spiritual or otherwise, is ultimately irrelevant; and viewing the Ultimate State of Consciousness as a particular altered state of consciousness is absolutely unacceptable. I am not at all denying that some very miraculous altered states of consciousness can certainly be attained—they can be attained for the simple reason that they are partial and exclusive and hence can be developed and perfected. But what has that to do with the all-inclusive Ultimate State of Consciousness? You can surely train yourself to enter alpha states; you can develop your ability with a mantra; you can learn to halt all thoughts from rising—but only because these are exclusive and partial states of consciousness apart from other states, and for that very reason can selectively be given more attention and effort than the others. But you cannot train yourself to enter that state of consciousness which you have never left and which includes all possible states of consciousness. There is just no place outside the Ultimate State of Consciousness where you can take up a position to train yourself in It. Listen to Huang Po once again:

> Bodhi (knowledge of the Buddha-Nature) is no state. The Buddha did not attain to it. Sentient beings do not lack it. It cannot be reached with the body nor sought with the mind. All sentient beings are already of one form with Bodhi.
>
> If you know positively that all sentient beings are already one with Bodhi, you will cease thinking of Bodhi as something to be attained. You may recently have heard others talking about this "attaining of the Bodhi-Mind," but this may be called an intellectual way of driving the Buddha away. By following this method, you only APPEAR to achieve Buddhahood; if you were to spend aeon upon aeon in that way, you would only achieve the Sambhogakaya (blissful states) and Nirmanakaya (transformed states). What connection would all that have with your original and real Buddha-Nature?[15]

Upon hearing this, many of us nevertheless feel that "Yes, I do understand that somehow I must already be one with the Absolute, but I still just don't know it!" But that is manifestly not true. The very fact that you are now seeking Buddha shows that you already know you are Buddha. "Console thyself," wrote Pascal, " 'thou wouldest not seek Me if thou hadst not found Me." And St. Bernard expressed the very same sentiment, "No one is able to seek Thee, save because he has first found." Or, as Blyth put it, "In order to be enlightened, we must first be enlightened."

Of course, individuals might indeed feel that they don't really know It, despite all the best assurances of the Masters. And the reason It might not seem evident to them is the somewhat peculiar nature of this ever-present Bodhi-knowledge; namely, it is nondual. A person doesn't seem to know It only because he is so used to seeing things dualistically, where he as subject holds out and looks at an object, either mental or physical, and feels that, yes, he sees that object very clearly, with "he" and "that object" being two different things altogether. He, as subject, then naturally assumes that he can also see Brahman in the same way, as an object out there to look at and grasp. It thus seems that he, the grasper, should be able to get Brahman, the grasped. But Brahman won't split into getter and got. In all of reality there is only One without a second, and yet out of habit the person tries to make It two, to split It so as to finally grab It and exclaim, "Aha! I've got It!" He tries to make it an experience to be grasped among other experiences. But Brahman is not a particular experience, being one without a second, and so he is left grasping at ghosts and clutching at smoke.

And so it is that we all inevitably end up feeling that we just can't see It, no matter how hard we try. *But the fact that we always can't see It is perfect proof that we always know It.* In the words of the *Kena Upanishad:*

> If you think that you know Brahman well, what you know of Its nature is in reality but little; for this reason Brahman should still be more attentively considered by you. . . . Whoever among us understands the following words: "I do not know It, and yet I know It," verily that man knows it. He who thinks that Brahman is not comprehended, by him Brahman is comprehended; but he who thinks that Brahman is comprehended knows It not. Brahman is unknown to those who know It and is known to those who do not know It at all.[62]

That is, the very state of not-knowing Brahman IS the Ultimate State of Consciousness, *and that is exactly how you feel right now.* Says a Zen poem:

When you seek to know It, you cannot see It.
You cannot take hold of It,
But neither can you lose It.
In not being able to get It, you get It.
When you are silent, It speaks.
When you speak, It is silent.
The great gate is wide open to bestow alms,
And no crowd is blocking the way.[124]

Since you are Brahman, you obviously can't *see* Brahman, just as, for instance, an eye cannot see itself and an ear cannot hear itself. The *Brihadaranyaka Upanishad* says, "Thou couldst not see the seer of sight, thou couldst not hear the hearer of hearing, nor perceive the perceiver of perception, nor know the knower of knowledge." And the *Zenrin* puts it simply, "Like a sword that cuts, but cannot cut itself; Like an eye that sees, but cannot see itself." In fact, if your eye tries to see itself, it sees absolutely nothing. Likewise, the Void is what you right now don't see when you try to look for Brahman. That Void is exactly what you have always been looking for and have always never found nor seen. And *that* very not-seeing is It. And since you always don't see It, you always know It. Because any individual, explains St. Dionysius, "by the very fact of not seeing and not knowing God, truly understands him who is beyond sight and knowledge; knowing this, too, that he is in all things that are felt and known."

As you rest in your present awareness, you might perceive some sensation in the body, or you might be aware of thoughts passing by in front of the mind's eye, or you might be seeing the clouds float by. But there is one thing you cannot see: you cannot see the Seer. You see thoughts, things, clouds, mountains, but never the Seer, never the Self, never the pure Witness. Precisely because it sees thoughts, it is not itself a thought; precisely because it sees things, it is not itself a thing—it is radically free of all such objects, all such sights, all such ripples in the stream.

So what is this Witness in you that is aware of you? Who is aware of your thoughts, your feelings, your self, right now? What is that pure awareness? Of course, you cannot see this Seer! Anything you see is just more objects: you see thoughts float by, clouds float by, sensations float by. But the Seer itself is not an object, and thus can never be seen.

And so, for just a moment, simply be the Seer. Simply rest as the Seer, rest as the Witness, rest as that which sees but cannot be seen. As you rest in that emptiness, that absence, that clearing, that opening, you will begin to sense a vast freedom, a vast release from things seen, a vast release from the pain of being an object. You will rest as Emptiness, as the ancient Unseen, as the primordial Unborn, floating in the great Liberation.

When you rest as Emptiness, you are in touch with your Original Face, the face you had prior to the Big Bang. This great Emptiness is the primordial background that has always already been your True Self, a Self never lost and therefore never found. This Emptiness is the great background in which the entire universe arises moment to moment. And this great background is—by any other name—God.

That which is aware of you right now, is God. That which is your own innermost awareness, right now, is God. That which sees but is never seen, is God. That Witness in you right now, ever present as pure Presence, is God. That vast Freedom, that great Emptiness, that primordial Purity, your own present state of awareness, right now, is God. And thus, most fundamentally and forever, it is God who speaks with your tongue, and listens with your ears, and sees with your eyes, this God who is closer to you than you are to yourself, this God who has never abandoned you and never could, this God who is every breath you take, the very beat of your tender heart, who beholds the entire majesty before your eyes, yet is never, never seen.

Still don't see It? How right you already are. For each and every one of us, "by the very fact of not seeing and not knowing God, truly understands him who is beyond sight and knowledge; knowing this, too, that he is in all things that are felt and known."

Epilogue

THE POSSIBILITY of a genuinely integral paradigm is an alluring notion. This book, of course, has presented no more than a few fragments of what such a paradigm might look like. In other books I have tried to suggest what form the paradigm might take in the fields of anthropology and history, developmental psychology, sociology, and psychotherapies (see *A Brief History of Everything* for a summary). The real point of this book, however, was not so much to present a final paradigm—we are decades away from such—as to point out some of the major obstacles now blocking its emergence. And we saw a half dozen or so: category error, the pre/trans fallacy, the confusion of legitimacy and authenticity, the confusion of structure and stage, the failure to grasp the paradox of spirit as goal and ground. For there are now a tremendous number of gifted scholars working on or toward a comprehensive paradigm, and yet most of them, in my opinion, fall into one or more of those fallacies. The most common seems to be to take the results from a monological science (physics, physiology, systems theory) and attempt to stretch them, as it were, to cover what in fact can only be covered with dialogical and translogical sciences. This is, of course, a profound category error. The next most common seems to be the pre/trans fallacy—especially in psychology and sociology; and next, structure-stage confusion.

But in any event, I have simply offered what seem to me to be several such fallacies or errors, with the hope that the quest for the new paradigm may more easily move forward. I have suggested and outlined what I think aspects of the new paradigm might look like. But what I most wanted to leave with the reader was not a final view, but hints on how better to reach that view; not a final knowledge, but a balance in the quest itself; not a way to stop, but a way to carry on. And, indeed, we might eventually discover that the new paradigm is nothing but the quest itself; that the only constant is the search; that Being, as Hegel said, is simply the process of its own becoming. When a famous Zen Master was asked the meaning and nature of absolute reality, he replied only: "Walk on."

References

1. Arieti, S. *The Intrapsychic Self.* New York: Basic Books, 1967.
2. Aurobindo. *The Life Divine/The Synthesis of Yoga.* Pondicherry: Centenary Library, XVIII-XXI, n.d.
3. Ayer, A. *Language, Truth and Logic.* New York: Dover, 1952.
4. Baldwin, J. *Genetic Theory of Reality.* New York: Putnam, 1915.
5. ———. *Thought and Things.* New York: Arno Press, 1975.
6. Barrett, W. (ed.). *Zen Buddhism: Selected Writings of D. T. Suzuki.* New York: Anchor, 1956.
7. Battista, J. "The Holographic Model, Holistic Paradigm, Information Theory and Consciousness." *ReVision,* vol. 1, no. 3/4, 1978.
8. Becker, E. *The Denial of Death.* New York: Free Press, 1973.
9. Berdyaev, N. *The Destiny of Man.* New York: Harper & Row, 1960.
10. Bernstein, J. "A Cosmic Flow." *American Scholar,* Winter-Spring 1979.
11. Beynam, L. "The Emergent Paradigm in Science." *ReVision,* vol. 1, no. 2, 1978.
12. Blake, W. *The Portable Blake.* A. Kazin (ed.). New York: Viking, 1968.
13. Blanck, G., and Blanck, R. *Ego Psychology: Theory and Practice.* New York: Columbia Univ. Press, 1974.
14. Blanco, M. *The Unconscious as Infinite Sets.* London: Duckworth, 1975.
15. Blofeld, J. *The Zen Teachings of Huang Po.* New York: Grove, 1958.
16. ———. *The Tantric Mysticism of Tibet.* New York: Dutton, 1970.
17. Bohm, D. "A Conversation with David Bohm." Conducted by Renée Weber. *ReVision,* vol. 1, no. 3/4, 1978.
18. Bohm, D., and Hiley, B. "Some Remarks on Sarfatti's Proposed Connection between Quantum Phenomena and the Volitional Activity of the Observer-Participator." Pre-print, Dept. of Physics, Birkbeck College, Univ. of London, 1975.
19. Branden, N. *The Psychology of Self-esteem.* New York: Bantam, 1971.
20. Brandt, A. "Self-confrontations." *Psychology Today,* October 1980.

21. Breger, L. *From Instinct to Identity.* Englewood Cliffs: Prentice-Hall, 1974.
22. Broughton, J. *The Development of Natural Epistemology in Adolescence and Early Adulthood.* Doctoral dissertation, Harvard, 1975.
23. Brown, D. "A Model for the Levels of Concentrative Meditation." *Internat. J. Clinical Exper. Hypnosis,* 25, 1977.
24. Brown, D., and Engler, J. "A Rorschach Study of the Stages of Mindfulness Meditation." *Journal of Transpersonal Psychology,* vol. 12, no. 2, 1980.
25. Brown, G. *Laws of Form.* New York: Julian, 1972.
26. Brown, N. O. *Life Against Death.* Middletown: Wesleyan Univ. Press, 1959.
27. Bubba (Da) Free John. *The Paradox of Instruction.* San Francisco: Dawn Horse, 1977.
28. Bull, N. *Moral Judgment from Childhood to Adolescence.* Beverly Hills: Sage, 1969.
29. Campbell, J. *The Masks of God,* 4 vols. New York: Viking, 1959–68.
30. Capra, F. *The Tao of Physics.* New York: Bantam, 1977.
31. Copleston, F. *A History of Philosophy.* New York: Image, 1959.
32. Crittenden, J. "A Review of Person/Planet." *ReVision,* vol. 2, no. 1, 1979.
33. Dean, S. (ed.). *Psychiatry and Mysticism.* Chicago: Nelson-Hall, 1975.
34. Deikman, A. "Deautomatization and the Mystic Experience." *Psychiatry,* vol. 29, 1966.
35. Descartes, R. *Rules for the Direction of the Mind.* Quoted in Copleston (reference #31, above).
36. Deutshe, E. *Advaita Vedanta.* Honolulu: East-West Center, 1969.
37. Erikson, E. *Childhood and Society.* New York: Norton, 1963.
38. Fairbairn, W. *An Object Relations Theory of the Personality.* New York: Basic Books, 1954.
39. Fenichel, O. *The Psychoanalytic Theory of Neurosis.* New York: Norton, 1945.
40. Feuerstein, G. *Textbook of Yoga.* London: Rider, 1975.
41. Flavell, J. "Concept Development." In P. Mussen (ed.), *Carmichael's Manual of Child Psychology,* vol. 1. New York: Wiley, 1970.
42. Flavell, J., and Wohlwill, J. "Formal and Functional Aspects of Cognitive Development." In D. Elkind and J. Flavell (eds.), *Studies in Cognitive Development: Essays in Honor of Jean Piaget.* New York: Oxford Univ. Press, 1969.
43. Freud, S. *Beyond the Pleasure Principle.* S.E. vol. 18. London: Hogarth, 1960.
44. ———. *The Ego and the Id.* S.E. vol. 19. London: Hogarth, 1961.
45. ———. *New Introductory Lectures.* S.E. vol. 22. London: Hogarth, 1962.
46. ———. *An Outline of Psychoanalysis.* New York: Norton, 1969.
47. ———. *A General Introduction to Psychoanalysis.* New York: Pocket, 1971.
48. Frey-Rohn, L. *From Freud to Jung.* New York: Dell, 1974.
49. Fromm, E. *Escape from Freedom.* New York: Farrar, Straus, & Giroux, 1941.
50. Gard, R. *Buddhism.* New York: Brazillier, 1962.
51. Gardner, M. "Quantum Theory and Quack Theory." *NYRB,* May 17, 1979.

52. Garfield, C. "Ego Functioning, Fear of Death, and Altered States of Consciousness." In C. Garfield (ed.), *Rediscovery of the Body*. New York: Dell, 1977.

53. Gilson, E. *The Unity of Philosophical Experience*. London: Sheed & Ward, 1938.

54. Goleman, D. *The Varieties of Meditative Experience*. New York: Dutton, 1977.

55. GTU research seminars, 1980–81. Jacob Needleman and Dick Anthony, coordinators.

56. Guénon, R. *Man and His Becoming According to Vedanta*. London: Luzac, 1945.

57. Guillaumont, P. (trans.). *The Gospel According to Thomas*. New York: Harper & Row, 1959.

58. Hall, C. *A Primer of Jungian Psychology*. New York: Mentor, 1973.

59. Hartmann, H. *Ego Psychology and the Problem of Adaptation*. New York: International Universities Press, 1958.

60. Hegel, G. *The Phenomenology of Mind*. J. Baillie (trans.). New York, 1949.

61. Hixon, L. *Coming Home*. New York: Anchor, 1978.

62. Hume, R. *The Thirteen Principal Upanishads*. London: Oxford Univ. Press, 1974.

63. Jacobson, E. *The Self and the Object World*. New York: International Universities Press, 1964.

64. Jakobson, R. "Child Language Aphasia and Phonological Universals." Quoted in H. Gardner, *The Quest for Mind*. New York: Vintage, 1974.

65. James, M. *The Apocryphal New Testament*. London: Oxford, 1924.

66. James, W. *Principles of Psychology*, 2 vols. New York: Dover, 1950.

67. ———. *The Writings of William James*. J. McDermott (ed.). New York: Random House, 1968.

68. Jung, C. "The Psychological Foundations of Belief in Spirits." *Collected Works*, vol. 8. Princeton: Princeton Univ. Press.

69. Kaplan, P. *Toward a Theology of Consciousness*. Doctoral dissertation, Harvard, 1976.

70. Kernberg, O. "Borderline Personality Organization." *Journal of the American Psychoanalytic Association*, vol. 15, 1967.

71. ———. "Prognostic Considerations Regarding Borderline Personality Organization." *Journal of the American Psychoanalytic Association*, vol. 19, 1971.

72. Klein, M. *Psychoanalysis of Children*. New York, 1966.

73. ———. *Narrative of a Child Analysis*. London: Hogarth, 1961.

74. Kohlberg, L. *The Philosophy of Moral Development*. San Francisco: Harper & Row, 1981.

75. Kohut, H. *The Restoration of the Self*. New York: International Universities Press, 1977.

76. Lacan, J. *The Language of the Self*. Baltimore: Johns Hopkins, 1968.

77. Lasch, C. *The Culture of Narcissism*. New York: Norton, 1979.
78. Loevinger, J. *Ego Development*. San Francisco: Jossey-Bass, 1976.
79. Mahler, M., et al. *The Psychological Birth of the Human Infant*. New York: Basic Books, 1975.
80. Marin, P. "The New Narcissism." *Harper's*, October 1975.
81. Maslow, A. *Motivation and Personality*. New York: Harper & Row, 1954.
82. ———. *Toward a Psychology of Being*. New York: Van Nostrand Reinhold, 1968.
83. ———. *The Farther Reaches of Human Nature*. New York: Viking, 1971.
84. McCarthy, T. *The Critical Theory of Jürgen Habermas*. Cambridge: M.I.T. Press, 1978.
85. McPherson, T. "Religion as the Inexpressible." In Flew and MacIntyre (eds.), *New Essays in Philosophy of Religion*. New York: Macmillan, 1964.
86. Mead, G. *Mind, Self, and Society*. Chicago: Univ. of Chicago Press, 1934.
87. Ogilvy, J. *Many Dimensional Man*. New York: Oxford Univ. Press, 1977.
88. Ornstein, R. *The Psychology of Consciousness*. San Francisco: Freeman, 1972.
89. Ouspensky, R. *A New Model of the Universe*. New York: Vintage, 1971.
90. Peck, R., and Havighurst, R. *The Psychology of Character Development*. New York: Wiley, 1960.
91. Piaget, J. *The Child's Conception of the World*. New York: Humanities Press, 1951.
92. ———. *The Construction of Reality in the Child*. New York: Basic Books, 1954.
93. ———. *The Essential Piaget*. Gruber and Voneche (eds.). New York: Basic Books, 1977.
94. Prince, R., and Savage, C. "Mystical States and the Concept of Regression." *Psychedelic Review*, vol. 8, 1966.
95. Ramana Maharshi. *The Collected Works of Ramana Maharshi*. A. Osborne (ed.). London: Rider, 1959.
96. Randall, J., and Buchler, J. *Philosophy: An Introduction*. New York: Harper & Row, 1971.
97. Reich, W. *Selected Writings*. New York: Farrar, Straus, & Giroux, 1973.
98. *ReVision*, vol. 1, no. 3/4, 1978.
99. Riesman, D. *The Lonely Crowd*. New York: Doubleday, 1954.
100. Rogers, C. *On Becoming a Person*. Boston: Houghton Mifflin, 1961.
101. Rogers, C., and Holdstock, T. "Person-centered Theory." In R. Corsini (ed.), *Current Personality Theories*. Itasca: Peacock, 1977.
102. Roszak, T. *Person/Planet*. New York: Anchor, 1978.
103. Russell, B. *A History of Western Philosophy*. New York: Simon & Schuster, 1945.
104. Sarfatti, J. "Implications of Meta-physics for Psychoenergetic Systems." *Psychoenergetic Systems*, vol. 1, 1974.
105. Schumacher, E. *A Guide for the Perplexed*. New York: Harper & Row, 1977.

106. Schuon, F. *Logic and Transcendence*. New York: Harper & Row, 1975.
107. ———. *The Transcendent Unity of Religions*. New York: Harper & Row, 1976.
108. Selman, R., and Byrne, D. "A Structural Analysis of Levels of Role-taking in Middle Childhood." *Child Development*, vol. 45, 1974.
109. Shepherd, A. *A Scientist of the Invisible*. Quoted in J. White and S. Krippner (eds.), *Future Science*. New York: Anchor, 1977.
110. Smith, H. *Forgotten Truth*. New York: Harper & Row, 1976.
111. Smuts, J. *Holism and Evolution*. New York: Macmillan, 1926.
112. Smith, H. *Forgotten Truth*. New York: Harper & Row, 1976.
113. Sullivan, C., Grant, M., and Grant, J. "The Development of Interpersonal Maturity: Applications to Delinquency." *Psychiatry*, vol. 20, 1957.
114. Sullivan, H. *The Interpersonal Theory of Psychiatry*. New York: Norton, 1953.
115. Suzuki, D. T. *Studies in the Lankavatara Sutra*. London: Routledge & Kegan Paul, 1968.
116. ———. *Essays in Zen Buddhism*. London: Rider, 1970.
117. Taimni, I. *The Science of Yoga*. Wheaton: Quest, 1975.
118. Tart, C. *States of Consciousness*. New York: Dutton, 1975.
119. ——— (ed.). *Transpersonal Psychologies*. New York: Harper & Row, 1975.
120. Thibaut, G. (trans.). *The Vedanta Sutras of Badaryana*. New York: Dover, 1962.
121. Van der Leeuw, J. *The Conquest of Illusion*. Wheaton: Quest, 1968.
122. Wachsmuth, G. "The Etheric Formative Forces." In J. White and S. Krippner (eds.), *Future Science*. New York: Anchor, 1977.
123. Washburn, M. "Observations Relevant to a Unified Theory of Meditation." *Journal of Transpersonal Psychology*, vol. 10, no. 1, 1978.
124. Watts, A. *The Way of Zen*. New York: Vintage, 1957.
125. ———. *The Supreme Identity*. New York: Vintage, 1972.
126. Welwood, J. "Self-knowledge as the Basis for an Integrative Psychology." *Journal of Transpersonal Psychology*, vol. 11, no. 1, 1979.
127. Werner, H. "The Concept of Development from a Comparative and Organismic Point of View." In Harris (ed.), *The Concept of Development*. Minneapolis: Univ. of Minnesota Press, 1957.
128. ———. *Comparative Psychology of Mental Development*. New York: International Universities Press, 1964.
129. Wescott, R. *The Divine Animal*. New York: Funk & Wagnalls, 1969.
130. Whitehead, A. N. *Science and the Modern World*. New York: Macmillan, 1967.
131. Whyte, L. *The Next Development in Man*. New York: Mentor, 1950.
132. Wilber, K. "The Ultimate State of Consciousness." *JASC*, vol. 2, no. 1, 1975–76 (revised as chapter 10 of this volume).
133. ———. *The Spectrum of Consciousness*. Wheaton: Quest, 1977.

134. ———. "A Developmental View of Consciousness." *Journal of Transpersonal Psychology,* vol. 11, no. 1, 1979 (expanded and revised as chapters 3 and 4 of this volume).

135. ———. "Eye to Eye." *ReVision,* vol. 2, no. 1, 1979 (revised as chapter 1 of this volume).

136. ———. *No Boundary.* Los Angeles: Center Press, 1979 (new edition: Shambhala, 1981).

137. ———. *The Atman Project.* Wheaton: Quest, 1980.

138. ———. "The Pre/Trans Fallacy." *ReVision,* vol. 3, no. 2, 1980 (chapter 7 of this volume).

139. ———. *Up from Eden.* New York: Doubleday/Anchor, 1981.

140. ———. "Odyssey." *Journal of Humanistic Psychology,* vol. 22, no. 1, 1982.

141. ———. *A Sociable God.* New York: McGraw-Hill, 1982.

142. Wittgenstein, L. *Tractatus logico philosophicus.* London: Routledge & Kegan Paul, 1969.

143. Zimmer, H. *Philosophies of India.* London: Routledge & Kegan Paul, 1969.

Afterword

FRANCES VAUGHAN

F OR MANY YEARS I have told students of transpersonal psychology that they must read Ken Wilber if they want to know how transpersonal theory integrates psychology and spiritual teachings from the world's religions. No one is expected to agree with everything he says, but they need to understand why his perspective is important.

The depth and scope of Ken Wilber's vision is not easy for most of us to encompass. Many of his critics take issue with the details of one small segment or another, but never address his philosophical position as a whole. It seems that there are few people who can challenge the overarching view that integrates so many disciplines and perspectives.

My own acquaintance with Wilber's work dates back to 1975, when I was an associate editor of the *Journal of Transpersonal Psychology* and we had the privilege of being the first to publish his paper "The Spectrum of Consciousness." When his book by the same title was published soon afterward, I realized what a great service he was doing for us all. His ability to articulate in a clear and coherent manner the integral vision that many of us had been attempting to formulate, with limited success, expanded the field of psychological and spiritual inquiry to encompass a truly global view of the spiritual quest.

Wilber is undoubtedly one of the greatest thinkers of our time. His cross-disciplinary syntheses encompass the psychology, philosophy, and religion of East and West, as well as sociology, anthropology, and postmodern thought. In the last two decades he has been widely recognized as an outstanding philosopher. Some people have compared him to

Hegel, but to my mind he is much easier to read! He has been hailed as the Einstein of consciousness studies, and his work offers a healthy antidote to the dogmatic reductive thinking in many disciplines. His contribution to psychology has been compared to that of Sigmund Freud, Carl Jung, and William James. His brilliant and fundamental reformulation of theories of human development and the evolution of consciousness have earned him an international reputation and the respect of scholars in a wide range of fields. I believe he offers a worldview that will, in time, affect all of our academic, social, medical, religious, and scientific institutions.

In his work Wilber demonstrates an indomitable warrior spirit that matches any adversary with fearless integrity. His dedication to service is evident in his uncompromising commitment to doing the work that he feels called to do, despite the arduous discipline that it demands. Through it all he remains open to feedback and keeps a cheerful sense of humor about his own human foibles in personal relationships. He has also demonstrated his willingness to revise his ideas in response to new information, as evidenced by the evolution of his own thinking, whose phases he calls Wilber I, II, and III.

When he responds to critics, Wilber often reflects the tone of their own remarks, and this leads some observers to feel that he can be unduly sharp. However, it seems to me that he has demonstrated both wisdom and compassion in his willingness to reply to critics who are familiar with only a small portion of his work. His compassion may seem ruthless at times, but I know his heart is open, and he writes from experience as well as a prodigious amount of reading. I have been a student of psychology, religion, and philosophy for nearly forty years and, with the possible exception of the Dalai Lama, I have yet to meet or read anyone who can match the laserlike quality of his intellect.

Wilber's rare intellectual genius is matched by an emotional intensity that we can feel by reading the account of his passionate love relationship with his late wife, Treya Kilham Wilber, as portrayed in his book about her life and death, entitled *Grace and Grit*. I know many people whose lives have been deeply affected by reading this book, and many who have been helped to deal with their own illness or loss of a loved one.

I have had the privilege of knowing Ken very well for the better part of two decades. He has been a spiritual friend, a teacher, and a shining star of inspiration. What I value most about his work is the fact that I see it always pointing to liberation and enlightenment. His exquisite mastery of language always points beyond itself to the ineffable mystery. For those inclined to jnana yoga, a thorough study of Wilber's work can be deeply rewarding. For those who feel confused on the spiritual path, his clarity is unmatched. For those who are familiar with the farther reaches of spiritual practice, his pointing-out instructions are a delight. In each of the dozen books he has written to date, his penetrating vision-logic brings a kaleidoscope of ideas into a meaningful pattern that offers us a window on the wisdom of the ages.

Sources

A Sociable God: A Brief Introduction to a Transcendental Sociology.
New York: McGraw-Hill, 1983. Reissued as *A Sociable God: Toward a New Understanding of Religion.* Boston: Shambhala Publications, 1984. © 1983, 1984 by Ken Wilber.

Eye to Eye: The Quest for the New Paradigm. Boston: Shambhala Publications, © 1983, 1990, 1996 by Ken Wilber.

Books by Ken Wilber

The Spectrum of Consciousness (1977)

No Boundary: Eastern and Western Approaches to Personal Growth (1979)

The Atman Project: A Transpersonal View of Human Development (1980)

Up from Eden: A Transpersonal View of Human Evolution (1981)

The Holographic Paradigm and Other Paradoxes: Exploring the Leading Edge of Science (1982)

A Sociable God: Toward a New Understanding of Religion (1983)

Eye to Eye: The Quest for the New Paradigm (1983)

Quantum Questions: Mystical Writings of the World's Great Physicists (1984)

Transformations of Consciousness: Conventional and Contemplative Perspectives on Development, by Ken Wilber, Jack Engler, and Daniel P. Brown (1986)

Spiritual Choices: The Problems of Recognizing Authentic Paths to Inner Transformation, edited by Dick Anthony, Bruce Ecker, and Ken Wilber (1987)

Grace and Grit: Spirituality and Healing in the Life and Death of Treya Killam Wilber (1991)

Sex, Ecology, Spirituality: The Spirit of Evolution (1995)

A Brief History of Everything (1996)

The Eye of Spirit: An Integral Vision for a World Gone Slightly Mad (1997)

The Marriage of Sense and Soul: Integrating Science and Religion (1998)

One Taste: The Journals of Ken Wilber (1999)

Integral Psychology (2000)

INDEX